Forgotten Faces

of Fantastic Films

One of the many forgotten faces—George Rosener as Otto, the butler, from *Doctor X* (1932)

Forgotten Faces of Fantastic Films

by James T. Coughlin

Foreword by Gregory William Mank

Midnight Marquee Press, Inc.
Baltimore, Maryland, USA, London, UK

ISBN 978-1936168-57-6
Library of Congress Catalog Card Number 2015912389
Manufactured in the United States of America
First Printing October 2015

Dedication

To my wife Mary and children Kerry & Brian
who have given me the gift of love that will never be forgotten

Table of Contents

Foreword

The faces are vivid, for many of us who are long-time disciples of the Golden Age of Horror. Indeed, after decades watching and re-watching the films, they are almost as engrained on our consciousness as the iconic stars they supported.

They were a strange and striking repertory, playing in Hollywood's nether world arena of Frankenstein's Monster, Count Dracula, the Mummy, the Invisible Man and the Wolf Man. Each and every one was a seasoned professional, but his or her name was usually far below the billing of a Karloff, Lugosi, Rains or Chaney ... and sometimes there was no billing at all. Each was aware, often painfully, that capricious luck was at least as responsible as God-given talent for bestowing celebrity; had fate been kinder, they might be marquee names, rather than day players.

In this book, *Forgotten Faces of Fantastic Films*, Dr. James T. Coughlin tells their fascinating stories.

They occupied various brackets of fame (or non-fame); some of these actors, as the author notes, are not actually "forgotten," but nevertheless, have never fully received the worthy attention they enjoy here. Ernest Thesiger is a horror genre legend for his Horace Femm of *The Old Dark House* and Dr. Septimus Pretorius of *Bride of Frankenstein*, both directed by his London chum, James Whale. This book offers the goods on Thesiger, including details of his World War I service as a rifleman, and his decidedly unconventional marriage. As for his career, you'll also learn that, on more than one occasion, Thesiger played one of the Three Witches in *Macbeth* ... and that, a year before his death, he received the Order of Commander of the British Empire.

Just so, we reverently remember Edward Van Sloan—in his Power-of-Good portrayals in *Dracula*, *Frankenstein*, *The Mummy*, and *Dracula's Daughter*—so reverently, perhaps, that it's hard to conjure up a young Van Sloan milking the laughs in stage comedy roles. In fact, as revealed here, Van Sloan enjoyed an early success in the star role of "Babbs," aka *Charley's Aunt*, cavorting in drag in that warhorse comedy.

Then there's the cackling Witch of Disney's *Snow White and the Seven Dwarfs*, or at least her unforgettable voice ... Lucille La Verne. Did you know Ms. La Verne had a very distinguished stage career ... and a flair, way back in far less politically-correct times, for playing roles in blackface?

Then there are the more minor roles. A burgomaster. A constable. A butler. A father. For those addicted to encore viewings of horror films, it's almost as if these figures are decorations, kept in mothballs until next time, rather like minor decorations stored in the attic until next Christmas, to be placed to the far side of the manger, or on the

Portrait of Ernest Thesiger

inconspicuous side of the tree. Yet the tableaus would never be complete without them. As this book shows, these players, despite often utilitarian service in Hollywood, all had careers that provided moments of glory—before, during and sometimes even after their stints in horror films.

A case in point: Halliwell Hobbes. We recall the bald, blustery Britisher, for example, in the 1931 *Dr. Jekyll and Mr. Hyde*, playing Brigadier-General Carew, the arch-establishment father of Rose Hobart's heroine, clucking disapprovingly of the experiments of Fredric March's Jekyll ... and, come the climax, savagely beaten to death by March's simian Hyde. He went on to play many supporting parts, including a butler in *The Invisible Man's Revenge*, released in the summer of 1944. That same summer, however, he starred on Broadway in Agatha Christie's *Ten Little Indians*, enjoying the plum role of the villainous Judge Wargrave, maniacally mad in the Act III climax, shouting insanely at the audience as he tries to murder the heroine.

These actors had traveled the world, learning their craft in touring companies, loving what they did, eventual-

Alec Craig, Heather Angel, Eily Malyon and Halliwell Hobbes, from *The Undying Monster* (1942)

ly settling in Hollywood. An example: E.E. Clive, best remembered as bewildered Constable Jaffers in *The Invisible Man* and the windbag Burgomaster in *Bride of Frankenstein*. As this book documents, Clive toured in the late 1890s as a proud member of "The Penny Gaff," a woebegone parade of wagons bearing actors, scenery, props and even benches for the audiences, eking its way through the hills of England, Wales, Ireland and Scotland. Result: E.E. Clive could proudly claim that he'd appeared in 1,139 plays.

"No small parts, only small actors" It was a credo they had to believe devoutly, lest they succumb to heartbreak and despair.

Telling the stories of these remarkable *Forgotten Faces* is Dr. James T. Coughlin, a film history archaeologist who's been excavating the sagas of these players for decades. This is research you won't find on the Internet, or anywhere else; it's a treasure-trove of people and places, titles and dates, studios and stages; over 40 years of discoveries by an ace researcher whose life-long fascination with these

actors goes back to his childhood. Jim and I very happily collaborated on the 1997 book *Dwight Frye's Last Laugh*, so I know first-hand how he enjoys the thrill of the hunt as far as finding long-lost information on players who richly deserve his attention and expertise.

A bonus: The photos. There are over 300 of them, showing the *Forgotten Faces* in action, with many stars and character players.

Solidly researched, profusely illustrated, this is a celebration of the classic horror genre from a rarely-taken angle, an overdue and affectionate tribute to actors and actresses long worthy of the attention. In this wonderful book they, at last, enjoy top billing.

Gregory William Mank
Delta, PA
February 23, 2015

Introduction

As part of the dedication to *Dwight Frye's Last Laugh*, a book I was privileged to co-author with Gregory William Mank and Frye's son Dwight David, I noted my appreciation to my late mother Jane for teaching me to pay attention to the character people in motion pictures. From an early age, I remember watching an old film on our antiquated TV set, with my mother pointing out Guy Kibbee, J. Farrell MacDonald or Mary Gordon. I recall while viewing *The Wizard of Oz* in the early sixties that my mom would inform me that Margaret Hamilton, the Wicked Witch, was also in *My Little Chickadee* with W.C. Fields and that Charley Grapewin, Uncle Henry, appeared with Henry Fonda in *The Grapes of Wrath*. As I got better at recognizing performers, she would quiz me on what else they had been in and tell me anecdotes about seeing their films when she was young.

Just as my favorite baseball players were relief pitchers like the Senators' Dave Baldwin and Dick Lines, my beloved actors and actresses were those stalwarts in support who, in my mind, added more to the story than did the leads. What that says about me psychologically is a whole other matter.

Back in 1975, I began a correspondence with the late actor Barry Brown. Barry had lent assistance to Calvin Beck and Bhob Stewart on *Heroes of the Horrors* and *The Scream Queens*. With his lifelong passion for the supporting players and those performers who receive little or no recognition, Barry was a natural to helm the third volume in Beck's "trilogy," *Unsung Heroes of the Horrors*. Barry had read my 1974 article on Dwight Frye in Leonard Maltin's *Film Fan Monthly* (#154). After a series of letters back and forth, he solicited my help on his project. Barry was primarily interested in players of the fifties and sixties, particularly those associated with the films of Roger Corman, like Dick Miller, Jonathan Haze, Mel Welles and Bruno VeSota. He realized my area of focus was the late silent period through the early forties, coming to the conclusion that our collaboration would allow each of us to focus on the people whose careers we were most comfortable in exploring.

For the most part, Barry divided the chapter assignments along these lines. He would handle the aforementioned Miller, Haze, Welles and VeSota, along with Allison Hayes, Katharine Victor, Richard Carlson, John Agar, Rondo Hatton, etc. I would work on Frye, Colin Clive, Edward Van Sloan, Lionel Atwill, George Zucco, Fay Wray, David Manners, Patric Knowles, Ernest Thesiger, Noble

Calvin Beck's *Heroes of the Horrors* brought writers Jim Coughlin and Barry Brown together, to embark upon a project of their own, never to be.

FORGOTTEN FACES OF FANTASTIC FILMS:

william v. mong
john miljan

JIM   COUGHLIN

WILLIAM V. MONG (1875-1940)

Although virtually ignored by film reference books, Mong was a veteran character actor who appeared in numerous silent pictures before winding up his career in the early talkies with his colorful portrayals of mean, miserly old men.

Born in Chambersburg, Pennsylvania, on June 25, 1875, he spent a number of years in vaudeville and legitimate theatre before entering films in 1910. In addition to acting, Mong did a great deal of directing (for Universal, Triangle, etc.) and scenario writing, while he gravitated from leading roles to character parts.

Mong was married to Esme Warde, who operated a chain of circulating libraries in and around Hollywood. The Mongs derived great pleasure from their ownership of a large aviary, which at one time housed over 200 rare birds from around the globe.

He passed away on December 10, 1940, in Studio City, California. Mong had not made any films the last two years of his life due to illness.

Film Career:

Mong appeared in over 200 films from 1910-1920, including THE SEVERED HAND (1916), THE HOPPER (1918), and MUTINY OF THE ELSINORE (1920). The New York Times found him "sufficient to his part" as Merlin the Magician, his first substantial fantasy role, in A CONNECTICUT YANKEE IN KING ARTHUR'S COURT (1921). Most of Mong's roles had been of a kindly nature until his powerful portrayal of a ruthless smuggler in the Barbara La Marr film, THY NAME IS WOMAN (1924), which typed him as a heavy henceforth.

Mong had a knack for chewing up the scenery with his scowls and sneers, such as his portrayal of the cook in ALL THE BROTHERS WERE VALIANT (1923) starring Lon Chaney Sr. and his devious Cognac Pete in WHAT PRICE GLORY? (1926).

Mong appeared in three horror-mystery endeavors of the noted Danish director, Benjamin Christensen. He was the caretaker in THE HAUNTED HOUSE (1928), involving a scheme by Edmund Breese to test presumptive heirs; the professor in SEVEN FOOTPRINTS TO SATAN (1929); and the "mystery man" who summons Chester Conklin and Louise Fazenda to visit their uncle in THE HOUSE OF HORROR (1929). His gaunt, evil countenance enhanced all such films.

A STRANGE ADVENTURE (1932) gave Mong a brief but meaty part as Silas Wayne, who summons his relatives for an early reading of his will and is murdered during the proceedings. THE VAMPIRE BAT (1933) featured Mong as Sauer, one of the villagers who wrongly drives Herman (Dwight Frye) to his death, believing him to be responsible for the peculiar goings-on in the town of Kleinschloss. Sauer the alderman further insists on pounding a stake into the misfortunate lad's heart. Mong met another early demise in a poverty row chiller, THE DARK HOUR (1936), as Henry Carson, wealthy and eccentric uncle of Irene Ware, who is found dead in his study of carbon monoxide poisoning.

Mong also graced many major non-horror films in the latter days of his career. He was Pew in MGM's TREASURE ISLAND (1934), the sniveling Cleon in LAST DAYS OF POMPEII (1935), and the old, judicious Sachem in THE LAST OF THE MOHICANS (1936). Mong's last film was THE PAINTED DESERT (1938), in which he played Heist.

Though certainly not a major star or a name familiar to even ardent film buffs, Mong is an actor worth watching for when his old films pop up, as his performances are invaria-

BELOW: A portrait of William V. Mong

BELOW: A portrait of John Miljan

The first page (of two) of the very first "Forgotten Faces of Fantastic Films" column that appeared in *Midnight Marquee* **#30, in the fall of 1981**

The official logo for Jim Coughlin's column appeared beginning in issue #35 of *Midnight Marquee*

Johnson, Maria Ouspenskaya and Beverly Garland. From the summer of 1976 through most of 1977, we would mail chapters back and forth, with updates, corrections and such. Unfortunately, progress slowed, mainly on my end due to graduate school commitments. What I failed to realize was that Barry was suffering from depression far deeper than I had comprehended. Barry's struggle culminated with his taking his own life on June 25, 1978 (the IMDb erroneously lists June 27, but a personal letter from Barry's brother James confirms the actual date).

In the weeks following Barry's death, Calvin Beck asked me to send to him all my written work on the book, as well as my stills related to the performers. He would combine all this with Barry's work and material from his own archives in an attempt to salvage *Unsung Heroes of the Horrors*. Barry's brother James, also a writer, preferred that we did not proceed with Beck's arrangement with Collier-Macmillan. I was presented with the choice of trying to market the book with James Brown, still utilizing Barry's work, or go it alone with just my own chapters. In that Barry was a far superior writer to me and had conducted in depth, sensitive interviews with most of the then still-living performers, I felt the best choice was to work with James in shopping the manuscript around for another publisher. James had a number of publishing contacts, but, after a few months of rejections, *Unsung Heroes of the Horrors* was scrapped altogether.

I had spent many hours in my youth reading *Famous Monsters of Filmland* and *Castle of Frankenstein*. During and after college, I began to acquire horror-related fanzines on my journeys to Cinemabilia, a motion picture-related book and materials store in New York's Greenwich Village. It was there that I first purchased *Gore Creatures*, edited by Gary J. Svehla. I greatly appreciated the intelligent writing of Svehla's 'zine and had used Gary D. Dorst's piece on Dwight Frye in *Gore Creatures* #19 as a main reference for my *Film Fan Monthly* article on Frye. I decided to write to Svehla to see if he had any interest in publishing any of my chapters from *Unsung Heroes of the Horrors* in article

form. Gary and I agreed to use my work on Edward Van Sloan as a test case of sorts. When Svehla ran "Edward Van Sloan: The Elder Statesman of Horror" in *Midnight Marquee* (the revised title of *Gore Creatures*) #28 (September 1979), I was elated. At least all my efforts on *Unsung Heroes of the Horrors* had not been in vain.

For *Midnight Marquee* #30 (1981), I once again submitted a chapter from the aborted *Unsung Heroes of the Horrors*. Gary ran the piece entitled "George Zucco: A Portrait of Evil Sophistication." I also tried something different for the same issue. Barry Brown and I had toyed with an encyclopedic tome on horror-related performers and technicians, tentatively titled *The World of Fantasy Performers*. We had exchanged sample entries on various actors and actresses to get a sense of format and layout, but that was the only work completed on our second project together. For *Midnight Marquee* #30, I decided to resurrect two sample short pieces on William V. Mong and John Miljan, submitting them as a prospective regular feature entitled "Forgotten Faces of Fantastic Films." That was the start of an ongoing collaboration between Gary and Susan Svehla and me that has spanned more than 35 years.

For the next six issues of *Midnight Marquee* (1982-1986), "Forgotten Faces of Fantastic Films" appeared regularly, featuring relatively brief profiles of two performers in each issue. The people covered were: Lionel Belmore and Gustav von Seyffertitz (#31), Una O'Connor and Montagu Love (#32), Brandon Hurst and Gene Roth (#33), Kamiyama Sojin and Doris Lloyd (#34), E.E. Clive and Arthur Edmund Carewe (#35) and Cesare Gravina and Fern Emmett (#36). For the 25th Anniversary issue of *Midnight Marquee* (#37, Fall 1988), the Svehlas requested more detailed submissions. I wrote about Ernest Thesiger, C. Henry Gordon, Robert Barrat and Patric Knowles for this special issue, providing additional in depth career coverage. From that point on, I attempted to be more thorough with the "Forgotten Faces" articles, aiming to go beyond just titles and roles, adding more personal data and some flavor to particular parts that exemplified each actor's work.

Beginning with *Midnight Marquee* #38, every entry of "Forgotten Faces" would feature greater detail, but only one player per issue. William Harrigan was the focus of #38. The expanded coverage allowed for the use of more rare stills, which enhanced the articles, in my opinion. This pattern continued with Olga Baclanova (#39), Forrester Harvey (#40), Halliwell Hobbes (#42), Murray Kinnell (#45), Edgar Norton (#46), and Maude Eburne (#48).

Midnight Marquee #49 was a special vampire film issue, so my submission was on the following supporting players of Universal's 1931 *Dracula*: Herbert Bunston, Frances Dade and Charles Gerrard. Due to life circumstances, there was a long gap (1995-1998) between that piece and my next submission for *Midnight Marquee*, which came with my career study of Lucille La Verne for Issue #58. As Gary and Susan Svehla were trying new things with *Midnight Marquee*, while also launching a new non-horror genre magazine, I decided to try something different as well, examining the lives and work of performers beyond just the fantasy genre, while also taking into account work in other media, such as theater, radio and television (when applicable).

The first such biographical piece, now just called "Forgotten Faces," was on actor Wyrley Birch, presented in the Svehlas' new *Mad About Movies* #2 (2001). This was followed by three more fairly long career explorations in *Mad About Movies* on Robert Gleckler (#3), Ivan Simpson (#5) and Neil Fitzgerald (#6). From 2007 to present, there have been no further installments of "Forgotten Faces" in either *Midnight Marquee* or *Mad About Movies*.

About three years back, Gary Svehla wrote to me regarding putting past installments of "Forgotten Faces" together in book form. I was enthusiastic about the opportunity to expand and correct some of my earlier pieces, but more so to bring long overdue recognition to a selection of performers whose efforts have delighted me since childhood. There was also the chance to investigate additional actors who have never had a career study in print. Charles Irwin and George Rosener both fall into this category.

Looking back on the close to 35 actors and actresses whose careers I had discussed in the pages of *Midnight Marquee* and *Mad About Movies*, some decisions had to be made as to who to include and who to omit. I decided to concentrate on those who had made some impact in the classic horror films of the 1930s. I also determined that I would group them by film, such as *Dracula* or *The Invisible Man*, rather than alphabetically or chronologically. I realize this was an arbitrary choice, but hopefully it makes some sense.

Some performers were not included because their careers have been thoroughly reviewed by esteemed colleagues, such as Greg Mank writing on Una O'Connor in *Women in Horror Films, 1930s*. Others, like Sojin and Cesare Gravina, did not make the cut, as they were predominantly

Jim Coughlin's original writing partner, the late Barry Brown, whose depression resulted in his early death.

silent film actors. Likewise, Gene Roth was eliminated, as most of his significant film work was post-1940.

Perhaps some of the choices, like Wyrley Birch and Murray Kinnell, impress as esoteric to some. Most of the people selected are, for one reason or another, personal favorites. I did feel that Edward Van Sloan, Ernest Thesiger and Noble Johnson had to be part of *Forgotten Faces of Fantastic Films*. I learned so much researching the careers of Edgar Norton, Ivan Simpson and Neil Fitzgerald that I wanted to share my discoveries with others. As a youth, as soon as I made the connection that the voice of the Wicked Witch in *Snow White and the Seven Dwarfs* and La Vengeance in *A Tale of Two Cities* were one and the same person, I became a lifelong fan of Lucille La Verne. Please forgive my indulgences in this matter of the choices made.

In any case, it is my wish that these neglected actors and actresses receive some modicum of recognition as a result of this book being published. In a small way, *Forgotten Faces of Fantastic Films* is my repayment to these individuals for all the joy their performances have given me over these many years.

Dracula (1931)

Edward Van Sloan (1882 - 1964)

It seems essential that the formula for a good horror film contains an influential figure, representing the side of good, to serve as an antithesis to the monster/villain, who symbolizes the forces of evil. The task of such a character is usually to convince the doubters and cynics around him that the fiend does in fact exist, in order to mobilize the powers that be to destroy it. As Van Helsing, in the person of Edward Van Sloan, stresses in *Dracula* (1931), "The strength of the vampire is that people will not believe in him." Van Sloan was a natural for roles of this nature, with his vivid characterizations of wise, venerable old doctors and professors, whose fund of mystical, unconventional knowledge inevitably proves to explain the inexplicable. Particularly as Dutch vampire hunter Abraham Van (Von)

Helsing in *Dracula* and *Dracula's Daughter*, his portrayal fit the mold. Van Sloan's performances in other horror classics, like *Frankenstein* and especially *The Mummy*, shared many commonalities in this vein. From time to time, Van Sloan would turn up as the evildoer himself, as in *Behind the Mask* and *Air Hawks*. For the most part, however, his presence in a horror film would provide a ray of hope for the innocent, as well as a thorn in the side of the monster or villain.

Edward Paul Van Sloun (he later changed the "u" to an "a" for professional purposes) was born in Chaska, Carver County, Minnesota, on November 1, 1882 (12 days after the birth of Bela Lugosi). He was one of seven children born to Martinus (Martin) Van Sloun (1848-1918) and the former Theresa Breher (1852–1931). Edward had four sisters (Marie Dorothea, Lenore Magdalena, Josephine A. and Alma Katherine) and two brothers (Frank Joseph and Karl L.).

As a teenager his father Martin immigrated from Born, a city in the province of Limburg, the Netherlands, to Minnesota. He and his family established a farm on

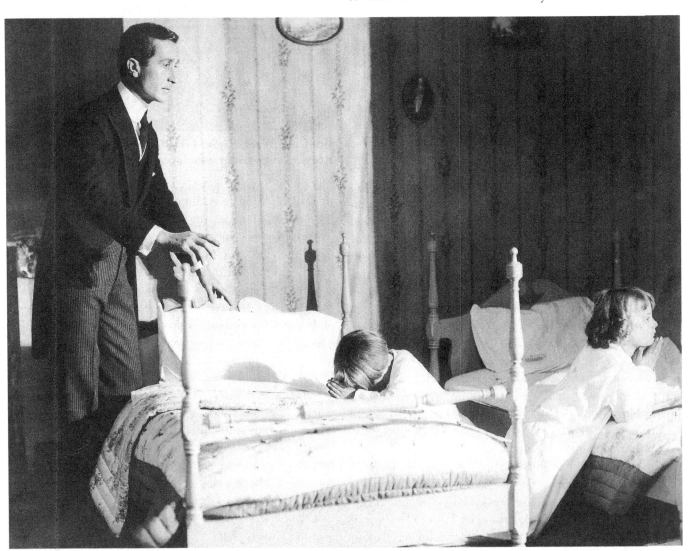

Slander (1916): **Edward Van Sloan as Joseph Tremaine, with children**

what is now Bavaria Road in Chaska. Martin married Illinois-born Theresa in 1875. Family historian Dennis Van Sloun has described Edward's parents' relationship as "non-traditional" (*Chaska Herald*, 5/6/2004, p. 13). Martin dabbled in different businesses, running a saloon and then a furniture store, before leaving his family in 1889. He then settled in Tacoma, Washington. Theresa remained in Minnesota, doing what she could to provide for her children. For a time in the mid-1890s, she ran a boarding house on Rice Street in St. Paul, Minnesota. Although Martin had returned from Tacoma by that point, Theresa opted to move with Edward, Marie, Lenore, Alma and Josephine to San Francisco, California. Martin, now working as a painter, stayed behind in Chaska. According to Dennis Van Sloun, the family spoke both Dutch and German at home, with Edward being heavily influenced by these cultures. Martin eventually died from a heart ailment in 1918, but Theresa lived until 1932, able to witness the beginning of Edward's film career.

Edward attended the University of California at Berkeley, with the intention of becoming an architect. His experience with weekly German theatrical productions gradually changed his mind regarding a career choice. Edward's architectural training helped spawn an interest in scene designing and stage lighting. He was putting some of his designs to the test for a school production of Shakespeare's *The Merchant of Venice*, when Edward was encouraged by the director and his peers to enact the role of Gratiano. Van Sloan was to lend his talents to many subsequent college plays as a producer, designer and actor. After finishing college, Edward dabbled with commercial art for a brief time, before deciding to devote his full energies to the theater.

Van Sloan went East in 1908, making his professional acting debut in H.V. Esmond's *Under the Greenwood Tree*, playing what Edward referred to as "the silly-ass Englishman." He then toured the provinces of Canada portraying a similar type as Lord Fancourt "Babbs" Babberley in *Charley's Aunt*. Babbs spends half the play in drag, masquerading as millionaire Donna Lucia. Van Sloan yearned for more diverse parts, stating: "I found myself in danger of becoming a specialist—a bad thing for a beginner who has ambitions … so I decided to serve my apprenticeship in stock" (*Dramatic Mirror*, 4/29/14).

During this early period of his career, Van Sloan met and married Myra M. Jackson Roop (1883-1960) in Pennsylvania. Edward and Myra would have a son Paul William (1911-1962). Paul, who had a lengthy military career (and is buried in Arlington National Cemetery), had a connection to film as well, working as a technical advisor on *The Beginning of the End* (1947) with Brian Donlevy. Paul and his wife Virginia (nee Hatteroth) would present Edward with a grandson, Warner L. Van Sloun, born in

Dracula **(1931): Two adversaries—Van Helsing (Van Sloan) and Count Dracula (Bela Lugosi)**

1930. Sadly, both wife Myra and son Paul would die before Edward himself

From 1911-1915, Edward was an integral member of the Brownell-Stork Company, which was based in Newark, New Jersey. Van Sloan also played stock and repertory in locations like Bridgeport, Connecticut and Niagara Falls, New York. Among the early stage roles Edward played were: Sir Christopher Deering in *The Liars*, Joe Brooks in *Paid in Full*, Gabot Arany in *The Concert*, Jack Brookfield in *The Witching Hour* and Tom Bennett in *Forty-Five Minutes From Broadway*. "No danger of specialty in that," (*Dramatic Mirror*, 4/29/14) Van Sloan commented.

Van Sloan starred in *The Amateur Husband* (5/21/16) at Proctor's Palace in Newark. *The Newark News* (5/22/16) commented, "The story is thin, so thin in fact that it verges on inanity. The trick is to save it, and this Mr. Van Sloan does by virtue of his brisk, staccato style in humorous expression."

Slander (1916), starring Bertha Kalich and directed by Will S. Davis, represents Van Sloan's only known silent film credit. Filmed at the Fox Studio at Fort Lee, New Jersey, *Slander* gave Van Sloan the role of Joseph Tremaine, who is accidentally shot and killed by his father (Eugene Ormonde) after it is discovered that both are in love with Kalich.

***Frankenstein* (1931): Dwight Frye, John Boles, Mae Clarke, Edward Van Sloan, Colin Clive and Boris Karloff**

Edward returned to the theater as part of the Metropolitan Stock Company in Cleveland, Ohio before venturing to Broadway and the realm of fantasy. Edward was featured as Richard Bradbury in *The Unknown Purple* (9/4/18), an updated version of *The Count of Monte Cristo* with a mysterious ray added into the plot for effect. After a few more seasons in stock, Van Sloan returned to the New York stage as Crawford Boswell in Guy Bolton's *Polly Preferred* (1/11/23), a comedy about the making of silent pictures. The review in *Variety* (1/12/23) read, "Edward Van Sloan as the effeminate movie director is remarkably effective, and is responsible for much of the laughter."

Van Sloan played Herr Hauser in *Morals* (11/30/25), about the suppression of vice in a mythical German city. In a foreshadowing of things to come, Edward was Dr. Burghardt Von Vierreck in *Schweiger* (3/23/26), concerned with the psychic healing of a child murderer's mind. Van Sloan appeared with the prestigious Theatre Guild as Captain Miguel Lopez in their production of *Juarez and Maxi-*

milian (10/11/26). Among those in a stellar cast were Edward G. Robinson, Morris Carnovsky and Dudley Digges. Edward assayed the part of Lieber in the short-lived *Lost* (3/28/27), which closed after only eight performances.

Horace Liveright, the publisher and producer who was intent on bringing the Hamilton Deane play *Dracula* to the New York stage, had seen Van Sloan on Broadway. After viewing one of Edward's performances, Liveright stated emphatically, "That's him! That's the man to play Van Helsing." *Dracula* opened on Broadway at the Fulton Theatre on October 5, 1927, running for 261 performances before closing May 19, 1928. The play, which began a lifelong association of the role of Count Dracula with its star Bela Lugosi, also featured Bernard Jukes of the London cast as Renfield and Herbert Bunston as Dr. Seward (a role he recreated in the 1931 film version). Of Edward's portrayal of Van Helsing, a "specialist in obscure diseases," Brooks Atkinson (*The New York Times*, 10/6/27) wrote, "Mr. Van Sloan is excellently mysterious and apprehen-

The Mummy (1932): Van Sloan as Doctor Muller

field (Dwight Frye). He turns to Dr. Seward (Herbert Bunston) and the others present to disclose that they are dealing with the undead—Nosferatu! When this statement meets opposition, Van Helsing counters, "I may be able to bring you proof that the superstition of yesterday can become the scientific reality of today!" After the learned professor is introduced to Renfield amidst the howling of wolves, Van Helsing probes the madman about his conversing with wild animals, producing wolfsbane in the process. Renfield, infuriated, recoils, exclaiming, "You know too much to live, Van Helsing." As Renfield is led away, Van Helsing cautions he must be carefully watched.

Later, as Mina (Helen Chandler) speaks with John Harker (David Manners) about her "bad dreams," Van Helsing discovers two marks on her neck, just as Count Dracula (Bela Lugosi) enters. Dracula notes, "Van Helsing—a most distinguished scientist whose name we know even in the wilds of Transylvania," thus setting the stage for the two adversaries. As the Count turns his attention to Mina, Van Helsing realizes Dracula casts no reflection in the mirror inside a cigarette box. Confronting the Count with this phenomenon, Dracula smashes the mirror, apologizes and abruptly departs. Van Helsing is emphatic that "Dracula is our vampire," but the resistance from Seward and Harker remains. As the Professor cites vampire lore, the cackling Renfield, in a moment of conscience, tells them to be guided by what Van Helsing says. Mina's unconscious body is discovered, with Van Helsing warning she is in far greater danger than death itself.

sive as the doctor." Following its run on Broadway, *Dracula* moved to the West Coast, playing the Biltmore Theatre in Los Angeles in June 1928, before returning to the East Coast that same September.

Van Sloan went on to play Dr. A.P. Workman, a spiritualist, in *Remote Control* at the Forty-eighth Street Theatre, New York (9/10/29). Workman is suspected of being involved in a jewel robbery at the radio station from which he broadcasts his show, but he is murdered at the microphone before any further light can be shed on the crime.

When director Tod Browning and Universal were in the process of casting the film version of *Dracula*, the decision as to who would play Van Helsing was perhaps the easiest they faced, given that Van Sloan gave such a definitive rendition of the role on stage. So, at the age of 48, Edward Van Sloan made his talking screen debut in what was destined to be one of the most famous horror films of all time, *Dracula* (1931).

Van Helsing is first observed in *Dracula*, following his arrival at Seward Sanitarium, analyzing a blood sample of the lunatic Ren-

It's Great to Be Alive (1933): **Gloria Stuart, Edward Van Sloan, Emma Dunn and players**

***The Crosby Case* (1934): Van Sloan and Wynne Gibson**

Van Helsing quarrels with Harker, who wants to take Mina away, before the escaped Renfield regales them with Dracula's promise of rats for his servitude. Van Helsing, left alone, finds himself in Dracula's presence, with a wonderful battle of wills ensuing, before the vampire is driven away by a crucifix. Eventually after Mina disappears, Van Helsing and Harker trail Renfield to Carfax Abbey. After Dracula kills Renfield, he retreats to one of his boxes filled with native soil. Van Helsing finds and impales the Count, driving a stake through his heart. Van Helsing tells Harker, who has found Mina alive, to leave, adding he must tend to unfinished business. The film ends here, but in its original release version, Van Sloan stepped out of character and delivered an epilogue, as he had done in the stage version. Although only fragments exist today, the speech went as follows:

> Please! One moment! Just a word before you go. We hope the memories of Dracula won't give you bad dreams—so, just a word of reassurance. When you get home tonight and lights have been turned out and you're afraid to look behind the curtains—and you dread to see a face at the window—why, just pull yourself together and remember … that, after all, there are such things!

Van Sloan's portrayal of Van Helsing is certainly memorable and, in this author's opinion, one of the highlights of supporting acting from the classic Universal horrors. Perhaps his delivery and mannerisms do not appear natural by today's standards, but they certainly enhanced the mood and atmosphere of *Dracula*, particularly in the context of what is considered by many to be stagy direction by Tod Browning.

Based on its success with *Dracula*, Universal was determined to bring Mary Shelley's *Frankenstein* to the screen. Robert Florey was slated to direct Bela Lugosi as the Monster, so Paul Ivano shot test footage on the Carfax Abbey set from *Dracula*. Lugosi, in make-up designed by Jack Pierce reportedly based on Paul Wegener's *Der Golem*, appeared with Van Sloan in these test reels. Van Sloan reflected that the Monster's head was "about four times normal size, and with a broad wig on it. He (Lugosi) had a polished, clay-like skin," adding that the overall effect was not especially frightening. Van Sloan claimed that Bela instead looked more like "something out of *Babes in Toyland*" (*Famous Monsters #31*). It remains uncertain as to how accurate Edward's memory was about the event as the footage has long been presumed lost. After James Whale took over as director on *Frankenstein* (1931), Jack Pierce revised the appearance of the Monster for its new portrayer, Boris Karloff.

Despite other cast changes for *Frankenstein*, Van Sloan was retained to play Dr. Waldman, Henry Frankenstein's former medical school instructor. Edward also was designated to deliver a prologue for the new film, just as he had done the epilogue for *Dracula*. Van Sloan steps to the front of a stage, addressing the film audience:

> Mr. Carl Laemmle feels it would be a little unkind to present this picture without a word of warning. We are about to unfold the story of *Frankenstein*, a man of science who sought to create life after his own image, without reckoning upon God. It is one of the strangest tales ever told. It deals with the two great mysteries of creation—life and death. I think it will thrill you. It may shock you. It may even horrify you. So, if any of you feel you'd not care to subject your nerves to such a strain, now's your chance to … er … well, we warned you!

Early on in *Frankenstein* (1931), Dr. Waldman lectures at Goldstadt Medical College, as Frankenstein's deformed assistant Fritz (Dwight Frye) watches through a window. Before dismissing class, Waldman points out the differences between a normal brain and that of a criminal whose "life was one of brutality, of violence and murder."

Concerned over the well-being of Henry Frankenstein (Colin Clive), his fiancée Elizabeth (Mae Clarke) and friend Victor Moritz (John Boles) seek out Waldman for both information and advice. The doctor tells them of Henry's advanced theories, as well as his unreasonable demands regarding bodies, which resulted in Frankenstein leaving the University. Waldman explains, "Herr Frankenstein

Air Hawks (1935): **Edward Van Sloan as crazed inventor Professor Schulter**

was interested only in human life … first to destroy it and then re-create it. There you have his mad dream." He agrees to accompany the pair to Henry's laboratory, but warns they won't be welcome.

Arriving at Frankenstein's lab housed in a tower, the trio's attempt to enter is at first thwarted by Fritz. Henry capitulates, allowing them to seek shelter from the terrible storm that is raging. Frankenstein permits them to see his lab, informing Waldman that he was wrong about the ultraviolet ray being the highest color in the spectrum. Henry brags about going beyond, discovering a ray that is the catalyst for life itself, but Waldman balks. Henry assures him that he is not experimenting with the dead, but with bodies that he himself has assembled. As all present witness the creation process, Henry, in ecstasy, has to be restrained.

Waldman later informs Henry that the Creature (Karloff) has an abnormal brain, admonishing, "You have created a monster and it will destroy you!" The creature calmly enters, but becomes enraged as Fritz waves a torch at it. The doctors are forced to subdue the Monster. As

Waldman and Henry peruse medical books, the Monster hangs his tormenter Fritz, leading the older man to sedate the Creature with a "half grain solution." Waldman promises the Baron (Frederick Kerr), who arrives to take home his son Henry, that he "will see that it (the Monster) is painlessly destroyed." As Waldman makes notes about dissecting the Creature, the Monster breaks loose, killing the doctor and escaping the laboratory.

Although Van Sloan's role of Waldman was not as significant as that of Van Helsing in *Dracula*, Edward still delivered a credible performance. Of course, Waldman fails to destroy the Monster, whereas Van Helsing had succeeded, perhaps lacking some of the occult awareness the latter so richly possessed. Van Sloan had the foresight to realize that *Frankenstein*, like *Dracula*, was deemed to be an important motion picture. He allegedly allayed Karloff's fears about the film ruining his career, declaring, "Not so, Boris, not so! You're made!"

After the two archetypal roles in *Dracula* and *Frankenstein*, Van Sloan appeared as the assistant to Paul Porcasi in *Under 18* (1931), starring Marian Marsh, who had made a

The Last Days of Pompeii (1935): **Kindly neighbor Edward Van Sloan gazes with admiration at Gloria Shea, Preston Foster and their infant son.**

recent impression in *Svengali* (1931). Edward followed this with his portrayal of a lawyer in *Manhattan Parade* (1931).

Behind the Mask (1932) offered Van Sloan a substantial villainous role as Dr. August Steiner, alias Dr. Alec Munsell, who runs a private hospital. The true identity of Steiner, actually a mysterious masked surgeon known as Mr. X, is unknown even to the gang of dope smugglers that he leads. Those who have closed in on Steiner's secret have been eliminated in a sadistic manner on the operating table. Hart (Jack Holt), a Secret Service agent, wins the confidence of Henderson (Boris Karloff), thus gaining entrance into Steiner's gang. When the agent's ruse is discovered, Hart is strapped down to the table as Steiner prepares to "operate." The daughter (Constance Cummings) of a previous victim from the gang shoots the doctor, armed with a scapel, to death, thus saving Hart. Van Sloan chewed some scenery in *Behind the Mask*, barely hiding his delight in engaging in a little mayhem of his own. *Behind the Mask*, although a Columbia title, was part of the "Son of Shock!" package distributed to television by Screen Gems in 1958.

Van Sloan played Moffat, the boss, in *Play Girl* (1932), starring Loretta Young. Again opposite David Manners, Edward was Mr. Walters, the French & Sprague manager, in *Man Wanted* (1932). *Forgotten Commandments* (1932), a drama of early Soviet Russia with Irving Pichel as a scientist, included Van Sloan as a doctor. Again as a doctor, Edward treated blind Charles Bickford in *Thunder Below* (1932). Van Sloan had a poignant moment as the Rabbi who visits convict George E. Stone just prior to his execution in *The Last Mile* (1932).

The Death Kiss (1932) brought together three *Dracula* alumni: Van Sloan, David Manners and Bela Lugosi. Edward was Tom Avery, the director of a motion picture being shot in a film-within-a-film. Avery orders a scene to be re-shot, until it is revealed that the leading man has been killed for real. Later, when the murder scene is being recreated, Avery is about to be exposed as the killer and falls to his death from a catwalk as he flees the scene.

At the onset of *The Mummy* (1932), Professor Muller (Van Sloan) warns Sir Joseph Whemple (Arthur Byron) and Norton (Bramwell Fletcher) not to open the coffin they have discovered through their archaeological efforts. Muller, a famous Egyptologist, translates the inscription on the golden box containing the mummy of Imhotep to read, "Death … eternal Punishment for anyone who opens this casket. In the name of Amon Ra, King of the Gods." Muller's fears are dismissed as superstition, but when Norton later reads from the Scroll of Thoth, the mummy (Boris Karloff) indeed comes to life.

Ten years hence, Muller is treating Helen Grosvenor (Zita Johann) for a psychological problem of a mysterious nature. Muller finds Helen at the Whemple home where Sir Joseph's son Frank (David Manners) has brought her after discovering the young woman in a daze near the Cairo Museum. Muller informs Sir Joseph that the newly unearthed mummy of Princess Ankh-es-en-Amon is the very person Imhotep had unsuccessfully tried to raise from the dead 3700 years before, resulting in his being buried alive as punishment. Muller and Sir Joseph are summoned to the museum where a guard has been found murdered. They discover the missing Scroll of Thoth near the body.

Muller makes the connection that Ardath Bey (Karloff) and Imhotep are one and the same, postulating that the mummy of Imhotep was not stolen, but rather brought back to life by the reading of the Scroll. Enraged, Ardath Bey threatens Muller, demanding that the Scroll of Thoth be turned over to Sir Joseph's Nubian servant (Noble Johnson), now the mummy's slave. Muller pleads with Sir Joseph to burn the parchment, but Ardath Bey induces cardiac arrest in the elder Whemple.

Muller attempts to elicit the help of the skeptical Frank, who does not accept the Professor's explanation of his father's death. Frank accepts an amulet depicting Isis from Muller as protection, but Imhotep causes the young man to pass out before he can rescue Helen. Muller and a revived Frank arrive just as Imhotep is about to plunge the sacrificial knife into Helen, so she can join him in immortality. The powerless men watch in amazement as Imhotep is destroyed by the powers of Isis in response to the pleas of Helen.

The role of Muller has numerous parallels to that of Van Helsing in *Dracula*. Muller, like Van Helsing, has a vast knowledge of the occult and obscure. He confronts Ardath Bey with the photo of the mummy taken by Norton, just as Van Helsing had flashed the mirror in the box at Count Dracula. Both Muller and Van Helsing had to contend with disbelieving heroes played by David Manners. Despite becoming rather typecast at the early juncture of his career, Van Sloan, as Muller, managed to render one of his best screen performances.

The Secret Seven (1940): Four of the elite crime solvers: Van Sloan, William Forrest, Howard Hickman and Bruce Bennett

Billion Dollar Scandal (1933), with Robert Armstrong and Olga Baclanova, included Van Sloan as Attorney Carp. *Infernal Machine* (1933), centered around a time bomb on an ocean liner, had Van Sloan fifth-billed as Professor Gustave Hoffman, one of the passengers. Van Sloan's appearance in Majestic's crime drama *The World Gone Mad* (1933) is unconfirmed. Edward was Mr. Briggs in *The Working Man* (1933) with George Arliss and Bette Davis. *Trick for Trick* (1933), about two magicians (Ralph Morgan and Victor Jory) matching their skills against one another, featured Van Sloan as John Russell, a guest invited to a gloomy mansion. *Silk Express* (1933), a tale of murder on a train with Neil Hamilton, had Edward as the mill owner in the association concerned with importing silk from Asia. Van Sloan was Dr. Wilton, Gloria Stuart's father, in the fantasy *It's Great to be Alive* (1933), in which all the men in the world but *one* (Paul Roulien) are left infertile by an epidemic of "masculitis." Edna May Oliver had an interesting part as an eccentric scientist who tries to create a synthetic man. *Baby-Face* (1933), with Barbara Stanwyck terrific as a pre-Code seductress, had Van Sloan as Jameson, a bank director.

Deluge (1933), combining the talents of the *King Kong* tandem of Willis O'Brien and Merian C. Cooper, involved drastic weather changes on Earth, resulting in a series of earthquakes and tidal waves. Van Sloan portrayed Professor Carlysle, one of the learned men trying to cope with the calamity. Edward played Professor C. Edson Hawley in Chesterfield's mystery *Murder on the Campus* (1933). Rounding out a busy year, Edward was seen as a judge in *Goodbye Love* (1933).

Van Sloan portrayed Professor Franz Lubeck, a nearly blind German suspect, in *The Crosby Case* (1934), a mur-

A Man's World (1942): **A portrait of Edward Van Sloan as Doc Stone**

der mystery with Onslow Stevens and Wynne Gibson. In *Manhattan Melodrama* (1934), with Clark Gable and William Powell as boyhood friends now on opposite sides of the law, Edward played Captain Swenson, a yacht skipper. *The Scarlet Empress* (1934), Josef von Sternberg's lavish production with Marlene Dietrich, offered Van Sloan the part of Herr Wagner. Edward was Jim Winters, the mercenary father of Ann Harding, in *The Life of Vergie Winters* (1934). *I'll Fix It* (1934), starring Jack Holt, had Van Sloan as Parkes. He played Komeoski opposite Fay Wray in *Mills of the Gods* (1934). Van Sloan was a board director in Universal's atmospheric tale of betrayal and revenge, *The Man Who Reclaimed His Head* (1934), with Claude Rains and Lionel Atwill. Although many references list Edward as Dr. Valle in the cast of *Death Takes a Holiday* (1934), Van Sloan does not appear in surviving prints and his scenes may have been cut before the actual film's release.

Grand Old Girl (1935), starring May Robson, had Van Sloan as Holland. As Professor Bostwick in *A Shot in the Dark* (1935), Edward was third-billed in a complex role. On the surface a kindly teacher, Bostwick, who earlier abandoned his wife (Doris Lloyd), proves to be involved with his son (James Bush) in a conspiracy to murder stepsiblings to gain an inheritance. *The Woman in Red* (1935), starring Barbara Stanwyck and directed by Robert Florey, had Van Sloan as Foxall, the prosecuting attorney. Edward played Dr. O'Neill in *Death Flies East* (1935). Van Sloan was

among those at rescued Helen Mack's bedside in *Captain Hurricane* (1935). *The Arizonian* (1935) featured Edward as Judge Cody. Van Sloan portrayed Doctor Gordon in *Three Kids and a Queen* (1935) and Klover in *Grand Exit* (1935).

Air Hawks (1935) is concerned with Independent Air Lines, headed by Barry Eldon (Ralph Bellamy), vying for the contract to deliver the mail. Arnold (Douglass Dumbrille), the malevolent leader of the opposition, who has the task of ruining Independent's chances, employs a crazed inventor, Professor Shulter (Van Slaon). Shulter devises a lethal electrical ray, which he directs at Independent's planes, causing them to explode in mid-air. Eldon heroically brings a halt to Shulter and Arnold's destructive activities.

The Last Days of Pompeii (1935), including some fine special effects by Willis O'Brien, had Van Sloan as Calvus, a family friend of the blacksmith Marcus (Preston Foster). Calvus consoles Marcus after his wife and baby son are killed by a nobleman's chariot. Marcus, quite embittered, turns to the arena as a gladiator and later becomes one of the most powerful men in Pompeii.

Van Sloan was provided with a minor yet important part in *The Black Room* (1935), starring Boris Karloff in a dual role as the twin De Berghman brothers. Early on Edward was seen as the doctor who delivers the twins and then minimizes the concern of the Baron (Henry Kolker) regarding the old prophesy that one twin will eventually murder the other.

Van Sloan played the chairman of the medical society in Warner Bros.' *The Story of Louis Pasteur* (1936), with Paul Muni winning an Academy Award in the title role. In *Road Gang* (1936), an exposé of brutality in Southern prison camps, Van Sloan portrayed Charles Dudley, a lawyer.

Dracula's Daughter (1936), with Edward back as Professor Von (not "Van" this time) Helsing, picks up where *Dracula* left off. Two policemen (Halliwell Hobbes and Billy Bevan) find the body of Renfield at the bottom of the Carfax Abbey stairs, while Von Helsing informs them of another corpse that has been dead "about 500 years." They find Count Dracula's body impaled by a stake and bring the suspect Von Helsing in handcuffs to Scotland Yard. The Professor attempts to explain the unnatural occurrences to Sir Basil Humphrey (Gilbert Emery), rebutting his skepticism with, "The strength of the vampire, Sir Basil, lies in the fact that he is unbelievable!" Sir Basil cautions Von Helsing that from the appearance of things, the Professor is headed either to the gallows or an institution for the criminally insane. Von Helsing, therefore, requests that his former pupil Dr. Jeffrey Garth (Otto Kruger), a psychiatrist, come to his defense.

Garth agrees to help his old mentor, but he cannot accept the occult explanations either. When a young girl (Nan Grey) exhibits two puncture marks on her neck following

The Mask of Diijon (1946): Edward Van Sloan tries his guillotine illusion on Jeanne Bates.

an attack, Von Helsing postulates to Garth and Sir Basil that one of Dracula's victims, now undead as well, might be responsible. Garth is finally convinced that Countess Zaleska (Gloria Holden) is indeed a vampire. Zaleska and her henchman Sandor (Irving Pichel) abduct Jeffrey's fiancée, so Garth follows them by plane to Transylvania. Von Helsing leads the police in pursuit to Castle Dracula. Sandor is shot after firing an arrow into Zaleska's heart out of jealousy. As the Countess expires, there is a comment on her beauty. Von Helsing ends the film, responding, "She was beautiful when she died—a hundred years ago!"

Although Von Helsing serves a different function in *Dracula's Daughter* than in *Dracula*, Van Sloan still commands the screen with his authoritative statements and presence. The screenwriters opted for the more sexually charged relationship between protagonist (Garth) and antagonist (Zaleska), versus the cerebral battle that existed between the

Count and Van Helsing in the original. Thus, Von Helsing became a far less significant character in *Dracula's Daughter*.

Despite resurrecting the role that first brought him screen notoriety, Edward Van Sloan's ensuing screen appearances were becoming less noticeable and frequently uncredited, as was the case with his brief appearance in *Kelly of the Secret Service* (1936). Van Sloan was not billed as the French Surete in *Fatal Lady* (1936), an Austrian Army doctor in *Sins of Man* (1936) and a medical board doctor in *The Man Who Found Himself* (1937). James Whale managed to include Van Sloan with many of his horror familiars (Dwight Frye, Marilyn Harris, E.E. Clive, etc.) as the president in post-World War I Germany in *The Road Back* (1937). The short *That Mothers Might Live* (1938) had Edward as the hospital chief of staff. Van Sloan played Dr. Rinewulf in *Penitentiary* (1938), an older man in *The Toy Wife* (1938) and a professor in *Campus Confessions* (1938). *Danger on the Air*

The Underworld Story (1950): **Edward Van Sloan (center) as the minister at the graveside service, with Paul Bryar, Frances Chaney, Dick Foote, Sue England and Lewis L. Russell.**

(1938), with Donald Woods trying to ascertain who killed a radio station's sponsor, featured Van Sloan as Dr. Leonard Sylvester, the physician of the murdered man who proves to be a charlatan and murder suspect. *Storm Over Bengal* (1938), starring Patric Knowles, gave Edward an interesting role as the old Maharajah of Lhanapur. *Honeymoon in Bali* (1939) provided another unbilled appearance for Van Sloan as a priest on the island of Bali.

The Phantom Creeps (1939), a Universal serial, reunited Van Sloan with Bela Lugosi, who played a crazed inventor seeking world domination. Edward was Chief Jarvis, who directs his G-men to follow the trail of the criminal mastermind. Van Sloan also recreated his stage portrayal of Abraham Van Helsing opposite Lugosi in a revival tour of *Dracula* around this time.

Abe Lincoln in Illinois (1940), with Raymond Massey marvelous as the would-be president, featured Van Sloan as Dr. Barrett. *Teddy the Rough Rider* (1940), a Warner Bros. short shot in Technicolor, included Edward as Secretary of State Elihu Root. Van Sloan played Dr. Burkardt in *The Doctor Takes a Wife* (1940), with Loretta Young and Ray

Milland. *The Secret Seven* (1940) had Van Sloan as Professor Holtz, one of a band of extra-legal crime experts assembled by ex-convict Bruce Bennett.

Before I Hang (1940) had Boris Karloff as Dr. John Garth, an elderly scientist who is sentenced to death for killing an old pauper during an experiment designed to combat old age. Garth befriends the prison physician, Dr. Ralph Howard (Van Sloan), with the two continuing this endeavor in the prison laboratory. On the day before his execution, Garth injects himself with serum derived from the blood of a hanged murderer, only to learn that he has been given a reprieve. Appearing years younger, Garth ironically learns his sentence has been commuted to life imprisonment. Under the influence of the killer's blood, Garth strangles Howard, his friend and colleague. Karloff and Van Sloan worked very well together, as they had in the early Universal horrors.

The Monster and the Girl (1941), with George Zucco as a mad doctor of sorts, had Van Sloan as Dave, the warden of the prison wherein a young man (Phillip Terry), framed for a murder he did not commit, is executed. Zucco later

24   **Forgotten Faces**

transplants Terry's brain into a gorilla (Charles Gemora).

Van Sloan was a minister in *Virginia* (1941) with Madeleine Carroll. He played a doctor at William Powell's sanity hearing in *Love Crazy* (1941). *The Men in Her Life* (1941), starring Loretta Young, had Van Sloan as the first doctor. In *A Man's World* (1942), a spy tale involving precious metal, Van Sloan was seen as Doc Stone.

Valley of Hunted Men (1942), with Bob Steele, Tom Tyler and Jimmie Dodd as the Three Mesquiteers, had Van Sloan as Dr. Heinrich Steiner. Nazis escaping from a Canadian prison kill Steiner's nephew (George N. Neise), with one of the escapees (Roland Varno) assuming his identity. Dr. Steiner, working on a project involving extraction of rubber to aid the Allies during the war, becomes a suspect due to his German heritage. The identity thief is revealed and the trio clear Steiner.

Edward was one of Irene Hervey's Dutch associates in *Destination Unknown* (1942), concerning hidden jewels being sought to aid the Chinese in their struggle with Japan. Van Sloan reverted to the Axis as the Chief Tribunal Judge in *Hitler's Children* (1943), a propaganda piece directed by Edward Dmytryk. *Hitler's Children* was a big money maker for RKO, and perhaps Van Sloan's most widely seen film. *Mission to Moscow* (1943), a pro-Russian film stressing the need for collective security at the height of World War II, included Edward as a German diplomat in Berlin.

Riders of the Rio Grande (1943) again linked Van Sloan with the Three Mesquiteers. As the disgraced Pop Owens, Edward arranges to have himself killed to cover his son's indiscretions, but he mistakes the three cowboys for his would-be assassins.

As Professor Bergstrom, Van Sloan was the inventor of a secret radio transmitter in *Submarine Alert* (1943), the cast of which included Dwight Frye and Richard Arlen. *The Masked Marvel* (1943), a Republic serial involving combating Japanese saboteurs, had Van Sloan as Professor A. M. MacRae. He was uncredited as a doctor in *The Song of Bernadette* (1943). As Gregory, the aide to Professor Lyman (Frank Reicher), Van Sloan appeared in the first two chapters of another Republic serial, *Captain America* (1943).

For the most part, Van Sloan's remaining screen appearances were little more than cameos. Edward was unbilled as an Admiral in *A Wing and a Prayer* (1944), directed

Edward Van Sloan, as Van Helsing from *Dracula* (1931), listens to lunatic Renfield (Dwight Frye) and manages to create one of the iconic performances from the Golden Age of classic horror.

by Henry Hathaway. Again uncredited, Van Sloan was the Dutch Underground leader in *The Conspirators* (1944), with Paul Henreid, Hedy Lamarr and Peter Lorre. *End of the Road* (1944), with John Abbott as a twisted killer, had Van Sloan as a judge. *I'll Remember April* (1945) gave Edward a small part as a board member.

Van Sloan's last significant film role was that of Sheffield, the magic store proprietor, in *The Mask of Diijon* (1946), starring Erich von Stroheim as a once famous magician. Sheffield, Diijon's neighbor, and Victoria (Jeanne Bates), Diijon's wife, devise a new guillotine illusion with the hope of stimulating the magician to return to work. Diijon, however, is more interested in "the power of the mind" and instead delves into hypnosis (and eventually murder). Although a borderline horror genre film, *The Mask of Diijon* gave Van Sloan ample screen time and dialogue.

As A.J.A. Woodruff, Van Sloan was at least listed in the credits in *Betty Co-Ed* (1946), starring Jean Porter. He had a small role as a German in *A Foreign Affair* (1948), directed by Billy Wilder. *Sealed Verdict* (1948), concerning Nazi war crimes, had Van Sloan as a priest.

Edward returned to the stage in 1948, being billed under his correctly spelled name of "Van Sloun" in *The Vigil*. *The Vigil* was a religious drama that utilized an American courtroom setting to examine what happened between the crucifixion of Jesus Christ and His Resurrection. A gardener (Tom Fadden) stands trial for stealing the body of Christ from His tomb in order to lend credibility to the divinity of Jesus. The audience, as jury, is left to decide after all the evidence is presented. *Variety* remarked, "Edward Van Sloun gives an intelligent and effective portrayal of the judge." *The Vigil* opened at the Coronet Theatre in Hollywood on March 10, 1948 and ran for three weeks. After subsequent tryouts, *The Vigil* came to the Royale Theatre on Broadway on May 21, 1948. It was not well-received and closed after only 11 performances.

Van Sloan's final two screen appearances were both uncredited. He portrayed a judge in *This Side of the Law* (1950), with Kent Smith of *Cat People* fame. Edward then was seen as the minister presiding over the funeral and graveside service in *The Underworld Story* (1950).

As stated earlier, Edward, while in his retirement, had to contend with the deaths of his wife Myra in 1960 and son Paul in 1962. The impact of these losses likely hastened his own physical deterioration, as Edward suffered from chronic bronchitis and other ailments in his later years. On the day after Thanksgiving, November 1963, *Famous Monsters of Filmland* editor Forrest J Ackerman and his wife Wendayne, along with young fan G. John Edwards, visited with Van Sloan at his final residence in San Francisco. Unfortunately, an opportunity was lost in that a substantial interview from that meeting did not transpire, although Ackerman did relate some anecdotes from Van Sloan in *Famous Monsters #31*.

Edward Van Sloan passed away on March 6, 1964 at 1:35 p.m. at his home at 241 Stanyan Street, San Francisco, California. The cause of death was listed as pulmonary emphysema and coronary artery disease. Van Sloan was cremated the following day. Edward's sister Josephine arranged through Carew and English Funeral Home in San Francisco to have his ashes shipped to Boehm Cemetery, Blue Bell, Montgomery County, Pennsylvania, so that Van Sloan could be interred with his wife Myra.

When one thinks of the early Universal horror films, Van Sloan and Van Helsing seem almost interchangeable. Edward Van Sloan certainly left fantasy buffs with a number of interesting characterizations to remember—Dr. Waldman in *Frankenstein*, Professor Muller in *The Mummy*, the evil Dr. Steiner in Columbia's *Behind the Mask* and so on. One of the reasons he became so well known to "Monster Kids" of the 1950s was that he was seen on TV in eight entries in the "Shock!" and "Son of Shock!" packages (*Dracula, Frankenstein, Behind the Mask, The Mummy, The Man Who Reclaimed His Head, The Black Room, Dracula's Daughter* and *Before I Hang*). Van Sloan's place in horror film history, however, has been secured by his deft interpretation of Abraham Van Helsing in *Dracula* (and to a lesser degree, Von Helsing in *Dracula's Daughter*). In conclusion, if you think for one minute that vampires don't exist, that mummies can't return to life or that a creature cannot be assembled from body parts and brought to life by lightning, remember the warnings issued on screen by Edward Van Sloan and permit yourself the catharsis of being shocked and terrified.

Sources

Ackerman, Forrest. "Great Horror Figure Dies," in *Famous Monsters of Filmland #31* (December 1964), pp. 40-49.

Bowman, David. "They Called Him 'Herr Doktor'; Edward Van Sloan, Universal's' House Physician of Horror," in *Filmfax #35* (October/November, 1992), pp. 63-66.

Chastain, George. "Edward Van Sloan," in *Classic Horror Players Directory* (http://myweb.wvnet.edu/-u0e53/edwardvansloan.html).

Coughlin, James T. "Edward Van Sloan: The Elder Statesman of Horror," in *Midnight Marquee #28* (September 1979), pp. 26-31.

Olson, Mark W. "The First 'Van Helsing': Chaska Native Starred in Original Movie Role," in *Chaska Herald* (Thursday, May 6, 2004), pp. 1,13.

Seymour, Blackie. "Edward Van Sloan: Nemesis of Evil," in *Classic Images* # 251 (May 1996), pp. C12-C13.

Van Sloan, Edward. *Wikipedia.com.*

Herbert Bunston
(1865 – 1935)

In a 1995 *Midnight Marquee* article on the supporting players of Universal's *Dracula* (1931), this author argued that Herbert Bunston belonged, with Charles Gerrard and Frances Dade, to a third tier of players from that film (Bela Lugosi comprising the first tier and Edward Van Sloan, Helen Chandler, David Manners and Dwight Frye making up the second). This was not to minimize Bunston's contribution to *Dracula.* His role of Dr. Seward is the one for which he is best remembered. Bunston came into films at a relatively advanced age (64) and died five years later, so he really did not have the career span of most of the performers covered in this work. It is fortunate, however, that there are a few other choice performances of Bunston's captured on film that can be viewed today, which might break, to some degree, the automatic association of the actor with the role of Seward.

Herbert Bunston was born on Trafalgar Day, October 21, 1865 (some sources wrongly state 1870 or 1874) in Charmouth, Dorset, England (Axminster, Devon, England has also been listed as his birthplace). He was the son of Anna Matilda Victoria Bond (1841-1870) and Thomas Bunston (1840-1918). Thomas and Anna Matilda had two daughters, Matilda Victoria (1869-1951) and Anna (1870-?) besides their son Herbert. Tragically, Herbert's mother died shortly after the death of his sister Anna. Thomas Bunston would then marry Isabella Murray Millard in 1872. Thomas' second marriage would result in three half-sisters for Herbert: Margaret, Isabella and Ethel.

Young Herbert was educated at King's School, Ely, Cambridgeshire and Cranleigh School, Surrey. There is little known of his early adulthood. By then, Bunston stood six-feet and weighed 160 pounds, with brown hair and blue eyes. Bunston was wed to Emily Fox Chaffey (1867-1939) in Hailsham, Sussex in July 1897.

Reportedly, Bunston made his stage debut in an 1897 production of *La Poupee.* His British stage career spanned the years 1897-1928, during which time he played in various companies both in London and toured the "provinces" of the United Kingdom. Bunston acted with many prestigious theatrical personalities of the time, including Frank

A theatrical portrait of Herbert Bunston (c. 1925)

The Lady of Scandal (1930)—Frederick Kerr, Ruth Chatterton and Herbert Bunston

Dracula (1927 Broadway stage): **Edward Van Sloan, Terence Neill, Bela Lugosi, Herbert Bunston and Bernard Jukes**

R. Benson, Herbert Beerbohm-Tree, Charles Hawtrey and Arthur Bourchier.

In the late summer of 1903, Bunston ventured to the United States for the first time, appearing as the juvenile lead in *Drink* (9/14/03), which played New York's Academy of Music for 40 performances. *Drink* then went on tour for six months before Bunston and the company returned to England.

Bunston played a variety of roles on the English stage in drama and comedies in theaters large and small. He portrayed Major Graves in *The Success of Sentiment* (9/27/08) at London's Court Theatre. He appeared with future horror film players Eva Moore and Halliwell Hobbes in *Company for George* (10/15/10) at the Kingsway Theatre. Also in the 1910/1911 theatrical season, Bunston was seen in Chekhov's *The Cherry Orchard* at London's Aldwych Theatre. Bunston enacted the role of Satine in Gorky's *The Lower Depths* (12/2/11) at the Kingsway. In early 1912, Bunston played both Prince's Theatre in Bristol and the

Garrick Theatre in London (2/7/12) in *The Firescreen*. He was prominently featured in *The Firescreen* as bacteriologist and professor Sir William Murdoch. Other 1911/1912 appearances came in *Find the Woman* at London's Garrick Theatre, with Roland Young, and *Esther Waters* at London's Apollo.

Herbert and his wife Emily resided at St Nicholas, 1 The Crescent, Burlington Lane, Chiswick St. Nicholas, Brentford, England at this time, according to the 1911 England Census. They had two children, daughter Margaret Chaffey Bunston (1899-1966), and son John Edmund Trenchard Bunston (1905-1949). John Edmund would receive a patent for an optical projection apparatus for working with Mercator charts just a few years before his death.

Returning to the Garrick during the 1912/1913 theatrical season, Bunston was seen in *Croesus*. Bunston toured with Matheson Lang, playing Bristol and elsewhere, in 1914/1915 in *Mr. Wu*, which was later made into a successful silent film with Lon Chaney. Herbert was featured along with Kyrle Bellew in *Find the Woman* at the Prince's Theatre in Bristol in 1915/1916. At the Playhouse in London, Bunston was part of a strong cast, including Gladys Cooper and Arthur Wontner, in *The Yellow Ticket* in 1917/1918. *The Witch of Edmonton*, featuring Sybil Thorndike, included Bunston amidst a large cast at the Lyric Hammersmith in London during the 1920/1921 season. For four years during the late 'teens, Bunston was part of the teaching faculty at the Royal Academy of Dramatic Arts in London.

Beginning in late 1922, Bunston began what became almost an annual ritual for the next six years of sailing back and forth between the United States and England. In the fall and winter of 1922/23, Bunston toured the western United States and Canada (playing cities like Ogden, Utah; Modesto, California and Winnipeg, Manitoba) as the kindly Hilchrist in Galsworthy's *The Skin Game*. Under the auspices of William A. Brady, Bunston was seen on Broadway as Rupert Smallwood, the husband of Winifred Frazer, in Arthur Wing Pinero's *The Enchanted Cottage* (3/31/23). The play, which ran for 65 performances at the Ritz Theatre, featured Katharine Cornell and ironically had Clara Blandick (Auntie Em from *The Wizard of Oz*) playing a witch. The historical drama *That Awful Mrs. Eaton!* (9/29/24), with Frank McGlynn as Andrew Jackson and Katherine Alexander in the title role, had Bunston as Sir Charles Vaughan, the British Ambassador. *That Awful Mrs. Eaton!*, also produced by Brady, ran for only 16 performances at the Morosco Theatre.

Set in France during World War I, *Simon Called Peter* (11/10/24) had a controversial plot wherein a priest (Leonard Willey) has a wartime affair with a nurse (Catherine Willard). Bunston portrayed the senior officer, Major Langston. The play had a run of 88 performances at the Klaw Theatre. John Van Druten's comedy *Young Woodley* (11/2/25), with Glenn Hunter as the title character, offered Bunston a change of pace. Bunston received critical acclaim for his complex portrayal of Frank Simmons, the Headmaster of Mallowhurst School. *Young Woodley* itself was a success, running for 260 performances at the famed Belasco Theatre. A young Helen Gahagan (the star of the 1935 *She*) had a prominent role in the production.

Bunston's final Broadway role was a significant one— Dr. Seward, the somewhat ineffectual administrator of the Purley "Sanitorium" bearing his name, in *Dracula* (10/5/27, 261 performances), Hamilton Deane and John Balderston's adaptation of Bram Stoker's famed novel. The stage role of Seward has more depth and lines than the screen characterization that would follow in 1931. In particular, more attention is paid to the doctor's angst,

The Lady of Scandal (1930): **Basil Rathbone, Ralph Forbes, Herbert Bunston and Ruth Chatterton**

as he witnesses the transformation of his daughter Mina (Dorothy Peterson) under the influence of Count Dracula (Bela Lugosi). From the original New York cast, Lugosi, Bunston and Edward Van Sloan would all repeat their stage roles when Universal brought *Dracula* to the screen four years later.

After gaining recognition on stage from both *Young Woodley* and *Dracula*, MGM signed Bunston to play Lord Elton, a role with which he was familiar from the London stage, in *The Last of Mrs. Cheyney* (1929). Lord Elton becomes infatuated with jewel thief Norma Shearer, making an error in judgment when he writes her an indiscreet letter containing information damaging to his associates. When the victimized group of socialites wants to turn Shearer in to the police, Elton's letter causes them to decide otherwise. Bunston had an interesting and touching moment in *The Last of Mrs. Cheyney* when he sang, accompanied by Ms. Shearer on piano, Thomas Moore's Irish ballad "Believe Me, If All Those Endearing Young Charms."

Also for MGM, Bunston was Lord Willie Crayle in *The Lady of Scandal* (1930) with Ruth Chatterton and Basil Rathbone. After his son (Ralph Forbes) announces his engagement to a famous actress (Chatterton), Lord Crayle

Dracula **(1931): In a scene cut from the final release print, Herbert Bunston and Edward Van Sloan search Carfax Abbey.**

summons him to discuss the dilemma. The solution is negated when she instead falls in love with Rathbone. Bunston had a musical interlude as well in *The Lady of Scandal*, when he dances by himself to a phonograph playing "Lulu Comes Home."

Bunston appeared as Mr. Brownbee in *Old English* (1930) starring George Arliss and his company of regulars, including Ivan F. Simpson, Murray Kinnell and Doris Lloyd. He was seen as Major Manners of the R.C.M.P., whose birthday banquet at the beginning of the film *Under Suspicion* (1930) set the tone for what ensues. In his early days in Hollywood, Bunston was under the management of Collier and Flinn.

The Wizard's Apprentice (1930) was a nine-minute short produced by William Cameron Menzies and foreshadowing to some degree "The Sorcerer's Apprentice" segment of Disney's *Fantasia* (1940). Among the special effects are hordes of multiplying marching brooms carrying pails of water, inevitably leading to a flood when directed by the less experienced apprentice (Fritz Feld) attempting to

impress a girl (Greta Granstedt). As the master wizard, Bunston is effective and understanding of his pupil, while providing a more imposing presence than in most of his screen portrayals.

Despite some controversy over who would play Count Dracula on the screen (before Bela Lugosi was chosen to repeat his stage success), Herbert Bunston was a fairly simple choice to recreate the role of Dr. John Seward, which he had performed so often on stage. After the setting in *Dracula* (1931) switches from the mountains of Transylvania to the refinement of London, England, Dr. Seward is first viewed while attending the symphony, being summoned for a fake phone call by a hypnotized usherette. This ruse was created by Count Dracula (Lugosi) in order to manipulate a meeting with Seward's theater party, including daughter Mina (Helen Chandler), her friend and guest Lucy Weston (Frances Dade) and John Harker (David Manners). For a time, Seward, who runs a sanitorium near Whitby, represents the conservative scientist, countering his colleague Van Helsing's claims about the "undead"

Dracula (1931): Dr. Seward (Herbert Bunston) is cautioned by Renfield (Dwight Frye).

with, "Modern science does not admit of such a creature. The vampire is pure myth. Superstition!" As Seward witnesses the Count interact with Van Helsing and becomes increasingly concerned with the well being of his daughter, he later evolves into the voice of reason. Seward convinces Harker not to take Mina away with matters unresolved, believing that would put his daughter in even graver danger. The doctor, whose previous expressions had mainly been of stoicism or confusion, now displays a look of horror when he witnesses Mina about to attack Harker, now realizing what this implies. Much of Bunston's screen time as Seward, however, is spent involved with the lunatic Renfield (Dwight Frye) and Van Helsing (Edward Van Sloan) in a number of interactions. The *New York Times* (2/13/31) summed up his performance thusly, "Herbert Bunston is a most convincing personality."

Bunston quickly established himself as a reliable character player on screen as he had been on stage. He portrayed Merson in *Always Goodbye* (1931), the Colonel in *I Like Your Nerve* (1931) and Roger Fenwick (the father of Geoffrey Kerr) in *Once a Lady* (1931). *The Last Flight* (1931) reunited Bunston with fellow *Dracula* players David Manners and Helen Chandler. Bunston's character is viewed with both Manners and Chandler in a compartment on a train bound for Portugal. *Ambassador Bill* (1931), starring Will Rogers, featured Bunston as the British Ambassador to the mythical strife-ridden kingdom of Sylvania.

The *New York Times* commented, "Herbert Bunston is capital as the excitable (Garrick) Ender-

ly," an abrupt and dismissive suspect, in *Charlie Chan's Chance* (1932), the third Warner Oland entry in the series (besides being a lost film). In Thackeray's *Vanity Fair* (1932), with Myrna Loy fine as Becky Sharp, Bunston was Mr. John Sedley, the wealthy merchant father of Becky's friend Amelia (Barbara Kent). Sedley goes bankrupt and dies penniless, but not before attempting to make amends to his daughter for his hubris during her upbringing. Working once again with William Cameron Menzies, now a director, Bunston was Lord Lavering in the borderline horror film *Almost Married* (1932), concerning a homicidal composer (Alexander Kirkland) who escapes from an asylum bent on revenge. Opposite Norma Shearer and Fredric March, Bunston was the minister in *Smilin' Through* (1932). Bunston's participation, according to studio call sheets, in *Westward Passage* (1932), an early Laurence Olivier film, and *The Mask of Fu Manchu* (1932), starring Boris Karloff, have not been verified. Herbert is also listed as appearing in MGM's star-laden *Dinner at Eight* (1933), but he is not identifiable and likely not in the release version of the film. As the Parisian banker Fauvel in *File 113* (1933), Bunston must contend with duplicity as well as his wife (Clara Kimball Young) being blackmailed.

When RKO Radio brought W.W. Jacobs' spooky short story *The Monkey's Paw* (1933) to the screen, Bunston was signed to play Mr. Sampson. After the meek clerk (Ivan F. Simpson) steals the paw, purported to grant its holder three wishes, from his friend and guest (C. Aubrey Smith), he chooses to ask for the sum of 200 pounds (with the hope

File 113 (1932): Lew Cody watches with amusement as Herbert Bunston berates George E. Stone.

The Moonstone (1934): Gustav von Seyffertitz, David Manners, Phyllis Barry, Herbert Bunston and player, with Jameson Thomas standing behind the sofa

of giving his son the ability to marry and have a good start). The next morning, however, it is the lawyer Sampson, representing the electric company for whom the clerk's son (Bramwell Fletcher) works, who arrives at the door with dire news. The son was killed during the night at the workplace when, telling the tale of the monkey's paw to colleagues, he laughed uncontrollably, causing him to fall into machinery that mangled him to death. As Samson consoles the clerk and his wife (Louise Carter), he presents the couple with a check for 200 pounds (the amount in the wish) as insurance compensation for an employee killed on the job. Unfortunately, *The Monkey's Paw* remains a lost film, other than some fragments.

Trick for Trick (1933) provided Bunston with another interesting role as psychic expert Professor King. King is actually Mr. Maxwell in disguise, whose daughter was murdered six months earlier. He attempts to avenge himself on magician Ralph Morgan, whom he holds responsible for his daughter's death, but accidentally stabs Victor Jory to death with a penknife by mistake. It turns out, in

a twisted turn of justice, that Jory was the murderer all along. William Cameron Menzies, again working with Bunston, handled the technical effects for this Fox film.

Long Lost Father (1934), starring John Barrymore and Helen Chandler, included Bunston as the Bishop. Back at MGM, Herbert was seen as Major Bagdall in *Riptide* (1934) with Norma Shearer and Robert Montgomery. Bunston was the doctor at the party in *Gambling Lady* (1934) with Barbara Stanwyck. He played Mr. Pettinghill in *Dr. Monica* (1934), starring Kay Francis. *The Age of Innocence* (1934), with Irene Dunne, John Boles and Lionel Atwill, had Bunston as lawyer W. J. Letterblair. Bunston was Uncle Fred in *Desirable* (1934), the first cabinet member in *British Agent* (1934) and Cavendish in *The Richest Girl in the World* (1934).

Monogram's above-average adaptation of Wilkie Collins' *The Moonstone* (1934) had Bunston, as Sir John Verinder. The cast of *The Moonstone* included horror film veterans David Manners, Gustav von Seyffertitz, Charles Irwin, and John Davidson. Verinder, once a distinguished scientist and dedicated physician, has become absent-minded

The Little Minister (1934): Herbert Bunston as Carfrae

Clive of India (1935), starring Ronald Colman, included Bunston as the first director of the East India Company. Bunston played the Cornwall College president in _A Shot in the Dark_ (1935), in which the usually benevolent Edward Van Sloan proves to be the villain. _After Office Hours_ (1935), with Clark Gable, had Bunston as Barlow, the butler of Billie Burke and her family. Bunston had a brief but strong appearance in the early going of _Les Miserables_ (1935) as the harsh judge at Favorelles, who sentences Jean Valjean (Fredric March) to 10 years as a galley slave for stealing a loaf of bread. _Cardinal Richelieu_ (1935), with George Arliss dynamic in the lead, provided Bunston with his final screen role as the Duke of Normandy. The Duke attempts to bribe Richelieu with 10 million francs, which the Cardinal shrewdly accepts, planning to use the money to help his sovereign, King Louis XIII (Edward Arnold), build an army rather than aiding the British as expected.

Herbert Bunston suffered a heart attack and died in Los Angeles, California on February 27, 1935. He was 69 years old (although _Variety_, 3/6/35, reported Bunston to have been 61). Funeral services were held on March 3, 1935. His widow Emily, whom he affectionately called Millie, and children Margaret and John survived him. Bunston had still maintained a home at 37 Harrowgate Road, Chiswick, Middlesex, England that was part of his estate that was probated in London on August 8, 1935.

If today's film fans remember Herbert Bunston, it is probably for his portrayal of Dr. Seward in _Dracula_. Some contemporary writers, like John Soister, have characterized Bunston's penchant for appearing "long suffering, slightly confused and not terribly capable" (2004, p. 140) as Dr. Seward and other characters. Other existing films, like _The Last of Mrs. Cheyney_, _The Lady of Scandal_, _Vanity Fair_ and _The Moonstone_, indicate that Bunston was far more versatile than that, providing evidence of the talent of this neglected performer. Herbert Bunston's existing body of work merits a reappraisal, while one can only long to have witnessed his stage successes or to have seen missing films like _The Monkey's Paw_.

with age, ignoring his financial situation to the point that he becomes involved with a notorious moneylender (von Seyffertitz). The elderly doctor alternately displays paternal concern for his daughter (Phyllis Barry) and anger, verbally sparring with his aged housekeeper (Elspeth Dudgeon, who gained some genre notoriety playing the elderly male Sir Roderick Femm in James Whale's _The Old Dark House_, 1932), whom he has been threatening to fire for 40 years. After making a house call to deliver a baby during a terrible storm, Sir John collapses into unconsciousness from pneumonia. Verinder's delirious ramblings in bed, however, help Inspector Cuff (Irwin) develop a plan to unravel the theft of the missing "moonstone." Other than the father-daughter relationship being similar, Verinder is a very different character than Dr. Seward in _Dracula_. Bunston, to his credit, handled both roles with range and conviction.

Set in the Scottish village of Thrum, _The Little Minister_ (1934), with Katharine Hepburn both headstrong and captivating, featured Bunston as Mr. Carfrae. Carfrae is the old minister being replaced by young and idealistic John Beal (in the title role).

Sources

Coughlin, Jim. "The Supporting Players of Universal's _Dracula_: Herbert Bunston, Frances Dade, Charles Gerrard," in _Midnight Marquee #49_ (Summer1995), pp. 63-67.

Soister, John T. _Up From the Vault: Rare Thrillers of the 1920s and 1930s_, Jefferson, NC: McFarland & Co., 2004.

Charles K. Gerrard
(1883 – 1969)

Of all the performers in the 1931 *Dracula*, Charles K. Gerrard was, aside from Bela Lugosi, the most established as a screen actor, having been prominently featured in silent films since 1916. He remains, however, one of the biggest enigmas of the cast of *Dracula*. He has largely been ignored by virtually every major film reference book. Why he left films for good in 1934 remains a mystery, although he did continue to act in the theater at least until 1950. Even the date and place of his death were not established until a few years back.

He was born Charles Kavanaugh in Carlow, Ireland, on December 20, 1883 (some sources wrongly report 1887). His mother's maiden name was McMurrough. Charles was the older brother of actor/director Douglas Gerrard McMurrough Kavanaugh, who, using the name of Douglas Gerrard, preceded his elder sibling to the screen in 1913. When Charles made his screen debut in 1916, he elected to follow the lead of his brother by using the name Charles Gerrard. On many occasions, he was billed as Charles K. Gerrard, with the "K" actually representing his last name "Kavanaugh." He was sometimes listed in screen credits as Charles Gerard (one "r") as well. A lean man, Gerrard stood five-foot 10 ½-inches. Charles went by the nickname of "Kit," as indicated by his World War II Draft Registration.

Details of Gerrard's early acting career are still undetermined. Following his emigration to the United States in 1907, Charles settled in Manhattan. He was first seen on Broadway as Watkins in *Officer 666* (1/29/12). Gerrard appeared with his brother Douglas and Edgar Norton in *The Spy* (1/13/13). *Secret Strings* (12/28/14), featuring Blanche Yurka and including Charles in the cast, was Gerrard's last Broadway venture until 1933.

Gerrard's first known film appearance was in *His Brother's Wife* (1916), starring Carlyle Blackwell. Charles' initial screen billing came as Jack Rodney, the Earl of Huntington in Selig's *The Prince Chap* (1916), directed by and starring Marshall Neilan. Opposite Alice Brady, Gerrard played Count Renier in *Miss Petticoats* (1916). Charles provided a villainous role as Craig Wells in *The Country That God Forgot* (1916), where he steals government funds, then shoots and deserts the leading lady (Mary Charleson). He portrayed fortune hunting Lord Percy in *The Plow Girl* (1916), by now exhibiting a propensity for playing aristocratic types of questionable character.

As Hamilton, Gerrard not only falsifies records but also murders his boss in *Melting Millions* (1917). *The Heart of Texas Ryan* (1917), the cast of which included Tom Mix, had Charles as Senator J. Murray Allison. Gerrard played the money-squandering Lawrence Topham in *A Woman's*

A portrait of Charles K. Gerrard (c. 1930)

Awakening (1917), coal-company manager Samuel Winter in *Little Miss Optimist* (1917) and brash Captain Francis Barold in *The Fair Barbarian* (1917), the latter two for Pallas Pictures starring Vivian Martin. *Down to Earth* (1917), with Douglas Fairbanks attempting to combat medical quackery at a clinic for wealthy hypochondriacs, featured Gerrard as socialite Charles Riddles, who loses his love Eileen Percy to Doug. *Down to Earth* and *The Heart of Texas Ryan* are two of Gerrard's early films that remain available for viewing.

Charles, as Grand Duke Orloff, worked with director Tod Browning for the first time in *The Legion of Death* (1918). Gerrard, as Tom Reardon, played opposite Lew Cody in *The Demon* (1918) and in *Beans* (1918), as Attorney Wingate. *Playthings* (1918), directed by brother Douglas Gerrard, included Charles as philandering Gordon Trenwith. He was Karl Wagner, an American-born German who turns to sabotage, in *The Hun Within* (1918), with Dorothy Gish. Other roles around this time for Gerrard were: Gerald Grant in *She Hired a Husband* (1918), gambler Maddie Knox in *Venus in the East* (1919), millionaire Hugh Varick in *Pettigrew's Girl* (1919) and scheming thief John Harland in *The Pest* (1919), starring Mabel Normand. As Thompson, Bryant Washburn's valet, in *Something to Do* (1919), Gerrard

The Darling of the Rich (1922): Leslie Austin, Betty Blythe and Charles Gerrard

masqueraded as "Lord Sidney." Gerrard had a meaty role as the evil dictator Theo Kameneff, who menaces Norma Talmadge, in *The New Moon* (1919). He did another villainous turn as the brutal Van Surdam in *The Isle of Conquest* (1919), again opposite Norma Talmadge. Rounding out the year, Charles played foreign adventurer Vincent Cortez in *Counterfeit* (1919) and murder-suspect Gordon Savage in *The Tooth of the Tiger* (1919), an Arsene Lupin tale.

By this point in his career, Charles Gerrard was virtually typecast as unscrupulous characters. He was William Gurson (aka "Will the Weasel"), who runs a shady cabaret and tries to take advantage of Dorothy Gish, in *Mary Ellen Comes to Town* (1920). *Why Women Sin* (1920) featured Gerrard as E.W. Wadsworth, who pretends to be phony nobleman Baron de Ville as part of a blackmail scheme. Charles played J. Dyke Sommers in *Whispers* (1920). *The World and His Wife* (1920) had Gerrard as Don Alvarado, who slanders beautiful Alma Rubens and is subsequently slain in a duel with Montagu Love. As Duval, Gerrard led a band of crooks that preyed upon the rich in *Blackbirds* (1920).

Gerrard played the unethical trustee Qualters in *The Passionate Pilgrim* (1921), John Stewart in *The Gilded Lily* (1921), Hurt Kilstrom in *Conceit* (1921) and was third-billed as Ned Ormsby in *Out of the Chorus* (1921). As French Pete, Gerrard hit a new characterological low as a criminal who fronts a bogus fund for war orphans in *Sheltered Daughters* (1921). *French Heels* (1922), starring Irene Castle, had Charles as Keith Merwyn. At the time the most expensive film made to date, *When Knighthood Was in Flower* (1922) starred Marion Davies and featured Gerrard as Sir Adam Judson. Financed by William Randolph Hearst, *When Knighthood Was in Flower* is another extant Gerrard silent feature. Gerrard also was seen as legal advisor Martin Tancray in *Heroes and Husbands* (1922), safe robber Dipley Poole in *Sure Fire Flint* (1922), Jim Slade in *The Lights of New York* (1922) and drug-addicted physician Dr. Crang in *Pawned* (1922). As Count Rostoff, Gerrard was involved in smuggling jewels in *Anna Ascends* (1922). Charles portrayed Torrence Welch in *The Darling of the Rich* (1923), Lord Altringham in *The Glimpses of the Moon* (1923), Sir Peter Dare in *The Dangerous Maid* (1923) and Charles Topping in *Her Temporary Husband* (1923). As the famed Sultan Saladin,

Off the Highway (1925): Charles Gerrard evokes the ire of William V. Mong.

Gerrard was second-billed to Wallace Beery in *Richard, the Lion-Hearted* (1923). *Loving Lies* (1924) had Gerrard as Tom Hayden, while *Lilies of the Field* (1924) included him as Ted Conroy. *Circe the Enchantress* (1924), starring Mae Murray, featured Gerrard as Ballard "Bal" Barrett.

Gerrard had an interesting role opposite the versatile and often overlooked William V. Mong in *Off the Highway* (1925). As drunken scoundrel Hector Kindon, Gerrard was the undeserving relative to whom Caleb Fry (Mong) changes his will, due to his disappointment in the choice of careers by his nephew (John Bowers). Fry feigns his own death, switching identities with his own servant (also played by Mong), who had just passed away. Fry, as the servant, is abused and cast out by the vile Kindon before being taken in by Bowers and his love (Margueritte De La Motte). Eventually, Fry is able to accumulate some money and cleverly uses it to ruin Kindon on Wall Street. The despairing Kindon commits suicide when he realizes the extent of his losses.

Continuing with morally challenged roles, Gerrard played Paul Glynn, a crook who befriends Robert Ames in order to steal jewels, in *The Wedding Song* (1925). As Creighton Deane in *California Straight Ahead* (1925), Gerrard actually kisses a chimp that he mistakes for Gertrude Olmstead. Charles portrayed Count Karaloff in *The Man on the Box* (1925), Lait Rodman in *Accused* (1925) and Reggie De Vere in *The Nervous Wreck* (1926).

The Better 'Ole (1926), starring Charlie Chaplin's older brother Sydney, is another Gerrard silent that still exists. Revealed as a German spy by Old Bill (Syd Chaplin) and his cronies Alf (Jack Ackroyd) and Bert (Harold Goodwin), Gerrard appeared as British Major Russett.

Now rarely playing a character to be trusted, Gerrard, as Dr. Carl Tanner, makes improper advances to the wife (Marie Prevost) of his best friend (Victor Varconi) in *For Wives Only* (1926). Gerrard was Steve, an international crook, in *The Cheerful Fraud* (1927). Aspiring to marry an heiress, Charles played the manipulative son of Scott (Charles Hill Mailes) in *Play Safe* (1927). As Arthur Remsen in *Framed* (1927), Charles sets up Milton Sills for stealing diamonds, but he later redeems himself by confessing to the deed on his deathbed at a penal colony to which he had been sent for another crime. Gerrard played Count Lazlos in *The Heart Thief* (1927), millionaire Raymond Tyson in *Painting the Town* (1927) and Robert Van Dorn in *Home Made* (1927).

Gerrard was DeLeon, the despicable owner of a dancing school, who is responsible for a young woman's suicide in *The Port of Missing Girls* (1928). Charles appeared as Joe in *Ladies of the Night Club* (1928), Mr. Roberts in *The Wright Idea* (1928) and Leonard Hardingham in *Romance of a Rogue* (1928), a melodrama starring H.B. Warner.

Caught in the Fog (1928), set aboard a houseboat off the coast of Florida, had Gerrard on hand as a criminal accomplice to May McAvoy. As "Silk Shirt" Harry, Charles barely hides his jewel thieving aspirations while masquerading as a cook. Although McAvoy assists Harry in pilfering a valuable pearl necklace, plot twists reveal the complexity of her character.

As duplicitous businessman Henry Lord, Gerrard is murdered for his indiscretions in *Circumstantial Evidence* (1929). *The Lone Wolf's Daughter* (1929), starring Bert Lytell as Michael Lanyard, gave Gerrard a prominent (third-billed) part as Count Polinac, an international jewel thief and extortionist. *Light Fingers* (1929), a crime drama starring Ian Keith, had Gerrard on hand as London Tower. Charles played Commander Weymouth of the Royal Navy in *Men Without Women* (1930), a John Ford-directed drama set aboard a submarine. *Anybody's Woman* (1930), directed by Dorothy Arzner and involving a romantic triangle of Ruth Chatterton, Clive Brook and Paul Lukas, featured Gerrard as Walter Harvey.

Journey's End (1930), directed by James Whale and featuring a fine cast including Colin Clive, David Manners, Ian McLaren, Billy Bevan and Anthony Bushell, had Gerrard in a significant role as Private Mason. As the cook in the dugout of the trenches of a World War I battlefield, Mason must make do with limited provisions to spice up teatime and meals for the British officers to whom he attends. Gerrard was quite good as Mason, providing with Billy Bevan some comic moments amidst a poignant, tragic story. James Whale was more adept at handling comedy

Light Fingers (1929): Ian Keith threatens Charles Gerrard.

Having viewed Gerrard's abler work in *Journey's End* and *Another Fine Mess*, the fault may be more with Tod Browning's misguided attempt to inject comedy, as well as that of the screenwriters (Garrett Ford, et al.). Perhaps Billy Bevan or Forrester Harvey could have done more with the role or maybe the cockney humor was out of place altogether.

Gerrard is first viewed in *Dracula* in the room of the patient Renfield (Dwight Frye). Martin attempts to prevent Renfield from eating a spider, even berating the madman for abandoning his former staple of flies. Martin finally gives in, uttering, "All right. 'ave it your own way!" Martin escorts Renfield to and from interviews with Dr. Seward (Herbert Bunston) and Professor Van Helsing (Edward Van Sloan), muttering about Renfield's ability to escape from his confinement. He tells Seward that it is unlikely Renfield can be put in a place from where he cannot get loose. Martin also provides the reference to what happened to Lucy (Frances Dade), as he

than was Tod Browning, which might explain why Gerrard was more subtly amusing in *Journey's End* than in his broader interpretation of Martin in *Dracula*.

Gerrard had an even greater opportunity to showcase his comedic skills in the Laurel and Hardy short, *Another Fine Mess* (1930). Charles played Lord Leopold Ambrose Plumtree, who, along with his new bride (Thelma Todd), attempts to see Colonel Buckshot (James Finlayson) about renting his "palatial residence." Laurel and Hardy, hiding from the police, have taken refuge in the home of the Colonel, who has left for a safari in South Africa. Hardy pretends to be the Colonel, engaging in humorous interplay with Gerrard about the rent, billiards and other topics, before Finlayson returns, chasing "Plummie" out of the house with a revolver.

Gerrard played Bert, the henchman of London gangster Montagu Love, in *The Lion and the Lamb* (1931). He portrayed Gibson in the Janet Gaynor and Charles Farrell drama, *The Man Who Came Back* (1931). What followed would be the role for which Gerrard is likely best remembered today—Martin, the sanitorium guard in *Dracula* (1931).

The role of Martin in the film version of *Dracula* (1931) is significantly different from that of Butterworth (originated on Broadway by Alfred Frith), the sanitorium attendant, in the theatrical treatment by Hamilton Deane and John L. Balderston. Martin's character has been rewritten from that of Butterworth with almost the sole purpose of providing comic relief, which does not impress as working well within the overall atmosphere of *Dracula*. Tom Weaver and the Brunas brothers in *Universal Horrors* label Gerrard's performance as Martin, "completely inept" (p. 16).

Another Fine Mess (1930): Gerrard as Lord Plumtree in the Laurel and Hardy comedy short

"What do you think of them, Trotter?"

Journey's End (1930): Billy Bevan, Charles Gerrard, Colin Clive and Anthony Bushell in a scene from the poignant anti-war film directed by James Whale

reads a newspaper article to the nurses about the "woman in white." To the maid (Moon Carroll), Martin states, "They're all crazy. They're all crazy except you and me. Sometimes I 'ave my doubts about you." When the maid concurs, Martin recoils with an exaggerated take. *Dracula* might not represent Charles Gerrard at his best, but without the role of Martin, he might hardly be remembered at all.

After a substantial career in silent films and a few noteworthy appearances in early talkies, of which *Dracula* was one, Charles Gerrard's screen career experienced a fairly rapid, unexpected decline. Gerrard had a small, unbilled bit in *Always Goodbye* (1931), which starred Elissa Landi and featured Charles' cast mate from *Dracula*, Herbert Bunston. Charles was the bailiff in *The Menace* (1932), which starred H.B. Warner and Bette Davis and included other "forgotten faces" like Halliwell Hobbes, Murray Kinnell and Forrester Harvey. *Devil's Lottery* (1932), with Elissa Landi and Victor McLaglen, had Gerrard on screen for just a brief glimpse as a man giving a toast.

Following an unbilled appearance in *Man About Town* (1932) for Fox, Charles Gerrard traveled to England, where he would act in two of his three final films. Gerrard was uncredited in the Stanley Lupino musical, *Facing the Music* (1933). He returned stateside to be seen (but not billed) in *If I Were Free* (1933), with Irene Dunne and Clive Brook. Gerrard's last known screen role came as Mr. Whitman, the father of Enid Stamp-Taylor, in the U.K. comedy *A Political Party* (1934), featuring a young John Mills.

Upon his return to the United States in late 1933, Gerrard focused his acting efforts exclusively on the stage. He played McGregor, the dogsled driver, in *The World Waits* (10/25/33), a play concerning a South Pole expedition. *Yellow Jack* (3/6/34) had Gerrard in the cast as Adrian Stokes of the West African Yellow Fever Commission. Bernard Jukes, the original stage Renfield from *Dracula*, also appeared in *Yellow Jack*, playing a laboratory assistant. Gerrard played Moran in the short-lived (four performances) *The Puritan* (1/23/36). It would be six years before Gerrard would be again seen on the Broadway stage.

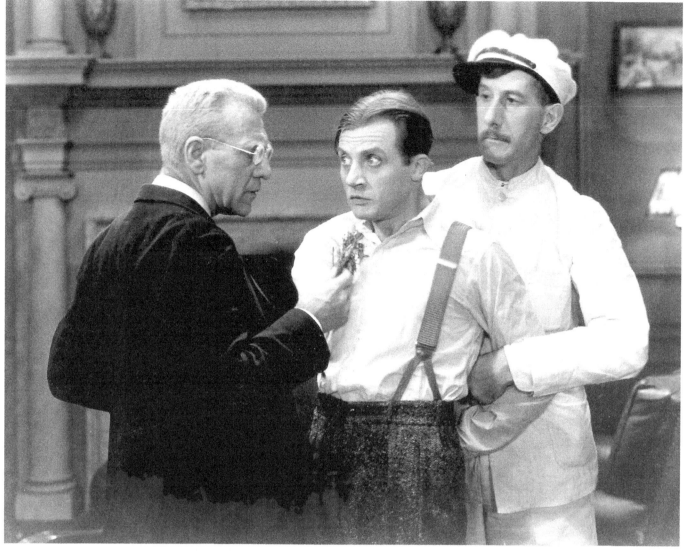

Dracula (1931): Van Helsing (Edward Van Sloan) uses wolfsbane to intimidate Renfield (Dwight Frye), who is being restrained by Martin (Charles Gerrard).

He played Rear Admiral Spring in *Plan M* (2/20/42), the cast of which included Lumsden Hare and Neil Fitzgerald. *Catherine Was Great* (8/2/44), headlining the colorful Mae West, had a decent run of 191 performances at the Shubert. Gerrard portrayed Count Panin as part of a large cast that prominently featured young Gene Barry. The final Broadway role for Gerrard was that of the warder in *The Gioconda Smile* (10/7/50), starring Basil Rathbone.

Charles Gerrard continued acting in the theatre for at least 16 years after leaving films, but the reason he never returned to the screen is unknown. There is minimal information, other than theater credits, for Gerrard from 1934 until his death at the age of 85 on January 1, 1969 in New York City. Brother Douglas, who passed away on June 5, 1950 at 58, preceded Charles in death by 19 years.

While it could be said that *Dracula* certainly typecast not only Bela Lugosi but also Dwight Frye and Edward Van Sloan for the rest of their performing lives, the film seemed to also mark the end of Charles Gerrard's days as a motion picture actor. Gerrard had been a well-established featured player in the silents, specializing in crooks, cads and other unscrupulous types. He worked for all the major studios, with important directors and major stars. How he could not have found a niche in similar roles in talkies is strange indeed. At least there are some silent films, like *Down to Earth* and *The Better 'Ole*, as well as important roles in *Journey's End*, *Another Fine Mess* and of course *Dracula* that can still provide evidence of the neglected talent of Charles Gerrard.

Sources

Coughlin, Jim. "The Supporting Players of Universal's *Dracula*: Herbert Bunston, Frances Dade, Charles Gerrard," in *Midnight Marquee #49* (Summer1995), pp. 63-67.

Dr. Jekyll and Mr. Hyde
(1931)

Edgar Norton
(1868 - 1953)

Although he had an acting career involving parts of seven decades, Edgar Norton has received minimal recognition in film and theater reference works. After a lengthy stage career, Norton made the adjustment to motion pictures, including some important contributions to the horror film genre (*The Man Who Laughs, Dr. Jekyll and Mr. Hyde* 1931, *Dracula's Daughter, Son of Frankenstein*, etc.). Norton worked for all the major studios. Unfortunately, Norton became typecast, mainly in butler/servant roles, but he usually managed to perform with distinction in even the smallest of parts. Edgar made an unsung contribution to the fantasy film genre by being a catalyst in bringing *Alice in Wonderland* (1933) to the screen.

Harry Edgar Mills was born in Islington, Middlesex (now part of London), England on August 11, 1868. Edgar was the fourth of eight children of Jane Anne (née Fleming) (1837-1880) and Frederic Mills (1837-1895), a British civil service clerk. The other Mills children (and year of birth) were: Percy Ransom (1861), Ethel Mary Josephine (1864), Lionel Fleming (1867), Annie J. (1872), Lilian Frederica (1874), Alice Muriel (1875) and Agnes Eveleen (1878). Contrary to what his appearance in later years might suggest, Edgar, as a young man, was an accomplished athlete. He excelled at swimming and enjoyed boxing, golf and tennis.

Already interested in the stage, Harry was thrilled when his father received a visit from noted actor Richard Mansfield in 1880, as Edgar related to a reporter from The *New York Times* in 1932:

> I was only 12 years old when I first saw Mansfield in *Dr. Jekyll and Mr. Hyde*. He had scored a tremendous hit in the play in New York the year before and Sir Henry Irving had induced him to come to London with the play. My father, who was in the English Government service, knew Mansfield and, when the great actor reached London in August of 1880, he came to our home for dinner. He was with us several times and I stared at him with open-eyed, and perhaps open-mouthed, idolization. I remember Mansfield asking me what I planned to make of myself and I stammered, to my family's amazement,

An early woodcut portrait of Edgar Norton (c. 1905)

> that I wanted to be an actor. Mansfield laughed and told me if I ever went on the stage to let him know and he'd give me a chance with his company.

Consistent with what he had told Richard Mansfield, young Mills followed through with his dream of becoming an actor. Billed as Edgar Norton, 18-year-old Harry Edgar made his theatrical debut on 12/23/1886 in *Alice in Wonderland: A Musical Dream Play, in Two Acts for Children and Others*. The operetta, presented by H. Savile Clarke with music by Walter Slaughter, starred Miss Phoebe Carlo. Norton, as the March Hare, was described as wearing a red waistcoat, as well as a wreath of roses around his left ear. Already a Lewis Carroll devotee, Norton was highly impacted by this production, which would prominently factor in his life 47 years hence.

In his early theatrical days, not only did Norton tour the provinces, but he also played major British theatres like the Globe and the Strand. At the latter, he portrayed suitor Benjamin Backbite in support of Kate Vaughan (as Lady Teazle) in *School for Scandal* (1887).

By 1889, Norton was a member of the theatrical company of noted Shakespearean actor Richard Mansfield, who was true to his word nine years prior about one day engaging young Edgar in his company. In Mansfield's production of *King Richard III* (3/16/1889), Norton appeared as Sir Thomas Vaughan. Norton sailed to America with Mansfield's troupe, departing from Liverpool, England on the Catalonia on 9/18/1889, and landing in Boston, Massachusetts on 9/22/1889. Among the roles Norton assayed on Broadway during the tour were: The Earl of Surrey in *King Richard III* (12/16/89), Poole in *Dr. Jekyll and Mr. Hyde* (1/2/90), a minor part in *Prince Karl* (1/27/90), the landlord in *Master and the Man* (2/5/90) and the loutish bailiff in *Beau Brummell* (5/19/90), written especially for Mansfield by Clyde Fitch. In addition to New York, Mansfield's company played Philadelphia; Washington, DC; Baltimore; Chicago; St. Louis; Cleveland; Rochester and Boston.

In a 1/3/32 *New York Times* piece, Norton reflected on the intensive and diversified theatrical training he received under Mansfield's tutelage, including the understudy system:

> One night we youngsters would play juveniles, and the next night we might be a character actor or an aged person. Each of us had to know every part in every play, which we might possibly portray.

Norton had understudied the character of Poole despite being only 22 at the time. When an actor departed the company, Mansfield entrusted Edgar with the role, even loaning the young man his "lucky wig" in order to play the much older Poole.

Edgar, then 22 years old, married Lillian Mabel Hubbard, 20, at St. James Cathedral in Toronto, Ontario, Canada, on 9/16/1890. J. Philip Dumoulin performed the wedding ceremony. His wife would go by the name of Mabel Norton.

After parting ways with Mansfield and his company, Norton found adequate demand for his services, mainly on the East Coast. In New York, Edgar was seen at the Union Square Theatre in *Adrift* (the curtain raiser) and *The Fabricator* (8/6/1892), both of which starred Robert Hilliard. Norton played Frank Elliott in the former and Wilber in the latter. In Philadelphia, Norton appeared in *The Voodoo* (4/18/1893).

While touring, Edgar's wife Mabel gave birth to their only child, Edgar Norton Mills, on March 27, 1893, in Chicago, Illinois. The younger Edgar would serve in the

A late 1920s portrait of Norton

United States Navy in World War I, marry shortly after the war (to Anne J. Mills) and have two children of his own (Annette E. Mills, born c.1921, and Edgar N. Mills, born 12/6/23).

Norton spent parts of two seasons with the Empire Theatre (Brooklyn, New York) Stock Company, appearing in works like *The House With Green Blinds* (10/16/1893). He then went on tour with a star-studded company, including Rose Coghlan, Maurice Barrymore, Ada Dyas and Effie Shannon. For Coghlan's troupe, Norton played Lord Alfred Rufford in Oscar Wilde's *A Woman of No Importance* (12/11/1893) and Wright in *Lady Barter* (1/2/1894). Norton enacted the role of the first mate in *John-a-Dreams* (3/18/1895), with Henry Miller. In the fall of 1897, Edgar played Boston and elsewhere as Chickwell, the servant, in the farce *The Mysterious Mr. Bugle*. Norton was seen on Broadway as the Manager in *The Christian* (11/28/1898), starring Viola Allen, in addition to touring extensively with the show (Albany, NY; Washington, DC; Providence, RI; etc.).

After the turn of the century, Edgar appeared on Broadway in a revival of *The School for Scandal* (1/31/02). Norton was part of a large company in an extremely popular musical comedy, *The Prince of Pilsen* (3/17/03). The

"WHO INVITED YOU TO THE PARTY?"

MARGUERITE CLARK
IN
"THE AMAZONS"
© 1917

The Amazons (1917): **Edgar Norton, Eleanor Lawson, Marguerite Clark, Helen Greene and Adolphe Menjou**

show, with book by Frank Pixley and music by Gustav Luders, provided the public with many enduring songs, including "Heidelberg (The Stein Song)."

In December 1903, Norton was playing Sir Archibald Blackett in *The Toreador* at the Broadway Theatre in Denver, Colorado. His oldest sibling Percy, 42 years of age, an actor himself in plays such as *The Burgomaster*, was suffering from consumption and, facing death, moved in with Edgar. During one particular performance, the press noted that Norton played his role with his eyes filled with tears, realizing he had said his final farewell to his brother on his way to the theater. Percy is said to have passed away during that performance of *The Toreador*. Norton continued to tour in *The Toreador* with the Jefferson De Angelis Opera Company, playing Atlanta in late January 1904. He frequently would get the biggest laughs of the show when he would sing "Everybody's Awfully Good to Me."

Back in New York, Norton, as Lord Triverton, performed in another musical with an interesting title, *The Maid and the Mummy* (7/25/04). The horror/mummy angle was just a hoax within the plot, however. Also on Broad-

way, Norton was seen in *The Rich Mrs. Repton* (11/16/04). Both Edgar, as the Duke of St. Kitts, and wife Mabel, as the comical charwoman Mrs. Cropper, toured with star Edna Wallace Hopper in *A Country Mouse*, playing California and Oregon in early 1905. Of his performance as the Reverend Mr. Denman in *The American Lord* (4/16/06), a Syracuse critic wrote, "Edgar Norton's curate was of the old *Private Secretary* type and as mirthful."

Edgar's wife, Mabel Norton, was an interesting, creative individual herself. On 11/9/07, Mabel filed a patent (#882789) for a stocking cap cover that would protect a woman's stocking on the upper part of the leg. The patent for her device was issued on 3/24/08. She continued to dabble with designing ideas over the years, once again applying for a patent (US1419940A) on 4/7/21 for an all-in-one woman's petticoat and drawers, which was granted on 6/20/22. While the Nortons lived in New York, Mabel was prominent in the Twelfth Night Club, a sister organization to the Lambs and the Players involving stage actresses and actors' spouses. When Edgar and Mabel permanently relocated to the West Coast, she resigned from her position

The World We Live In (1921 Broadway play): Edgar Norton as Ichneumon Fly, with Grace Dougherty

to accept the chairmanship of the drama section of the Women's Club of Hollywood.

Mabel also had some unwanted notoriety when she was arrested on 10/20/09 for an unpaid hotel bill exceeding $500 owed to the Hotel Remington on 129 W. 46th Street in New York City. When the Nortons were first pressured to settle up on their bill, Edgar was in a play in Chicago. Mabel, on her lawyer's advice, had removed her belongings from their lodging and moved to the Hudson Grand View Apartment House on Clermont Avenue, where the arrest took place. Edgar had returned to New York and with his son forcibly blocked the entrance of a detective to their apartment. As a result, Edgar was also charged with interfering with a policeman. Both Edgar and Mabel spent the night at the 123rd Station. Subsequently, Mabel filed suit for false arrest and malicious prosecution. Mabel claimed the stigma of the arrest adversely impacted her performing career and also caused emotional distress. The case went on for three years, during which time Mabel was awarded $5000 in damages, only to have the decision reversed and then reinstated.

On Broadway, Edgar played Harold Percy Montague in *Nearly a Hero* (1/24/08) and Algernon Graham in *The Boys and Betty* (11/2/08), while also appearing in *An Englishman's Home* (3/22/09). Other theatrical performances for Norton during this period were: Ricky Van Riker in *A Little Brother of the Rich* (12/27/09), the Chevalier in the operetta *Madame Troubador* (10/10/10) and Bertrand de

Mauret in *The Spy* (1/13/13), with Charles K. Gerrard (Martin in the 1931 *Dracula*). At the Cort Theatre in Chicago, Norton was Arthur Stabler in the musical *When Love is Young* (10/28/13). Back in New York, Edgar was featured in *The Beautiful Adventure* (9/5/14), *A Full House* (5/10/15) and as Mortimer in Arnold Daly's revival of *Beau Brummell* (4/24/16). In the sort of role in which Norton would be very familiar on screen, he was the valet to Cyril Maude in *The Basker* (10/30/16).

Like many Broadway performers in the 'teens, Norton obtained work in some early silent feature films. Edgar's presumed film debut came in *The Ocean Waif* (1916), a print of which still exists, although some sections have badly deteriorated. Norton was Hawkins, the valet to novelist Carlyle Blackwell, both of whom attempt to move into a presumed deserted house by the sea that is occupied by squatter Doris Kenyon. Edgar played Lord Tweenways in *The Amazons* (1917), a comedy about three sisters, including Marguerite Clark, who rebel against a male-dominated society. He reprised his Broadway role of Valentine Borroyer ("a boring and stodgy man of wealth") in *The Beautiful Adventure* (1917). As Martin, Norton was seen with Francis X. Bushman in *A Pair of Cupids* (1918).

Norton still considered himself primarily a stage performer, despite his occasional forays into motion pictures. He appeared in New York as Ethelbert Briggs in *Stranger Than Fiction* (3/5/17), starring E.H. Southern. The musi-

Men (1924): Edgar Norton as the Baron

Tiger Love (1924): **A portrait of Norton as Don Victoriano Fuentes**

satirical fantasy *The World We Live In* (aka *The Insect Comedy*, 10/31/22). The play, written by Josef and Karel Capek, Czech playwrights also responsible for *R.U.R.* and the term "robot," received good notices, while running for 111 performances. In a revival of Shakespeare's *As You Like It* (4/3/23), featuring a star-laden cast including Ian Keith, A.E. Anson, Marjorie Rambeau and Walter Abel, Norton played LeBeau. *As You Like It* would turn out to be Edgar's final Broadway appearance. From then on, Norton would turn his professional attention almost exclusively to motion pictures.

Norton did play a rather unusual role outside of either film or theater. He was engaged for many years to be the double for William Gibbs McAdoo, to whom Edgar bore a strong resemblance. McAdoo had been Secretary of the Treasury (1913-1918) under Woodrow Wilson and would later serve as U.S. Senator from California (1933-1938). Occasionally, photos of McAdoo have been misidentified as Norton and vice versa.

As Peters in *The Light in the Dark* (1922), Norton had the opportunity to work alongside Lon Chaney. For Famous Players/Lasky, for whom Edgar made a number of silents, Norton was Cecil Updyke, an exotic musician in *Woman-Proof* (1923). Despite its title, *The Wolf Man* (1924) was not a horror film, but starred John Gilbert ("a beast when

cal *The Melting of Molly* (12/30/18) had Norton as St. Clair McTabb. Again with wife Mabel, Edgar was featured in the Victor Herbert musical *The Velvet Lady* in Chicago (10/18/19) and elsewhere. Norton made his only film in a four-year span, playing Thomas in *The New York Idea* (1920), with Alice Brady and Lowell Sherman.

Norton had the wonderful opportunity to tour with Fred and Adele Astaire in the musical variety *Apple Blossoms* in 1921. Reviewing that show when it played at Toledo, Ohio's Saxon Auditorium, the *Toledo Blade* critic wrote, "The laughs were mostly supplied by Edgar Norton as a valet, and by Ruth Lee (with whom Edgar sang *The Marriage Knot*), as Julia, a maid, to whom are given the snappiest lines in the piece." Again with the Astaires and Marjorie Gateson, Edgar was back on Broadway playing the head waiter in the musical *The Love Letter* (10/4/21). One of Norton's most intriguing Broadway roles was that of Ichneumon Fly, who preys on unsuspecting crickets, in the

Lost: a Wife (1925): **Adolphe Menjou (left) with a disconsolate Edgar Norton**

The Love Parade (1929): Edgar Norton with Maurice Chevalier

drunk") and featured Norton as Sir Reginald Stackpoole. Of his role in *Men* (1924), the *New York Times* (5/5/24) noted, "Mr. Norton is especially good as the Baron" (who lures Pola Negri to Paris, only to abandon her).

Often playing older than his actual age, Norton was seen as the elderly actor in the theatrical rooming house in *Broadway After Dark* (1924). Edgar had the flamboyant role of Don Victoriano Fuentes in *Tiger Love* (1924). He played Clyde Wiel in *The Female* (1924), with Betty Compson and Warner Baxter. Again with Betty Compson and Adolphe Menjou, Edgar was Archie Wells in *The Fast Set* (1924).

Learning to Love (1925), starring Constance Talmadge, had Norton in a role to which he would become very accustomed (playing a manservant in more than 50 films)—the butler. *Lost: A Wife* (1924) provided Norton the interesting role of Baron Deliguieres, who has his wife (Greta Nissen) stolen away by Adolphe Menjou. Other parts for Edgar at this juncture were: William Blake in *Enticement* (1925), Dick Mayne in *The Marriage Whirl* (1925), the valet in *A Regular Fellow* (1925) and Hugo Jensen in *The King on Main Street* (1925).

Norton portrayed the Hon. Charles Darnely (Blanche Sweet's father) in *The Lady From Hell* (1926). Edgar was uncredited in *The Boy Friend* (1926) and played Beadon in *Marriage License?* (1926), which starred Alma Rubens. *Diplomacy* (1926), a Paramount film featuring genre character players like Sojin, Arthur Edmund Carewe and Gustav von Seyffertitz, included Norton as the servant at the British Embassy. Norton was the Englishman in *Fast and Furious* (1927), Ernie Whitehead in *Singed* (1927) and Jennings, the butler, in *My Friend From India* (1927).

Of his work in *The Student Prince in Old Heidelberg* (1927), *The New York Times* stated, "Edgar Norton gives a fine character study as Lutz, the smileless and haughty servant." In Universal's *The Man Who Laughs* (1928), with fine direction by Paul Leni and a bravado performance by Conrad Veidt, Norton played the Lord High Chancellor.

Norton was the insipid Lord Braggot, who gets "stood up" by his betrothed (Colleen Moore), in *Oh, Kay!* (1928). He played a valet in *A Certain Young Man* (1928). As private investigator Hilary Galt in *Behind That Curtain* (1929), with E.L. Park as Inspector Charlie Chan, Norton threatens to

Dr. Jekyll and Mr. Hyde (1931): **The loyal Poole (Edgar Norton) serves Dr. Jekyll (Fredric March).**

expose damaging information on Warner Baxter, but gets murdered by Phillip Strange before he can complete his dirty work. *The Love Parade* (1929), starring Maurice Chevalier and Jeanette MacDonald, had Norton on hand as the sympathetic Master of Ceremonies.

In the early days of sound, Norton was becoming more and more typecast as a servant. He was Fredric March's butler in *Sarah and Son* (1930), Alfred (Marie Dressler's butler) in *The Girl Said No* (1930), Dawes in *The Man From Blankley's* (1930), Ronald (Mary Astor's butler) in *Ladies Love Brutes* (1930), Williams (Lloyd Hughes' butler) in *The Runaway Bride* (1930), Morton in *A Lady of Scandal* (1930) and the butler in *A Lady Surrenders* (1930). Other roles ranged from a party guest in *Strictly Unconventional* (1930) to characters of distinction, such as Colonel Wunderlich in *One Romantic Night* (1930) and Lord Markham in *Sweet Kitty Belairs* (1930). Norton appeared in *Monte Carlo* (1930), directed by Ernst Lubitsch. Edgar played Renal in *Du Barry, Woman of Passion* (1930) and Thomas in *East is West* (1930). Round-

ing out a busy year, Norton was Halliwell Hobbes' lawyer in the comedy *Charley's Aunt* (1930).

Norton was colorful as Bolton, C. Aubrey Smith's servant, in *Bachelor Father* (1931). He played Dobbs, Gilbert Emery's butler, in *The Lady Refuses* (1931). Norton was Williams in *Meet the Wife* (1931), Tipton in *Compromised* (1931) and a fox huntsman in Cecil B. DeMille's remake of *The Squaw Man* (1931).

Dr. Jekyll and Mr. Hyde (1931), directed by Rouben Mamoulian and starring Fredric March in an Academy Award-winning dual role, gave Norton the key role of Poole, Jekyll's loyal, caring servant. Norton is first seen as Poole in the restored opening sequence of *Dr. Jekyll and Mr. Hyde*. Poole is later viewed knocking at Jekyll's laboratory door, voicing concern over the doctor's lack of sleep. Poole then delivers a note from Muriel Carew (Rose Hobart). Later, when Dr. Lanyan (Holmes Herbert) calls on Jekyll, Poole attempts to cover for his employer's increasingly erratic behavior ("He isn't well," claims the servant). Poole

Blind Adventure (1933): Edgar Norton and Robert Armstrong

(John Halliday's secretary) in *The Man Called Back* (1932), a butler in *Enemies of Society* (1933), Roberts the butler in *Sing, Sinner, Sing* (1933), George the butler in *Only Yesterday* (1933), the butler in *The Big Brain* (1933) and again a valet in *The Worst Woman in Paris?* (1933). In the Maurice Chevalier/Jeanette MacDonald musical *Love Me Tonight* (1932), audiences not only witnessed Norton again playing a valet, but also heard him sing a verse of Rodgers and Hart's "The Son Of A Gun Is Nothing But a Tailor."

Looking Forward (1933), a sentimental film set in the Depression featuring Lionel Barrymore, Lewis Stone and Colin Clive, had Norton as Mr. Elliott. Edgar was the maître d'hotel who interacts with Robert Armstrong in *Blind Adventure* (1933). Norton temporarily broke away from his

is relieved when Jekyll makes a display of discarding the key to the back door of the lab (symbolic of abandoning his experiments), but then is dispatched with a message for Miss Ivy (Miriam Hopkins). Poole's joy over Jekyll's upcoming wedding to Miss Carew abates as the doctor resumes his scientific endeavors. One night, Poole finds himself confronted by Mr. Hyde and attempts to block the way to Jekyll's front door. Poole then assists the police in gaining access to Jekyll's lab, thinking he is aiding his master. When he witnesses Hyde being shot, however, it is Poole who is the first to realize that he is actually Dr. Jekyll. Poole weeps, grasping his hands, as the film concludes. Norton rendered a fine characterization of Poole, whose dedication and trustworthiness help establish the kind of man Jekyll was prior to delving into areas "best left alone."

When interviewed (the *New York Times*, 1/3/32) on the set of the 1931 film, Norton was quite nostalgic about his experience in the role of Poole in Richard Mansfield's Company 33 years prior:

> When we hear of how *Dr. Jekyll and Mr. Hyde* frightened audiences, we only bear a portion of the real thrills. Mansfield actually frightened the members of his cast who had been with him for years. My heart always beat furiously during my scenes with him as Hyde.

To say that Norton was now pigeonholed by Hollywood is an understatement. Edgar was Robert Montgomery's butler in *Letty Lynton* (1932), Tompkins (Henry Stephenson's butler) in *Red-Headed Woman* (1932), Donaldson

A candid shot of Norton and his wife Mabel in the midst of negotiations for the sale of the rights of *Alice in Wonderland* to Paramount (c. 1933).

East of Java **(1935): Frank Albertson reads information displayed by Edgar Norton.**

screen typecasting when he returned to the stage in California in a production of *The Cat and the Fiddle* (11/32) with Olga Baclanova of *Freaks* fame.

As stated, the works of Lewis Carroll had long intrigued Norton, holding the belief that *Alice's Adventures in Wonderland* and *Through the Looking-Glass* could be translated into wonderful film adaptations. Although the books had become public domain in the United States, Edgar seized on the idea of obtaining the English rights, which would also include all British colonies and provinces, to these works. Norton spent years checking records, tracking down heirs, and corresponding with those connected to the estate of Lewis Carroll. He also sought out relatives of H. Savile Clark, who brought *Alice ...* to the stage, and Walter Slaughter, who had composed the original musical version of *Alice ...* in which Edgar had appeared in 1886. Eventually, Norton was able to secure all the English rights from the three estates.

Norton first approached the film industry via an ad taken out in trade publications in 1927. In the ad, Edgar made the claim that he had the rights to Carroll's works, adding they "would make the most perfect motion picture ever produced" (*The Ogden Standard Examiner*, 12/17/33). Norton began a "campaign of persuasion" (the *New York Times*, 1/7/34), going from studio to studio, exhausting all his Hollywood contacts to no avail. Although no studios at the time took Norton up on his offer, the fact he held the English rights discouraged Mary Pickford, Walt Disney and others from attempting to do a film version of *Alice in Wonderland*.

Because of an upsurge in public interest in Lewis Carroll and his works, Mabel Norton, who now was managing husband Edgar's career, decided the time was right to renew an effort to bring *Alice in Wonderland* to the screen. Mabel took manuscripts and documents to Sidney Kent of Paramount, with whom a deal was finally consummated in April 1933. The Nortons sailed to London in July 1933 to tie up all loose ends, returning to the United States in September 1933. Paramount's production of *Alice in Wonderland* began in late September, with a release date of 12/22/33. Edgar Norton's long-time dream had finally been realized. The only disappointment was that he was not able to secure his desired role of the Mad Hatter (it went to Edward Everett Horton) for himself.

Norton may not have appeared in Paramount's *Alice ...*, but his services remained in demand by the studios, with nine film parts in 1934 alone. Admittedly, the bulk of his roles had a familiar quality to them: The butler in *The Richest Girl in the World* (1934), Owen (Constance Bennett's butler) in *Outcast Lady* (1934), the butler at the party in *Imitation of Life* (1934) and Higgins the valet in *Sons of Steel* (1934). In a role reminiscent of some of Edgar's silent film efforts, Norton portrayed Baron Passeria in *Thirty-Day Princess* (1934), with Sylvia Sidney in the lead. Edgar played the first aide to

Rulers of the Sea **(1939): The shipping magnates—Vaughn Glaser, Edgar Norton, Montagu Love and Leonard Mudie**

Son of Frankenstein (1939): With Ygor (Bela Lugosi) and the Monster (Boris Karloff) in the background, Wolf (Basil Rathbone) is assisted by Benson (Edgar Norton).

the governor (Reginald Owen) in *Stingaree* (1934). He was Meadows in *Strictly Dynamite* (1934), Meigs in *Million Dollar Ransom* (1934) and a judge in *We Live Again* (1934).

As Lewis, Edgar was Reginald Denny's chauffeur in *Vagabond Lady* (1935). He played Katharine Alexander's butler in *The Girl From 10th Avenue* (1935). The short *Manhattan Monkey Business* (1935) included Norton as a doorman. Universal's borderline horror/adventure tale *East of Java* (1935), directed by George Melford of 1931 Spanish *Dracula* notoriety, had Edgar on hand as an eccentric island resident. Norton's scenes did not survive the final cut of *I Dream Too Much* (1935) and his role of the herald in *Trouble for Two* (1936), adapted from Robert Louis Stevenson's *The Suicide Club*, may have suffered the same fate. Edgar did appear as the London hotel manager in Fred Astaire's *Top Hat* (1935), Gibbs in *When a Man's a Man* (1935), Grimsby in *August Weekend* (1936) and for a brief moment in Laurel and Hardy's *The Bohemian Girl* (1936).

Dracula's Daughter (1936), an underrated Universal horror entry with Gloria Holden providing an interesting interpretation of the title role, gave Norton only one scene as Hobbs, servant to Scotland Yard's Sir Basil Humphrey (Gilbert Emery). After Dr. Jeffrey Garth (Otto Kruger) comes to realize that Countess Zaleska (Holden) is likely culpable for some bizarre murders, he phones Sir Basil, who is busy in his bed at home sorting stamps. As Hobbs hands the telephone to his employer, he is directed to search for "the Bolivian Blue." After Sir Basil's conversation with Garth concludes, Hobbs triumphantly announces that he has located the missing stamp. His joy is short lived, as Sir Basil chides him for actually finding "the Guatemalan Red." Hobbs clears away the stamp collection, asking if Sir Basil is ready for his "barley water." Sir Basil instead insists on his topcoat and revolver, as he is off to hunt vampires! Hobbs deadpans, "I always understood you went after them with a checkbook, sir," only to be told not to be

Practically Yours (1944): Edgar Norton, Fred MacMurray and Cecil Kellaway

facetious. "No sir!," Hobbs retorts, with an expression that combines condescension with confusion. Tom Weaver and the Brunas brothers in *Universal Horrors* claim that *Dracula's Daughter* is laden with excessive humor, some better fitting "a drawing room comedy." Norton's scene with Emery, however, is truly one of the film's amusing moments.

The House of Secrets (1936), an atmospheric low-budget thriller with genre veterans Holmes Herbert and George Rosener in colorful roles, featured Norton as Mr. Henry Shippam, the arthritic husband of the woman (Rita Carlyle) who tends to the titled old mansion. It was back to business as usual, with Edgar as Jenkins the servant in *Give Me Your Heart* (1936). He played James, the butler on stage, in *On the Avenue* (1937). Norton was Jarvis the butler in *Bill Cracks Down* (1937) and Rivers (Onslow Stevens' butler) in *You Can't Buy Luck* (1937). Edgar's already minor roles were further diminishing in size, but from time to time Norton would be seen in a major production, as when he played impresario John Barrymore's secretary in MGM's lavish *Maytime* (1937). Edgar portrayed Van Brunt, one of the old-timers taken with Jane Withers, in *45 Fathers* (1937). *Thoroughbreds Don't Cry* (1937), with Judy Garland and Mickey Rooney, featured Norton as Mr. Fox, Ronald Sinclair's teacher.

In the late 1930s, Edgar made a number of radio appearances for the *Lux Radio Theatre* (CBS). Some of these were abridged versions of fairly recent films with original cast members, such as "Mr. Deeds Goes to Town" (2/1/37) starring Gary Cooper and Jean Arthur. Norton

was also heard in the following *Lux* productions: "Peg O' My Heart" (11/29/37), "The Thirty-Nine Steps" (12/13/37), "Mad About Music" (4/18/38) and "Lady for a Day" (5/1/39) with May Robson and Warren William. Another radio program that featured Norton was the popular *I Love a Mystery* (NBC, c. 1939).

The Big Broadcast of 1938 (1938) featured Norton as the secretary to T.F. Bellows (W.C. Fields). He played James in *Campus Confessions* (1938) and the Smith family servant in *The Cowboy and the Lady* (1938). *Just Around the Corner* (1938), starring an adolescent Shirley Temple, had Edgar as the butler to Mrs. Ramsby (Cora Witherspoon). Unfortunately, all of Norton's scenes in John Ford's *Four Men and a Prayer* (1938) ended up on the cutting room floor.

Perhaps Norton's most familiar role, at least for horror film fans, is Thomas Benson, the Frankenstein family butler, in *Son of Frankenstein* (1939). As Wolf (Basil Rathbone), Elsa (Josephine Hutchinson) and Peter (Donnie Dunagan) von Frankenstein arrive at the ancestral Frankenstein home, they are greeted by the loyal Benson, who provides an umbrella and escorts them inside. Benson leads Wolf to the library, while explaining that the other servants had to be hired from another province as none of the locals would work for the Frankensteins after the horrors of the previous generation. Entering the huge room, Wolf sees his father's portrait over the fireplace, with Benson commenting, "I think you're rather like your father, sir!" (that proves to be prophetic). Wolf reads from his father's documents, illuminated by the flash of lightning, while Benson hands him a glass of brandy. Benson next shows up when Inspector Krogh (Lionel Atwill) appears. Later, in the reconstructed laboratory, Benson aids Wolf, despite the objections of Ygor (Bela Lugosi), with the Monster (Boris Karloff) on the operating table. Taking notes regarding the physical condition of the Monster, Benson observes Wolf pointing out bullets lodged in the creature's heart with the use of a fluoroscope. When the Monster eventually opens his eyes, he sees Benson, who defensively picks up a scalpel. It is no surprise when Benson, who was last observed taking a tray of food to little Peter's room, goes missing. (Extant stills bear out that scenes were filmed of Benson's death at the hands of the Monster, who then proceeds to eat the food intended for Peter). When Krogh finds Benson's watch with Peter (a gift from the "giant" who visits the boy), the servant's fate is made clear. There are many fine supporting pieces of acting in *Son of Frankenstein*, with Norton's work as Benson qualifying, blending nicely with the atmosphere created onscreen.

Captain Fury (1939), set in Colonial Australia, had Norton as Hamilton, aide to the Governor (Lawrence Grossmith). *The Man in the Iron Mask* (1939), directed by James Whale, included Norton as the second servant (Dwight Frye being the first) to the evil Fouquet (Joseph Schildkraut). As Fouquet prepares for the royal wedding, Norton's character ushers in a sheepherder with a plate containing a message for Fouquet revealing the identity of the man in the titled mask (after the Musketeers had switched the bad twin for the good one, both played by Louis Hayward). Norton portrayed Mr. McKinnon in *Rulers of the Sea* (1939), with Douglas Fairbanks, Jr. He also had an unconfirmed role in *The Mad Empress* (1939), which featured Lionel Atwill. Norton is credited as appearing once again with Laurel and Hardy in his role as Professor Witherspoon in *A Chump at Oxford* (1940), but his scenes may not have survived in the final release version. In *Brother Orchid* (1940), with Edward G. Robinson in a complex part, Edgar was Meadows, the London butler.

The House of the Seven Gables (1940), derived from Hawthorne's classic tale, featured Norton as Phineas Weed, secretary to the devious, immoral Judge Jaffrey Pyncheon (George Sanders). As Michael Mark, Harry Stubbs and other locals at a tavern peruse a newspaper alluding to the Pyncheon "treasure," Weed enters, seeking Holgrave (Dick Foran). The secretary is intercepted by Alan Napier, who greets Weed, teasing, "Oh, Annie, glass of buttermilk for the gentleman!" Spotting Holgrave, Weed implores him to see Judge Pyncheon on a "matter of great urgency." The townspeople mock Weed's employer, while the frail man struggles to deliver his message and maintain his dignity. Weed escorts Holgrave to the Judge's office. As Judge Pyncheon reviews documents, Weed brings in the mail and informs his employer that Deacon Foster (Miles Mander) had called, seeming "quite disturbed." Foster, who has been victimized by one of the Judge's schemes, barges past Weed, who vainly tries to prevent his entrance. The Judge then informs Weed he is leaving to go to the "House" of the title, where the conflicts reach a violent resolution. Although more of a Gothic tale than pure horror, *The House of the Seven Gables* represented Norton's final genre role.

In the 1940s, Norton's screen appearances became fewer and fewer, with his roles growing smaller and smaller. Edgar played the barber of Baron Colonna (Akim Tamiroff) in *The Corsican Brothers* (1941). Norton was Paul in *Rings on Her Fingers* (1942), the captain of waiters in *Happy Go Lucky* (1943), the butler for a high society family in *Are These Our Parents?* (1944) and Harvey, Cecil Kellaway's manservant, in *Practically Yours* (1944). *The Suspect* (1944), with Charles Laughton superb as a sympathetic murderer, had Norton as Mr. Frazer. *Kitty* (1945), with Paulette Goddard, offered Norton a fairly substantial part as the Earl of Compton. Again with Charles Laughton, Edgar played a nobleman in the company of King William III (Henry Daniell) in *Captain Kidd* (1945). *Doll Face* (1945), a musical

starring Vivian Blaine and Dennis O'Keefe, gave Norton another well-etched butler role as Soho, who is the valet to Stephen Dunne.

In *Devotion* (1946 release, but filmed in 1943), concerned with the literary Brontë family, Norton was briefly on view as a club member. Edgar played a butler one final time in *Our Hearts Were Growing Up* (1946), with Gail Russell as Cornelia Otis Skinner. *Thunder in the Valley* (aka *Bob, Son of Battle*, 1947) included Norton as Parson Leggy Hornbut, who is involved in the judging of the sheepdog contest near the film's conclusion. In Alfred Hitchcock's *The Paradine Case* (1947), starring Gregory Peck, Edgar portrayed a courtroom attendant. Edgar Norton's last screen role was that of an asylum night clerk in the atmospheric *The Woman in White* (1948), with Alexis Smith and Eleanor Parker.

Very little is known of Edgar Norton's life from his retirement from the motion picture industry in 1948 until his death in Los Angeles, California on February 6, 1953, at the age of 84. Edgar's wife Mabel had predeceased him on March 22, 1949. Norton had been suffering from coronary sclerosis for at least four years. The actual cause of Norton's death, according to his death certificate, was acute coronary occlusion. Edgar had been a resident of the Motion Picture Country Home for three years prior to his passing. Pierce Brothers of Hollywood handled Norton's funeral arrangements. Edgar was buried on February 11, 1953 in a grave with no marker in Valhalla Memorial Park, North Hollywood. When he died, there was no obituary for Norton in *Variety* or the *New York Times*, which is somewhat perplexing in that Edgar devoted over 60 years of his life to the acting profession.

Edgar Norton may not have been a major film actor, but he certainly did render many enjoyable performances over the years. In the horror genre alone, Edgar imbued his characters, such as Dr. Jekyll's Poole, Sir Basil's Hobbs (in *Dracula's Daughter*) and the Frankenstein family's Benson with more depth and wit than the screenwriter or viewer might have expected. Although he rarely broke away from the mold of butler or stodgy nobleman, Norton was able to display a wide range of emotions, including sympathy, humor, concern, and anguish, in normally one-dimensional roles. Norton's screen efforts were rarely dull and worth revisiting to this day.

Sources

Coughlin, Jim. "Forgotten Faces of Fantastic Films: Edgar Norton," in *Midnight Marquee #46* (1994), pp. 56-60.

"The Nortons and the Film of Alice," The *New York Times*, 1/7/34.

"Screen Role Awakens Memories of Mansfield," The *New York Times*, 1/3/32, p. X6.

Halliwell Hobbes
(1877 – 1962)

Halliwell Hobbes was an extremely versatile actor who brought an air of refinement and culture to his craft through his manner of speech and appearance. Hobbes' acting career spanned almost 60 years, mostly in the theater, but also marked by roles in more than 100 films and significant appearances on television during its "Golden Age." Halliwell was commonly seen on screen as butlers and valets, as well as police constables, statesmen, church officials and elderly relatives. He played opposite a wide spectrum of performers, from George Arliss to the Bowery Boys. Hobbes' contributions to the horror/fantasy genre include portrayals in *Dr. Jekyll and Mr. Hyde* (1931), *Dracula's Daughter* (1936), *Here Comes Mr. Jordan* (1941), *The Undying Monster* (1942) and *The Invisible Man's Revenge* (1944). Although he is classified herein as a "forgotten face," Halliwell Hobbes distinctive long countenance and balding pate make him recognizable to most fans of old movies.

The son of William Albert Hobbes and the former Marion Dennis, Herbert Halliwell Hobbes was born in Stratford-upon-Avon, England, on November 16, 1877.

Romeo and Juliet (1908 London stage): Matheson Lang as Romeo and Halliwell Hobbes as Tybalt

Herbert Halliwell was the seventh of eight children born to the couple, including brothers Robert, William and Francis, and sisters Ada, Gertrude, Laura and Kathleen. The family lived (c. 1880) at 4 Chapel Street in Stratford. Halliwell was educated in Stratford and later Trinity College, studying law before finally selecting the stage as his profession. Hobbes made his theatrical debut in January 1898 in Glasgow, Scotland, with Frank R. Benson's Repertory Company, remaining with them for a few seasons. Halliwell, who dropped the first name Herbert for the stage, toured South Africa in 1901 with William Haviland's Company. Hobbes played on tour with such theatrical luminaries as Ellen Terry and Mrs. Patrick Campbell before returning to Benson's troupe in 1905 when they journeyed to the West Indies. With Johnston Forbes Robertson and company, Hobbes ventured to the United States, appearing for the first time on Broadway at the New Amsterdam Theatre in Shaw's *Caesar and Cleopatra* (10/30/06).

As a young man, Hobbes, who stood 5-foot-8 ½-inches, was an avid sportsman. He played and enjoyed watching cricket, while also keeping fit with tennis and swimming.

Returning to England from the U.S., Hobbes was seen as Tybalt in *Romeo and Juliet* (March 1908), starring Matheson Lang, at London's Lyceum. Becoming established in London's West End theater community, Hobbes played roles such as Prince Michael in *The Prince and the Beggar Maid* (June 1908), the Corporal in *Private Nobody* (November 1908), the Archbishop of Canterbury and Mountjoy in *King Henry V* (November 1908), Hanks in *Hannele* (December 1908), Horatio in *Hamlet* (March 1909) and Sir Walter Blunt in *King Henry IV (part I)* (May 1909).

Hobbes was seen as Pope Pius IX in *The Eternal Question* (August 1910), Ewan Mylrea in *The Bishop's Son* (Fall 1910) and Septimus Spring in *Company for George* (October 1910). At the Royalty Theatre in February 1911, Hobbes played Dr. Rank in Ibsen's *A Doll's House* and Chernoyarsky in *The Career of Nablotsky.*

In early 1911, Hobbes toured the provinces as Sherlock Holmes in *The Speckled Band*. As a member of Ethel Irving's Company, Hobbes sailed to Australia in May 1911. While "down under," the troupe staged such plays as *The Witness for the Defense*, *His House in Order* and *Lady Frederick*. Back in England, Hobbes remained busy on stage as Homo in *The Open Door* (October 1912), Don Guzman de Soto in *Westward Ho!* (February 1913), Horatio in *Hamlet* (March 1913) and Reason in *Every-wife* (April 1913). Hobbes once again ventured to Australia in the summer of 1913, this time as part of Lewis Waller's Company, touring the country while appearing in works like *A Fair Highwayman* (September 1913) as Bob Heathfield.

With war on the horizon, Hobbes came back to England. At the age of 37, Hobbes enlisted in the British Army

Jealousy **(1929): Halliwell Hobbes as Rigaud**

in the early days of World War I. He was commissioned a Lieutenant in the 7th Battalion of the Royal East Kent Regiment, referred to as "The Buffs." Hobbes saw action in France and elsewhere, being promoted to Captain before the end of the war.

In April 1915, in Croydon, Surrey, England, Hobbes was wed to Nancie Brenda Marsland (1893-1988), who was originally from Knutsford, Cheshire, England. Going by the name of Nancie B. Marsland on the stage, she acted extensively with Halliwell in both England and the United States, although only on rare occasions after 1929 when the family moved to Hollywood. Marsland also collaborated on a number of popular songs, writing the words for, among others, "Nightfall at Sea" (1912), "Twilight's Silent Hour" (1913), "Almost Blossoms" (1914), and "The Mill O' Dreams" (1915).

On March 27, 1917, Nancie Marsland gave birth to the Hobbes' only child, son Peter Halliwell Hobbes (1917-1995). Peter would later embark on an acting career of his own, appearing frequently on the London stage. He also was seen in films like *The Barretts of Wimpole Street* (1934) and *Curse of the Demon* (1957).

After leaving military service in April 1919, Hobbes went on a theatrical tour, playing Captain de Corlaix in *In the Night Watch* (May 1919). He then toured throughout most of 1920 with Phyllis Neilson-Terry's troupe, portraying the Laird in *Trilby*. On the London stage, Hobbes was Roger Blair in *The Crossing* (September 1920), Venturewell the merchant in *The Knight of the Burning Pestle* (November 1920), Massingham in *The Ninth Earl* (March 1921), Robert Heathcote in *A Matter of Fact* (April 1921) and Tornaquinci in *The Love Thief* (September 1921). At the Duke of York Theatre, Hobbes played both John Cam Hobhouse and Count Guiccioli in *The Pilgrim of Eternity* (November 1921). He then was seen at the Liverpool Playhouse as Takeramo in *Typhoon* (April 1922). Back in London, Hobbes portrayed Dr. Charrier in *The Risk* (July 1922), Dr. Livesey in *Treasure Island* (December 1922) and Edward Eversley in *Success* (June 1923).

Along with his wife Nancie, Basil Rathbone and Philip Merivale, Hobbes sailed from Liverpool to New York to appear with Eva Le Galliene at the Cort Theatre in Molnar's *The Swan* (10/23/23). *The Swan* was a hit, running for 255 performances, opening new doors for Hobbes' act-

Scotland Yard (1930): Donald Crisp, Edmund Lowe and Halliwell Hobbes

ing career. Hobbes next appeared as Colonel Whittaker in Noel Coward's *Easy Virtue* (12/7/25, 147 performances) with noted actress Jane Cowl. *Slaves All* (12/6/26), with Hobbes as Reverend Matthew Holdsworth, closed at the Bijou after only 8 performances. Nancie B. Marsland was in the cast of all three of these Broadway shows with her husband.

The Adventurous Age (2/7/27, 16 performances) starred Mrs. Patrick Campbell and included Hobbes as Leonard Rivers. Hobbes and Marsland returned briefly to England, where Halliwell portrayed Snittle Timberry in *When Crummles Played* (June 1927) at the Lyric Theatre. Back in New York, Hobbes was Lord Warminster in *Caste* (12/23/27, 11 performances). He played John Barthwick, M.P., in Galsworthy's *The Silver Box* (1/17/28, 23 performances). Hobbes both directed and appeared in *When Crummles Played* (10/1/28, 40 performances) at the Garrick Theatre. The play was actually two shows in one, with Hobbes portraying Vincent Crummles in the title satire and Thorowgood in *George Barnwell or the London Merchant*. As Bishop Bradford, Hobbes played opposite Spring Byington, with whom he would later interact so humorously in *You Can't Take it With You* (1938), in *Be Your Age* (2/4/29, 32 performances).

Hobbes made his motion picture debut as the Earl of Balkerry, the uncle of star Morton Downey, in *Lucky in Love* (1929). *Jealousy* (1929) featured Hobbes as Rigaud, an elderly boulevardier who purchases a gown shop for Jeanne Eagels who later discovers him murdered when she seeks him out for financial help. As Ruddick in *Grumpy* (1930), Hobbes found himself in the first of his numerous manservant roles as the valet to Cyril Maude. *Scotland Yard* (1930), with Edmund Lowe and Donald Crisp, included Hobbes as Lord St. Arran. As Stephen Spettigue, the object of deception in *Charley's Aunt* (1930), Halliwell falls for Charles Ruggles (in drag), thus enabling the marriage of his niece (June Collyer).

The Bachelor Father (1931), starring Marion Davies, had Hobbes as Larkin, the butler. He was the Siegneur, a benevolent older man who loves Loretta Young, in *The Right of Way* (1931). As Sir James, Hobbes was the Courtney family barrister in *The Lady Refuses* (1931). Again opposite Marion Davies, Hobbes played Hopkins in *Five and Ten* (1931). He portrayed Barton, O.P. Heggie's butler, in *The*

"Merridew! After him quick – Hold him!"

***Grumpy* (1930): Halliwell Hobbes tries to prevent Paul Cavanagh from interfering with Cyril Maude.**

Woman Between (1931). Hobbes continued this typecasting pattern, playing Roget, Lewis Stone's butler, in *The Sin of Madelon Claudet* (1931) with Helen Hayes and the Schuyler family butler in *Platinum Blonde* (1931), which helped propel Jean Harlow to stardom.

Hobbes' first horror film role was pompous Brigadier General Carew in Paramount's *Dr. Jekyll and Mr. Hyde* (1931), with Fredric March in the Oscar-winning title role(s). Carew, an overprotective father, refuses to grant Jekyll permission to marry his daughter Muriel (Rose Hobart) in the near future. The haughty Carew prides himself on never having been late for dinner in 40 years. The General's refusal provides the impetus for Jekyll's delving into experimental drugs. On the day he is to announce his engagement to Muriel, Jekyll deteriorates into Hyde, attacks his beloved and kills General Carew, before his eventual downfall. Carew, selfish, hypocritical and petty, is a departure from the kind and genial characters frequently played by Hobbes. Many years later, Rose Hobart commented to interviewer Tom Weaver on the actor who played her father in *Dr. Jekyll and Mr. Hyde*, "He was just a charming English gentleman" (Weaver, p. 164).

Directed by Frank Capra and starring Barbara Stanwyck, *Forbidden* (1932) afforded Hobbes the unbilled role of the florist. *Lovers Courageous* (1932) had Hobbes as Mr. Smith, a rigid father who attempts to convince his young son (Jackie Searl) not to attempt to advance his station in life. Roy William Neill directed *The Menace* (1932) and in-

cluded Hobbes as Phillips. Hobbes was Kibbee, the loyal and wise family butler, in *Love Affair* (1932). He played Lord Litchfield, a wealthy newspaper magnate with designs on Elissa Landi, in *Devil's Lottery* (1932). *Man About Town* (1932) featured Hobbes as Hilton the valet, who advises Warner Baxter to close his gambling casino. *Week Ends Only* (1932) had Hobbes as Martin, the former butler, who now owns a speakeasy and hires his ex-employer Joan Bennett to work there. In a tale about restoration of life, *6 Hours to Live* (1935), Hobbes portrayed Baron Emil von Sturm. *Payment Deferred* (1932), with Charles Laughton as the murderer, included Hobbes as a prospective tenant. *Cynara* (1932), starring Ronald Colman, featured Hobbes as the outraged coroner at the inquest.

The poignant *Looking Forward* (1933), starring Lionel Barrymore, had Hobbes as Mr. James Felton. As Dearing, one of the Scarlet Ring protecting stolen Chinese jewels, Hobbes was found murdered in *A Study in Scarlet* (1933), with Reginald Owen as Sherlock Holmes. Hobbes played Churchill in *Midnight Mary* (1933), starring Loretta Young, and the British Major General in *Captured!* (1933), with

Personal photo from 1931 of Halliwell Hobbes on the beach with his wife, Nancie B. Marsland and their dog

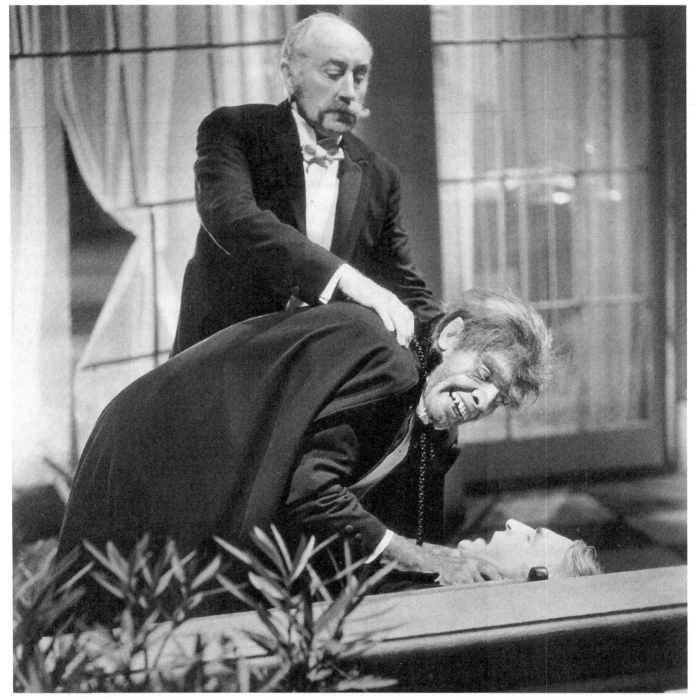

Dr. Jekyll and Mr. Hyde (1931): **Carew (Halliwell Hobbes) tries to pull Hyde (Fredric March) off a servant (G.L. McDonnell).**

Leslie Howard and Douglas Fairbanks, Jr. *The Masquerader* (1933) had Hobbes as Brock, the valet to the recently deceased Sir John Chilcote, who convinces and coaches drug-addicted Loder (Ronald Colman in a dual role as both men) to assume the identity of his late master for the good of country. Working again with director Frank Capra in *Lady for a Day* (1933), Hobbes was wonderful as John, the butler for Annie (May Robson), at the chaotic reception staged by Warren William. During an exchange with Ned Sparks, Hobbes as John challenges, "If I had choice of weapons with you, sir, I'd choose grammar!"

The butler roles continued for Hobbes, with his portrayals of Louis in *Should Ladies Behave* (1933) and Burford, Clive Brook's servant, in *If I Were Free* (1933). Sporting a beard, he played Dr. Lorenzo, the noted surgeon who tends to star Lilian Harvey, in *I Am Suzanne!* (1934). Mordaunt Hall in the *New York Times* (1/10/34) commented on his portrayal of Lorenzo, "Mr. Hobbes is an artist to his fingertips, and although his role is a minor one he makes an indelible impression." Other parts for Hobbes at this time were Colonel Dawson Ames in *Mandalay* (1934) and Bollard in *Riptide* (1934). As Henry Clarendon in *All Men Are*

Enemies (1934), Hobbes tried to encourage a match between his son (Hugh Williams) and Mona Barrie. He played Mr. Chase from Tiffany's, who brings a string of pearls to Evelyn Venables in *Double Door* (1934). *The Key* (1934), with William Powell and Colin Clive as adversaries in 1920's Ireland, featured Hobbes as General C.O. Furlong. *Bulldog Drummond Strikes Back* (1934) had Hobbes as a bobby. Hobbes portrayed George Dane in *She Was a Lady* (1934), Sir Walter Carrister in *British Agent* (1934), the English ambassador in *Madame Du Barry* (1934) and a government official in *We Live Again* (1934). In *Menace* (1934), Hobbes was Skinner, seemingly a villainous butler, who turns out to be a detective trailing Ray Milland. *Father Brown, Detective* (1934) had Hobbes as aristocrat Sir Leopold Fischer, whose "Flying Star" diamonds are the target of jewel thief Paul Lukas.

Hobbes played Sir Stephen Barr, a medical specialist, in *The Right to Live* (1935), with Colin Clive and Josephine Hutchinson. He was Monsieur Paulet, the finance minister who wants to buy Maurice Chevalier's stock in a mine, in *Folies Bergere de Paris* (1935). Hobbes was uncredited as the father of a little girl in *Vanessa: Her Love Story* (1935). Third-billed as Father Joseph, Hobbes appeared opposite George Arliss in *Cardinal Richelieu* (1935). *Jalna* (1935) included Hobbes as aspiring writer Uncle Ernest, one of the elderly sons of 99-year-old Whiteoak family matriarch Jessie Ralph. He was seen as Police Commissioner Watkins, an old friend of Chan (Warner Oland), who erroneously arrests Jon Hall in *Charlie Chan in Shanghai* (1935). *Millions in the Air* (1935) had Hobbes as Theodore. Hobbes was unbilled both as Lord Sunderland in *Captain Blood* (1935), which helped make a star of Errol Flynn, and as Mr. Gordon in *Rose Marie* (1935), with Jeanette MacDonald and Nelson Eddy. Set on an ocean liner, *Here Comes Trouble* (1936) provided Hobbes with the colorful role of Professor Howard, reputed to be a noted archaeologist and ethnologist, who turns out to be Piccadilly Joe, a clever jewel thief. With Paul Muni shining in the title role of *The Story of Louis Pasteur* (1936), Hobbes gave a modulated performance as Dr. Joseph Lister.

Dracula's Daughter (1936), starring Gloria Holden, had Hobbes as Constable Hawkins, who, with colleague Albert (Billy Bevan), investigates what has transpired at Carfax Abbey (supposedly picking up right at the conclusion of the 1931 *Dracula*). The two policemen find the body of Renfield at the foot of the enormous staircase and then discover Dracula impaled by a stake in a coffin. When the still-loitering Von Helsing (Edward Van Sloan) confesses to the staking, the baffled pair arrest him. While they keep watch over the corpses, Countess Zaleska (Holden) hypno-

Cardinal Richelieu (1935): Halliwell Hobbes as Father Joseph

tizes Albert and removes Dracula's body, later destroying the remains by fire.

Changing of the Guard (1936), shot in an early Technicolor process, featured Hobbes as the aging Colonel who regales his granddaughter (Sybil Jason) with tales of his military career in the Highlander regiment, leading to an elaborate dream sequence. *Hearts Divided* (1936), with Marion Davies, had Hobbes as Cambaceres, second consul to Napoleon (Claude Rains). In *The White Angel* (1936), with Kay Francis excellent as Florence Nightingale, Hobbes was the sympathetic Lord Raglan, commander-in-chief of the British forces in the Crimea, who intervenes on the nurse's behalf. Hobbes' roles often were not significant, as witnessed by minor parts as Beuhl the butler in *Spendthrift* (1936), a man in *Mary of Scotland* (1936), Oliver in *Give Me Your Heart* (1936) and Hotchkiss in *Love Letters of a Star* (1936).

Maid of Salem (1937) featured Hobbes as Jeremiah Adams, the recluse uncle of Fred MacMurray, who is murdered by a seaman while traveling to Florida with his nephew. Hobbes was the Archbishop of Canterbury, presiding over the coronation of the true Edward (Bobby

Dracula's Daughter (1936): **Sergeant Hawkins (Halliwell Hobbes) discovers Dracula's corpse.**

Mauch), in *The Prince and the Pauper* (1937). *Parnell* (1937), MGM's unsuccessful biopic of the Irish statesman starring Clark Gable, included Hobbes as W.H. Smith. Hobbes had a rare villainous turn in a comedy, *Fit For a King* (1937), as Count Strunsky, the former prime minister who plots to assassinate the Princess (Helen Mack) before being thwarted by Joe E. Brown. Hobbes played Dean J. M. Meredith of Winfield College in the Dick Powell musical *Varsity Show* (1937).

It was back to typecasting as a butler once again for Hobbes as John in *The Jury's Secret* (1938) and in *Service de Luxe* (1938). *Bulldog Drummond's Peril* (1938), however, offered Hobbes a more substantial role as Professor Bernard Goodman, the father-in-law of Algy (Reginald Denny). Goodman, working on a secret formula, presents a 15 carat diamond to Drummond (John Howard) as a wedding gift. He is later presumed dead when his laboratory explodes, but Goodman survives (although his formula does

not). In *Kidnapped* (1938), Hobbes was Dominie Campbell, who runs a countryside school for boys, including David Balfour (Freddie Bartholomew).

Perhaps Hobbes' most colorful and eccentric performance was that of DePinna, one of the many offbeat characters in the Sycamore household, in Frank Capra's screen version of Kaufman and Hart's *You Can't Take it With You* (1938). DePinna, an iceman who made a delivery to the Sycamores and Vanderhofs one day and never departed, toils in the basement making fireworks with Samuel S. Hinds. He is at his most amusing, though, dressed as an ancient Greek discus thrower, serving as a model for aspiring artist Spring Byington.

Hobbes played Sir John Galt in *Storm Over Bengal* (1938), the clergyman slipping on the sidewalk in the Reginald Owen version of *A Christmas Carol* (1938) and Captain Matthews in *Pacific Liner* (1939). When the Hardy family wrongly believes they are heirs to a two million dollar fortune in *The Hardys Ride High* (1939), Hobbes was their temporary butler Dobbs in a mansion in Detroit. In *Tell No Tales* (1939), Hobbes, as Dr. Lovelake, is found in possession of a hundred dollar bill that had been part of ransom money from a kidnapping. Hobbes was back at Winfield College, this time as Dean Burton, in *Naughty But Nice* (1939), another Dick Powell musical. He had an uncredited bit as a British chaplain in *Nurse Edith Cavell* (1939) with Anna Neagle. Hobbes portrayed Williams the butler in *Remember?* (1939). He was the doctor who informs Ronald Colman he is going blind from a head blow received in the Sudan in *The Light That Failed* (1939).

Hobbes was heard on CBS Radio in *The Gulf Screen Guild Theatre* dramatization of "Smilin' Through" (12/17/39), starring Norma Shearer and Basil Rathbone.

Opposite Robert Montgomery, Hobbes portrayed the Lord Chancellor in *The Earl of Chicago* (1940). He was the Vicar at St. Matthew's in the remake of *Waterloo Bridge* (1940), who tells Roy (Robert Taylor) and Myra (Vivien Leigh) that they cannot be married after 3:00 p.m. and should return the next morning. Hobbes was briefly seen as the astronomer in *The Sea Hawk* (1940) with Errol Flynn. *Third Finger, Left Hand* (1940) featured him as Burton. As the judge, Hobbes presided over a difficult divorce and custody battle involving Mrs. Leslie Carter (Miriam Hopkins) in *Lady With Red Hair* (1940). Hobbes took a brief hiatus from the screen to return to Broadway, playing Capulet in a revival of *Romeo and Juliet* (5/9/40, 36 performances), starring Laurence Olivier and Vivien Leigh. His work must have impressed the couple because when he returned to the screen Hobbes played the Reverend Nelson, the father who begs his son Horatio (Laurence Olivier) to give up the title character (Vivien Leigh), in *That Hamilton Woman* (1941). The musical *Sunny* (1941) had Hobbes uncredited as Johnson.

In the fine fantasy *Here Comes Mr. Jordan* (1941), Hobbes portrayed Sisk, the valet of the murdered Farnsworth, who hands Joe (Robert Montgomery) his saxophone easing his transition into his new body. Hobbes was the minister in *Dr. Kildare's Wedding Day* (1941), during which the fiancée (Laraine Day) of Kildare (Lew Ayres) is tragically killed prior to the marriage ceremony. *Son of Fury: The Story of Benjamin Blake* (1942), starring Tyrone Power, had Hobbes as Purdy. Ernst Lubitsch's classic *To Be or Not to Be* (1942) featured Hobbes as General Armstrong who directs airman Robert Stack to return to Poland to stop the professor (Stanley Ridges) who has vital information on the Polish RAF flyers' families that could endanger them all. As Bennett, the family butler, in *The War Against Mrs. Hadley* (1942), Hobbes secretly becomes an air raid warden to contribute to the war effort.

For *Lux Radio Theatre* (CBS), hosted by Cecil B. DeMille, Hobbes was heard over the air in "A Tale of Two Cit-

***Maid of Salem* (1937): Tavern keeper Lionel Belmore serves a pint to Halliwell Hobbes.**

ies" (1/12/42), with Ronald Colman recreating his screen success as Sydney Carton.

The Undying Monster (1942), an atmospheric horror tale from 20th Century Fox, had Hobbes as Walton, the Hammond family butler. Walton attempts to protect John Howard, later revealed to be a werewolf, burning his bloodied scarf to mask murder evidence. Walton, along with his eerie wife (Eily Malyon), acts in a suspicious manner in general. Hinting at the Hammond curse of lycanthropy, Walton recites, "When stars are bright on a frosty night, beware the bane on the rocky lane."

Along with screen wife Doris Lloyd, Hobbes, as Mr. Barrie, was a prospective foster parent for Margaret O'Brien and Peter Severn in *Journey for Margaret* (1942). The childless elderly couple showers the children with gifts, but things do not work out. Hobbes then played a doctor in *Forever and a Day* (1943).

Sherlock Holmes Faces Death (1943) provided Hobbes with another substantial role as Alfred Brunton, the eccentric Musgrave family butler. Brunton, inclined to spout verse, has an amusing encounter with Dr. Watson (Nigel Bruce), while toasting his employers, the Musgraves. "Some were murderers and some worse, but they all knew how to keep a secret—and so do I." Dismissed for insubordination, the heavy drinking butler disappears, but his body turns up in the old crypt beneath the cellar (actually the old *Dracula* set).

As Charney the butler, Hobbes encountered Leo Gorcey and the East Side Kids in *Mr. Muggs Steps Out* (1943). In the Deanna Durbin musical *His Butler's Sister* (1943), Hobbes portrayed Willebrandt. After playing Leutnant

You Can't Take it With You (1938): Halliwell Hobbes as DePinna

sequently arranging their murders, feigning his own death in the process. Later, quite alive as well as quite mad, Wargrave unsuccessfully attempts to kill the heroine. He is then found really dead, a bullet hole in his head, wearing a judge's wig, as if presiding on the bench in court. It is a shame that Hobbes never had such a substantial role on the screen. When *Ten Little Indians* was adapted for film in 1945 as *And Then There Were None*, Hobbes did not recreate the role of the judge, which instead went to Barry Fitzgerald and was renamed Quinncannon. Hobbes later opened as Archdeacon Pennyfeather at the Plymouth Theatre in *Hidden Horizon* (9/19/46), based on Christie's *Murder on the Nile*. *Hidden Horizon*, whose cast included David Manners and Diana Barrymore, did not enjoy the success of the earlier Christie adaptation, closing after only 12 performances.

Hobbes resurfaced on the screen as Clenchfield in *Canyon Passage* (1946), directed by Jacques Tourneur. He was the coroner in *If Winter Comes* (1947), with Deborah Kerr and Walter Pidgeon. Set during the War of the Roses, *The Black Arrow* (1948), starring Louis Hayward, featured Hobbes as the Bishop of Tisbury.

The Linden Tree (3/2/48), written by J.B. Priestley, gave Hobbes the opportunity to act on Broadway with Boris Karloff and Una O'Connor. Unfortunately, the reviews were dismal and *The Linden Tree* lasted only seven performances at the Winter Box Theatre.

The comedy *You Gotta Stay Happy* (1949), with James Stewart and Joan Fontaine, had Hobbes as Martin. *That Forsyte Woman* (1949), with a stellar cast including Greer Garson, Errol Flynn and Robert Young, included Hobbes as the wealthy Nicholas Forsyte.

Hobbes, now in his seventies, began shifting his acting pursuits back to the theater and the relatively new medium of television. He played John Marks in "Reclusive Sisters" (1949, season 2, episode 15), a segment of the NBC series *Martin Kane*. For the suspenseful early TV series *Lights Out* (NBC), Hobbes appeared in "Dr. Heidegger's Experiment" (11/20/50, season 3, episode 13) and as O'Haggis in "The Devil in Glencairn" (7/16/51, season 3, episode 47). As part of *Robert Montgomery Presents* (NBC), Hobbes was seen with Helen Hayes in "Victoria Regina" (1/15/51, season 2, episode 10), with Leslie Nielsen in "Happy Birthday, George" (3/3/52, season 3, episode 18) and opposite Cedric Hardwicke in "A Criminal Assignment" (10/12/53, season 5, episode 7). With Brian Aherne as the pirate Henry Morgan, Hobbes was featured in "The Buccaneer" (6/15/51, season 1, episode 37), part of *Pulitzer Prize Playhouse* (ABC). Hobbes also was viewed on *Lux Video Theatre* (CBS) as Justin in "The Treasure Trove" (3/26/51, season 1, episode 26), with Bruce Cabot, and as Fitz James in "No Will of His Own" (11/12/51, season 2, episode 12), starring Gene Lockhart. On *Goodyear Theatre* (NBC), Hobbes

Eberhard in the short *Information Please* (1944), Hobbes was seen in two major films as Mr. Muffin in *Gaslight* (1944) at MGM and as Soames, Bette Davis' servant, in *Mrs. Skeffington* (1944) for Warner Bros.

Returning to the realm of horror, Hobbes played Cleghorn, the butler of Lester Matthews and Gale Sondergaard, in *The Invisible Man's Revenge* (1944). *Casanova Brown* (1944), a comedy starring Gary Cooper, had Hobbes as Charles, the butler.

Hobbes once again elected to return to Broadway, appearing in two Agatha Christie works. As Sir Lawrence John Wargrave, the "hanging" judge who sentenced an innocent man to death, Hobbes was prominent in the long-running (426 performances) play *Ten Little Indians* (6/27/44). The role of Sir Lawrence was a bravura one for Hobbes, as he actually turns out to be the mastermind behind assembling all the guests on Indian Island and sub-

Ten Little Indians (1944 Broadway stage): Halliwell Hobbes as Sir Lawrence Wargrave

appeared with a young Walter Matthau in "Tour of Duty" (2/3/52, season 1, episode 9).

Back on stage as Dean Frederick Damon in a revival of *The Male Animal*, Hobbes enjoyed a lengthy run (over 300 performances), first at the City Center (4/30/52) and then the Music Box Theatre (5/15/52). This contrasted with an all too short (seven performances) run at the ANTA Playhouse in *Portrait of a Lady* (12/21/54), in which Hobbes played Mr. Touchett, at whose Gardencourt home the work is set. Based on the novel by Henry James, the play starred Jennifer Jones. *Tonight in Samarkand* (2/16/55, 29 performances), with Louis Jordan and Theodore Bikel, had Hobbes as Perignolles. Halliwell Hobbes' final Broadway appearance came at the ANTA with his portrayal of David Anson, the father of Hume Cronyn's character, in *A Day By the Sea* (9/26/55, 24 performances).

As the Reverend Garland in "The Small Servant" (10/30/55, season 1, episode 2), Hobbes was back on the small screen for *The Alcoa Hour* (NBC). Hobbes then toured in November and December of 1955 in *A Quiet Place*, playing New Haven, Boston, Cleveland and Pittsburgh before winding down at the National Theatre in Washington, DC. Set in Italy's Amalfi Coast, *A Quiet Place* featured Hobbes as Mr. Metcalfe, a retired author and neighbor of a troubled American couple played by Tyrone Power and Leora Dana. Unfortunately, the play closed in Washington, DC, never reaching Broadway.

His final film was *Miracle in the Rain* (1956), in which Hobbes played Eli B. "Windy" Windgate, a former millionaire yachtsman who lost his fortune in the Crash of 1929. Van Johnson, a G.I. stationed in New York who is also an aspiring reporter, recognizes the old man, senses a great human interest story and cajoles Windgate into allowing himself to be interviewed. Hobbes was Father Benedict in "The Flower of Pride" (3/12/56, season 8, episode 26) on *Studio One in Hollywood* (CBS). Portraying Helen Hayes' doorman in "Mrs. Gilling and the Skyscraper" (6/9/57, season 2, episode 18) for NBC's *The Alcoa Hour* was Halliwell Hobbes' last acting assignment. Now 79 years old and in failing health, Hobbes, who had been living in New York at 10 East 81st Street, chose to retire, moving back to California.

On February 20, 1962, Halliwell Hobbes suffered a heart attack and died at his home at 701 Ocean Avenue, Apartment 11, in Santa Monica, California. He was 84 years old. Nancie B. Marsland, his wife of 48 years, and their son, actor Peter Hobbes, survived him. Hobbes' ashes were scattered in the Rose Garden of the Chapel of the Pines Crematory in Los Angeles, California.

Halliwell Hobbes epitomizes the legion of steady, talented character actors, whose efforts enhanced so many films and whose work film historians neglected far too long. Hobbes was a technically adept, forceful presence, ever ready to lend a dramatic or comedic touch, depending on the demands of a role. Along with Eric Blore, Halliwell remains one of the screen's quintessential butler/valets. Horror film fans should pay attention in particular to his contributions when given the chance to view films like the Fredric March *Dr. Jekyll and Mr. Hyde*, *Dracula's Daughter*, *The Undying Monster* and *The Invisible Man's Revenge*. These films, however, barely scratch the surface of the body of Hobbes' screen work, which fortunately populates many classic movies that are still regularly seen today.

Sources

Coughlin, Jim. "Forgotten Faces of Fantastic Films: Halliwell Hobbes," in *Midnight Marquee* #42 (Summer 1991), pp. 22-24.

Hoey, Michael A. *Sherlock Holmes & the Fabulous Faces: The Universal Pictures Repertory Company*, Albany, Georgia: BearManor Media, 2011.

Weaver, Tom. *Attack of the Monster Movie Makers*, Jefferson, N.C.: McFarland and Company, Inc.,1994.

Murders in the Rue Morgue (1932)

Noble Johnson
(1881 – 1978)

Portrait (c. 1918) of Noble Johnson

An extremely versatile actor, Noble Johnson was able to avoid the stereotypical roles given to most other black performers of his time due to his light features, as well as his athletic physique and prowess. In addition to playing roles often reserved for blacks, like servants and native chiefs, Johnson portrayed a whole spectrum of races and nationalities, including Native Americans, Mexican bandits, Asian royalty, Cossack henchmen, Cuban zombies and more. He was actually of mixed race, stating that black, Caucasian and Native American ancestors were among his lineage. A fellow actor once said of him, "He was like his name—noble," in that his off-screen personality was highlighted by his sincerity and gentleness. These are not the character traits, however, that have endeared Johnson to horror film fans. Rather, it was Noble Johnson's memorable hulking, menacing, frightening performances in such motion pictures as *Murders in the Rue Morgue*, *The Most Dangerous Game*, *The Mummy*, *King Kong* and *The Ghost Breakers* that have established him as perhaps the most significant of the unheralded players in the fantasy genre.

Noble Mark Johnson was born on April 18, 1881 in Marshall, Salina County, Missouri. He was the son of Perry Johnson (1852-1929) and the former Georgia Reed (1861-1885). Noble was the second of their four children, with brother Virgel (1879-1967) being the firstborn. Soon after Noble's birth, the family moved to Ivywild, Colorado, a subdivision of Colorado Springs (where it has erroneously been reported that Noble was born). Perry Johnson, a proficient horse handler, breeder and trainer, had found work in the Colorado Springs area, dealing with the horses of wealthy ranchers and families who had made a fortune in gold mining. Noble's sister Iris Hazel (1883-1939) was born in Ivywild, followed by younger brother George Perry Johnson (1885-1977). Unfortunately, Georgia Reed Johnson suffered complications during George's birth and passed away two days later. Despite all his work demands, Perry managed to raise four children, with some assistance from a neighboring servant.

Noble attended both the Lowell School and the Lincoln School in Colorado Springs. One of his schoolmates was Lon Chaney. Noble and Lon allegedly became friends and often rode horses together. Much of Johnson's youth was spent involved in rugged outdoor endeavors, which led to the development of both his impressive six-foot-two, 215 pound muscular frame and skills he would later put to use in films, performing daring stunts and handling ani-

mals. Thanks to the amazing research of Bill Cappello, a great deal has been learned about Noble Johnson's early years prior to his lengthy film career.

Dropping out of school and leaving home at the age of 15, Johnson traveled extensively, supporting his passions in a variety of occupations. He spent two summers traveling the horse racing circuit with his father Perry, learning the intricacies of training and handling thoroughbreds. Noble had aspirations of becoming a cowboy, while working at different trades in the offseason, including delivering supplies to miners, cooking and cutting down trees. Over the next few years, Johnson worked for a major cattle ranching concern, the Sanborn and Kaiser Company in Jefferson, Colorado, as well as other cattle ranches from Colorado to Wyoming. Noble would often return home to Colorado Springs in the winters, where he would train ponies and other animals, while also keeping active by boxing and wrestling in a gym he had helped construct.

In the winter of 1903, Johnson spent four months trapping in the mountains, where the temperature dropped as

Bull's Eye (1917 serial): Vivian Reed rides with Noble Johnson in Episode 7.

low as 55 degrees below zero. He eventually sold his pelts, worked for a timber company, tried some gold mining and returned once again to Colorado Springs, where he dealt with a serious bout of pneumonia. Following his recovery and having the wanderlust, Noble left Colorado for New York City in the spring of 1905. He traveled with polo ponies and other horses to be sold, and then secured work from a Mr. Blackmer in Ossining, New York. Noble moved on to Huntington, Long Island, where he trained horses for wealthy J.S. Farlee. He handled many tasks for the Farlee family, including serving as their coachman. With his zest for physical fitness, which remained a passion all through his life, Noble joined the West Side Athletic Club in Manhattan. There, Johnson boxed and exercised on a regular basis. He worked for the Durland Riding Academy and Tichnor-Grand Stables in New York City, where he also learned to train dogs, a skill that would prove valuable in later years. Noble continued to box, using assumed names, until he broke his hand in June 1907. Out of idle frustration, Johnson returned to Colorado.

Noble worked for a few years at the Mosier Ranch near Florrisant, Colorado, while also attempting to run a Wild West Show with a partner one summer. He moved to Los Angeles in the fall of 1910, securing a position at White's Garage, where he became proficient at servicing automobiles. Johnson next ventured up the West Coast, working in the lumber mills in Gray's Harbor, Washington and for the Jackson Fruit Company in North Yakima. Back in Colorado, Noble served as a cook for a government-surveying outfit. Johnson was married for the first time (of three) to Ruth Thornton in Denver, Colorado, on October 19,

1912. When and why this marriage ended has not been ascertained.

Noble returned to Los Angeles in 1913, re-establishing himself at White's Garage, where he was promoted to a foreman. Soon after, he would again travel the Northwest, finding positions in Portland, Seattle and Vancouver, British Columbia. Whatever his occupation at any point, Johnson would make time to run cross country, box and keep physically active in general.

In the spring of 1914, Johnson drove an automobile party from Denver to Kansas City and back, before going home to Colorado Springs. Soon after Noble returned to Colorado Springs in mid-1914, he was recommended to Romaine Fielding, an actor/director with the Lubin Film Manufacturing Company, who was on location shooting a film entitled *The Eagle's Nest* (1915). Although Johnson was initially employed to handle horses for the company, Noble was enlisted to enact the part of an Indian chief following an injury to a Lubin player. Johnson remained with Lubin for about a year, appearing in *Mr. Carlson of Arizona* (1915), *From Champion to Tramp* (1915), *A Species of Mexican Man* (1915), *The Valley of Lost Hope* (1915) and *A Western Governor's Humanity* (1915). He shot films at Lubin's Philadelphia, Pennsylvania, studio as well as western locations.

Johnson had a minor role as a Babylonian soldier in D.W. Griffith's *Intolerance: Love's Struggle Throughout the Ages* (1916). Noble then signed a contract with Universal Pictures, commencing with his appearance in the short *The Lady from the Sea* (1916). He played Romero Valdez in

The Bronze Bell (1921): Noble Johnson as Chatterjii

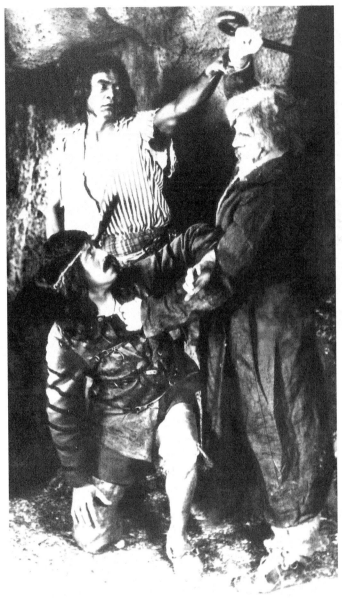

The Adventures of Robinson Crusoe (1922 serial): Noble Johnson (top left) and players

Kinkaid, Gambler (1916), set in Mexico. Johnson also was seen in the early silent version of Jules Verne's *20,000 Leagues Under the Sea* (1916).

Johnson—being bright and ambitious—envisioned many possibilities within the motion picture industry. With a group of blacks in Los Angeles, including actor Clarence Brooks, Noble helped form the Lincoln Motion Picture Company and was named the firm's first president. Lincoln's first production was *The Realization of a Negro's Ambition* (1916), which featured Johnson as James Burton, a Tuskegee Institute engineering graduate, who goes West to the oil fields of California, only to be denied a job because he is black. Burton, however, saves the life of the daughter of a rich white oilman and is rewarded with a position, as well as the opportunity to prospect for oil. After bringing in a gusher, Burton, now well off, returns home to the

South and marries the girl he left behind. Although only two reels and lacking in some technical aspects, the film was well received by black audiences.

The Trooper of Company K (1917), Lincoln's second venture, again starred Johnson as a shiftless Buffalo soldier, part of the black Tenth Cavalry, who redeems himself with the heroic rescue of a white captain during the battle of Carrizal. Noble's brother, George Johnson, formerly a postal worker in Omaha, Nebraska, had joined Lincoln prior to the release of *The Trooper of Company K* and quickly established himself, handling the film bookings. While in essence moonlighting for Lincoln, Noble was becoming firmly established at Universal, eventually resulting in Universal exerting pressure on Johnson to stop making "race movies."

Johnson was appearing in serials, shorts and features for Universal by 1917. He portrayed Johnny Little Bear who helps Jack Mulhall discover a rich mine in *Fighting for Love* (1917). Johnson played the cannibal king in *Love Aflame* (1917), Mike Tregurtha in *The Terror* (1917), Blackfoot in *The Indian's Lament* (1917), Thomas Jefferson Jones in *Mr. Dolan of New York* (1917), a Native American in *The Hero of the Hour* (1917) and undetermined roles in *A Soldier of the Legion* (1917) and *The Last of the Night Riders* (1917). Noble was prominently featured in two Universal serials, as Little Bear in *The Red Ace* (1917) and as Sweeney Bodin in *Bull's Eye* (1917), a Secret Service tale with Eddie Polo.

Meanwhile, back at Lincoln, George Johnson was growing in influence and favored a merger with black nov-

Adventure (1925): Pauline Stark interacts with cannibal chief Noble Johnson.

The King of Kings (1927): Noble Johnson as the charioteer for Mary Magdalene (Jacqueline Logan)

elist Oscar Micheaux. Noble blocked the move, believing Micheaux's views too radical for the time. Speaking of one particular Micheaux property, Noble proclaimed, "Unless we would change it so decidedly that it would hardly be recognizable, we could not expect much support from white houses" (Cripps, 1977). Despite being sympathetic, Noble could not betray his own integrity or business sense, so Micheaux went on to produce his own pictures.

The Law of Nature (1917) was to be Johnson's last effort as Lincoln's leading player. Noble portrayed a Western ranch foreman who is persuaded by his wife to go East; she then deserts him. Johnson's character returns West with his child, followed by his broken, repentant wife, now abandoned by her new lover. In melodramatic fashion, the wife dies with the baby in her arms. Although *The Law of Nature* was fairly successful, Johnson received the expected ultimatum, Lincoln or Universal! Noble was compelled to resign as Lincoln's president, concentrating on his contractual obligations to Universal. Lincoln would last a few more years, folding in 1922. Noble's brother George would then return to postal work, this time in Los Angeles, while also managing a clearing house for black press known as the Pacific Coast News Service.

Johnson was involved in two Hoot Gibson Universal shorts, *Play Straight or Fight* (1918) and *The Branded Man* (1918), as Trovio Valdez. He also was seen in *The Human Tiger* (1918), with Eileen Sedgwick. As Silent Andy in

the serial *The Lure of the Circus* (1918), Noble was reunited with Eddie Polo. Johnson then played Spike in another serial, *The Midnight Man* (1918), starring former heavyweight boxing champion James J. Corbett. *Lightning Bryce* (1919), a National serial featuring Jack Hoxie, had Noble in two roles, Dopey the henchman, and the Arnold family butler. *The Red Glove* (1919), a Universal serial with Marie Walcamp, included Johnson as an Indian chief.

Directed by Rex Ingram, *Under Crimson Skies* (1920), with Elmo Lincoln, had Noble as Baltimore Bucko. *The Adorable Savage* (1920) featured Johnson as Ratu Madri, a Fiji island ruler. Noble henceforth would still make films at Universal, but he began to freelance with many studios and major directors.

The Leopard Woman (1920) had Johnson as Chake, the slave that Louise Glaum dispatches to (unsuccessfully)

Topsy and Eva (1927): Noble Johnson as Uncle Tom

Redskin (1929): **Richard Dix (left) confronts an ornery Noble Johnson.**

Ten Commandments (1923). Johnson portrayed the Lion, a Parisian gangster, in *A Man's Mate* (1924); a deputy sheriff in *The Midnight Express* (1924); a minion of Hell whipping a woman in *Dante's Inferno* (1924); Marimba, the cannibal chief, opposite Jackie Coogan in *Little Robinson Crusoe* (1924); and a cannibal leader once again in *The Navigator* (1924), starring Buster Keaton.

As for his first significant role in a fantasy film, Douglas Fairbanks' lavish *The Thief of Bagdad* (1924), the *New York Times* (3/2/24) commented, "Noble Johnson figures as the Indian Prince. He is effective and true to type, with a splendid imitation of an Indian beard." Noble was among the royals, along with the Mongol Prince (Sojin) and the Persian Prince (Mathilde Comont), who seek to find a special gift to win the hand in marriage of the Princess (Julanne Johnston), the daughter of the Caliph. The Prince of the Indies brings back a crystal ball with magic powers taken from the eye of an idol. The gifts from the various princes are initially used to save the Princess' life, but then become elements of the evil Mongol's plan to take over Bagdad.

Johnson played Ponfilo in *The Dancers* (1925), starring Alma Rubens. He was Googomy, the native leader who attacks the plantation, in *Adventure* (1925), with Pauline Starke and Wallace Beery. The odd character names continued as Noble portrayed Wabigoon in *The Gold Hunters* (1925). Johnson could be viewed among the crowd in MGM's spectacular *Ben-Hur: A Tale of the Christ* (1925).

murder House Peters. The serial *Daredevil Jack* (1920) had an episode wherein Johnson boxed with the then current heavyweight champ, Jack Dempsey. As the Crow, a vile henchmen, Noble achieved some redemption when, mortally wounded, he clears Buck Jones of murder in *Sunset Sprague* (1920). An interesting part, in terms of visual impact, was that of Conquest, one of the titled characters in MGM's *The Four Horsemen of the Apocalypse* (1921), starring Rudolph Valentino. John Ford's *The Wallop* (1921), with Harry Carey, included Johnson as Espinol. Noble played Chatterjii in Thomas Ince's *The Bronze Bell* (1921), set in India.

Johnson assayed a number of Latino roles around this time, including El Capitan Ramirez, whose band of brigands takes over the town of Magdalena, in *Serenade* (1921); Blackie Lopez, a rustler and kidnapper who covets Hoot Gibson's sweetheart, in *The Loaded Door* (1922); and Leon Serrano, masquerading as a deputy sheriff to cover up his cattle rustling, in *Tracks* (1922). Noble was prominently on hand as Friday in the Universal serial *The Adventures of Robinson Crusoe* (1922), with Harry C. Myers in the title role. *Captain Fly-by-Night* (1922), with Johnnie Walker, had Johnson as an Indian.

In *Drums of Fate* (1923), Noble played the friendly native king who saves the life of Maurice Flynn. He was a villain in the Ruth Roland serial *The Haunted Valley* (1923) and an Indian in *The Courtship of Miles Standish* (1923). *Burning Words* (1923), a Mounties story with Laura LaPlante, had Johnson as Bad Pierre. Noble was "the Bronze Man" in the prologue of Cecil B. DeMille's *The*

Moby Dick (1930): **left to right—Stubbs (Walter Long), Ahab (John Barrymore) and Queequeg (Noble Johnson)**

Kismet (1930): Otis Skinner (center) faces the axe of executioner Noble Johnson (far right), while Richard Carlyle, John St. Polis, Edmund Breese, Ford Sterling and players revel in the moment.

Noble portrayed Sitting Bull in both *Hands Up!* (1926) and *The Flaming Frontier* (1926), set at the Battle of Little Big Horn with Dustin Farnum as Custer. He was third-billed as Martell in *The Law of the Snow Country* (1926). Johnson was seen in *Aloma of the South Seas* (1926) and the Universal short *The Little Warrior* (1926). *The Lady of the Harem* (1926), whose cast included Sojin and Brandon Hurst, included Noble as the imposing tax collector.

Red Clay (1927) afforded Johnson another Native American role as Chief Bear Paw. Cecil B. DeMille made good use of Noble's physical presence and stunting skills, casting him as the charioteer transporting Mary Magdalene (Jacqueline Logan) in *The King of Kings* (1927). Johnson was Bimbo, the hulking Lascar ship's cook who is shot by Leatrice Joy aboard a tramp steamer in Donald Crisp's *Vanity* (1927). In Thomas Cripps' insightful *Slow Fade to Black* (1977), he notes that the Duncan sisters' (Vivian and Rosetta) production of *Topsy and Eva* (1927) was " ... relieved only by Noble Johnson's staunch effort to preserve Tom's dignity." Noble's Uncle Tom withstood the lashes of Gibson Gowland (of *Greed* fame) as Simon Legree. *When a Man Loves* (1927), starring John Barrymore, included Johnson as an apache in France during the reign of Louis XV. *Soft Cushions* (1927), with Boris Karloff as the chief conspirator, featured Johnson as the powerful Captain of the Guard.

The Gateway of the Moon (1928), about the construction of a Bolivian railway, had

Noble as Soriano. *Something Always Happens* (1928), a haunted house thriller with Esther Ralston and Sojin, billed Johnson as "the Thing." Set on the island of Pago Pago, *Why Sailors Go Wrong* (1928) had Johnson as a native. He played cardsharp Doc Mellis in *Manhattan Knights* (1928). Noble appeared in the Western *The Black Ace* (1928) and played Li Wong Foo, involved in drug trafficking, in *Yellow Contraband* (1928). Warner Bros.' ambitious production of *Noah's Ark* (1928) had Johnson as a slave broker. In *Sal of Singapore* (1928), Noble was the first mate to Erickson (Alan Hale). *The Yellow Cameo* (1928), a Pathé serial about buried treasure near an old Spanish mission, had Noble menacing heroine Allene Ray. Johnson reportedly had a bit role in *West of Zanzibar* (1928), which, if true, would refute the statement that he never appeared in any films with childhood friend Lon Chaney.

As the troublesome Pueblo Jim, a Navaho Indian, in *Redskin* (1929), Noble was in conflict with Richard Dix, who is trying to bring opposing tribes together. *Black Waters* (1929) featured Johnson as Jeelo. *The Four Feathers* (1929) had Noble as Ahmed, who bravely aids maligned Richard Arlen. *The Four Feathers* marked Johnson's first association with producer Merian C. Cooper and director Ernest B. Schoedsack, the men who would eventually call upon him

The Mummy (1932): The Nubian (Noble Johnson) stirs the pot, with Ardath Bey (Boris Karloff) and Helen (Zita Johann) in the background.

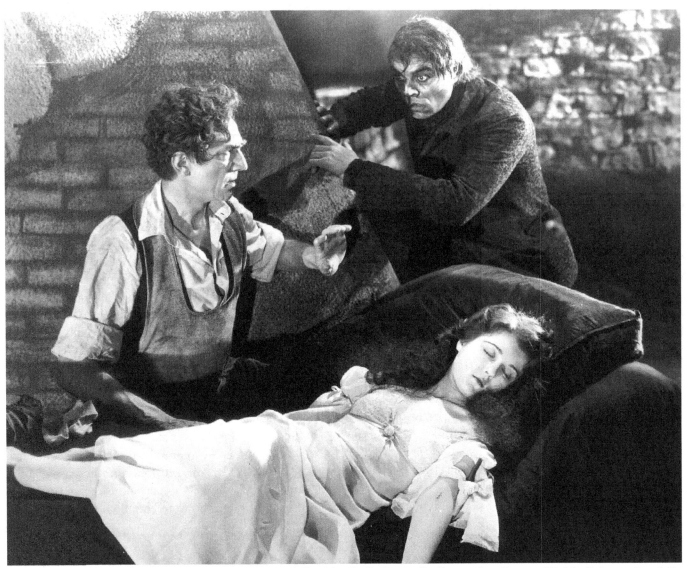

Murders in the Rue Morgue **(1932): Professor Mirakle (Bela Lugosi) dispatches Janos (Noble Johnson), while Sidney Fox lies unconscious.**

to play his most famous role, the native chief in *King Kong* (1933). *The Mysterious Dr. Fu Manchu* (1929) featured Noble as Li Po, star Warner Oland's henchman.

According to the United States Census of 1930, Johnson, now using the private name of Mark Noble, was living at 181 West Maple Street, Glendale, California, with his second wife Mae [or May] (1880 - ?), whose father was from France and mother from Spain. The date of Noble's marriage to Mae and when it terminated are, like the end of his first marriage, unknown at present. In any case, it was apparent that Johnson was becoming more and more of a private person, valuing his anonymity despite his screen success.

Set in German East Africa, *Mamba* (1930) had Johnson as Hassim, a native who identifies Jean Hersholt as being responsible for the death of his daughter. Another of Noble's powerful portrayals was that of Queequeg, the exotic tattooed harpooner and faithful companion of Captain Ahab (John Barrymore), in *Moby Dick* (1930). Johnson was

Youssef, an Arab, in *Renegades* (1930), which featured a pre-*Dracula* Bela Lugosi. Johnson's impressive physique was in evidence in his role of the executioner in *Kismet* (1930), starring Otis Skinner, David Manners and Loretta Young.

Johnson was a guard in the courtroom sequence of *Son of India* (1931). He played Osman in *East of Borneo* (1931), with Charles Bickford and Rose Hobart. The moody pre-Code *Safe in Hell* (1931), with Dorothy Mackaill marvelous in the lead, had Noble as Bobo, the black police sergeant on the corrupt Caribbean island.

Murders in the Rue Morgue (1932), directed by Robert Florey and starring Bela Lugosi, can be viewed somewhat as a compensatory project for both, after Universal removed them from the production of *Frankenstein* (1931). Johnson played Janos, the "Black One," mute servant to Dr. Mirakle (Lugosi), who runs a carnival as a ruse to cover his experiments with apes. After an exhibition, Janos is dispatched by Mirakle to follow Camille (Sidney Fox), to whom Erik the ape has become attracted. Later, following

The Most Dangerous Game (1932): **Henchmen Steve Clemente and Noble Johnson (right) restrain Joel McCrea (center).**

the death of a prostitute (Arlene Francis) after her blood has been mixed with that of the ape, Janos must dispose of her body. Taking an axe, he severs the ropes holding her hands and feet to X-shaped beams, with the corpse plunging through a trapdoor into the river below. At the film's climax, Janos spots the police through a window and is directed by Mirakle to hold them off. Descending the same staircase Dwight Frye as Fritz did in *Frankenstein*, Janos is shot to death by an officer. As often was the case, Johnson's physical appearance brought more to the role of Janos than did his acting.

In *Mystery Ranch* (1932), a George O'Brien Western, Johnson played Mudo (whose tongue had been cut out), one of the henchmen of the evil Charles Middleton. This was followed by another mute henchman role as Ivan, the black-hearted Cossack, in *The Most Dangerous Game* (1932). Ivan delights in torturing those who refuse to be hunted

by the malefic Count Zaroff (Leslie Banks). As Ivan follows a pack of vicious dogs through a swamp in quest of Zaroff's prey (Fay Wray and Joel McCrea), a hastily made and cleverly placed spear impales him. Noble was quite menacing in the role.

Johnson was billed as the Nubian in Universal's *The Mummy* (1932), starring Boris Karloff. The Nubian, the servant of Sir Joseph (Arthur Byron), is the victim when Ardath Bey (Karloff), actually Imhotep incognito, places him under a hypnotic spell. Sir Joseph suffers a heart attack induced by Imhotep while attempting to burn the Scroll of Thoth. The Nubian steals the Scroll, burning other papers in an attempt to deceive Dr. Muller (Edward Van Sloan) into thinking the ancient document has been destroyed. As Imhotep later enters with Helen (Zita Johann), the Nubian, viewed stirring a cauldron, is compelled to block her escape so that she can be forced to join the mummy in

King Kong (1933): **Noble Johnson as the Chief of Skull Island**

Forgotten Faces

eternal life. Johnson, whose role was not very substantial, was still effective in this classic horror opus.

After appearing as the head boatman in *Nagana* (1933), with Melvyn Douglas seeking a cure for sleeping sickness in the tropics, Johnson was signed by RKO for their upcoming production of *King Kong* (1933). For his part as the native chief, Noble wore a wig, had his skin darkened and was covered with ceremonial markings, besides being attired in an elaborate headdress and grass skirt. As Denham (Robert Armstrong), Captain Englehorn (Frank Reicher), Jack Driscoll (Bruce Cabot), Ann Darrow (Fay Wray), and the rest of the landing party from the Venture look on, the inhabitants of Skull Island are apparently involved in a sacrificial ritual. The chief (Johnson) and witch doctor (Steve Clemente) stand beside a young maiden, while the natives chant and dance. The interlopers are spotted, bringing a halt to the ceremony. The chief approaches, signaling two warriors to accompany him, with their every step being accentuated by Max Steiner's musical score. Englehorn assures the chief that the party comes in friendship, but the chief wants them to immediately leave the island.

Roman Scandals (1933): Even the torturers Leo Willis (left) and Noble Johnson (right) laugh at the antics of Eddie Cantor.

The witch doctor spots Ann, however, causing the chief to demand the "golden woman" for the bride of Kong, offering six of his women in return. The ship's party cautiously retreats to their vessel, but natives come aboard the Venture and kidnap Ann during the night. With Ann tied to an altar, the chief stands before a huge gong above the high wooden gates, invoking Kong to accept their offering. He shouts, "Kara Ta ni, Kong … O Taro Vey, Rama Kong," before the fantastic ape arrives and chaos ensues. Although not a complex role on paper, the part of the native chief would not have been as impressive in lesser hands than those of Noble Johnson.

Johnson again played a native chief, this time leading an uprising against foreigners on a Malayan rubber plantation, in *White Woman* (1933). Noble was one of the soldiers attempting to torture Eddie Cantor in *Roman Scandals* (1933). Johnson was then asked to reprise his role of the native ruler for RKO's sequel *Son of Kong* (1933). Noble's appearance in *Son of Kong* was briefer than planned, as footage involving the natives was eliminated before the film's release. Four castaways, including Denham and Englehorn from the original *King Kong*, land on Skull Island near the Great Wall. The chief, blaming the whites for causing the destruction of their village, leads his subjects in giving them a hostile reception. Denham and the others retreat to the sea, keeping the natives at gunpoint in order to escape.

Massacre (1934), starring Richard Barthelmess, had Johnson as an Indian leader. *Murder in Trinidad* (1934) featured Noble as the villainous Queechie, who serves as a guide for Nigel Bruce through the dangerous Caroni swamp. He played an attendant in *Kid Millions* (1934), another Eddie Cantor film. Over the years, many comedians, including Buster Keaton, Cantor and Bob Hope, made use of the threatening figure of Johnson as a counterpoint to their own weakness for comic purposes.

Set in the northwest frontier of India, *The Lives of a Bengal Lancer* (1935), starring Gary Cooper, had Noble as Ram Singh. He was the Amahaggar Chief who threatens Randolph Scott, Helen Mack and Nigel Bruce early on in RKO's *She* (1935). Johnson was dressed as a devil as part of the carnival attraction in *Dante's Inferno* (1935), having already acted in the 1924 version. Johnson played Bisco, a convict, in *Escape from Devil's Island* (1935), with Victor Jory. *My American Wife* (1935), with Francis Lederer, had Noble as the Native American Nation leader.

Mummy's Boys (1936), a Wheeler and Woolsey comedy, featured Johnson as the tattoo artist. Cecil B. DeMille's *The Plainsman* (1936), starring Gary Cooper, had Johnson as the Native American with Painted Horse (Victor Varconi). Both Indians follow Calamity Jane (Jean Arthur) into a cabin, where Noble comically tries on one of her hats before getting angry, smashing a mirror and throwing his tomahawk. Later, he ties Hickok (Cooper) to a pole and hauls him over a fire. *Lost Horizon* (1936) included Noble as the leader of the porters on the return journey from Shangri-La. Johnson was seen in two films for director John Ford, as a Sikh policeman in *Wee Willie Winkie* (1937) with Shirley Temple, and as a native in *Four Men and*

She (1935): **Nigel Bruce, Helen Mack and Randolph Scott face Noble Johnson, the imposing Amahaggar Chief.**

a Prayer (1938). He played Roustan in *Conquest* (1937), with Charles Boyer as Napoleon. *Mysterious Mr. Moto* (1938), the fifth entry in the "Mr. Moto" series with Peter Lorre, had Noble as a native sergeant on Devil's Island.

Noble earned the trust of Gary Cooper during their work together and was hired to train Cooper's Afghan wolfhound. Putting the skills to use that he had acquired years earlier in New York, Johnson also trained dogs for Richard Arlen and Bruce Cabot (Hathcock, p. 48), as well as Mischa Auer, Ruth Chatterton and others. For a time, he operated kennels in Glendale and North Hollywood, California.

The Republic serial *Hawk of the Wilderness* (1938) provided Johnson with the substantial role of Mokuyi, who survives a shipwreck along with a baby who grows up to be Herman Brix (as Kioga). An expedition comes to the island 22 years after the wreck, resulting in Mokuyi being captured by the treacherous William Royle. Mokuyi, having been rescued by Kioga, tries to convince the natives that the white man's magic will calm the active volcano. Unfortunately, the volcano does erupt, but, in true serial fashion, a plane rescues all the protagonists in the nick of time. Mokuyi then reveals a pouch of valuable gems, indicating a favorable future for Kioga and himself.

Johnson played Luke Johnson in *Frontier Pony Express* (1939) with Roy Rogers. He had little to say, but his pres-

ence was unmistakable as General Regules in *Juarez* (1939), starring Paul Muni. Again for Cecil B. DeMille, Johnson was viewed as the Native American shooting the piano in *Union Pacific* (1939). A particularly villainous role for Noble was that of Hannibal, the brutal guard on an Amazon rubber plantation who proves a nemesis for Richard Arlen and Andy Devine, in *Tropic Fury* (1939). John Ford's *Drums Along the Mohawk* (1939) had Johnson as the Native American invading the home of obstinate Edna May Oliver, setting her bed afire. Noble was a captured Delaware Indian wading in the river in *Allegheny Uprising* (1939), with John Wayne. James Whale's penultimate feature film *Green Hell* (1940) concerned itself with a hidden temple in the jungle, and featured Johnson as a hostile tribal chief.

Once again the horror genre beckoned Noble for *The Ghost Breakers* (1940), played mostly for laughs by Bob Hope, but strictly for chills by Johnson as a zombie. Nightclub entertainer Mary Carter (Paulette Goddard) inherits a supposedly haunted castle on an island near Cuba. She ventures there with Larry Lawrence (Hope), who is fleeing gangland reprisal for an exposé he provided. The zombie (Johnson), completely bald and clad in native garb, is kept in a small hut near the boat landing by an old custodian. The zombie lies motionless on his back, his blank eyes staring upward, until the call of his keeper compels him to arise. There is a very good sequence wherein he chases Mary to the castle and up a sweeping staircase. Hope refers to the creature as "only the colored caretaker," but Noble's zombie enhances the terror amidst the laughter with his menacing strolls.

Noble was among the Native Americans confronting Gary Cooper and Preston Foster in *Northwest Mounted Police* (1940), another Cecil B. DeMille production. He was Lobo, henchman of the vile Henry Brandon, in the Roy Rogers Western *The Ranger and the Lady* (1940). *Seven Sinners* (1940), with Marlene Dietrich and John Wayne, included Johnson as an irate Russian. The Hope and Crosby *Road to Zanzibar* (1941) had Noble on hand as a tribal chief. As Chief Poison Arrow in *Hurry, Charlie, Hurry* (1941), Johnson meets Leon Errol, on a fishing trip, and makes him an honorary member of the tribe. *Aloma of the South Seas* (1941), another volcanic island tale with Dorothy Lamour and Jon Hall, featured Noble as Moukali. *Shut My Big Mouth* (1942) had Johnson as Chief Standing Bull, who demands the scalp of star Joe E. Brown.

The Ghost Breakers (1940): Noble Johnson as the haunting zombie

Johnson was Elan, the ruler of a South Sea island, in *The Mad Doctor of Market Street* (1942). Elan proclaims Dr. Benson (Lionel Atwill) a god after the latter apparently brings Tanao (Rosina Galli), the chief's wife, back from the dead. Later Elan consigns Benson to his doom when he realizes the man is quite human after all. Noble was a Sikh in Zoltan Korda's *The Jungle Book* (1942), with Sabu. Johnson was excellent as the great Shawnee warrior Tecumseh in *Ten Gentlemen from West Point* (1942), particularly in the scene where he humbles the captured Laird Cregar. *Danger in the Pacific* (1942) had Noble as the chief of the tribe of headhunters. Johnson played Carney, the former bodyguard of a murdered blackmailer, in *Night in New Orleans* (1942).

Thank Your Lucky Stars (1943), featuring virtually every performer on the Warner Bros. lot, had Johnson as Charlie the Indian. The musical *The Desert Song* (1943), directed by Robert Florey, featured Noble as Abdel Rahmen. From here on, Noble's screen appearances were becoming both rare and brief.

A Game of Death (1945), RKO's remake of *The Most Dangerous Game*, did give Johnson another henchman role, this time as Carib. Assisting Kreiger (Edgar Barrier) in his perfidy, Carib's character was quite reminiscent of Noble's portrayal of Ivan in the original. John Loder and Audrey Long were seen in the Joel McCrea and Fay Wray parts. Johnson's last fantasy-related role was that of a trustee in Hell in *Angel on My Shoulder* (1946), with Paul Muni.

As Wassac, the tribal leader involved in peace talks despite the murder of his son, Noble was seen with Bill Elliott in *Plainsman and the Lady* (1946). He even managed to find his way into a Bowery Boys film as Hasson in *Hard Boiled Mahoney* (1947). Johnson was a native guard in *Slave Girl* (1947), with Yvonne DeCarlo, and an Indian chief in *Along the Oregon Trail* (1947), with Monte Hale.

Unconquered (1947) represented Johnson's final appearance in a Cecil B. DeMille opus. He played the tall Ottawa Indian, while Boris Karloff was seen as the Chief of the Seneca. As Comanche Chief Black Eagle, Noble re-

Ten Gentlemen from West Point (1942): **Mighty warrior Tecumseh (Noble Johnson) stands over his humbled captive (Laird Cregar).**

ceived stolen rifles from villainous Bruce Cabot in *The Gallant Legion* (1948). He was a bartender in *Dream Girl* (1949), with Betty Hutton.

Johnson's most noteworthy performance in the latter part of his career was that of Chief Red Shirt in John Ford's *She Wore a Yellow Ribbon* (1949). Red Shirt stands firm that shifty Harry Woods' demand of $50 is too much for a wagon full of rifles, slaying the gun dealer with his bow during the ensuing tirade. Much later, as Captain Brittles (John Wayne) bravely enters the Native American encampment, Red Shirt shoots an arrow into the ground at his feet as a warning to advance no further. Brittles defiantly snaps the arrow in half, gaining an audience with the various Indian leaders, to the chagrin of Red Shirt.

Rock Island Trail (1950), concerned with railroad expansion and starring Forrest Tucker, had Noble as Bent Creek. Johnson's final screen role was that of Nogura, the Oseka Chief, in Republic's *North of the Great Divide* (1950), with Roy Rogers in the lead. Nogura is concerned when his tribe loses their food supply after traps prevent salmon from reaching their fishing waters. Nogura is arrested and later kidnapped, before Rogers rights all wrongs. Noble played the role in a dignified manner, bringing to conclusion a long, significant film career.

Perhaps a greater mystery than any he was involved in onscreen was what happened to Noble Johnson after he retired from films. Apparently he had invested in real estate in California and Nevada while still in the motion picture industry. Noble continued to buy and sell houses and properties after 1950. He and third wife Gladys Blackwell (1905-2000), more than 20 years Noble's junior, trav-

eled the West in a mobile home, living at different points in time in Northern California, Oregon and Washington. Going now exclusively by the name of Mark Noble, Johnson was virtually estranged from his family. Noble reportedly (Cappello, February 1992) would call his niece, Virgel Elizabeth Johnson Browne, George's daughter, on occasion to see how they were doing, but that was about the only familial contact he maintained. After George had donated his papers and memorabilia to the U.C.L.A. Library Special Collections division, Noble paid a one-time visit there in October 1969. He was adamant that he did not want any material related to him, his life or career available for public viewing, to which the university librarians complied. Johnson resisted the notion of anyone prying into his past. His wife Gladys informed Bill Cappello that Noble destroyed all his own movie memorabilia just prior to his death.

Noble Johnson died in Yucaipa, San Bernadino County, California, on January 9, 1978, at the age of 96. His death certificate gave the name of Mark Noble and listed his occupation as rancher, with 35 years in the cattle business. There was no mention of his having been involved in motion pictures. The cause of death was arteriosclerotic heart disease, compounded by myelopathic atrophy, a degeneration of the spinal cord, which had progressively hindered Noble in his later years. Johnson was cremated, with his ashes interred in the Garden of Peace at Eternal Valley Memorial Park, Newhall, California.

Thomas Cripps (1977, p. 130) stated Noble's influence thusly:

> Of all the blacks, Noble M. Johnson exemplified both the plight and achievement of the Negro actor. His boyhood in Colorado prepared him to be a stuntman and an animal trainer, both of which stood him in good stead during dry spells in a career that stretched from Lubin in Philadelphia to Hollywood and John Ford's *She Wore a Yellow Ribbon* (1949). His coppery-bright skin and square features opened up a wide range of roles that allowed him to obliterate his racial identity in white circles while receiving praise from the black press. For blacks of the 1920s Johnson's career was a kind of victory within a context of despair, a black presence that went beyond menials to substantive roles

Noble Johnson had been a staple in the film industry for four decades, but seemed largely forgotten by the early 1950s. Perhaps it is not so surprising that he in kind turned his back on his past career.

North of the Great Divide (1950): **Douglas Evans, Roy Rogers, Noble Johnson and Gordon Jones, in Johnson's final film**

For horror and fantasy film fans, Noble Johnson's ominous ubiquity fit the proper mood in films like *The Most Dangerous Game*, *Murders in the Rue Morgue* and *The Mummy*. The classic *King Kong* would not be the same if Johnson were not present on Skull Island. Although a largely unheralded performer, in part due to his own choice, Noble Johnson is worthy of long overdue notice, not just for his contributions to the horror genre, but for his importance to the motion picture industry in general.

Sources

Brown, Barry, & Coughlin, Jim. *Unsung Heroes of the Horrors*, Unpublished manuscript, 1978.

Cappello, Bill. "Noble Johnson—Part I," in *Classic Images #199*, January 1992, pp. 42-43, 63.

Cappello, Bill. "Noble Johnson—Part II," in *Classic Images #200*, February 1992, pp. 50-51.

Cripps, Thomas. *Bright Boulevards, Bold Dreams: The Story of Black Hollywood*, New York: One World/Ballantine, 2006.

Cripps, Thomas. *Slow Fade to Black: The Negro in American Film, 1900-1942*, New York: Galaxy Books, 1977.

Cripps, Thomas. *Toms, Coons, Mulattoes, Mammies and Bucks: An Interpretative History of Blacks in Films*, New York: Viking Press, 1973.

Everett, Eldon K. "Noble Johnson, the First Black Movie Star," in *Classic Images #52*, 1976, p. 39.

Hathcock, Luther. "Whatever Happened to Noble Johnson," in *Classic Images #129*, March 1986, pp. 48-49, 51.

Leifert, Don. "Noble Johnson: Portrait in Black," in *Gore Creatures #24*, 1975.

Sampson, Henry T. *Blacks in Black and White: A Source Book on Black Films*, Metuchen, NJ: The Scarecrow Press, 1977.

Brandon Hurst
(1866 – 1947)

Among the reasons that performers fall into the realm of "forgotten faces" is that their major portrayals occurred in films that are now lost, or in silent or other vintage pictures that are rarely viewed. Such is the case with Brandon Hurst, a marvelously wicked villain of the silent screen. Hurst had a wonderfully expressive countenance with devious eyes that would often gleam in anticipation of havoc he was about to wreak. Although reduced to minor parts as butlers and English statesmen in the early sound era, Brandon Hurst made some significant contributions to the fantasy genre in silent films like *Dr. Jekyll and Mr. Hyde* (1920), *The Hunchback of Notre Dame* (1923), *The Thief of Bagdad* (1924) and *The Man Who Laughs* (1928), as well as the early sound chiller *Murders in the Rue Morgue* (1932).

Brandon Hurst was born in London, England, on November 30, 1866. After a standard British boarding school upbringing, Hurst spent four years studying linguistics, history and literary criticism at London's Philological College. At that point, Hurst stood five-foot-eleven, weighed 150 pounds, and had brown eyes and brown hair. Eventually, Hurst became a riding master in the 1st King's Dragoon Guards, a noted cavalry regiment of the British army. A growing interest in theater arts, however, caused Hurst to embark on a stage career as an actor, playwright and producer.

Although Hurst was married in 1891, there is no known record of the exact date and location of the wedding, nor of his wife's name. By 1914, Hurst listed himself as "divorced," but, when that event occurred is undetermined as well.

In May 1892, Hurst was seen in Derby, England, in the title role of Charley Wyckenham in one of the earliest productions of *Charley's Aunt*. Hurst gained fame as a comedian, both in vaudeville and on the legitimate stage in England. He is said to have written over 25 one-act plays, one of which was *A Losing Hazard* (4/11/1892).

In 1898, theater impresario Charles Frohman recruited Hurst to venture to the United States. The prodigious Frohman, who produced more than 700 plays and nurtured such talent as William Gillette, Julia Marlowe and Ethel Barrymore, would eventually lose his life aboard the Lusitania when it was sunk by a German submarine in 1915.

Frohman initially engaged Hurst to be part of his noted "Charles Frohman's Comedians," who played most of the major cities of the East Coast of the United States. Hurst also spent time in Chicago as part of the Dearborn Stock Company. At Hoyt's Theatre in New York, Brandon was seen in the farce *Coralie and Company, Dressmakers* (2/5/1900). Hurst performed in a number of comedies in Manhattan around this time, including *The Money Makers* (1/16/05), *Mademoiselle Marni* (3/6/05) and *Gallops* (2/12/06). Under the production of Weber and Fields, Hurst was seen on Broadway in *Personal* (9/3/07). Brandon toured with Maude Fealy in *The Stronger Sex*, playing, among other locations, the Grand Opera House in Seattle (12/8/07). Hurst continued to dabble in play writing, co-authoring the three-act *The Making of a New Man* (3/24/09) with Charles de Lima.

Two Women (11/29/10), at the Lyric Theatre on Broadway, garnered Hurst favorable reviews opposite Mrs. Leslie Carter. Other New York stage roles for Hurst came in *Mrs. Avery* (10/23/11), as George Demarest in *Within the Law* (9/11/12) and in a revival of *The Second Mrs. Tanqueray* (2/3/13), again with Mrs. Carter. Hurst spent the summer of 1913 in Rochester, New York with the Manhattan Players at the Lyceum Theatre in a company that included future film performers Maude Eburne and Ernest Cossart.

Hurst made his film debut as Edward Pinckney in Pathé's *Via Wireless* (1915), filmed in Green-

1913 portrait of Brandon Hurst with the Manhattan Players, Rochester, NY

The Hunchback of Notre Dame (1923): A character portrait of Brandon Hurst as Jehan

act he will regret when Hyde kills him after discovering the secret of the transformation. As the elitist Carewe, Hurst held his own with Barrymore in this compelling dramatization of Robert Louis Stevenson's classic.

A Dark Lantern (1920) featured Hurst as Colonel Dereham. *The World's Applause* (1923), with Bebe Daniels, Lewis Stone and Adolphe Menjou, included Brandon as James Crane. *Legally Dead* (1923) gave Hurst the interesting part of Dr. Gelzer, who uses adrenaline to restore the life of wrongly executed Milton Sills.

Hurst's most famous horror role was that of Jehan Frollo, the wicked brother of Dom Claude (Nigel de Brulier), in the enduring classic *The Hunchback of Notre Dame* (1923). The screenwriters deviated from Victor Hugo's novel with their presentation of Jehan as the evil master of the unfortunate Quasimodo (Lon Chaney). Hurst further embellished the part with his leers and gesticulations, suggesting dubious intentions, particularly when it comes to the Gypsy girl Esmeralda (Patsy Ruth Miller). When Jehan makes it clear he wants Esmeralda for his own, the Gypsy declares she would rather die than love him. Near the climax, as Quasimodo fights off the hordes storming the Cathedral of Notre Dame, Jehan attempts to seize Esmer-

wich, Connecticut. Brandon lived on W. 30th Street in Manhattan at the time, focusing his efforts on Broadway, including *Rich Man, Poor Man* (10/5/16). *Theatre Magazine* (November 1916, p. 394) found Hurst to be "excellent" as Peter Beeston in this drama. Although nearing 50 years old, Hurst, with his prior military experience, enlisted in the British Army during World War I, being named a captain in the Remount Service.

Returning to the United States, Hurst appeared at the Fulton Theatre in *Her Honor, the Mayor* (5/20/18). As Li Fu Yang, Hurst was seen in *The Lady of the Lamp* (8/17/20), Earl Carroll's elaborate fantasy of ancient China. Although now increasing his commitment to motion pictures, Brandon helped organize the Players' Assembly in New York, producing and acting in two works with the group: *Montmartre* (2/13/22) as Jean Tavernier and *The Night Call* (4/26/22) as Edward Howe.

Hurst firmly established himself in film circles with his portrayal of Sir George Carewe in *Dr. Jekyll and Mr. Hyde* (1920), with John Barrymore in fine form in the lead role(s). Carewe, the father of Jekyll's fiancée (Martha Mansfield), also serves as an evil influence upon the doctor. Sir George taunts Jekyll about being afraid of temptation, an

The Hunchback of Notre Dame (1923): Quasimodo (Lon Chaney) with his evil "protector" Jehan (Hurst)

The Man Who Laughs (1928): The wicked Olga Baclanova seeks counsel from the cunning Brandon Hurst.

"What's the news today -- Prince of Scandalmongers?"

alda. Quasimodo turns on his master, killing Jehan, but receiving a fatal knife wound in the process. Although *The Hunchback of Notre Dame* will always evoke Chaney's bravura performance, Hurst's efforts have held up well over the years.

The Thief of Bagdad (1924), a fantasy extravaganza for its time, had the swashbuckling Douglas Fairbanks headlining a cast including Sojin, Anna May Wong and Noble Johnson. As the Caliph of Bagdad, Hurst is eager to find a husband for his beautiful daughter (Julanne Johnston) and has the suitors set out on a difficult quest to prove they are worthy of her hand in marriage. Hurst again rendered a steady performance, showing the evolution of the Caliph's character from judgmental to frightened to gracious and understanding, as he presents Johnston to be Fairbanks' bride.

Hurst played Daniel Randon in *Cytherea* (1924), Count Beetholde in *One Night in Rome* (1924), Herrold the reporter in *The Silent Watcher* (1924) and Bertrand in *The Lover of Ca-*

mille (1924). Again opposite Lon Chaney, Brandon played a clown in *He Who Gets Slapped* (1924). *The Lady* (1925) starred Norma Talmadge as a humble woman who splits with her cheating upper class husband while pregnant with their child. As St. Aubyns, Sr., Hurst was the aristocratic father-in-law who, after the death of his son, coldly seeks out Talmadge with a court order to obtain custody of his grandson. When MGM remade *The Lady* as *The Secret of Madame Blanche* (1933), Irene Dunne had the lead and Lionel Atwill excelled in Hurst's role.

Lightnin' (1925) featured Hurst as Everett Hammond and would represent his first of seven appearances in films directed by John Ford (who was noted for utilizing actors whom he considered reliable over and over as a type of stock company). Hurst played the Pharaoh in an Egyptian flashback sequence of *Made for Love* (1926). Brandon appeared in successive films with leading lady Florence Vidor, as Jasper Doak in *The Enchanted Hill* (1926) and Matard in *The Grand Duchess and the Waiter* (1926). Hurst played a

The Greene Murder Case (1929): Sproot (Brandon Hurst) addresses Philo Vance (William Powell).

be assayed by Basil Rathbone in MGM's sound remake, *Anna Karenina* (1935).

Another film based on a Victor Hugo novel, *The Man Who Laughs* (1928), gave Hurst one of his meatiest screen roles. He played Barkilphedro, the jester, who knows everyone's business and plays all the angles to gain the confidence of King James II (Sam de Grasse), Queen Anne (Josephine Crowell) and Duchess Josiana (Olga Baclanova). The tale centers on Gwynplaine (Conrad Veidt), who as a child had his face maimed into a permanent smile because of his father's politics. Barkilphedro discovers Gwynplaine is heir to a peerage. In an attempt to avenge himself against the rejecting Josiana, the jester convinces Queen Anne of the benefits of a marriage between Gwynplaine and the Duchess. Barkilphedro's efforts are thwarted, however, as are his wicked designs on the innocent Dea (Mary Philbin). Hurst uses many non-verbal devices as Barkilphedro, including eye rolls, sneers and grimaces, main-

butler, a role with which he would become very familiar, in *Secret Orders* (1926). *Paris at Midnight* (1926) had him as Count Tallefer, the father of Mary Brian. John Ford's *The Shamrock Handicap* (1926) included Hurst as the procurer of taxes. Hurst played Doyle in *The Rainmaker* (1926), Andre de Chauvalons in *Volcano* (1926) and Peterby in *The Amateur Gentleman* (1926). *The Lady of the Harem* (1926), with Sojin as the Sultan and Noble Johnson as a tax collector, had Hurst as a beggar.

After a minor part in Cecil B. DeMille's *The King of Kings* (1927), Brandon was seen as Uncle George in the noteworthy silent *Seventh Heaven* (1927), which brought leading lady Janet Gaynor the first ever Academy Award for Best Actress. *Annie Laurie* (1927), starring Lillian Gish amidst the battling Scottish clans of Campbell and MacDonald, featured Brandon as the treacherous Campbell chieftain. Hurst was billed as Mr. Golden in *High School Hero* (1927), directed by David Butler.

Of his portrayal of Greta Garbo's rigid and wronged spouse Karenin in MGM's *Love* (1927), the *New York Times* (11/30/27) offered, "Brandon Hurst contributes an excellent character study as Anna's husband." A still in William K. Everson's *The Bad Guys* provides evidence that Hurst replaced Lionel Barrymore, who was said to have overshadowed Garbo, in *Love*. The role of Karenin, which was a significant one for Hurst playing opposite the studio's rising star, Garbo, would

The Connecticut Yankee (1931): Brandon Hurst as the devious Merlin, the Magician

Young as You Feel (1931): Brandon Hurst, Will Rogers and Donald Dillaway

taining the balance of staying in character while not going completely over the top playing such a scoundrel.

News Parade (1928) had Hurst as A.K. Wellington, a camera-shy millionaire. Brandon played Inspector Haynes in *Interference* (1928) with William Powell. Hurst was Dr. Isaacs, an aged inventor who is murdered by his butler, in *The Voice of the Storm* (1928). In *The Greene Murder Case* (1929), with William Powell as Philo Vance, Brandon was the Greene family butler and a murder suspect. He played Sturgess in *The Wolf of Wall Street* (1929), Sir Emmett Wildering in *Her Private Life* (1929), Jowles in *High Society Blues* (1930), Mr. Taine in *The Eyes of the World* (1930) and the Crown attorney in *The Right of Way* (1931). In the early 1930s, Hurst was managed by Gardner and Vincent, and, later, by Edward Small.

A Connecticut Yankee (1931) gave Hurst a dual role, playing both Merlin the Magician and the doctor at the mansion tending to William Farnum, whom Will Rogers travels to see during a fierce storm. As Merlin in the Camelot sequences, Hurst was back at his scene-chewing villainy, threatened by the arrival of Sir Boss (Rogers), while plot-

ting against the King (Farnum) with the treacherous Morgan le Fay (Myrna Loy). *A Connecticut Yankee* was Brandon's second appearance in a movie directed by David Butler, who would go on to utilize Hurst in 13 more of his films between 1931 and 1948. Hurst must have inspired loyalty with both directors and fellow performers. Will Rogers would have Brandon in two more of his films as well: *Young as You Feel* (1931), as Robbins, and *Down to Earth* (1932), as Jeffrey the butler.

Directed by Frank Strayer, who would soon direct *The Vampire Bat* (1933), *Murder at Midnight* (1931) had Hurst as Lawrence the butler. Lawrence suspiciously sets a clock ahead after a murder, finds an incriminating letter, then dies while on the telephone to the police as he is about to exonerate himself and expose the actual killer.

Murders in the Rue Morgue (1932), starring Bela Lugosi and directed by Robert Florey, featured Brandon prominently as the Prefect of Police. The Prefect is skeptical when medical student Pierre Dupin (Leon Ames) attempts to convince him that Dr. Mirakle (Lugosi) and his ape Erik are culpable for the rash of grisly murders plaguing Paris.

White Zombie (1932): **Butler Silver (Brandon Hurst, left) looks on as Bela Lugosi shows off Madge Bellamy to Robert Frazer.**

After finally agreeing to investigate, the Prefect leads his gendarmes to Mirakle's lair, with the commotion prompting the ape to turn on and kill his master. The role of the Prefect of Police did not have much depth, but Hurst imbued it with more dimension than would have a lesser actor.

The atmospheric *White Zombie* (1932), again with Lugosi in the lead as Murder Legendre, featured Hurst as Silver, servant to Beaumont (Robert Frazer). When en-

countering one of Legendre's zombies (George Burr Macannan), Silver screams and faints. Silver later meets his demise when the zombie bodyguards throw him into an underground river.

In *Scarface* (1932), with Paul Muni rendering a powerful performance, Hurst was seen as a citizens' committee member. Brandon played the district attorney in *The Midnight Lady* (1932), a personal secretary in *Sherlock Holmes* (1932), a staff general in *Rasputin and the Empress* (1932), and

Bombay Mail (1934): A striking portrait of Brandon Hurst as the rebellious Pundit Chundra

John Ford's classic *The Lost Patrol* (1934), highlighted by the fine work of Victor McLaglen and Boris Karloff, had Hurst as Corporal Bell, one of the first of the patrol to be killed off by the unseen enemy. Again with Karloff, Brandon was seen as a stock trader in *The House of Rothschild* (1934), the cast of which included virtually half the founders of SAG (Ivan Simpson, Murray Kinnell, Noel Madison, C. Aubrey Smith, Karloff, etc.). Again cast as an Indian, Hurst was a Hindu priest in *House of Mystery* (1934), concerning a curse that follows Clay Clement who, 20 years prior, killed a sacred monkey in a Hindu temple. Other roles for Hurst at this time were Bramley, a consulting doctor, in *Have a Heart* (1934); a statesman in *Viva Villa!* (1934); an English officer in *Crimson Romance* (1934); the Magistrate in *Red Morning* (1934) and Anders Strothers in *The Little Minister* (1934).

Hurst had a sympathetic role as Higgins, the butler, who, with his wife (Jane Darwell), takes a caring interest in Shirley Temple in *Bright Eyes* (1934). *The Woman in Red* (1935), directed by Robert Florey and starring Barbara Stanwyck, included Hurst as Uncle Emlen Wyatt. He was Grondal, the Federie family butler, in *While the Patient Slept* (1935), the doctor who treats Preston Foster in *Annie Oakley* (1935), Middleton the butler in *The Great Imperson-*

The Lost Patrol (1934): Brandon Hurst as Corporal Bell

a Gilbert and Sullivan operetta actor in *Cavalcade* (1933). Hurst had an intriguing role in *Bombay Mail* (1933) as Indian Pundit Garnath Chundra, who spends much of his time in meditation, but is actually an anti-British rebel.

In the spring of 1933, Hurst became one of the early members (SAG card #26) of the Screen Actors Guild. Many years prior, Brandon had been involved in the formation of Equity. He had the reputation of being a fair man who placed the good of his peers and profession over his individual needs.

ation (1935), a military policeman in *Bonnie Scotland* (1935) and had a minor role in *A Tale of Two Cities* (1935). Hurst showed his comedic touch as the sheriff in the Edgar Kennedy short, *Gasoloons* (1935).

John Ford utilized Hurst in four of his significant films in a two-year period. Hurst was Airan, one of the Scottish lairds, in *Mary of Scotland* (1936). He played Sergeant Tinsley, who searches for Irish rebels, in *The Plough and the Stars* (1936). Again opposite Shirley Temple, Brandon was Bagby in *Wee Willie Winkie* (1937). *Four Men and a Prayer* (1938) had Hurst, unbilled, as the jury foreman.

The Charge of the Light Brigade (1936) had Hurst as Lord Raglan. *Stolen Holiday* (1937) included Brandon as a police detective. In one of a number of films he did for director Frank Lloyd, Hurst was the tithing man in *Maid of Salem* (1937), centered on the witch hysteria in 17th-century Massachusetts. Hurst appeared in two musicals with Jeanette MacDonald, as the master of ceremonies in *Maytime* (1937) and an English general in *The Firefly* (1937).

On June 21, 1937 NBC broadcast a 45-minute version for radio of *Hamlet*, staring John Barrymore in a very familiar role. Hurst was heard as Claudius, King of Denmark.

In the Harold Lloyd comedy *Professor Beware* (1938), Brandon was Charlie the butler. Hurst played Doomster in *Kidnapped* (1938), a beggar in *If I Were King* (1938), Franz Liszt in *Suez* (1938), a doctor in *The Sun Never Sets* (1939) and Sir Henry Forrester in *Stanley and Livingstone* (1939). In a bit of a role reversal for Halliwell Hobbes, Hurst played his butler in *Tell No Tales* (1939). Again directed by David Butler, Brandon began another long association, this time with Bing Crosby, as C. Aubrey Smith's butler in *East Side of Heaven* (1939). Hurst would appear in five Crosby features, plus three "Road" pictures with Crosby and Bob Hope, and four additional Hope films as well.

The Blue Bird (1940), Maeterlinck's fantasy with Shirley Temple and Gale Sondergaard, had Brandon as a footman. He played Hedges in *If I Had My Way* (1940), Wilton in Frank Lloyd's *The Howards of Virginia* (1940) and Bates in *Rhythm on the River* (1940), with Bing Crosby. *Sign of the Wolf* (1941), based on a Jack London story, had Hurst as Dr. Morton. Brandon was the head waiter in a café in *Birth of the Blues* (1941). Given his appearance in the stage production 49 years before, it was fitting that Hurst had a role (as a coach) in *Charley's Aunt* (1941), with Jack Benny and Richard Haydyn as Charley. Revisiting familiar territory once again (having appeared in the 1920 silent version), Brandon played Briggs, the butler of Lanyon (Ian Hunter), in Victor Fleming's *Dr. Jekyll and Mr. Hyde* (1941), starring Spencer Tracy.

Hurst spent his later years living at the St. Elmo Apartments, 6358 Yucca Street, Hollywood. It was from this address in March of 1942 that Hurst wrote a letter

Mary of Scotland **(1936): Brandon Hurst as Airan, one of the Scottish lairds**

to Kenneth Thomson of the Screen Actors Guild (SAG), requesting some assistance, while also enclosing a poem he had written in the wake of the Japanese attack on Pearl Harbor. It was entitled *December 7, 1941* (and here is presented with the indentations and punctuation as Hurst had submitted it to SAG):

> They made their play on a Sabbath morn
> > With peace talks on their lips,
> And left an island blasted and torn
> > With bombs from their mother ships.
> They lied and stalled, this gangster crew,
> > Whilst they held out a friendly hand

The Green Years (1946): Brandon Hurst (as the bookseller) deals with Charles Coburn.

And all the time these bastards knew
 The treachery they had planned.
But out of the wreck of that fatal day,
 A slumbering people awoke
And from shore to shore of the U.S.A.
 The voice of a nation spoke
And they made a vow that for every man
 Who gave his life that day
Ten thousand heads of the murdering clan
 Should be the price they'll pay
So we'll gird our loins and drive this band
 Back into their nooks and niches
And Blight and darkness will cover the land
 Of these rising sons of bitches.
     — Brandon Hurst

Hurst had another fantasy-related role as the ghost of Chief Justice John Marshall, one of the spirits of founding fathers who come to the aid of accountant William Holden, in *The Remarkable Andrew* (1942). Brandon was Hans, among the irate villagers, in *The Ghost of Frankenstein* (1942). Hurst portrayed the Smythe butler in *The Mad Martindales* (1942), the majordomo in *The Pied Piper* (1942), a senator in *Tennessee Johnson* (1942) and Swayne in *Road to Happiness* (1942). *Road to Morocco* (1942), the third entry in the Hope-Crosby "Road" series, had Brandon on hand as the English announcer. He would also be seen in the fourth and fifth "Road" pictures.

Brandon Hurst even found his way into a Val Lewton RKO horror as the cemetery gatekeeper in the moody *The Leopard Man* (1943). Hurst's roles seemed to be steadily diminishing in size, as evidenced by his playing a bit in *The Constant Nymph* (1943), a dignified man in the audience in *Dixie* (1943), a government official at the railroad station in *The Man From Down Under* (1943), a cab driver in the "Good Night, Good Neighbor" segment of *Thank Your Lucky Stars* (1943), a Lowood School trustee in *Jane Eyre* (1943) and a watchman in *Shine On Harvest Moon* (1944). Brandon, as a Shakespearean actor, even appeared in an "Our Gang" short, *Radio Bugs* (1944). He played another

East Side of Heaven (1939): Brandon Hurst with Robert Kent and Irene Hervey

Hurst as Mr. Todd, the landlord. Brandon was almost 80 years old when he played Brown in *Magnificent Doll* (1946) for another of his familiar directors, Frank Borzage.

All of Hurst's final seven films would involve either director David Butler or actors Bob Hope and Bing Crosby. *The Time, the Place and the Girl* (1946), directed by Butler, had Brandon as Simpkins, the butler for S.Z. Sakall and Florence Bates. *My Favorite Brunette* (1947), with Bob Hope, gave Hurst his final butler role. Brandon had a small bit in *Welcome Stranger* (1947) with Crosby. Again with Hope, Hurst portrayed a floorwalker in *Where There's Life* (1947). *My Wild Irish Rose* (1947), with Butler directing Dennis Morgan as the great Irish tenor Sidney Olcott, included Hurst as Michael the gardener. *Road to Rio* (1947), the fifth Hope-Crosby "Road" venture and Hurst's third, had Brandon as a barker. It is fitting that David Butler, utilizing Brandon for the 15th time, directed Hurst's final film, *Two Guys From Texas* (1948), with Dennis Morgan and Jack Carson. *Two Guys From Texas* was released well after Hurst's death.

Brandon Hurst passed away at the age of 80 in Hollywood, California, on July 15, 1947. The cause of death was arteriosclerosis. Hurst was buried in an unmarked plot in Pierce Brothers Valhalla Memorial Park, North Hollywood.

While Brandon Hurst's extensive body of film work might not be familiar to all but ardent film buffs, he still left behind a legacy of major roles in important productions, like Jehan in *The Hunchback of Notre Dame* and Barkilphedro in *The Man Who Laughs*. Even his supporting efforts in films directed by John Ford and David Butler, among others, reflect a versatile, capable performer who brought a little something special to each character he took on. He often could say more with his eyes than with words. Brandon Hurst, like so many other players from the silent and early sound eras, is clearly worthy of belated recognition.

historical figure, Ralph Waldo Emerson, in *The Adventures of Mark Twain* (1944), which starred Fredric March. *The Canterville Ghost* (1944), featuring marvelous interplay between Charles Laughton as the titled spirit and young Margaret O'Brien, had Hurst as Mr. Peabody. Brandon was again a footman in *Mrs. Parkington* (1944) with Greer Garson. *The Princess and the Pirate* (1944), with Bob Hope, had Hurst humorously on hand as Mr. Pelly.

Hurst's role of Dr. Geissler in *House of Frankenstein* (1944) offered him the classic line, "The jugular vein is severed—not cut—but torn apart as though by powerful teeth." *The Man in Half Moon Street* (1945) represented Hurst's last fantasy film appearance. Brandon was Simpson, the butler, whose 120- jiweyear-old master Julian Karell (Nils Asther) maintains his youth by obtaining hormones from the glands of victimized medical students.

Emlyn Williams' *The Corn is Green* (1945), starring Bette Davis, featured Hurst as Lewellyn Powell. Brandon played The Prince of Wales' valet in *The Great John L* (1945), the sea lawyer in *The Spanish Main* (1945), a man on the train in *Confidential Agent* (1945) and a gambler in *San Antonio* (1945) with Errol Flynn. He had an interesting turn as the old bookseller who deals with Charles Coburn in *The Green Years* (1945). Once again with Hope and Crosby, Hurst was one of the men at Professor Zambini's mind reading act in *Road to Utopia* (1945). Hope again called for Brandon to play the Marquis in *Monsieur Beaucaire* (1945). *Sister Kenny* (1946), with Rosalind Russell an inspired heroine, had

Sources

Coughlin, Jim. "Forgotten Faces of Fantastic Films: Brandon Hurst," in *Midnight Marquee #33* (Fall 1984), pp. 24-25.

Doctor X
(1932)

Arthur Edmund Carewe
(1881 - 1937)

Many of the character actors associated with fantasy films have left behind a long legacy of portrayals for viewers to savor for years to come. There have also been those who have only whetted the appetite for what might have been, having made colorful contributions to only a few genre films due to untimely deaths or other factors. Arthur Edmund Carewe is a case in point for the latter. A suave villain in the silent era, with occasional horror/fantasy roles such as the third screen Svengali in *Trilby* (1923), Carewe appeared to be on his way to a noteworthy second career as a supporting player in early sound films. Dynamic performances in Warner Bros. *Doctor X* (1932) and *Mystery of the Wax Museum* (1933) revealed Carewe's ability for assaying macabre roles. Personal problems, illness and finally suicide, however, assured that Arthur Edmund Carewe's potential would never be fully realized.

As is the case with many early film performers, Arthur Edmund Carewe's beginnings are shrouded with some mystery, in part due to the machinations of studio publicists. Carewe (sometimes billed without the "Edmund" or as "Carew" minus the "e") was born in Trabzon (Trebizond), Armenia (now Turkey) on December 30, 1881 (although some sources wrongly claim either 1884 or 1894). His birth name was Hovsep Hovsepian, although it has also been erroneously reported as Jan Fox. At one time there were claims that Carewe was not Armenian at all, but rather a Native American of Chickasaw descent.

Following the 1882 death of his father Garo Hovsepian, an influential businessman and legislator, and the Hamidian massacres of 1894-96 (during which approximately 300,000 Armenians were slaughtered by the Ottoman Empire), the Hovsepian family was compelled to emigrate. Young Hovsep and brother Ardasches arrived in the United States aboard the *Augusta Victoria*, landing in New York Harbor on August 7, 1896. Older brother Garo had preceded them to America and their mother joined them in the U.S. in 1897.

Carewe was educated at the Cushing Academy in Ashburnham, Massachusetts. For a time, he and brother Garo ran a rug business in New York City, but Carewe had an inclination toward the arts, taking classes in both painting and sculpting. Eventually Carewe enrolled in the famed American Academy of Dramatic Arts (AADA) on Madison Avenue in Manhattan, graduating in March 1904. Carewe was awarded the prestigious David Belasco Gold Medal for Dramatic Ability.

Portrait of Arthur Edmund Carewe (c. 1925)

Now going by the stage name of Arthur Carew (soon he would add the "e"), he was involved in a notorious incident on February 5, 1910. Carewe was part of a concocted publicity scheme concerning actress Nance Gwynn, during which he was arrested at her flat brandishing a gun and threatening to kill himself. Carewe narrowly averted six months in the workhouse.

The next five years proved frustrating for Carewe, as he struggled to secure significant stage roles in the New York tri-state area. Carewe then moved to Chicago, Illinois where he continued to supplement his acting with a job in the rug and furnishings business. He was married to soprano Irene Pavlowska (formerly Irene Levi) on February 17, 1915. In Cook County, Illinois, on June 28, 1918, Carewe became a naturalized United States citizen. Soon after, he ventured to Hollywood to test his skills in silent pictures. With his handsome, brooding appearance (six-foot tall, 165 pounds, black hair and dark brown eyes), Carewe appeared a natural for the screen.

Sham **(1921): Tom Ricketts, Ethel Clayton and Arthur Edmund Carewe**

The earliest film credit for Carewe came with his role of Maddy Knox in *Venus in the East* (1919), starring Anna Q. Nilsson and directed by Donald Crisp. *Romance and Arabella* (1919), starring Constance Talmadge and featuring Carewe as Claude Estabrook, is often listed as his first film, but it was actually released a month later. Carewe played the duplicitous publisher Joseph Rayberg (as well as the dual role of Baron Landsandhome), who tries to seduce his employee Madge Kennedy, in *Daughter of Mine* (1919). He portrayed Eliot Slade, who pursues star Shirley Mason, in the comedy *The Rescuing Angel* (1919). *Girls* (1919), starring Marguerita Clark, had Carewe as Wilbur Searles. *The World and Its Women* (1919), directed by Frank Lloyd, featured Carewe as Count Alix Voronassof, who is killed in the Russian Revolution of 1917. *Dangerous Waters* (1919) included Carewe as Victor DeLara, the spoiled, self-centered suitor of Marguerite De La Motte. Carewe played Archibald Loveday in *Bonnie Bonnie Lassie* (1919), directed by Tod Browning for Universal.

In the Western *Rio Grande* (1920), with Rosemary Theby, Carewe was Don Jose Alvarado. *Children of Destiny* (1920) had Carewe third-billed as the Count Di Varesi. *The Breath of the Gods* (1920), set during the Russo-Japanese War, gave Carewe the role of Prince Hagane, betrothed to a Japanese girl for political reasons. *Burning Daylight* (1920) had Carewe as Arthur Howison. Carewe's countenance and presence, however, often led to his being cast in villainous roles. In *The Palace of Darkened Windows* (1920), for example, Carewe was the Rajah, who attempts to add captive European women to his harem.

Opposite Carmel Myers, Carewe played Christiansen in *The Mad Marriage* (1921). He was Heminway in *The Easy Road* (1921), with Thomas Meighan and a young Gladys George. In *Sham* (1921), a society tale involving debt and deception, starring Ethel Clayton, Carewe portrayed Bolton. Carewe played Stinson, the crooked cattle buyer in the Buck Jones Western *Bar Nothing* (1921). *Her Mad Bargain* (1921) had him as Grant Lewis, who slanders model Anita Stewart.

On a personal note, Carewe and Irena Pavlowska were divorced in 1921. Although primarily a screen actor, Carewe often welcomed the opportunity to return to the stage, as he did in 1921, playing Prinzivalle in Maeterlinck's *Monna Vanna*.

Returning to the screen and stepping up his perfidy, Carewe was John Brainerd, a blackmailer and bigamist, in *His Wife's Husband* (1922). He played "Con" Arnold, the man who exposes benevolent Monte Blue's criminal past, in *My Old Kentucky Home* (1922) and Colonel Fentress, who abducts a judge's wife and kills a man on his wedding day, in *The Prodigal Judge* (1922). A film whose title, *The Ghost Breaker* (1922), promised more than was delivered, included Carewe in the major role of the Duke D'Alba. The Duke is actually responsible for devising a supernatural scheme in an attempt to locate hidden treasure in an old castle and win the hand of heroine Lila Lee. Hero Wallace Reid thwarts D'Alba on both counts.

Trilby **(1923): Svengali (Arthur Edmund Carewe) plays the piano, while Zouzou (Maurice de Canange) accompanies on violin.**

The Phantom of the Opera (1925): The Phantom (Lon Chaney) hovers menacingly over Arthur Edmund Carewe, Norman Kerry and Mary Philbin.

The Claw **(1927): A romantic moment between Claire Windsor and Arthur Edmund Carewe**

As Svengali in George du Maurier's *Trilby* (1923), Carewe drew critical raves. The *New York Times* (7/30/23) commented:

> It is Arthur Edmund Carewe's revelation of Svengali that dominates this production. His make-up is true as steel. He has the long fingers, the sharp, aquiline nose, the hollow, cadaverous cheeks, the black, matted beard and unkempt hair of the Svengali of the book. His dark eyes are scintillating and gruesome. He is the sleek, sloppy, greasy Svengali. He wears shapeless trousers, a filthy shirt and an Inverness cape. In the latter portion of the film he is garbed in a narrow-shouldered dress suit and straight trousers, in which costume he gasps his last in an uncomfortable position.

Svengali, as in the later John Barrymore version (1931), becomes enamored of Trilby (Andree Lafayette). He uses hypnosis to place her under his influence, train her to sing and steal her affections from Little Billee (Creighton Hale). A musical genius, Svengali transforms Trilby into a world-renowned concert singer, until he suffers a fatal heart attack during a performance. Ironically, Trilby joins Svengali in death just as Billee believes he has finally recaptured his true love.

Daddy (1923), a Jackie Coogan vehicle, provided Carewe with a sympathetic role for a change as Paul Savelli, whose wife takes their son and leaves him in the wrong belief he has been unfaithful. Savelli fights depression and eventually becomes a great violinist, leading to an emotional reunion with son Coogan at the climax. Carewe also appeared uncredited as an Israelite slave in DeMille's *The Ten Commandments* (1923).

In early Hollywood, however, it was difficult to break away from typecasting, so Carewe was next handed a series of villainous characters to portray. He was Prince Ferdinand, who tries to destroy evidence of a rightful ruler and take over a kingdom, in *Refuge* (1923). In a film scripted by Frances Marion, Carewe played Ramlika, the evil Arab chieftain opposed by Norma Talmadge, in *The Song of Love* (1923). *The Price of a Party* (1924) had Carewe as a contemporary fiend, broker Kenneth Bellwood, who manipulates all those around him to suit his own purposes. *Sandra* (1924) featured Carewe as banker Henri La Flemme, who has an affair with star Barbara LaMarr and is later arrested for embezzlement.

A Man's Past **(1927): Arthur Edmund Carewe kisses the hand of Barbara Bedford.**

***Uncle Tom's Cabin* (1927): A character portrait of Arthur Edmund Carewe as George Harris**

The character of "The Persian" in Gaston Le Roux's novel *The Phantom of the Opera* plays a significant part of Erik's backstory and eventually reveals much of the Phantom's past history. As portrayed by Carewe in the 1925 Lon Chaney, Sr. version of *The Phantom of the Opera*, the opera house managers first mistake Inspector Ledoux for the Phantom. Ledoux is the only individual besides Erik, the Phantom (Chaney), to know of the remains of medieval dungeons and torture chambers on which the Paris Opera House is built. After Erik abducts Christine (Mary Philbin) to his underground lair for the second time, her lover Raoul (Norman Kerry) solicits the assistance of "the

Persian," Ledoux. Now an agent of the French police, Ledoux reveals Erik is a madman, but also a brilliant musician and master of the dark arts who returned to Paris after escaping exile on Devil's Island. Ledoux helps Raoul navigate the catacombs in pursuit of Erik and Christine. The two men fall victim to the Phantom's heat trap and are nearly burned alive. Unless Christine consents to marry him, Erik will allow Raoul and Ledoux to die, while also unleashing explosives that will result in numerous fatalities. Christina agrees, but the Phantom reneges, attempting to drown both men. The complex Erik again changes heart, permitting them to live, before being chased to his own watery death by the hostile Parisian mob. Obviously the film was dominated by Chaney's bravura interpretation of the Phantom, but Carewe also gave a well-delineated performance as Ledoux. Carewe's characterization of the knowledgeable Persian predates later horror film characters, such as Professor Van Helsing in *Dracula* (1931).

Set in a sanitarium, *The Boomerang* (1925), with Anita Stewart, included Carewe as Poulet. Carewe played Prince Yussuf opposite Ramon Novarro in *A Lover's Oath* (1925). *The Only Thing* (1925) had Carewe as Gigberto, the chief revolutionary who is smitten with a princess (Eleanor Boardman) and abducts her. When Gigberto is later captured and sentenced to die with the princess, Harry Vane (Conrad Nagel), who also loves her, switches places with the revolutionary.

Over the next couple of years, Carewe provided some colorful portrayals in important films. When Greta Garbo resurfaces as La Brunna, the toast of the Paris Opera, in

***God's Gift to Woman* (1931): Arthur Edmund Carewe tends to Frank Fay.**

Doctor X (1932): A portrait of Carewe as Dr. Rowitz

thony Kinsella in *The Claw* (1927). Of particular note for genre fans, however, was his role of Harry Blythe in Paul Leni's atmospheric *The Cat and the Canary* (1927), one of the early haunted house thrillers that developed the formula for so many others yet to come. Blythe, a nephew of the late Cyrus West, is one of the avaricious relatives gathered in an eerie setting for a reading of the uncle's will, 20 years after his death! Having Carewe in the mix with such scene stealers (and potential villains) as Lucien Littlefield, Martha Maddox, Tully Marshall, and George Siegmann helped to divert the attention of the audience from the real culprit, Forrest Stanley.

Directed by George Melford, *A Man's Past* (1927) starred Conrad Veidt as Dr. La Roche and featured Carewe as Lieutenant Destin. During a chess game, another doctor (Ian Keith) shoots Destin, the prison governor's assistant, who is about to expose La Roche as a convict. La Roche, however, operates on Destin, saving his life and earning a pardon.

Dealing with unspecified health issues and personal problems, Carewe took a three-year hiatus from the screen (until 1930). In 1926, he had scripted two screenplays for First National that were never produced. Carewe also traveled to Germany in 1928 to Universum Film AG (UFA) with his own script for a proposed film. This project also never reached fruition. Whether his disappointment

Torrent (1926), Carewe was prominently on hand as Salvatti, her mentor. In *Diplomacy* (1926), a film that also included fellow "forgotten faces" like Sojin, Gustav von Seyffertitz and Edgar Norton, Carewe was the pompous Count Orloff. *The Silent Lover* (1926), with Milton Sills, had Carewe as Captain Herault. As Maurice Sequineau, the judgmental brother of Ricardo Cortez in *Volcano* (1926), Carewe tried to prevent his sibling's marriage to Bebe Daniels, whom he has labeled a "mulatto." He played the sympathetic role of George Harris, of mixed race himself, in Universal's adaptation of *Uncle Tom's Cabin* (1927), starring James B. Lowe. George's plan to marry his beloved Eliza (Margarita Fischer) is thwarted by their "master," resulting in the couple being separated for years. While traveling with a band of refugees, George finds his young son and is eventually reunited with Eliza as well.

Carewe attracted the attention of then 10-year-old moviegoer Robert Bloch with his portrayal of Major An-

Mystery of the Wax Museum (1933): The fiending Arthur Edmund Carewe breaks down before Edwin Maxwell.

Mystery of the Wax Museum (1933): Carewe as the drug-addicted Professor Darcy (aka "Sparrow")

over these setbacks, coupled with illness, had adversely impacted his career at this point is just conjecture. Carewe had a marvelous speaking voice, so that was not a factor in his making a delayed transition to talking pictures.

In any case, Carewe returned to the screen as Dr. Beaudine, who hypnotizes amnesia victim Frank Fay with humorous and complicated results in the French farce, *The Matrimonial Bed* (1930). While clearly called Dr. Beaudine on the screen, Carewe's character was listed as Dr. Fried in the film's credits. *Sweet Kitty Bellairs* (1930), an early musical set in 1793 England and involving mistaken identities, starred Walter Pidgeon and Claudia Dell, while featuring Carewe as Captain Spicer. *God's Gift to Women* (1930) reunited Carewe, as Dr. Louis Dumont, with Frank Fay, who herein enacted a Casanova type, captivating, among others, Laura LaPlante, Joan Blondell and Louise Brooks. Carewe's scenes as the fake count in *The Life of the Party* (1930) were reportedly deleted. Carewe had a minor role (the "suave man") in *The Gay Diplomat* (1931), set in Bucharest, with Ivan Lebedeff chasing a beautiful spy. Carewe was said to have been one of the actors, along with Ian Keith, Paul Muni and others, considered for the lead in Universal's *Dracula* (1931), which, of course, went to Bela Lugosi.

Captain Applejack (1931), with Ambrose Applejohn (John Halliday) contemplating the sale of his family's an-

cestral castle, had Carewe as Ivan Borolsky, allegedly a spy in pursuit of Anna Valeska (Kay Strozzi). Borolsky, however, denies being a spy and contends that Anna had betrayed him. In Ambrose's dream sequence, Halliday, Carewe and Strozzi are all seen as pirates involved with hidden treasure that is supposedly still stashed at the castle. Back in the present, Borolsky (aka Jim), actually a thief, returns with confederates to seek the treasure, but is captured by the Coast Guard, who have been summoned by Ambrose. Carewe played Borolsky with flair and bravado, in line with the serio-comedic mood of this pre-Code Warner Bros. sound adventure.

Doctor X (1932), filmed in an early two-color Technicolor process, starred Lionel Atwill as Dr. Xavier, with Fay Wray cast in her first horror role. Sporting a black patch over one eye, Carewe was Dr. Rowitz, one of a group of scientists (John Wray, Harry Beresford and Preston Foster are the others) at Xavier's Academy of Surgical Research, all of whom have bizarre behavioral or professional histories. Rowitz, who, along with Dr. Haines (John Wray), had been stranded in a boat and involved in an act of suspected cannibalism, is interested in the psychological effects of the moon on behavior. When a rash of murders appears to implicate his staff, Dr. Xavier has three of the scientists, including Rowitz, locked to chairs and connected to a special apparatus, while a murder is experimentally recreated. Something goes awry, however, and the lights go out. When power is restored, Rowitz is found dead in his chair. Doctor Wells (Preston Foster), eerily making use of "synthetic flesh," is later revealed to be the madman and murderer. Mordaunt Hall in the *New York Times* (8/4/32) commented, "Arthur Edmund Carewe, who years ago gave a striking performance as Svengali in a silent film of *Trilby*, is in his element as one of the scientists."

Mystery of the Wax Museum (1933), again starring Lionel Atwill and Fay Wray, was also photographed for Warner Bros. in the two-color Technicolor process. Carewe had an even more substantial role than he did in *Doctor X*. *Mystery of the Wax Museum* featured him as Professor Darcy, better known as "Sparrow," a cocaine fiend. Sparrow is first viewed with a group of men carrying an oblong box to the residence of Worth (Edwin Maxwell). Worth initially denies Sparrow his drug payoff, instead threatening him for talking too much and then striking him. Noting Sparrow's desperation, Worth has an associate fetch a parcel of cocaine, but then sadistically slaps the addict's face before he departs. Later, Sparrow is viewed in service for Igor (Atwill), providing figures for the disfigured man's wax museum. Igor refers to him as Professor Darcy, noting, "He has been my hands for years," ever since the terrible fire had rendered the formerly talented Igor's hands useless for sculpting. Igor keeps Sparrow supplied with cocaine in return for a variety of services, including keeping him appraised of the whereabouts of Worth, who was responsible for the fire that destroyed Igor's London waxworks.

After the police are tipped off that Sparrow could be involved in a recent series of murders, he is roughed up and apprehended. At the police station, the Captain (DeWitt Jennings) claims, "He's a junky. He'll talk in a little while. Just lock him up." Carewe plays the deterioration of Sparrow very well, first denying all charges, then weakening, giving some information and begging for drugs. The withdrawal is too much for Sparrow. He breaks, revealing that people were murdered because of their resemblance to historical figures. Sparrow tells the police that Judge Ramsey, among other victims, can be found in Igor's Wax Museum encased in wax. "He's a statue of Voltaire, with all the other corpses! The whole place is a morgue—do you hear? A morgue!" The *New York Times* (2/18/33) wrote, "Arthur Edmund Carewe, who appears as the Sparrow, Igor's emissary, does his bit to make the flesh crawl." Carewe turned in a haunting, well-developed characterization as Sparrow, seeming to point the way to future horror/fantasy roles, which unfortunately never materialized.

Thunder in the Night (1935): Arthur Edmund Carewe is held back by Edmund Lowe.

In fact, Arthur Edmund Carewe would only appear in two more films. *Thunder in the Night* (1935), starring Edmund Lowe, gave Carewe an interesting role as Professor Omega, a mystic. Omega warns of impending disaster due to his vision of "thunder in the night." The Professor had toured in vaudeville with Katherine Szabo ((Gloria Roy), the mistress of Szegedy (Cornelius Keefe), who is found murdered. Although evidence points to the Professor being in the murdered man's room, he confesses to stealing the already dead Szegedy's money, but not to the homicide.

Charlie Chan's Secret (1936) represented Carewe's final screen role. He played Professor Alfred Bowan, the husband of a medium (Gloria Roy, with whom he was also featured in *Thunder in the Night*). Bowan, supported financially by Mrs. Lowell (Henrietta Crosman), fears losing her patronage and becomes a suspect following a murder. As the Professor, Carewe is once again a red herring, although at one point he turns on the electrical current to a device that renders Charlie Chan (Warner Oland) unconscious. Chan later vindicates Bowan of the murder, but compels him to leave town because of his other insidious deeds.

Carewe's later years had been marked by a series of setbacks, both in terms of his career and personal life. The culmination of these misfortunes occurred shortly after filming was completed on *Charlie Chan's Secret*, when Carewe suffered a paralytic stroke. Frustrated by past failures, limited in the present by the effects of the stroke and despondent about the future, Arthur Edmund Carewe chose to end his life with a self-inflicted gunshot wound to his head on April 23, 1937. Carewe was found dead in his car in the parking lot of a motel near the beach in Santa Monica, California. He was 55 years old.

Far from a famous actor, yet a very capable one, Arthur Edmund Carewe never had the opportunity to fulfill his potential. Although this could be said of many performers who die relatively young, Carewe had shown, in the fantasy genre in particular, wonderful glimpses of his range and capabilities. Fortunately, existing films such as *The Phantom of the Opera*, *The Cat and the Canary*, *Doctor X* and *Mystery of the Wax Museum* still bear witness to the talents of this neglected actor.

Sources

Carewe, Arthur Edmund. *Wikipedia.com*
Coughlin, Jim. "Forgotten Faces of Fantastic Films: E.E. Clive, Arthur Edmund Carewe," in *Midnight Marquee #35* (Fall 1986), pp. 32-33.

George Rosener
(1884 - 1945)

It can be argued that George Rosener is one of those performers whose overacting often enhanced rather than detracted from the films in which he was featured. He thrived in parts in which his character was demented, eccentric, or just plain peculiar. Rosener also had the ability to inspire dread in some of his roles, making him a natural for horror films. Unfortunately, this vein was rarely mined, with the exception of *Dr. X* (1932).

He was born George Michael Rosener in Brooklyn, New York on May 26, 1884 (some sources claim 1879, yet various Census reports and Draft Registration support 1884), the oldest of four children of John J. Rosener (1861-1920) and Margaret Flowers (one source says "Held," 1864-1908). George's paternal grandparents, Johan Heinrich Rosener and Maria Elizabeth Jost, were émigrés from Prussia. At various times, the Rosener family lived in Long Island City, Queens and Ward 13 in Brooklyn during George's formative years.

George Rosener was strongly attracted to performing from an early age. He allegedly had begun his acting career as a circus clown while still a teenager. Leaving his family behind in Brooklyn, Rosener secured various entertainment jobs, including tent and medicine shows, eventually touring with various stock companies. Drawn to writing as much as to acting, Rosener for a time worked as a journalist while also writing plays and sketches in his spare time.

While still in his teens, Rosener was a member of the Vincentian Stock Company in New York. In late 1902, George joined the Jefferson Dramatic Stock Company, also based in New York City. For the Jefferson troupe, he played Benjamin Butternut in *She Would be a Widow* (11/27/02) and Obadiah Dawson in *Captain Rackett* (12/21/02). With the Carroll Dramatic Society of Brooklyn, Rosener portrayed Captain Molineaux in *The Shaughran* (1903) and Dunston Kirke in *Hazel Kirke* (1903).

In early 1906, Rosener was part of the May Hillman Stock Company, touring the Mid-Atlantic region of the United States. In February 1906, the Hillman Company presented *Children of Satan*, written by Rosener, in Frederick, Pennsylvania. On April 17, 1906, the Cumberland, Maryland *Evening Times* reviewed another Hillman stock offering written by Rosener entitled *Floodtide*. In addition to authoring the play, the paper noted:

> George Rosener gave a pleasing rendition of the hero's part. Mr. Rosener is a former journalist who, upon completion of his play, gave up his newspaper work to star in his own production and is making a hit.

An early portrait (c. 1920) of George Rosener

Rosener also wrote and performed in *Claire of Old New York* (May 1908) for Hillman's company.

Rosener remained in Cumberland, succeeding James Lee as the manager of the Family Theatre for a brief time in 1908. Rosener then returned to Brooklyn, once again residing with his father and younger brother Henry (1892-1969). His sister Josephine Rosener (1886-1909) tragically passed away shortly after their mother's death in 1908. The fourth Rosener sibling, John, Jr., (1891-1891) had died during infancy. George secured another newspaper position, writing for the *New York World*.

Now penning plays on a regular basis, Rosener churned out the following works between 1909 and 1912 alone:

> 1909: *Coast Folks* (a rural drama in five acts)
> 1910: *Let Me Pass*, *Where the Trail Ends*, *When Ann Acted*, *The Frozen Trail* (a four-act drama) and *Sleepy Hollow* (a three-act "romance of the Revolution")
> 1911: *Relations* (a vaudeville sketch), *The Irish Eden* (a three act comedy-drama),

***My Maryland* (1927 Broadway musical): George Rosener as Zeke Bramble**

Sheriff of Tuckahoe (a one-act sketch) and *Cohen's Divorce* (a one-act vaudeville sketch); 1912: *College Days* (a three-act comedy), *A Successful Failure* (a one-act farce), *Lonesome Mile* (a two-act western comedy-drama), *The Great Winglebury Duel* (a one-act farce), *A Cure for Husbands* (comedy) and *Under London* (a one-act dramatization of *Oliver Twist*)

On February 9, 1913 May Hillman, for whose stock company Rosener served as stage manager, actor and writer on and off for seven years, died in Brooklyn, New York from complications of an unstated disease. The *New York Dramatic Mirror* (2/26/13) reported that her husband, George Rosener, with whom she had collaborated in vaudeville and literary endeavors, survived her. Other details of their marriage are not known. Nonetheless, her death was a terrible loss for George.

By 1914, Rosener had established residence at 1402 Broadway, Room 230, in Manhattan, New York. He authored the three-act drama *The Heart of a Shamrock* (1914), while yearning to perform once again. Rosener soon took to the road, playing in vaudeville as a character singer, impersonator and comedian. He wrote and performed in *The Question Mark* (1914), a "comedy dramatic playlet." Reportedly, Rosener and his colleagues filmed one of their playlets, *Red and White*, concerning Native Americans, in April 1914.

Another portrait (c. 1930) of George Rosener

Doctor X (1932): **George Rosener looking menacing as Otto the butler**

Rosener worked for the Shubert Organization on and off for almost 20 years, as actor, director and writer. Early on, while touring the Shubert vaudeville circuit, Rosener often received favorable plaudits, as evidenced by the *Utica Herald-Dispatch* (1/13/15) review, "George M. Rosener as a character man is one of the most pleasing features of the bill."

In the summer of 1916, Rosener wrote the play *The Lady from Lonesome Town* for actress Nancy Boyer. Touring the Midwest, the play received fine notices, such as this one from *The Englewood Economist* (Chicago, Illinois, 8/30/1916):

> Together they (Boyer and Rosener) have put over a play that will live as long as we have that lofty ideal of American womanhood.

On January 2, 1917, Rosener wed Adele R. Oswald (1889-1942). A talented performer in her own right, Adele had an interesting background. While in her teens, the Illinois born Oswald had studied voice with Madame Marchesi of France as well as with famed tenor Jean de Reszke. Oswald made her stage debut in the chorus of *His Honor the Mayor* at the Chicago Opera House in early 1906. She was featured in vaudeville in 1906/1907 in *The Land of Nod* and *My Cinderella Girl*. A gifted soprano, Adele eventually became the prima donna of the Colonial Opera Company, touring the West Coast in the summer of 1909. In late 1909, she moved to the Top of the World Company, playing cities in Texas and Arizona. In addition to her skills as an actress and vocalist, Oswald was a noted horsewoman, achieving fame (and winning blue ribbons) astride the Kentucky jumper Vladimer in competitions in Chicago, St. Louis, Louisville and elsewhere. After Adele's marriage to George, the two Roseners occasionally played

Doctor X (1932): **Joanne Xavier (Fay Wray) is alarmed by Otto (George Rosener).**

on the same bill in vaudeville. For example George and Adele appeared together in *The Woman of It* (1917), which was written by Rosener.

The *New York Clipper* (2/14/17) wrote of Rosener's vaudeville appearance at the Alhambra:

> George M. Rosener, with his English "dope" and G.A.R. (Grand Army of the Republic) types, had no trouble in going over big. This last type is particularly well portrayed, but would gain in effect with just a little less of the affected melodrama in the portrayal. He responded to the applause with the remark that "to an actor applause is the sweetest harmony of all."

He played the Colonial two weeks later, with the *New York Clipper* (2/28/17) now less favorable in noting that, "Rosener resorts to much low comedy for laughs and his change from one character to another, even though done on stage, takes considerable time."

The *Duluth* (Minnesota) *News-Tribune* ran the following item on June 3, 1917:

> George Rosener, character actor now playing in Orpheum vaudeville, is one of the latest vaudeville actor recruits to the colors. He has joined the Twenty-first Artillery of New York (training in Fort Wilson, Texas).

In actuality, Rosener's draft registration card, completed at Local Board 153, 59 Washington Square, New York City, is dated September 12, 1918, two months prior to the Armistice (11/11/18) ending World War I.

For Labor Day 1917, Rosener wrote *The Missing Log*, which was part of a pageant presented by the Boy Scouts of America at the Yale Bowl in New Haven, Connecticut. In September 1917, Rosener signed a 40-week contract with the Loew's vaudeville circuit. He would play the Proctor, Keith and Orpheum circuits as well, but he would inevitably find his way back to the Shubert Organization.

Alias the Doctor (1932): George Rosener, as the hospital chief of staff, uses an early telephone to summon Richard Barthelmess from the operating room.

Rosener also made his sole contribution to the silent film era when *The Wild Girl* (1917), based upon his original story, was made into a film by Selznick starring Eva Tanguay (known as "The I Don't Care Girl").

By now well established as a "character singer and impersonator" (*Indianapolis Star*, 10/17/15), Rosener still found time to focus on his writing, grinding out sketches and plays such as *The Reunion of Featherbed Lane* (January 1918). In November 1920, Rosener wrote *A Cycle of Manhattan* for his wife Adele in which she sang a series of songs in different dialects corresponding to various ethnic sections of New York City. Earlier that year, Rosener had toured the Southeast on the Keith circuit. The Columbia, South Carolina *State* (4/18/20) reported, "George Rosener heads Keith bill—*The Anthology of an Old Actor*—a "Palmy Day Tragedian." Rosener's performing specialty continued to be characterizations, often of old men. When he played the Belasco in Washington, DC, the *Washington Post* (10/25/21) noted:

> The rapid changes made by George M. Rosener in sight of the house added to the interest in his impersonations. His act, "The Anthology of an Old Actor," gave him splendid opportunity and he held the full attention of the audience.

Obviously George had improved his changing technique over time.

The Devil is Driving (1932): George Rosener as the Dummy, with Wynne Gibson

Rosener remained a versatile individual, appearing in vaudeville, while expanding his writing horizons. In 1921, he became the editor of a quarterly digest magazine known as *Rosener's Pan*, featuring a variety of articles "done in essay, epigram, story and philosophy" (according to the claim on the cover of Issue #3). In addition to serving as editor, Rosener wrote a significant portion of the articles. The magazine sold for 25 cents per copy, with the first issue appearing in June 1921. Some of the contents, however, proved too salacious for the taste of the time. On January 14, 1922, members of the New York Police Department seized the contents of the 1400 Broadway office of George J. Wetzel, partner in Stagelore Publishing Co. and the publisher of *Rosener's Pan*, following a complaint from an agent of the Society for the Suppression of Vice. The charge was that more than three-quarters of the magazine involved writing of an obscene nature. The police seized and destroyed all copies, including the bulk of the third issue of *Rosener's Pan*. On April 31, 1922, Wetzel was convicted of publishing an indecent magazine and fined $250.00. Max Greenberger, Wetzel's attorney, had offered to bring Rosener, who was then touring in vaudeville,

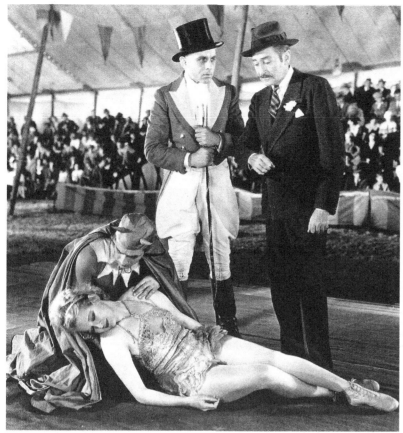

The Circus Queen Murder (1933): **Ringmaster George Rosener and detective Adolphe Menjou observe as Donald Cook cradles the fallen Greta Nissen.**

Paris Edition, 6/24/25, 416 performances), the reliable Rosener was again on hand. In the chorus were a young Jack Oakie and Billy De Wolfe.

On June 23, 1926, Adele Rosener gave birth to her and George's only child. Although named George Michael Rosener, Jr. (1926-1988), he was usually referred to as Michael, presumably to differentiate him from his father.

Rosener made his most noteworthy Broadway appearance in another Shubert success, the musical romance *My Maryland* (9/12/27), which ran for 312 performances. *My Maryland* was based on the Civil War play *Barbara Frietchie* by Clyde Fitch and featured stirring songs by Sigmund Romberg. Rosener portrayed Zeke Bramble, a comic character and opportunist who manages to ingratiate himself to both the Union and Confederates. Zeke would change his allegiance according to the victors at the moment. He also had strong and protective feelings toward Barbara (Evelyn Herbert). Rosener played the banjo and took part in four musical numbers ("Mexico," "Something Old, Something New," "Boys in Gray" and "Country Dance") during the proceedings.

While Rosener was appearing in *My Maryland*, the melodrama *Speak Easy* (9/26/27, 57 performances) that he had co-written with Edward

in Toledo, Ohio, back to Manhattan to testify as to the meaning of the articles. The court determined, however, that Rosener's testimony would be "incompetent," so he was not summoned at that time. The three-issue run of *Rosener's Pan* was over. Rosener returned to more conservative writing territory, authoring the three-act comedy *The Bells of Shannon* (1922), a follow-up to his *True Hearts of Erin* (1921).

In the spring of 1923, Rosener toured Pennsylvania and upstate New York with the noted dancer Irene Castle. The *Oswego Daily Palladium* (4/6/23) wrote of his contribution to the bill:

> George Rosener, who gave character interpretations, displayed great skill. He was true to his title as "That Entertaining Chap."

Later in 1923, Rosener made his first appearance on Broadway in the Shubert musical revue *Artists and Models—1923* (8/20/23, 312 performances). Comedian Frank Fay was among the headliners, while Rosener performed various character sketches. When the Shuberts updated their revue two years later as *Artists and Models—1925* (aka

The House of Secrets (1936): **Holmes Herbert, George Rosener and David Thursby**

The Case of the Black Cat (1936): **Nedda Harrigan grabs hold of George Rosener, whom Craig Reynolds is about to murder.**

Knoblock opened at the Mansfield Theatre. Set in New York's Hell's Kitchen and utilizing realistic "street" dialogue that Rosener had experienced in his years in Brooklyn and Manhattan, *Speak Easy* featured Leo G. Carroll and two youngsters who would soon after venture to Hollywood: Edward Woods (*The Public Enemy*) and Ruthelma Stevens (*The Circus Queen Murder*).

In early 1928, Rosener authored the play *The Five-Leaf Clover*, which never reached Broadway. Rosener's next effort as a playwright, the farce *She Got What She Wanted* (3/4/29), had a better fate, opening on Broadway at Wallack's Theatre and running for 120 performances. In the meantime, Rosener spent a few months on the B.F. Keith vaudeville circuit in 1929, touring the Northeast.

Rosener made his film debut in a one-reel Vitaphone short directed by Murray Roth entitled *The Fallen Star* (1930). This appearance gave George the opportunity to present onscreen one of his many characterizations from his vaudeville days.

With the advent of talking pictures, there was a demand in Hollywood for individuals who could pen realistic dialogue. Rosener was brought in by Warner Bros. to add colorful lines to the adaptation by Henry F. Thew of the play *Penny Arcade*, retitled *Sinners' Holiday* (1930). Among those benefitting from Rosener's written contributions were James Cagney, Joan Blondell and Lucille La Verne.

Also for Warner Bros., Rosener wrote the screenplay for Cagney's second film, *The Doorway to Hell* (1930), which included a pre-Renfield Dwight Frye as a gangster named Monk. Some critics commented that Rosener's dialogue was dated and cliché-ridden, but the film did earn an Academy Award nomination for Best Original Story. *The Doorway to Hell* also had Rosener in a minor role as Slick.

Rosener adapted his own comedy play, *She Got What She Wanted* (1930), for the screen. The film version starred Betty Compson, Lee Tracy and Alan Hale. Rosener then began to focus more on working in front of the cameras in films like *Union Depot*.

Set at a busy Midwest Metropolitan train station, *Union Depot* (1932) was a fascinating study of human behavior during the Great Depression. The establishing opening scenes depict many interesting interactions and feature cameos by, among others, Lucille La Verne, a very young Dickie Moore, Lilian Bond and Maude Eburne. After the main characters, Ruth (Joan Blondell) and Chick (Douglas Fairbanks, Jr.), are introduced, a villainous figure arrives at the station. Initially viewed exiting a cab is Dr. Bernardi, as played by George Rosener, an insidious looking individual with dark glasses, a limp and a cane. Bernardi initially forgets to pay his fare, explaining he is in a "great hurry" looking for someone. Ruth provides the backstory, telling Chick that Bernardi, a fellow resident of a low rent boarding house, has been paying her, an injured dancer, 50 cents an hour to read suggestive books ("from Europe") to him as his eyes are bad, despite knowing that this arouses him. The previous night, however, Bernardi had removed his glasses, disturbing Ruth with his "horrible" looking eyes and evil laugh, before coming on to her,

Park Avenue Logger (1937): Crippled George Rosener, with Ward Bond and George O'Brien

so she fled from this madman. Chick agrees to assist her. Bernardi, now hiding behind a newspaper, spots Ruth with Chick, overhearing her plans to travel to Salt Lake City to rejoin her theater troupe. While she is shopping, a Red Cap (Johnny Larkin) brings her a ticket for a drawing room in "car 59," which Ruth wrongly assumes was purchased for her by Chick. When Ruth boards the train and enters the compartment, screams are heard as an unseen Bernardi confronts her. As Chick rushes to her aid, Bernardi, who has jumped out of the window, is seen hobbling on the tracks just prior to being hit and killed by an oncoming train. Although Bernardi was prevented from harming Ruth, his vile intentions seemed evident, so no one appears to react at all to his death. Rosener, with minimal dialogue, gave a wonderful performance of a despicable, degenerate character.

As Dr. Franz von Bergman in *Alias the Doctor* (1932), Rosener was the chairman of the board of directors of the Vienna Hospital wherein skilled surgeon Dr. Brenner (Richard Barthelmess) operates. Von Bergman learns from Lucille La Verne, Barthelmess' foster mother, that Brenner had assumed his late brother's identity and is not actually a certified physician. In fact, he is an ex-convict, which von Bergman verifies, who went to prison to shield his brother who botched an operation on his girlfriend. Von Bergman summons Brenner to the boardroom, just as the surgeon is about to operate on his own mother, who has an embo-

lism and is facing death. At first, von Bergman is opposed to letting the young man operate on his mother because, if something went wrong, "we'd all be found guilty with you." Responding to Brenner's impassioned plea, von Bergman allows the operation to proceed, adding from the gallery when all goes well, "He's done it!"

According to the *Charleston Daily Mail* (1/4/33), Warner Bros. make-up artist Perc Westmore had told Rosener that he had achieved "synthetic flesh." Rosener, whether he realized Westmore was joking or not, reportedly then went to Warner Bros. with the story idea for *Dr. X* (1932). Although uncredited as a writer, Rosener is generally acknowledged as having contributed to the screenplay construction for the film.

To look at George Rosener's make-up in *Dr. X* (1932) as Otto, the butler at the Medical Research Institute headed by Dr. Xavier (Lionel Atwill), one might think he is a ghoul of some sort. Gaunt, with dark circles around his eyes, Otto could well be mistaken for the undead. Otto does take odd delight in instructing the maid (Leila Bennett) that she must wear the clothes of a murder victim as part of Xavier's experiment to recreate an actual killing that has recently occurred in the vicinity. After Dr. Rowitz (Arthur Edmund Carewe) is murdered during the failed experiment, Otto discovers reporter Lee Taylor (Lee Tracy) in a closet overcome by gas fumes. This takes place prior to another reenactment. As Xavier takes Rowitz's place handcuffed to a chair and connected to an electri-

The Secret of Treasure Island (1938): George Rosener lurks in the background (center), while Grant Withers menaces Gwen Gaze.

cal apparatus, as are two other scientists (John Wray and Harry Beresford), Otto is instructed to bolt the door. Wells (Preston Foster), the actual fiend, assaults and strangles Otto before turning his attention to Joanne (Fay Wray), now playing the victim in the second experiment. Taylor intervenes and Wells plunges to his death through a window. *Dr. X* (1932) is George Rosener's only major horror credit. He is successful in the role, with his offbeat, semi-crazy, creepy portrayal adding to the general eerie atmosphere of this underrated film.

Following this horror venture, Rosener was seen as Ortello, a gangster associate of gambler Lew Cody in *70,000 Witnesses* (1932). He then assayed the role of a crooked fight manager in *Madison Sq. Garden* (1932), starring Jack Oakie. The film featured many boxing notables, including fighters Jack Johnson, Sailor Sharkey and Tommy Ryan, as well as sportswriters Damon Runyan and Grantland Rice as themselves.

The Devil is Driving (1932) featured Rosener as a sinister deaf mute known as the Dummy, actually the mastermind of a car theft ring operating out of an eight story New York City garage. The Dummy dispatches a henchman to steal an expensive sedan, but, while driving away, the stolen car accidentally hits the nephew (Dickie Moore) of star Edmund Lowe. When garage employee James Gleason confronts the Dummy and slimy Jenkins (Alan Dinehart) about a paint job masking the accident, they have him murdered. After being exposed by Lowe, the Dummy and Jenkins escape in a car only to crash into a vehicle coming the opposite way up the ramp. The escape car plunges

down the elevator shaft, killing both antagonists. Rosener's performance as the Dummy, like his work as Dr. Bernardi in *Union Depot*, showed how menacing he could be without dialogue.

The Circus Queen Murder (1933), based on a novel by Anthony Abbot (Fulton Oursler), was the second Thatcher Colt mystery released by Columbia. A vacationing Colt (Adolphe Menjou) comes across a traveling circus in the upstate New York town of Gilead. Co-owner and ringmaster of the circus John T. Rainey (Rosener) beseeches Colt to lend assistance as, "somebody's out to wreck our circus." While searching for the missing Flandrin (Dwight Frye), Colt has Rainey direct all the clowns to remove their make-up, but to no avail. Despite death threats, the show does go on, with Rainey proclaiming that the audience is about to witness "the greatest aggregate of circus performers ever presented to the public." Rainey provides introductions for aerialists Donald Cook and Greta Nissen. When the latter is murdered during her act, it is Rainey who attempts to calm the crowd and have them remain in their seats. Rosener was very effective as Rainey, obviously benefitting from his own experience as a circus performer to lend credibility to the portrayal.

When Jack Kirkland adapted Erskine Caldwell's novel about Georgia sharecroppers, *Tobacco Road*, for the stage in 1933, Rosener was the original choice to play Jeeter Lester, the tenant farmer family patriarch. Unfortunately for George, however, during out-of-town tryouts the decision was made to replace him with Henry Hull in the lead prior to *Tobacco Road* opening on Broadway (12/4/33). The show would run for over three thousand performances.

Rosener continued to find work as a writer as well. He contributed to the screenplay of *Goodbye Love* (1933), which featured Charles Ruggles, Verree Teasdale and Sidney Blackmer.

On March 8, 1934, Rosener filed copyright infringement charges against Earl Carroll and his play, *Murder at the Vanities* (9/12/33). Rosener alleged that the show appropriated elements from two of his own plays, *Grease Paint* (1929) and *Murder to Music* (1931). It is not known whether Rosener received any settlement in the matter.

Rosener resumed writing for the Broadway stage, providing sketches and staging the dialogue for the musical revue *Keep Moving* (8/23/34, 20 performances), which featured the Singer Midgets, some of whom would later appear in *The Wizard of Oz* (1939). He directed his first Broadway show, the musical comedy *Music Hath Charms* (12/29/34, 25 performances), starring Constance Carpenter. Rosener also wrote some of the music and lyrics for this short-lived show, which marked his final collaboration with the Shubert Corporation. *If a Body* (4/30/35, 45 performances), co-written by Rosener and his old colleague Edward Knoblock, was a murder mystery and was staged by George at the Biltmore Theatre. Rosener's final Broadway effort, *One Good Year* (11/27/35), a comedy that he staged, enjoyed a more successful run (215 performances) than its three predecessors.

Returning to the screen, Rosener played a trapper in *The Test* (1935), with Rin Tin Tin, Jr. helping to track down fur thieves.

Set at "The Hawk's Nest," a large estate outside of London, *The House of Secrets* (1936) provided an interesting role to Rosener as Hector Munson, a crazed madman who is actually a famous scientist believed to be dead. Leslie Fenton, who has inherited the estate, and others are jeopardized by the release of poison gas. Munson is jarred back to sanity and claims there is an antidote in the adjacent tank. The scientist has been working on a revolutionary formula for a gas that would instantly counteract any poison gas, but had become temporarily insane, either from stress or chemical interactions, resulting in him murdering his assistant. Cross (Ian McLaren) and Evans (Holmes Herbert) had arranged for his release from prison, while Dr. Kenmore (Morgan Wallace) had been treating Munson for his mental fragility. Despite erratic ties to reality, Munson helps alleviate the dire situation.

The Case of the Black Cat (1936), a Perry Mason tale with Warren William in the lead as Mason, had Rosener as Charles Ashton, the caretaker for the estate of Peter Laxter (Harry Davenport). With Laxter presumed dead, Ashton asks Mason to keep Sam Laxter (William Elliott) away from his beloved cat. Ashton is seen acting in a suspicious manner around a safe deposit box and in the garage. He gives his cat to Wilma (Jane Bryan) for safekeeping before going to see Frank Oafley (Craig Reynolds) and Daisy DeVoe (Nedda Harrigan). Frank, suspecting Ashton is hiding diamonds in his crutch, kills the caretaker with the help of Daisy. Ashton represents another of Rosener's eccentric and excessive characterizations that he seemed to take pleasure in performing.

Ellis Island (1936) reveals that 10 years prior, three men, including Theodore Kedrich (George Rosener), had robbed a federal reserve bank of one million dollars, money that was never recovered. Now 10 years later, Kedrich is released and about to be deported when Solo (Bradley Page), posing as a treasury agent, offers to grant him freedom in exchange for a 50-50 split of the hidden money. A gang of thieves (Jack LaRue, Maurice Black, etc.) abducts Kedrich, beat him and hide him in a warehouse. Ked-

Colorado (1940): **Lt. Burke (Roy Rogers) meets General U.S. Grant (Joseph Crehan), while the Secret Service official (George Rosener) looks on.**

rich's niece (Peggy Shannon) had come to Ellis Island to bid farewell to her Uncle Ted, but has to solicit the aid of Donald Cook and Johnny Arthur to find the man. Solo helps Kedrich escape, bugs the niece's apartment and learns the location of the money. The money, buried in a coffin in a false grave, is unearthed, with Solo escaping with it, followed by the thieves and the niece's party. Donald Cook releases a swarm of bees and helps the real government agent (Bryant Washburn) round up the villains. Although made by a Poverty Row studio (Invincible), *Ellis Island* represents a substantial, multidimensional role for Rosener, the type that he was rarely able to secure from the major studios.

Park Avenue Logger (1937) had Rosener as Matt O'Shea, the wheelchair-bound father of Peggy (Beatrice Roberts). O'Shea, the owner of a lumber firm and rival of the Timberlake Logging Corporation, has had his business decimated by the duplicity of his field boss (Ward Bond), who has been buying up O'Shea's bank notes and sabotaging his lumber shipments. George O'Brien, the son of the Timberlake boss, helps put an end to the villainy and win Roberts' affections.

New Faces of 1937 (1937) showcased Rosener's comedic side. As Pete, the theater doorman, Rosener has two encounters with Joe Penner, the comic known for the line, "Wanna buy a duck?" Initially Penner confronts the doorman, who is sleeping at his desk, in an attempt to secure

Arkansas Judge (1941): Townsmen Harrison Greene, Monte Blue, George Rosener and Barry Macollum congregate and plot.

a tryout for a new show. Pete resists Penner's ruses to enter, despite the comic's grandiose claims, finally throwing out the aspiring talent not once but twice. In a later scene, when Penner returns, now claiming to be a dramatic actor, mentioning Shakespeare, the doorman starts quoting from *Othello*, strangling Penner while doing dialogue from the play. Pete claims, "Oh, to live those glorious moments of triumph," as if he were a star in his younger days. Penner tries to switch to *Romeo and Juliet*, with Pete then enacting Romeo to the mortified comic's Juliet.

Super-Sleuth (1937), with Jack Oakie as an actor who portrays a clever detective and inadvertently solves a real crime, had Rosener as one of the long-suffering policemen putting up with Oakie's antics. *The Big Shot* (1937) featured Rosener as Phillips, the accountant, in a tale of a small-town veterinarian (Guy Kibbee) who inherits two million dollars and attempts to use his wealth to combat crime.

Concerned with an Asian rubber plantation and set in the province of Semang, *Jungle Menace* (1937) was the first serial released by Columbia. *Jungle Menace* was co-directed by George Melford, who directed the Spanish version of *Dracula* (1931), with Rosener one of many who contributed to the screenplay. The serial starred Frank Buck of "Bring 'Em Back Alive!" fame and featured Rosener as the Professor. Although the Professor is clearly a villain, helping dump a body in the harbor, he also delivers some humorous lines. Of Clarence Muse, the intellectual Professor inquires, "By any chance, my Senegambian friend, do you dally with a ham?" In many cases, Rosener could have beeen alluding to himself with such a statement.

The Mysterious Pilot (1937) was the second Columbia serial that Rosener co-wrote with George M. Merrick and others. Rosener also appeared in chapters 3, 4, 5, 9, 14, and 15 as Fritz, a colorful German character who operates a trading post. Fritz attempts to assist the protagonists, headed by Frank Hawks, a real-life famed aviator, who was killed in a flying accident not long after the serial's release.

As Captain Hook (aka Emerson), Rosener appeared to delight in the absurdity that was *Sh! The Octopus* (1937). When two inept detectives, Dempsey (Allen Jenkins) and Kelly (Hugh Herbert), are dispatched to inspect an old deserted lighthouse, they are confronted by Hook, the caretaker, a one-handed, volatile old salt who explodes in a rage in response to the ticking of a clock. Hook turns over the keys and checks the documents of Paul (John Eldredge) before threatening Cobb (Brandon Tynan), another bizarre character, while denying that he had arranged for people to come to the lighthouse. Hook later re-enters, carrying Polly (Margaret Irving), whom he had rescued from a motorboat wrecked on the reef. Almost all the characters have alternate identities, with Hook actually being Emerson of the "Intelligence Department," who has "been working on this case for nine years." The details of the matter at hand are never adequately explained, nor do motives make any sense. Hook runs into opposition from Nanny (Elspeth Dudgeon), who transforms into "the Octopus," the titled evil mastermind. Tentacles appear within the lighthouse and drag the loony captain away. At the film's return-to-reality denouement, Rosener is the doctor hovering over Hugh Herbert, whose wife has given birth to babies that look suspiciously like Allen Jenkins. When allowed latitude in a farcical comedy like *Sh! The Octopus*, Rosener would stretch the limits of over-acting.

The Secret of Treasure Island (1938), the third Columbia serial produced by Samuel Weiss in which Rosener appeared, perhaps represents the screen apex for the actor. Rosener also served as dialogue coach and co-wrote the screenplay based on a pulp magazine story by L. Ron Hubbard, of all people. In that he scripted the character of Captain Samuel Cuttle for himself, Rosener pulls out all the stops as an old sea dog who turns out *not* to be as crazy as he acts. Captain Cuttle lives in a wrecked ship converted into a house on a volcanic island off the coast of Mexico where pirate treasure is allegedly buried. Cuttle, sarcastic and bombastic, plays with his pet raven and sings humorous sea chanties about grizzly deaths and such. Although Cuttle appears in league with the villainous Collins (Walter Miller), he does not fear him and ends up aiding the protagonists. The peculiar old man helps lead William Farnum and his daughter (Gwen Gaze), as well as hero Don Terry, through a tunnel to the mainland, as the island explodes at the serial's climax. With Cuttle's character being unbalanced and unpredictable, Rosener was able to alternately act silly and threatening, while dispensing rather bizarre but funny dialogue. Rosener would never again enjoy this amount of screen time nor the opportunity to take his histrionics to the hilt.

In July 1938, Rosener arranged a Los Angeles tryout for the musical comedy *Thumbs West*, concerning hitchhikers, that he had written. George had hopes that the show would eventually reach Broadway, but critical response was mediocre at best, derailing Rosener's dream.

Rosener contributed to the screenplays of the serial *The Great Adventures of Wild Bill Hickok* (1938), starring Bill Elliott, and an entry in the "Renfrew of the Royal Mounted" series, *Fighting Mad* (1939), with James Newill as the singing Mountie.

Flying G-Men (1939), Rosener's fourth serial for Columbia (and the studio's sixth overall), had George (uncredited) as Hopkins, a spy who uses a historical study group as a front. The story involved three pre-World War II flyers opposing spies attempting to destroy strategic American defenses.

Rosener is viewed fairly early on in *Confessions of a Nazi Spy* (1939) as Klauber, a ship's officer on board the *S.S. Europa* bound from Germany to New York. Klauber protests to the captain about the promotion of an engineer solely based on his being a Nazi, but the entrance of Gestapo leader George Sanders interrupts him. After Sanders departs, Klauber states, "Perhaps we have lived too long, Captain," with both men fearing for the safety of their families back in Germany.

They All Come Out (1939), the first feature film directed by Jacques Tourneur, had Rosener as Barney, one of the prison inmates. Starring Tom Neal, the film was a commentary on rehabilitation, or the lack thereof, in the federal prison system.

In Name Only (1939), concerning a love triangle involving Cary Grant, Carole Lombard and Kay Francis, included Rosener as Dr. Hastings, the physician at the hotel. *5th Avenue Girl* (1939) had Rosener portraying a hobo in the sequence where millionaire Walter Connolly, while wandering in Central Park, stumbles upon Ginger Rogers.

Near the opening of *The Great Commandment* (1939), Rosener, as a bearded old merchant, is viewed riding a donkey, transporting an injured man (Earl Gunn) he found near death on the road. The man had escaped Roman tax collectors. The merchant complains to John Beal and other concerned Israelites, about the situation in Judea, noting, "A nation without a king is a nation lost." Irving Pichel (Sandor from *Dracula's Daughter*) directed *The Great Commandment*.

Hitler—Beast of Berlin (1939) concerned the efforts of Elsa (Steffi Duna) to have her husband Hans (Roland Drew) released from a German prison camp. She is instructed to hire Wunderlich (Rosener), a lawyer with good connections with the Nazis, to help her with the process. The prison camp commandant (Walter O. Stahl), who considers Hans a traitor, thwarts Elsa's efforts.

Set in Chicago after the great fire, *Three Sons* (1939) starred Edward Ellis as an ambitious department store owner attempting to build a dynasty in the wake of disaster. Rosener was briefly seen as the man taking the cigarette butt. His roles were clearly diminishing. In *Joe and Ethel Turp Call on the President* (1939), starring William Gargan and Ann Sothern, Rosener played Mr. Belknap, although he was not listed in the credits.

Abe Lincoln in Illinois (1940) featured Rosener as Dr. Chandler, who tends to Ann Rutledge (Mary Howard) when she collapses at a dance. After first allaying concern, Chandler asks Ann's tavern keeper father (Edmund Elton) if she has been "ailing lately." The doctor follows the Rutledge carriage to their home. It develops that she is much sicker than originally thought ("Brain fever" is what Howard Da Silva tells Raymond Massey as Lincoln). Chandler

Arkansas Judge **(1941): Vengeful villagers George Rosener and Monte Blue (center) incite the mob with torches.**

looks appropriately somber as he exits Ann's room, with Lincoln entering to witness his first love die. Rosener herein gave a restrained performance in this historical drama based on the play by Robert Emmett Sherwood.

Florian (1940), set in Austria and featuring magnificent Lippizaner stallions in its plot, had Rosener as the riding school inspector. Robert Young starred in this film that Edwin L. Marin directed for MGM.

The Carson City Kid (1940) was the first of five films Rosener would make near the end of his career with Roy Rogers at Republic Pictures. As Judge Tucker, Rosener is viewed near the film's climax, presiding over a trial of sorts for Noah Beery, Jr., accused of being the title character. The judge questions Hal Taliaferro about a safe robbery and Francis McDonald about his former partner, with both incriminating Beery. Rogers, the actual Carson City Kid, interrupts the proceedings in order to clear Beery and expose villain Bob Steele as the murderer of Rogers' brother. Rosener was convincing in the relatively undemanding role. Again working with Rogers at Republic, Rosener had an even smaller part as the Secret Service official on hand when Roy's character meets General U.S. Grant (Joseph Crehan) in *Colorado* (1940).

Victory (1940), adapted by *Dracula*'s John Balderston from Joseph Conrad's novel, starred Fredric March and Cedric Hardwicke, with Rosener convincing as a Dutch clerk. *So Ends Our Night* (1941), based on a novel by Erich Maria Remarque, was involved with refugees, including Fredric March and Margaret Sullavan, who attempt to flee from one country to the next. Rosener had the minor part of a customs guard.

Arkansas Judge (1941), starring the Weaver family of Grand Ole Opry fame and featuring Roy Rogers, included Rosener as Mr. Beaudry. An instigator, Beaudry is one of the judgmental townspeople of Peaceful Valley who descend upon wrongly accused Spring Byington's house, wielding torches like the crowd in a *Frankenstein* film. Beaudry helps put her home to the torch, hoping to drive the woman out of town, but Byington becomes trapped in the burning edifice as a result.

Rosener and Oliver Drake scripted *City of Missing Girls* (1941), while old colleague Elmer Clifton (with whom George worked on *The Secret of Treasure Island*) directed. Rosener played Officer Dugan, who is first seen reminiscing with his captain (H.B. Warner) at the Bureau of Missing Persons. Dugan later brings in Herb Vigran, who works for evil Philip Van Zandt at the Crescent School of Fine Arts, a cover for prostitution. When the "students" are brought in for a line-up, it is Dugan who directs them to turn right and left, stop chewing gum and the like. When Rosener would write his own roles, he would often go the route of eccentric, over-the-top characters, but here he functions in a supportive, somewhat sympathetic manner.

Rosener's last screen roles came in two additional Roy Rogers' Westerns. *In Old Cheyenne* (1941) offered George the villainous role of town boss Sam Drummond, who tries to pin his crimes on Gabby Hayes. The devious Drummond orders murders and forces ranchers from their lands with the aid of hired henchmen, all the while remaining free from suspicion. Rogers, playing a young journalist, is fooled for a time and vilifies Hayes, but eventually realizes the true culprit and exposes the corrupt boss. Rosener had a smaller role as an official in *Sheriff of Tombstone* (1941). Serving as dialogue director one final time, Rosener lent his skills to the screenplay of *I'll Sell My Life* (1941), starring Rose Hobart and Michael Whalen.

As Rosener's career was declining, tensions had increased between George and his wife Adele. The couple decided to divorce in 1940. The Roseners' teenage son Michael, however, managed to arrange reconciliation between his parents. George and Adele Rosener remarried on January 2, 1942, the 25th anniversary of their original wedding. Unfortunately, Adele became progressively ill and passed away a few months later on June 18, 1942.

George Rosener spent the wartime years in retirement at his residence at 5258 Sunset Boulevard in Hollywood. He lived long enough to see his son Michael enlist in the U.S. Navy, serving as a RM2 (Radioman Second Class) during the latter stages of World War II. George Rosener died on March 29, 1945, at the age of 60. His son Michael (actually George Michael Rosener, Jr.), following his wartime service, would marry (Barbara, on December 24, 1954) and work as a salesman in locations like Dayton, Ohio, and Palo Alto, California. Michael died on May 6, 1988, in San Diego, California, and was buried in Lakeland Hills Memorial Park in Burnet, Texas.

George Rosener never had the full opportunity to display his talents on the screen. Viewed today, some of his performances, like the Professor in *Jungle Menace*, Captain Hook in *Sh! The Octopus* and Captain Cuttle in *The Secret of Treasure Island*, impress as over-the-top, perhaps carrying over some traits from Rosener's many years in vaudeville. Yet Rosener was also capable of giving carefully sketched, modulated portrayals as well in films like *Alias the Doctor*, *Ellis Island* and *Abe Lincoln in Illinois*. Rosener's creepy interpretation of Otto the butler in *Dr. X* evidences how well he fit in the golden age of horror. Perhaps his most insidious role, Dr. Bernardi in *Union Depot*, indicates Rosener could play a memorable villain capable of lechery and unspeakable acts. Rosener always seemed to be enjoying his work on screen, even if he was guilty of chewing the scenery at times. Beyond his surviving film roles, Rosener left behind an extensive amount of written work (mainly plays and sketches), displaying his talent and versatility. It is hoped that this tribute will lead others to enjoy his legacy as well.

The Vampire Bat
(1933)

Lionel Belmore
(1867 – 1953)

The formula for many horror films, especially those taking place in Central or Eastern Europe, includes a number of stereotypical characters (e.g., a mad scientist, a distressed heroine, a hunchbacked henchman, vindictive villagers, etc.). The Burgomaster is also often a key character in films set in 19th-century Europe. Perhaps the actor most associated with that role is the robust Englishman Lionel Belmore. Belmore was so much more than that character—a successful stage actor, a silent film director and a colorful performer in so many parts (innkeepers, officers, nobles, etc.)—that it is perhaps unfair to pigeonhole him into one type of role. Conversely, it is as a Burgomaster (*Frankenstein*, *The Vampire Bat*) that most film fans seem to remember Lionel Belmore.

He was born William Lionel Belmore Garstin on May 12, 1867, in Wimbledon, Surrey, England, to parents George Benjamin Belmore Garstin (1830-1875) and Alice Maude Mary Ann Cooke (1844-1911). He was baptized on August 14, 1868. Young Lionel, as he preferred to be addressed, and his siblings, which included brothers George, Paul and Herbert Norman, and sisters Alice Maude, Mary Ann, Lilian and Daisy Gertrude, were raised at 14 St. George's Road in Wimbledon, a suburb of London. Not only did Lionel pursue a career in the theater, but Paul, Herbert, Alice and Daisy did as well. All acted under the name of "Belmore," abandoning the "Garstin."

Following his education at Bedford College, Lionel embarked on a long, illustrious stage career, performing with such notables as Lily Langtry and Wilson Barrett during the formative years. Some early appearances on the London stage for Belmore included Dr. Wheeler in *The People's Idol* (1890), Desmoulins in *The Lady of Lyon* (1890), Bronson in *The Silver King* (1891), Jabez Gawn in *Ben-My-Chree* (1891) and Bernardo in *Hamlet* (1891).

On June 7, 1891 Lionel Belmore married the former Emmeline Florence Carder (1865-1961) at St. James Church, Clapham Park, England. Lionel and Emmeline would have two daughters, Violet Emmeline Terry Belmore Garstin (1897-1983) and Rosamund Maude Belmore Garstin (1901-1997). Lionel and Emmeline lived apart, initially due to the demands of the theatrical profession, soon after the birth of Rosamund. It is uncertain as to the nature of Lionel's relationship with Emmeline and his daughters in subsequent years.

Belmore spent 16 years in the company of Sir Henry Irving, touring the world with Ellen Terry and other

A Shocking Night (1921): **Clark Comstock and Lionel Belmore**

stage greats. Lionel served in many capacities with Irving's troupe, including stage manager, production assistant, script prompter and actor. With Irving on the London stage, Belmore played Sir Nicholas Vaux in *Henry VIII* (1892), the third secretary in *Richelieu* (1892), the herald in *King Lear* (1892), Stephano in *The Merchant of Venice* (1893), Brander in *Faust* (1894), Oatcake in *Much Ado About Nothing* (1894) and Sir Hugh de Morville in *Becket* (1894). Irving had a long run (105 performances) in *King Arthur* (1895), in which Lionel played Sir Gawaine. Belmore played roles of various sizes in Irving productions, such as the first cavalier in *Charles I* (1895), Durochat in *The Lyons Mail* (1895), Beauchamp in *The Corsican Brothers* (1895) and the messenger in *Macbeth* (1895).

Occasionally, Belmore would appear independently of Irving, as when he played Ravachol in *An Old Song* (12/10/96) at the Criterion. For the most part, however, Lionel was under Irving's employ, usually at London's Lyceum Theatre, where Belmore played Sir Richard Ratcliff in *Richard III* (1897), De Brigode in *Madame Sans Gene*

The Man Who Fights Alone (1924): **Lionel Belmore as Meggs**

Bardelys the Magnificent (1926): **Lionel Belmore as the Vicomte de Lavedan**

(1897), Prince Dolgorovski in *Peter the Great* (1898), Carrots in *The Medicine Man* (1898) and Gorlov in *The Convert* (1898). For much of 1899, Belmore was the stage manager at the Prince of Wales Theatre for productions like *My Milliner's Bill*, *The Ordeal of the Honeymoon* and *Variations*.

Belmore traveled to the United States with Irving and Terry in the fall of 1899, performing such works as *Robespierre* (10/31/1899) on Broadway. Over the next seven years, Lionel would be back and forth between London and New York, as well as on tour, with the Irving company. Among the Irving productions in which Belmore appeared on Broadway were: *The Merchant of Venice* (as Salarino), *The Bells* and *Charles I* (in repertory, October/November 1901) and *Mauricette*, *Markheim*, *The Lyons Mail* (as Dorval), *King Rene's Daughter* and *Paolo and Francesca* (all in repertory, Oc-

tober/November 1906). The *New York Mirror* (10/27/06) noted that, "Lionel Belmore is good as the Marquis of Huntley" in the Irving/Dorothea Baird Company revival of *Charles I.*

Having parted ways with Irving, Belmore joined the company of actress Olga Nethersole for her tour of the United States in 1908. On Broadway, in repertory in February/March 1908, Belmore was seen with Nethersole in *The Second Mrs. Tanqueray*, *Camille*, *Magda*, *Sapho*, *Carmen*, *I Pagliacci*, *The Enigma*, *Adrienne Lecouveur* and *The Awakening.* Belmore then became part of the company of William Faversham, a turn-of-the-century matinee idol, performing with him on Broadway as Genaro in *The World and His Wife* (11/2/08), *The Barber of New Orleans* (1/15/09), as the physician in *Herod* (10/26/09) and in *The Faun* (1/16/11).

With The Drama Players, whose ranks included Hedwiga Reicher (Frank Reicher's sister), Herbert Kelcey and Effie Shannon, Belmore was back on Broadway in repertory as Professor Arnholm in *The Lady From the Sea* (11/6/11), as well as in *The Learned Ladies* (11/9/11) and *The Thunder-*

The Demi-Bride (1927): **Lionel Belmore as Monsieur Girard**

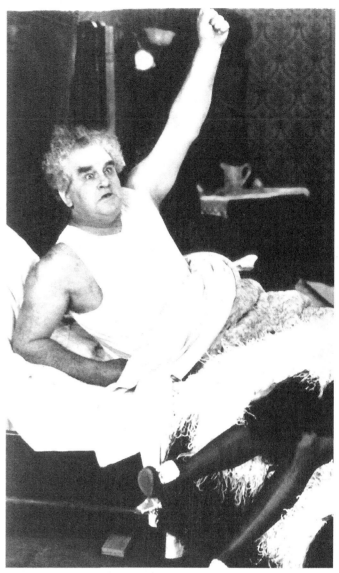

The Matinee Idol (1928): **A startled Lionel Belmore**

bolt (11/16/11). Lionel rejoined Faversham in a revival of *Julius Caesar* (11/4/12) at Broadway's Lyric Theatre. Belmore signed with the Shuberts to appear in the musical comedy *The Midnight Girl* (2/23/14) as Gustave Criquet III. He directed but did not appear in *The Marriage of Columbine* (11/10/14). The year 1914 marked Belmore's earliest association with motion pictures, initially as a director. Lionel would make only one more Broadway appearance thereafter, being seen, again for the Shuberts, in *Somebody's Luggage* (8/28/16), which also featured Beryl Mercer.

While living in New York in 1914, Belmore secured work as an assistant director to James Young at Vitagraph Studios. He worked under Young on *My Official Wife* (1914) and *The Violin of M'sieur* (1914), both featuring Clara Kimball Young, the director's wife. Belmore also made his film-acting debut with the Youngs as Jim, the husband, in *Taken By Storm* (1914).

Belmore began directing Vitagraph shorts starring Edith Storey, including *Hope Foster's Mother* (1914), *The Old Flute Player* (1914), *In the Latin Quarter* (1915), *The Silent Plea* (1915), *The Quality of Mercy* (1915) and *The Ruling Power* (1915). He both directed and appeared (as ranch owner John Benham) in *West Wind* (1915). Other Belmore directorial efforts for Vitagraph were: *Out of the Past* (1914), *His Bunkie* (1915), *From the Dregs* (1915), *Britton of the Seventh* (1916) and *Billie's Mother* (1916).

Belmore had a small role in Premo Films' *The Greater Will* (1915), with Montagu Love, and directed Robert Warwick in *The Supreme Sacrifice* (1916) for the same company. After appearing as Peters, the cruel farmer who enslaves orphan Zena Keefe, in *Shame* (1917), Belmore signed a player's contract with World Film Company in Fort Lee, New Jersey. Although focusing on acting, Belmore directed *The Wasp* (1918) for World, while also playing the part of Brazsos, a German spy. Other acting roles for Belmore

***Heart Trouble* (1928): Lionel Belmore and Madge Hunt**

at World were: General Israel Putnam in *The Beautiful Mrs. Reynolds* (1918), General Malcoff in *His Royal Highness* (1918), Giuseppe in *Wanted: A Mother* (1918) and Carl Hoffman in *Leap to Fame* (1918). For Universal, Lionel was seen in the comedy short *Maid Wanted* (1918).

Next inking a contract with Goldwyn Pictures, also based at the time in Fort Lee, Belmore made three films with their star Will Rogers. He portrayed Jake Bloom, who runs a gambling house, in *The Strange Boarder* (1920), the corrupt Belcher in *Jes' Call Me Jim* (1920) and Armstrong in *Guile of Women* (1920). Also for Goldwyn, Belmore, as M. Robert Parissard, played opposite Pauline Frederick in

Madame X (1920). In addition, Lionel was seen in the following parts: Rosenthal in *Duds* (1920), Richard Sibley, Sr. in *Milestones* (1920), Mark Bullway in *The Man Who Had Everything* (1920), the Impresario in *The Great Lover* (1920) and an undetermined role in *Godless Men* (1920).

Belmore played Montana millionaire Bill Bradford in the Lee Moran comedy *A Shocking Night* (1921). He was Angus Ferguson, the owner of a Scottish steel mill who is murdered during an attempted robbery, in *Courage* (1921). *The Sting of the Lash* (1921), with Pauline Frederick, had Belmore as Ben Ames. Lionel played James Rutledge, Marie Prevost's butler, in *Moonlight Follies* (1921). *Two Minutes to Go*

(1921), starring Charles Ray, included Belmore as Mary Anderson's father.

The Barnstormer (1922) featured Belmore as the manager of a traveling acting troupe who hires Charles Ray. He played John Burroughs, Wallace Reid's father, in *The World's Champion* (1922). Raoul Walsh directed Lionel as the Laird of Tyee in *Kindred of the Dust* (1922). *Iron to Gold* (1922), a Dustin Farnum Western, had Belmore as the sheriff. *Head Over Heels* (1922), a Mabel Normand comedy, included Lionel as Al Wilkins. Belmore played cattleman "Five-Notch" Arnett in *The Galloping Kid* (1922), starring Hoot Gibson. He was Colonel Rome Woolrich in *The Kentucky Derby* (1922), with Reginald Denny. As Archimede in *Enter Madame* (1922), Belmore was reunited with Clara Kimball Young. *Peg o' My Heart*

***The Unholy Night* (1929): Lionel Belmore (center, pointing), surrounded by fellow officers John Loder, Philip Strange, John Roche, Richard Travers and Gerald Barry**

(1922), King Vidor's screen version of Laurette Taylor's stage success, had Belmore as Hawks.

Jazzmania (1923), set in the Balkans and starring Mae Murray, included Belmore as Baron Bolo. Lionel was part of a ring of narcotics smugglers trailed by Richard Dix in *Quicksands* (1923). He was Irwin, Lew Cody's attorney, in *Within the Law* (1923). Belmore played Foster in *Railroaded* (1923). Lionel portrayed Alden Murray in *Red Lights* (1923), an early science fiction film involving a machine that utilizes telepathic suggestion. *Forgive and Forget* (1923) had Belmore as a butler. His appearance in the Buster Keaton comedy *Three Ages* (1923) is unconfirmed.

As Sir Geoffrey Wildairs, Lionel was the father of Virginia Valli in *A Lady of Quality* (1924). Belmore played Herbert Lorington in *A Fool's Awakening* (1924), Timothy Perrin in *Try and Get It* (1924), the Uncle in *Racing Luck* (1924) and Meggs in *The Man Who Fights Alone* (1924). The Jackie Coogan vehicle *A Boy of Flanders* (1924) featured Lionel as Baas Cogez. Belmore again had the opportunity to work with director Frank Lloyd in *The Sea Hawk* (1924), as Justice Anthony Baine, and in *The Silent Watcher* (1924), as Barnes the campaign manager. *Eve's Secret* (1925) with Betty Compson, featured Belmore as the Baron. He played Gaston Larrieau in *Never the Twain Shall Meet* (1925), directed by Maurice Tourneur. Lionel was Honest Tom Massingham in *Without Mercy* (1925). *The Storm Breaker* (1925), a sea saga with House Peters, had Belmore as the parson. Belmore, as Seth Corwin, played opposite famed female impersonator Julian Eltinge in *Madame Behave* (1925).

Stop, Look and Listen (1926), a Larry Semon comedy, had Lionel as the sheriff. *The Blackbird* (1926), directed by Tod Browning and starring Lon Chaney, featured Lionel as the nightclub owner. Belmore played Joel Corbin, the owner of an automobile manufacturing company, in *The Checkered Flag* (1926). Other roles for Lionel around this time were: John Beacon in *Shipwrecked* (1926), Mr. Stover in *Speeding Through* (1926), Crane in *The Self Starter* (1926), Reverend Bartholomey in *The Return of Peter Grimm* (1926) and Jacques St. Claire in *The Return of Grey Wolfe* (1926). He also appeared in the Billy West comedy short *Oh Billy, Behave* (1926). *The Dice Woman* (1926) gave Belmore the meaty part of Rastillac, the hotel owner who preys on employee Priscilla Dean. *Bardelys the Magnificent* (1926) provided another colorful character for Lionel as the Vicomte de Lavedan, opposite star John Gilbert.

Winners of the Wilderness (1927), with Tim McCoy, had Belmore as Governor Dinwiddie of Virginia. He played Monsieur, the father of Norma Shearer, in *The Demi-Bride* (1927). Cecil B. DeMille found a place for Lionel as a Roman noble in *The King of Kings* (1927). Belmore portrayed a

The Doll Shop (1929): Lionel Belmore as the doll maker

of star Harry Langdon. Lionel was Beezicks, part of a circus company that "adopts" orphan Frankie Darro, in *The Circus Kid* (1928).

Belmore's powerful voice and verbal delivery made for a seamless transition from silent films to talkies, as his 20 film appearances in 1929/30 attest. Lionel was Amos Sewald, a member of a Central American jungle expedition who is mysteriously slain by an arrow, in *Stark Mad* (1929). He played McDougal in *The Yellowback* (1929), Senor Carroles in *From Headquarters* (1929), the innkeeper in *Evidence* (1929), a convict in *Condemned* (1929) and yet another innkeeper in *Devil-May-Care* (1929). *The Doll Shop* (1929), an MGM two-strip Technicolor short, had Belmore in the lead role as the toymaker/doll shop proprietor. As Father Colomb, Lionel prevented Dolores Costello from vengefully killing Conrad Nagel in *The Redeeming Sin* (1929). The lavish *The Love Parade* (1929), starring Maurice Chevalier, had Belmore prominently on display as the Prime Minister.

Directed by Lionel Barrymore and featuring an intriguing cast including Boris Karloff and Sojin, *The Unholy Night* (1929) was concerned with a post-war reunion of a group of British officers who were part of the "Doomed Regiment" that fought at Gallipoli. Belmore was Major Endicott, who must contend with four of his colleagues being murdered before the killer is revealed to be one of their own, the scarred, vindictive Major Mallory (John Miljan).

party guest in *The Tender Hour* (1927), the first mate in Syd Chaplin's *The Missing Link* (1927), Jack McTeague in *The Sunset Derby* (1927), John D. Sommers in *Roaring Fires* (1927) and John Palfrey in *Sorrell and Son* (1927). Lionel appeared in *Topsy and Eva* (1927), the screen debut of Vivian and Rosetta Duncan. He played a "stout student" (at age 50!) in *The Student Prince in Old Heidelberg* (1927), with Ramon Novarro and Norma Shearer.

As millionaire Cyrus Todd, Belmore again played an automobile magnate and Shirley Mason's father in the Ben Turpin comedy, *The Wife's Relations* (1928). *Run, Girl, Run* (1928) had Belmore as the Dean of the college for which track star Carole Lombard competes. Lionel portrayed Henri Duray in *Rose-Marie* (1928), the Greek florist in *The Play Girl* (1928) and the General in *The Good-Bye Kiss* (1928). Belmore had a substantial role as Jasper Bolivar in *The Matinee Idol* (1928), directed by Frank Capra. Bolivar, the father of Bessie Love, is the producer and director of a small local acting troupe who unwittingly hires star theater performer Johnnie Walker. *Heart Trouble* (1928) featured Belmore as the struggling German immigrant father

Alexander Hamilton (1931): Hamilton (George Arliss) with General Schuyler (Lionel Belmore)

Frankenstein (1931): **Lionel Belmore (center), as the burgomaster, leads the villagers, including Michael Mark (to his right), after the Monster.**

Lionel was seen in the French language version of *The Unholy Night*, known as *Le spectre vert* (*The Green Ghost*, 1930), wherein he again played Endicott.

Love Comes Along (1930), directed by Rupert Julian and set on the island of Caparoja, included Lionel as Brownie, the conniving, vile owner of a cantina. *Playing Around* (1930), a musical featuring Alice White, had Belmore as Morgan the Pirate in the nightclub show at the Pirate's Den. He played the Colonel of the Hussars in *Captain of the Guard* (1930), with John Boles and Laura La Plante. Belmore was seen as Ossman in *The Rogue Song* (1930), Monsieur Dupont in *Hell's Island* (1930), a Mountie in *River's End* (1930) and the Minister of War in *The Boudoir Diplomat* (1930). The musical costume drama *Sweet Kitty Bellairs* (1930) had Belmore in pompous form as Colonel Villiers. *Monte Carlo* (1930), another musical, featured Lionel as Duke Gustav von Liebenheim, the father of weak Claud Allister who hopes to wed Countess Helene (Jeanette MacDonald). At one point, the old Duke tries to propose to Helene, to no avail.

Very little is known about Lionel Belmore's offscreen life. He lived in what was jokingly referred to as a British "colony," a section of Hollywood known as "Little Tooting." Belmore would meet regularly with fellow countrymen like Percy Marmont and Eric Snowden for kippers or Yorkshire pudding. Many of the Brits would also get together at cricket matches in the Los Angeles area, some of which featured participants, including C. Aubrey Smith, Murray Kinnell and Boris Karloff, who were involved in the motion picture industry.

Lionel had an uncredited bit as the café manager in *Kiss Me Again* (1931) with Walter Pidgeon. The musical *One Heavenly Night* (1931), with John Boles, had Belmore as Baron Zagon. As Bill the bartender, Belmore dealt with problem drinker William Farnum in *Ten Nights in a Barroom* (1931). He played Herr Kessner opposite Ramon Novarro and Helen Chandler in *Daybreak* (1931). *A Woman of Experience* (1931), set in wartime Vienna, had Lionel as the recruiting speaker. Belmore was General Philip Schuyler, the father-in-law of the title character played by George

Clive of India (1935): Lionel Belmore introduces Loretta Young and Ronald Colman to those assembled.

Tower of London (1939): Lionel Belmore as Beacon

Arliss, in *Alexander Hamilton* (1931). As "the Knitting Swede," Belmore was a notorious shanghaier who supplies unwilling sailors to dubious captains like Noah Beery, Sr., in *Shanghaied Love* (1931). A member of the Masquers Club, Belmore appeared in their short *The Great Junction Hotel* (1931). On an island populated by seedy denizens like Gustav von Seyffertitz and Morgan Wallace, Belmore played the judge at the murder trial of Dorothy Mackaill in *Safe in Hell* (1931). He was seen in the Thalians short *Hollywood Halfbacks* (1931) with Johnny Mack Brown, a former All-American football player at the University of Alabama. Belmore, as indicated in the Warner Bros. shooting schedule, played a lawyer in the John Barrymore *Svengali* (1931). Unfortunately, his scenes did not appear in the final release print of the film.

James Whale had a real flare for selecting colorful character actors to inhabit his films. Consistent with this, Whale chose Belmore to assay the role of Burgomaster Vogel in *Frankenstein* (1931). Vogel is first observed in one of the film's lighter moments visiting Baron Frankenstein (Frederick Kerr), inquiring about the wedding of his son Henry (Colin Clive) and giving flowers to the prospective bride (Mae Clarke). When the Baron insults him,

Vogel abruptly departs. Later, the Burgomaster organizes the townsmen into three groups to seek out the Monster (Boris Karloff). Vogel spots the Monster and Henry atop the windmill while leading the lake party. When Henry is hurled to the ground and likely killed, Vogel instructs his men to carry Frankenstein back to the village. Belmore established himself in horror film lore with his characterization of the Burgomaster in *Frankenstein*.

Police Court (1932) had Belmore as Albert Furman, the president of Masters Pictures Corporation, who refuses to hire down-and-out former silent star Henry B. Walthall. As Sir Pitt Crawley, Belmore was the lecherous father of Conway Tearle in *Vanity Fair* (1932). Edna Ferber's *So Big!* (1932), with Barbara Stanwyck in the lead, featured Lionel as Reverend Dekker. He appeared in two Masquers Club shorts, as the General in *Read 'Em and Weep* (1932)

The Hunchback of Notre Dame (1939): **Lionel Belmore (center, with bishop's hat) is among those waiting for the contestants for King of the Fools.**

and in *The Engineer's Daughter; or, Iron Minnie's Revenge* (1932). Belmore was Mr. Cartright in *The Man Called Back* (1932), directed by Robert Florey. He played Buck, the bartender, in *Malay Nights* (1932), with Johnny Mack Brown. Belmore was briefly viewed as the Roman citizen betting "300 silver" in Cecil B. DeMille's *The Sign of the Cross* (1932).

Lowly Majestic Pictures not only utilized some Universal sets for their production of *The Vampire Bat* (1933), they also signed some character actors, such as Dwight Frye and Belmore, who had worked on *Dracula* and/or *Frankenstein*. Belmore was a natural selection to portray Gustav Schoen, the Burgermeister of Kleinschloss, where *The Vampire Bat* is set. Schoen looks on while Dr. von Niemann (Lionel Atwill) examines the corpse of Martha (Rita Carlyle), noting that her body has been drained of blood. This fuels the villagers in their belief that vampires are

responsible. Schoen attempts to control the townspeople, who in typical horror film fashion pursue bat-keeping Herman (Frye) into the night with torches blazing. When Herman leaps to his death in a cavern, Schoen is unable to stop Sauer (William V. Mong) from driving a stake into his heart. Belmore was in good form as the Burgermeister (alternate spelling of Burgomaster), just as he had been in *Frankenstein*.

Cavalcade (1933), which won Oscars for Best Picture and director Frank Lloyd, featured numerous British expatriates in Hollwood, including Belmore as Uncle George. Lionel, as Mr. Bumble, appeared in Monogram's early sound version of *Oliver Twist* (1933), with Irving Pichel as an effective Fagin. Bumble, the parish beadle, takes custody of young Oliver after birth, but then, years later, turns the nine-year-old Twist (Dickie Moore) over to the workhouse.

Diamond Frontier **(1940): Victor McLaglen, Lionel Belmore, Evelyn Selbie (seated) and players**

The Constant Woman (1933) had Belmore as the character man in the Ohio stock company early in the proceedings. Lionel played Homer, the poet and companion of Theseus (David Manners), who is captured by the Amazons in *The Warrior's Husband* (1933). *Meet the Baron* (1933), with Jack Pearl as Munchausen, included Lionel as the explorer with the newspaper. Belmore was a puppeteer and was also seen as Satan in *I Am Suzanne!* (1933). Noel Coward's *Design for Living* (1933), with Fredric March, Miriam Hopkins and Gary Cooper, had Belmore as a theater patron.

The Man Who Reclaimed His Head (1934), Universal's atmospheric piece with Claude Rains and Lionel Atwill, had Belmore on board as the train conductor. Belmore was the second aide to the Governor (Reginald Owen) in *Stingaree* (1934), set in Australia. *Range Riders* (1934), a Buddy Roosevelt Western, featured Belmore as Mike the bartender. He played the prison governor in *The Count of Monte Cristo* (1934), with Robert Donat excelling in the lead role. Monogram's above average version of *Jane Eyre* (1934),

starring Virginia Bruce and with Colin Clive as Rochester, included Lionel as Lord Ingram. Belmore was a member of the court in *The Affairs of Cellini* (1934), with Fredric March. *Caravan* (1934), with Charles Boyer romancing Loretta Young, had Belmore in the role of the stationmaster. He portrayed Fidius in DeMille's *Cleopatra* (1934), starring Claudette Colbert. Lionel was the storekeeper in *Red Morning* (1934), with Steffi Duna.

As the official at the reception, Belmore greeted the title character (Ronald Colman) in *Clive of India* (1935). Belmore was the warden at Old Bailey Prison in *David Copperfield* (1935). He portrayed Will Leathwaite opposite Helen Hayes in *Vanessa: Her Love Story* (1935). Again with George Arliss, Belmore was seen as an agitator in *Cardinal Richelieu* (1935). Lionel had a colorful moment as the blacksmith, pounding out Laurel and Hardy's "Cuckoo" theme music on the anvil as the duo approach, in *Bonnie Scotland* (1935). He was the proprietor of the King and Peasant Inn in *The Three Musketeers* (1935). The musical *Dressed to Thrill* (1935)

The Son of Monte Cristo **(1940): Innkeeper Hercules Snyder (Lionel Belmore) is harassed by Lanen's soldiers, including the Captain (Theodore von Eltz, right).**

included Belmore as Pierre. Belmore was the innkeeper in the tavern during the early press gang sequence wherein Clark Gable and Wallis Clark "acquire" additional seamen in *Mutiny on the Bounty* (1935), directed by Frank Lloyd. *Forced Landing* (1935) had Lionel as the warden of the prison who directs Onslow Stevens to keep careful watch on a recently released kidnapper. *Hitch-Hike Lady* (1935), featuring a touching performance by Alison Skipworth, had Belmore as Mr. Harker, the green grocer.

Little Lord Fauntleroy (1936), with Freddie Bartholomew, had Belmore as Higgins, one of the townspeople. Lionel played the stage doorman in *One Rainy Afternoon* (1936), starring Francis Lederer (later to star as the Count in 1958's *Return of Dracula*). The short *Master Will Shakespeare* (1936) featured Belmore as Burbage, the theater manager, and first employer of young Shakespeare (Anthony Kemble Cooper). Belmore played a British Captain in the Crimean War in *The White Angel* (1936), with Kay Francis as Flor-

ence Nightingale. In *Mary of Scotland* (1936), Belmore was the fisherman, who, with wife Doris Lloyd, tries to assist Mary (Katharine Hepburn) during her escape. Belmore played a patroon in *The Last of the Mohicans* (1936), starring Randolph Scott as Hawkeye.

Maid of Salem (1937), set during the witch hunts and trials in late 1600s Massachusetts, had Belmore serving ale as a tavern keeper. He played a coachman in the short *The Romance of Robert Burns* (1937). Back to his frequent occupation, Lionel was the innkeeper in *The Prince and the Pauper* (1937), with Errol Flynn, Claude Rains and the Mauch twins. Belmore played a bank guard in *Topper* (1937), with ghosts Cary Grant and Constance Bennett causing havoc for Roland Young. *The Toast of New York* (1937), with Edward Arnold, had Belmore as the president of the board. Lionel was Friar Lawrence in the play (*Romeo and Juliet*) within the movie *It's Love I'm After* (1937), starring Leslie Howard and Bette Davis. Belmore was the butler for Calverton (C. Aubrey Smith) in *Thoroughbreds Don't Cry* (1937), with Judy Garland.

The Adventures of Robin Hood (1938), which firmly put Errol Flynn in the limelight, featured Belmore as Humility Prim. Lionel was the chief steward in *If I Were King* (1938), starring Ronald Colman. *Service de Luxe* (1938), featuring a young Vincent Price, had Belmore as Wade. He again played an innkeeper in *The Declaration of Independence* (1938), an Oscar-winning short from Warner Bros. *Pie a la Maid* (1938), another short, had Lionel as Dr. Kornbloom, contending with star Charley Chase.

Belmore's last significant horror film role was that of Emil Lang, the apothecary, in *Son of Frankenstein* (1939). Lang was among the jurors whose verdict led to the hanging of Ygor (Bela Lugosi) and, as a result, has been marked for death by the still living, demented shepherd. Belmore has a well-constructed death scene, wherein Ygor plays his horn from the castle tower as the Monster (Boris Karloff) pulls the shade on the window of Lang's shop. As Lang sits pensively beneath his clock, he realizes something is amiss, only to rise to face the Monster's wrath. Lang's murder leads to an angry display by the villagers, who storm Frankenstein's castle, but are halted by Inspector Krogh (Lionel Atwill) and his gendarmes.

The Sun Never Sets (1939), with Basil Rathbone and Lionel Atwill amidst a marvelous cast, had Belmore uncredited as a member of the selection board. Lionel had a small part as a villager in *Rulers of the Sea* (1939), concerned with the development of the steam engine for ships. *Tower of London* (1939), also directed by Rowland V. Lee at Universal, had another spectacular cast including Basil Rathbone, Boris Karloff, Vincent Price, Barbara O'Neil and a good portion of the studio's horror "stock company." Here Belmore portrayed Beacon, a chamberlain to King Edward IV (Ian Hunter).

Early on in *The Hunchback of Notre Dame* (1939), Belmore can be viewed wearing Bishop's attire near the "ugly face" contest that leads to Quasimodo (Charles Laughton) being crowned King of the Fools. Belmore also makes an appearance later in the film as one of the judges at the trial of Esmeralda (Maureen O'Hara).

My Son, My Son! (1940) featured Belmore as Mr. Moscrop, the baker, who, after being defended from a thug by Brian Aherne, hires the young man at his shop. He had a familiar role as the tavern keeper in *Tom Brown's School Days* (1940), with Jimmy Lydon and Freddie Bartholomew. As Boer settler Piet Bloem, Lionel played opposite the villainous Victor McLaglen in *Diamond Frontier* (1940), set during the diamond rush in South Africa. *The Son of Monte Cristo* (1940), directed by Rowland V. Lee, featured a number of character players associated with horror films in minor roles, including Dwight Frye, Michael Mark, Michael Visaroff, Ted Billings and Lawrence Grant. Belmore por-

trayed Hercules Snyder, the innkeeper. The actress portraying Snyder's wife, Margaret Fealy, had been Dwight Frye's drama teacher when he was a teenager in Denver.

In the opening scenes of *The Ghost of Frankenstein* (1942), Belmore is one of the village elders at the town hall. As the villagers demand action against the threat of Castle Frankenstein, the first councillor (Belmore) contradicts the dubious Burgomaster (Lawrence Grant), arguing, "The people are right," leading to the demolition of the edifice. *The Ghost of Frankenstein* would be Belmore's third and final appearance in a Universal *Frankenstein* film.

Belmore's small part in *Forever and a Day* (1943) was deleted from the final release version. *Forever and a Day* represented the 13th film on which Belmore worked with director Frank Lloyd. Lionel's last screen appearance was a brief bit as a laughing townsperson in *I Was a Criminal* (1945), starring Albert Bassermann. The film was actually shot as *Passport to Heaven* in 1941, but ran into issues due to its German setting in the midst of World War II, delaying its release for more than three years. *I Was a Criminal* was also known as *The Captain of Koepenick*. *The Ghost of Frankenstein* therefore actually constitutes Belmore's final role. Belmore did not act on screen or stage during the final 10 years of his life.

On Friday, January 30, 1953, Lionel Belmore died in Woodland Hills, California at the age of 85. He had been a resident of the Motion Picture Country House in Woodland Hills since it had opened in 1942. His sister Daisy Belmore Waxman (1874-1954), who, among her screen roles, had been a coach passenger with Carla Laemmle and Dwight Frye in the opening sequences of *Dracula* (1931), survived him. Belmore's former wife, Emmeline Carder, and daughters, Violet and Rosamund, were not mentioned in any of his print obituaries (although they were all still living at the time).

Lionel Belmore rendered many deft, comedic touches to numerous films with his pompous, self-important characterizations. His wild hair and excessive girth enhanced his comedy roles. Belmore was also capable of sensitive dramatic portrayals, playing kindly fathers and such, while also enacting a convincing villain when the script required. For horror film fans, however, Belmore, due to his performances in *Frankenstein* (1931) and *The Vampire Bat* (1933), remains the definitive burgomaster.

Sources

Coughlin, Jim. "Forgotten Faces of Fantastic Films: Lionel Belmore, Gustav von Seyffertitz," in *Midnight Marquee #31* (Fall 1982), pp. 14-15.

Maude Eburne
(1875 – 1960)

One of the truly funny, distinctive actresses of the screen, Maude Eburne was capable of stealing scenes from even dominant personalities like W.C. Fields and Bob Hope. She had a marvelous droll delivery and expressive face. Maude was often able to convey more with a frown and a sniff in a brief cameo than many performers could using many emotive techniques over the course of an entire film. Eburne had particularly amusing moments that counterbalanced the more eerie and serious events in genre films like *The Vampire Bat* and *Among the Living.* Her appearance also enhanced other fantasy-related movies like *The Bat Whispers, Return of the Terror, The Boogie Man Will Get You* and *The Secret Life of Walter Mitty.* Eburne was commonly seen as an eccentric aunt, a nosy neighbor, a zany maid, a scowling matron, or a feisty landlady. All in all, Eburne made nearly 120 films, ranging from major MGM productions to Chesterfield quickies, supporting elite performers like Alfred Lunt and Lynn Fontanne, to working with Western stars like Roy Rogers, Gene Autry and Buck Jones.

Of Scottish-Irish descent, Ella Maude Eburne Riggs was born on November 11, 1875 in Bronte-on-the-Lake, Oakville, Ontario, a suburb of Toronto, Canada. She was the last of 15 children (having 10 brothers and four sisters) born to John Riggs (1820-1901) and Mary Robinson (1826-1885). Her mother Mary died when Ella Maude was only 10 years old. Young Maude, as she became known, was educated in Toronto schools, including Havergal College, a preparatory boarding school for girls. While studying elocution in school, Eburne became enamored of the theater, eventually aspiring to a stage career. Her father, however, had serious reservations about his youngest child becoming an actress. Eburne told the *New York Times* (3/29/14) some years later, "If my father knew I was on the stage he would not rest in peace, and he had the same habit of thinking during his lifetime." Following school, Maude worked for a time in the newspaper business.

While visiting with one of her brothers in Buffalo, New York, Eburne began to formulate plans to become an actress, despite her father's objections. When Maude's father John passed away in 1901, she decided it was time to pursue her dream. One of Eburne's early theater experiences (c. 1903) was an engagement with the Howard-Dorset Company, headed by manager George H. Howard. Among the plays the com-

pany performed in repertory were: *The Man from Mexico, Held by the Enemy, My Lady Nell* and *The Pearl of Savoy.* A few years later, Maude secured a position with the Shubert Stock Company at the Teck Theatre in Buffalo, establishing herself as a character woman. In the early phase of her career, Maude played both stock and repertory, differentiating the two thusly (the *New York Times,* 3/29/14):

> The stock company experience was more pleasant because there is a constant variation of parts. In a repertory company you have your part in several plays, and you must keep at it all the time with very little relief; furthermore, they expect constant variety from you in these parts. If, as character woman, you have, for instance, as I had, six Irish parts at one time, the brogue

A Pair of Sixes (1914 Broadway stage): **Maude Eburne as Coddles**

A Pair of Queens (1916 Broadway stage): A portrait of Maude Eburne

on's only known screen appearance came (uncredited) as an unwed expectant mother at a halfway house in the Fox film *Bondage* (1933), starring Dorothy Jordan.

Maude Eburne spent 13 years struggling and dealing with the frustrations of the theater in the early part of the 20th century. Virtually every year, Maude would travel to New York City and make the rounds of the offices of managers and producers in the hope of career opportunities. She did land a role on Broadway in the short-lived (16 performances) *The Old Firm* (2/3/13), which played the Harris Theatre and featured Alison Skipworth. After that experience, it was back to the road as Eburne signed for a 22-week engagement with a stock company in Columbus, Ohio. By chance, however, Maude was introduced to Edward MacGregor, who was assembling a troupe to form the summer 1913 ver-

in every one must be a little different. It is drudgery of the worst sort, and the irony of it is that the more proficient you become in your work, the more you are removing yourself from real opportunity. That is because if you tell the manager in looking for an engagement that you have had experience in stock and repertoire, they immediately refuse to consider you for anything else.

Another of Eburne's employers in her formative theatrical years was the Myrkle-Harder Company, headed by leading lady Emma Myrkle and Will H. Harder. The company would travel from city to city, primarily in the Northeast (New York, Pennsylvania, Massachusetts, New Jersey, etc.), typically performing six plays in rep in each stop along the season's tour.

Eburne fell in love with and eventually married (c. 1906) the Myrkle-Harder business manager, Eugene Johnson Hall (1874-1932). Maude would give birth to a daughter, Marion (or Maryon) Birdsee Eburne Hall (1907-1960), on May 7, 1907 in Hamilton, Ontario, Canada. (Some sources list Eburne's husband and daughter's last name as "Hill," and Marion's birth year as "1917," but both are incorrect.) Marion (married name Sebby) also acted with the troupe, later known as the Harder-Hall Players, first as a child performer, then an ingénue and finally as leading lady. One of Marion Eburne Hall's early leading roles for the Harder-Hall company was that of Manette Fachard, the young French girl in *The Storm* (October 1927). Mari-

The Guardsman (1931): Maude Eburne and Lynn Fontanne

The Vampire Bat (1933): Herman (Dwight Frye) offers a bat to Gussie (Maude Eburne).

sion of the Manhattan Stock Company in Rochester, New York. What was unique about this company was that they didn't just perform old stock standards, but would try out new plays, some of which would actually reach Broadway. MacGregor asked Maude if she could leave for Rochester that same day and be ready for rehearsals the following morning. She readily agreed. One of the new works put on by the Manhattan Players was *The Party of the Second Part* by Edward Peple, later to be reworked and renamed *A Pair of Sixes.*

After another tryout in Hartford, Connecticut, *A Pair of Sixes* (3/17/14) opened in New York at the Longacre Theatre to great reviews. Eburne achieved almost immediate fame as Coddles, the lovesick Cockney maid. Maude worked a number of gimmicks into the role, including a dramatic manner of expressing her frustration, throwing her hands up and falling to the floor. The moment became a show-stopper, although Maude had feared it would bring to mind the theatrical cliché, "If you can't get a laugh, do a fall." Reflecting on the instant notoriety, Eburne stated (the *New York Times*, 3/29/14):

Actors who attain sudden notice are supposed to suffer invariably with conceit, but that idea is impossible in my case. If this had come several years ago I suppose I might have been unduly elated about it, but when the thing you have worked for unceasingly comes just as you had about decided to give up on account of weariness, you feel entirely different about it. There is a certain impersonal element of simple reward for labor and you are too seasoned to lose your balance over it. That is the way I feel.

A Pair of Sixes ran on Broadway for 207 performances, closing in September 1914 and then going on the road.

Eburne joined the Hall Players, an offshoot of the Myrkle-Harder Company, playing Washington, DC and elsewhere in plays like *A Bachelor's Romance* (1915/1916). She was seen with Wilton Lackaye in *Everyman's Castle,* touring in the spring of 1916. Eburne returned to Broad-

Lazy River (1934): Maude Eburne receives help from Robert Young.

way in *A Pair of Queens* (8/29/16), again at the Longacre Theatre, but the show only ran for 15 performances, failing to duplicate the success of *A Pair of Sixes*. Her next Broadway venture, *Here Comes the Bride* (9/25/17), was better received, lasting for 63 performances.

A Pair of Sixes (1918) was adapted for the silent screen as a vehicle for Taylor Holmes, who was fairly prominent in motion pictures at that time. Eburne was chosen to repeat her breakthrough role as Coddles, who pines for Holmes' character after the latter has lost a bet and been forced to become a servant for a year. Maude's only other silent film appearance came with her role of Sweet Genevieve in *Taxi* (1919), which also starred Taylor Holmes.

Eburne had another bravura part on Broadway in the musical comedy *The Canary* (11/4/18), with which she also toured on the road after almost six months in New York. Maude was Mary Ellen, an unattractive widow who was more than eager to marry once again.

Maude Eburne honed her comedy skills on stage playing opposite some of the best of the time, including Will Rogers and Fred Stone. A bright, creative woman, Eburne

also wrote essays on comedy, including "Women Who are Funny Off the Stage" (*Theatre Magazine*, October 1919), in which Maude described how she borrowed and developed comic mannerisms from serious women she had observed in everyday life.

Eburne spent the 1920s exclusively on the stage, often in New York, but also touring the United States. On Broadway, Maude portrayed Maggie Green in the musical comedy *The Half Moon* (11/1/20), Hildegard in the operetta *Love Dreams* (10/10/21), Piplete in the melodrama *Bavu* (2/25/22), Caroline in the musical comedy *Lady Butterfly* (1/22/23) and Medora in the comedy *Puppy Love* (1/27/26). At the Hollis Street Theatre in Boston, Eburne played a neglected but resourceful wife in *The Cradle Snatchers* (December 1926). The farce *Storm Center* (11/30/27) had Maude as Lena, a sharp-tongued servant, a characterization she would later repeat time and again in films. Other Broadway roles for Eburne were Queen Ysobel in the musical comedy *Three Cheers* (10/15/28), Mazie Brown in *Great Day* (10/17/29) and Smithy in the comedy *Many a Slip* (2/3/30).

Happiness C.O.D. (1935): Maude Eburne is very protective of her nephew, Frank Coghlan, Jr.

When director Roland West decided to rework the shadowy silent *The Bat* (1926) as *The Bat Whispers* (1930), he secured the services of Maude Eburne to play Lizzie Allen. As Lizzie, loyal maid to Grayce Hampton, Eburne did some extreme emoting, alternating hysterics with eye rolls. From this point until the late 1940s, Eburne would be one of the busiest character actresses in films. Maude was the boisterous Mrs. Mantel, mother of Esther Ralston, in *Lonely Wives* (1931). Eburne performed the song "Baby Feet" in the film. She played the advice-giving comic foil Aunt Kate in *Indiscreet* (1931). Eburne portrayed Esther in *The Man in Possession* (1931), Mrs. Petrick in *Stranger in Town* (1931), Mrs. Chauncey in *Bought!* (1931), Aunt Harriette in *Her Majesty, Love* (1931), the maid in *Local Boy Makes Good* (1931) and Mrs. Snyder in *Blonde Crazy* (1931) with James Cagney and Joan Blondell. MGM's production of Ferenc Molnar's *The Guardsman* (1931) offered Maude the opportunity to play opposite stage legends Alfred Lunt and Lynn Fontanne (in their only sound film). Eburne had the colorful role of "Mama," the doting but sarcastic long-time companion of Fontanne.

Eburne played Mrs. McCarthy in *Under 18* (1931), starring Marian Marsh, who had received fine notices for her work as Trilby in *Svengali* (1931). Maude was Rhoda

in *This Reckless Age* (1932) and the dowager party guest in *The Woman from Monte Carlo* (1932). *Union Depot* (1932), with Joan Blondell and Douglas Fairbanks, Jr. fine as the leads, featured a plethora of character performers in cameos at the train station, including Eburne as a passenger at the information desk. *Panama Flo* (1932) gave Eburne a chance to display her range as Sadie, the horrible boss of a Central American tavern. Showing her flamboyant side, Sadie sings "Happy Days are Here Again." Sadie, also quite vindictive, fires her dancers, including Helen Twelvetrees, showing total disregard that the girls have no means of getting back to the States.

Maude appeared in both *The Passionate Plumber* (1932) and its French-language version, *Le plombier amoureux* (1932), as Aunt Charlotte who comes to visit her niece, disapproving of her relationships with men. In *Polly of the Circus* (1932), Eburne was Mrs. Jennings, the Irish nurse tending to Marion Davies. Maude played Mrs. Elizabeth Hardy in *The Trial of Vivienne Ware* (1932), Emily Livingston in *The First Year* (1932), Martha Jenkins in *Divorce in the Family* (1932) and had a bit in *Faithless* (1932). *Robbers Roost* (1932), a Western with George O'Brien and Maureen O'Sullivan, had Eburne fourth-billed as deaf Aunt Ellen.

Despite being made by Majestic, a small independent production company, *The Vampire Bat*

Doughnuts and Society (1936): Nouveau riche Maude Eburne brushes up on the rules of etiquette.

Poppy **(1936): Catherine Calhoun Doucet hears some well-intentioned gossip from Maude Eburne.**

(1933) featured a fine cast headed by Lionel Atwill, Melvyn Douglas and Fay Wray, with horror film veterans Dwight Frye, Robert Frazer, Lionel Belmore, and William V. Mong in support. As Gussie Schnappman, Eburne was Wray's hypochondriac aunt, who pesters Dr. von Niemann (Atwill) for free medical advice and treatment (while proposing her own medical "theories"). Aunt Gussie is involved in a humorous sequence wherein she faints after being offered a bat by Herman Gleib (Frye). When she comes to, a large Great Dane is hovering over her, which Gussie naturally believes is Herman in another form. Gussie cries, "Out of the way, Herman! I know ya! I know ya!," as she tries to avert the advances of the playful dog. At the film's conclusion, von Neimann has a posthumous revenge of sorts upon the bothersome Gussie, as the final mixture of chemicals he had advised her to take for one of her maladies turns out to be a laxative. Gussie bolts up the stairs as *The Vampire Bat* draws to a close.

In *Ladies They Talk About* (1933), Eburne was Aunt Maggie, an elderly con woman who serves as a den moth-er of sorts to a group of incarcerated women, including star Barbara Stanwyck. A former madam, Maggie sits in a rocking chair in the prison, reminiscing about her old business venture, referring to it as "a beauty salon." Maude then played Lady Higby, the wife of the Admiral (Henry Kolker), in *Hell Below* (1933). As Buria, Eburne was a loyal Amazon officer to Queen Hippolyta (Marjorie Rambeau) in *The Warrior's Husband* (1933), loosely based on Greek mythology, with David Manners as Theseus. The musical *My Lips Betray* (1933) had Maude as Mama Wattscheck, acting as manager to Lilian Harvey, whom she encourages to persevere with her singing. Eburne was Mrs. Gibson in *Shanghai Madness* (1933), Mme. Fifi in *Ladies Must Love* (1933), the coroner's wife in *Big Executive* (1933), Mrs. Jackson in *Fog* (1933), Mrs. Ryan the landlady in *Havana Widows* (1933) and Mrs. Conway in *East of Fifth Avenue* (1933).

As Miss Minnie Lescalle, the mother of Jean Parker, Eburne locked horns with the vile C. Henry Gordon in *Lazy River* (1934). Minnie's shrimp business is in danger of a hostile takeover until Robert Young and two other ex-cons she had helped rally to Lescalle's aid. Maude played Mme. Bertha Smith, who protects her three young ladies (prostitutes), in *Love Birds* (1934). When Warner Bros. decided to remake the early sound horror film *The Terror* (1928) as *Return of the Terror* (1934), the result was disappointing and not very suspenseful. Eburne, as Mrs. Elvery, was part of a supporting cast of horror veterans, including J. Carrol Naish, Frank Reicher and Robert Barrat that should have yielded better results. *Here Comes the Navy* (1934) had Eburne as the mother of Droopy (Frank McHugh), who sends her money so she can obtain false teeth to better sing in the choir (Maude warbles "Oh, Promise Me") and "eat meat." *The Girl From Missouri* (1934), with Jean Harlow and Lionel Barrymore, included Eburne as the landlady, a role she also assayed in *Maybe It's Love* (1935). *When Strangers Meet* (1935), a mystery set in a bungalow park, featured Maude as Nell Peck.

Eburne provided another strong performance as "Ma" Pettingill, the tough but down-to-earth Western woman who takes the displaced British butler (Charles Laughton) under her wing in *Ruggles of Red Gap* (1935). Although wealthy herself, Ma despises the pretentiousness of her daughter (Mary Boland), allying herself with son-in law (Charles Ruggles) and the servant (Laughton) he brought to the Northwest. *Party Wire* (1935), with Jean Arthur, had Eburne as Clara West, the biggest gossip in

Valiant is the Word for Carrie (1936): Maude Eburne, Gladys George and Dudley Digges

town. Maude was Little Ellen Purdy, a champion husband-caller, in *Don't Bet on Blondes* (1935). Eburne portrayed Aunt Addie, Donald Meek's sister and housekeeper, who helps raise his three children, in *Happiness C.O.D.* (1935).

As Phoebe Leavenworth in *The Leavenworth Case* (1936), Eburne was the spinster sister of the murdered man, whom she is revealed to have poisoned by injecting eggs for his milk with arsenic. Phoebe, before taking the arsenic herself, justifies her deed, claiming her brother was a thief and a scoundrel who stood in the way of the marriage of his niece and ward (Jean Rouverol). For her work as Mrs. Hoggins in *Man Hunt* (1936), the *New York Times* (1/30/36) noted, "Maude Eburne gives a good character performance as the nagging wife of Chic Sale." Maude, as Belle Dugan, was paired with Louise Fazenda as partners in the Totem Coffee Shop in *Doughnuts and Society* (1936). Belle believes she has struck it rich when she sells her land holdings in the Klondike, only to later be crushed to discover the gold veins are barren. In between, however, Belle wreaks havoc on her ex-partner's party by turning the sprinklers on the guests. Republic had hoped to emulate MGM's success in the early 1930s with Marie Dressler and Polly Moran by having Eburne playing off Fazenda, but no subsequent films were made with the two actresses acting together. Republic used Eburne as Mrs. Pruitt in a John Wayne Western, *The Lonely Trail* (1936).

Poppy (1936), starring W.C. Fields, had Eburne as the kindly Sarah Tucker, who knew the Putnam family and recognizes Rochelle Hudson to be the missing heiress (which Fields unwittingly was trying to pass her off as in the first place). Tucker, being mindful of both town history and gossip, helps assure that the Countess (Catherine Doucet) receives her comeuppance as well. *Valiant is the*

Word for Carrie (1936), with Gladys George excelling as the title character, gave Eburne the colorful role of Maggie Devlin, the secretary who stands up to boss Dudley Digges at a struggling literary agency. *Reunion* (1936), featuring the Dionne quintuplets, had Maude as Mrs. Barton.

Champagne Waltz (1937), with Fred MacMurray, included Eburne as Mrs. Scribner. Maude was Mrs. Basscombe, the nouveau riche wife of Edgar Kennedy and mother of Joe E. Brown's girlfriend (Suzanne Kaaren), in *When's Your Birthday?* (1937). As Violet Butler, Eburne was a feisty ranch owner being threatened by Charles Middleton and his protection racket in *Hollywood Cowboy* (1937). Other roles for Eburne at the time were Maggie Casey in *Paradise Express* (1937), Mrs. Crump (Mickey Rooney's Ma) in *Live, Love and Learn* (1937) and Nadya, the Gypsy, in *Fight for Your Lady* (1937), as well as an uncredited bit in *Every Day's a Holiday* (1937) with Mae West.

Maude and Spencer Charters played the married couple on the train in *Vivacious Lady* (1938). Eburne was Mrs. Peggy Garth, the owner of thoroughbred Black Knight, who is kidnapped by gamblers, in the "Three Mesquiters" Western, *Riders of the Black Hills* (1938). Maude portrayed

Hollywood Cowboy (1937): Maude Eburne as Violet Butler

Fight for Your Lady **(1937): Gypsy Maude Eburne stands over fallen Charles Judels.**

Mrs. Magruder, the landlady, in *Convict's Code* (1939), Mrs. Minnow, the neighborhood harridan, in *Undercover Agent* (1939) and Mrs. Smith, the wife of the justice of the peace, in *Exile Express* (1939). Audiences got to hear Eburne sing "Put On Your Old Grey Bonnet" as "Ma" Hutchins, who is in danger of losing her ranch, in the Gene Autry Western, *Mountain Rhythm* (1939). Eburne's scenes as Senora Moreno were unfortunately deleted from the release print of *The Magnificent Fraud* (1939). Maude did play Mrs. Hopkins in *Sabotage* (1939), not to be confused with the 1936 Alfred Hitchcock film of the same name. *The Amazing Mr. Williams* (1939), with Melvyn Douglas and Joan Blondell, again had Eburne portraying a landlady.

Eburne had ongoing roles in two film series at this point in time. In two entries of the "Higgins Family" comedies, *My Wife's Relatives* (1939) and *The Covered Trailer* (1939), Maude portrayed the Widow Jones, who sets her sights on Grandpa Higgins (Harry Davenport). Eburne also had the recurring part of Mrs. Hastings, the housekeeper to the title character (Jean Hersholt), initially in *Meet Dr. Christian* (1939). Maude would reappear as the housekeeper in the

ensuing five "Dr. Christian" films: *Courageous Dr. Christian* (1940), *Dr. Christian Meets the Women* (1940), *Remedy for Riches* (1940), *Melody for Three* (1941) and *They Meet Again* (1941), which found Mrs. Higgins delving into astrology.

The Golden Fleecing (1940), with Lew Ayres, found Maude in her familiar role as a landlady. In *Colorado* (1940), starring Roy Rogers, Eburne, as Etta Mae, changes Gabby Hayes' negative opinion of women with her cooking prowess. As Hurricane Hattie McGuire, colorful owner of a hotel and bar, Eburne was again Gabby Hayes' love interest in *The Border Legion* (1940). Maude played Dogpatch denizen Granny Scraggs, who urges granddaughter Martha O'Driscoll to marry, in *Li'l Abner* (1940).

West Point Widow (1941) featured Eburne as Mrs. Willits, Anne Shirley's slovenly landlady. As Ella the cook at Henry Fonda's mansion in *You Belong to Me* (1941), Maude displayed a fondness for adding brandy to flavor her dishes. Eburne played a real eccentric, Borax Betty, who lives as a recluse in the desert, in *Glamour Boy* (1941). Betty mistakes Jackie Cooper for a "maniac kidnapper," before her fears are put to rest.

Among the Living (1941), a psychological thriller set in a Southern mill town, featured Albert Dekker in a dual role as twins, one, a sane businessman, and the other, a homicidal maniac. The film also provided Maude with a "quintessential landlady role," according to late film historian Doug McClelland, an unabashed Eburne aficionado. As Mrs. Pickens, Eburne has a wonderful scene wherein she rents a room to Paul, the recently escaped and dangerous twin. Mrs. Pickens cautions Paul not to trip over the vacuum cleaner, informs him that "foy-er" is French, before going into a discourse on how a previous French boarder had kissed her hand to the point "he'd like to pull the skin off." She then admonishes Paul, "No cooking allowed and no foul language," adding that they recently had a roomer who used language that "would have melted your gold tooth!" Paul starts dating Mrs. Pickens' daughter Millie (Susan Hayward). Waving to Millie and Paul as they are about to go shopping, the landlady states, "Us Pickenses always had a weakness for refinement!," proceeding to grab at her housedress stuck to her behind. *Among the Living* may have been intended as a suspense film, but Eburne's humorous antics stole the show.

To Be or Not to Be (1941), Ernst Lubitsch's memorable satirical comedy, had Eburne as Anna, Carol Lombard's cynical maid. The musical comedy *Almost Married* (1942), with Jane Frazee and Robert Paige, included Maude as Mrs. Clayton.

Eburne was in three *Henry Aldrich* films, but not in a recurring role. She was the wife of Principal Bradley (Vaughan Glaser), upon whom Henry (Jimmy Lydon) and Dizzy (Charles Smith) cause havoc while trying to sell her a vacuum cleaner, in *Henry and Dizzy* (1942). *Henry*

Aldrich, Editor (1942) had Maude as Mrs. Norris, the meddlesome deaf Irish neighbor who brings the supposedly ill Mr. Aldrich (John Litel) soup and leaves in a fit when she mishears Henry's use of the word "well" as "hell." In *Henry Aldrich Plays Cupid* (1944), Henry and Dizzy spot Eburne (listed as the "homely woman") at the train station and mistake her for the prospective bride of the now single Mr. Bradley. Dizzy exclaims, "Even old Bradley doesn't deserve that!" (perhaps an in-joke, as Eburne had earlier played his wife in the series).

Eburne played Agatha in *There's One Born Every Minute* (1942) and Juli, the woman with the checklist at the wedding banquet, in the Rodgers and Hart musical *I Married an Angel* (1942). *The Boogie Man Will Get You* (1942) provided Maude with another horror-related role. Professor Billings (Boris Karloff), who likes to experiment on people in his basement, sells his old Colonial Inn to Jeff Donnell, with the provision he can continue to reside in the cellar. Eburne was Amelia Jones, the zany housekeeper, who informs Donnell about the professor, of whom she is highly protective, "You don't know *how* good he is. Even when he was a baby he never cried—not even when we dropped him."

The Boogie Man Will Get You (1942): **Maude Eburne as the slightly demented Amelia Jones**

Dawn on the Great Divide (1942), Buck Jones' final film before his tragic death in the Cocoanut Grove fire, had Eburne as Sarah Harkins, heading west with her daughter (Christine McIntyre). *Lady Bodyguard* (1943) featured Maude as Mother Hodges, an elderly hat check girl, who becomes one of the greedy beneficiaries of pilot Eddie Albert's inflated insurance policy—and does her part to try to collect by putting sleeping powder first in a cake and then in his soup. Eburne played Maggie, the radio station cleaning woman, in *Reveille with Beverly* (1943), with Ann Miller. Maude was Miss Edna Counihan in *The Chance of a Lifetime* (1943), Dakota in *Ladies Courageous* (1944) and the dowager in the cable car in *Up in Arms* (1944), which starred Danny Kaye.

The year 1944 found Eburne firmly typecast in landlady roles. *Rosie the Riveter* (1944), a Jane Frazee musical comedy, featured Eburne as Grandma Quill, who runs an offbeat boarding house during wartime, renting rooms to airplane factory workers. As the landlady for Johnny (Rob-ert Livingstone), Maude appeared in the musical *Goodnight, Sweetheart* (1944). *I'm from Arkansas* (1944) found Eburne as Matilda Alden Jenkins, called "Ma," who not only runs a boarding house, but owns a special pig named Matilda (who gives birth to 18 piglets). As Madame Alda in *Bowery to Broadway* (1944), Maude operates the boarding house where Susanna Foster resides. Perhaps Eburne's most colorful landlady part came with her portrayal of the proprietress of the Boar's Head Inn in *The Princess and the Pirate* (1944). In *The Princess and the Pirate*, Maude smokes a pipe while renting a room to Bob Hope, whom she informs can have the clothes left behind by the previous tenant, who died of "non-payment of rent."

The Town Went Wild (1944) provided Eburne with a change of pace as Judge Bingle, who rules that, as babies, Freddie Bartholomew and Jimmy Lydon were switched at birth. The judge orders them now, as adolescents, to be sent to the opposite families. Bingle later has to undo the ensuing mess when it is revealed that the switch never occurred in the first place.

Eburne played Mrs. Packer in the Charles Laughton thriller, *The Suspect* (1944). In *Leave it to Blondie* (1945), Maude was Madame Magda, a phony gypsy fortune teller, who explains variations in her readings to using a "differ-

The Princess and the Pirate (1944): Maude Eburne as the intimidating landlady, with Virginia Mayo and Bob Hope as the prospective roomers

Story (1949), Hallmark's filmed production of the Lawton, Oklahoma Passion Play. In the modern day (c. 1926) segment of the film, Henrietta shames Taylor's character into attending the Easter pageant with his niece (Ginger Prince). Hallmark's *The Prince of Peace* (1951), also featuring Maude as Henrietta, perhaps an expanded re-working of *The Lawton Story.* Maude Eburne's last screen role was an unbilled appearance as a woman companion at the Stock Exchange in *Belle Le Grand* (1951), with Vera Ralston.

On October 15, 1960, at the age of 84, Maude Eburne passed away in Hollywood, California. The cause of her death is unknown to this writer. Eburne was buried at the Hollywood Forever Cemetery in Los Angeles, although her exact spot is unknown. She may have been cremated with her ashes scattered. Maude had been retired from the acting profession for more than nine years at the time of her death. Eburne had suffered the profound loss of her beloved only child Marion earlier in 1960, which likely hastened her own demise.

Maude Eburne's expressive, almost elastic face is clearly one that should not be forgotten and probably has not been by those who have been tickled by some of her offbeat screen characterizations. Even a mad doctor like Lionel Atwill in *The Vampire Bat* had to grin at her antics. Eburne was a true "character" woman in every sense of the word.

ent brand of tea." Magda causes problems for Dagwood (Arthur Lake) when she predicts a black-eyed brunette will come into his life. *Man from Oklahoma* (1945) had Eburne as Grandma Lane (grandmother to Dale Evans' character), who is the head of the feuding clan at odds with Gabby Hayes' family. Again with Dale Evans, Maude played Mrs. Randall in the musical *Hitchhike to Happiness* (1945).

Eburne had a minor bit as a fitter in the Danny Kaye fantasy, *The Secret Life of Walter Mitty* (1947). *Mother Wore Tights* (1947), starring Betty Grable, featured Eburne as Mrs. Muggin, the theatre company's character woman. In *Slippy McGee* (1948), Maude played Mrs. Dexter, who works in a parish house and discovers the burglar tools of Skippy (Donald Barry). The Western *The Plunderers* (1948) had Eburne as the "old dame" at the wedding of Rod Cameron and Adrian Booth before the justice of the peace. Eburne played the wisecracking Grandma of Anne Gwynne in *Arson, Inc.* (1949).

Nearing the end of her film career, Eburne was seen as Henrietta, the housekeeper of Ferris Taylor, in *The Lawton*

Sources

"Coddles Awakes at Last to Find Herself Famous," in the *New York Times"* (3/29/1914).

Coughlin, Jim. "Forgotten Faces of Fantastic Films: Maude Eburne," in *Midnight Marquee #48* (Winter 1995), pp. 93-95.

Eburne, Maude. "Women Who are Funny Off the Stage," in *Theatre Magazine* (October 1919), vol. 30, p 230, 232.

McClelland, Doug. "Maude Eburne," in *Film Fan Monthly #149* (November 1973).

Stumpf, Charles. "Queen of the Zanies: Maude Eburne," in *Classic Images #292* (October 1999), pp. 6-8.

William V. Mong
(1875 - 1940)

Mention the name of William V. Mong to the average film buff and the odds are the response will be, "Who?" Even an ardent scholar of old movies would at best associate Mong's name with an actor who played irritable old men in some early talkies. William V. Mong, however, was so much more than that. He was a stalwart in the developmental days of motion pictures, initially as a scenario writer, actor and director for the Selig Polyscope Company. Mong served the same function for the Pike's Peak Company before making contributions as actor, writer and director for fledgling Universal Pictures—all before 1920. In the twenties, Mong was a significant character player, working for all the major studios and alongside stars such as Lon Chaney, John Gilbert, Wallace Beery and many more. Directors like Benjamin Christensen and Edward Sloman clamored to have him cast in their films. In the late silents and early talkies, Mong's appearances ranged from important films like *What Price Glory?*, *Noah's Ark*, *The Sign of the Cross* and *Cleopatra* to quickies for independent studios like Chesterfield and Mayfair. While some of his noteworthy villainous roles in genre films like *Ransom* and *Code of the Air* are regrettably lost (as is most of his early screen work), Mong left behind a legacy of colorful portrayals, both evil and sympathetic, large and bit parts, that warrant overdue recognition for this prolific performer.

William Clyde Mong was born in Chambersburg (Ward 3), Franklin County, Pennsylvania, on June 25, 1875. He was the fourth of five children born to the former Louisa Denig Barnitz (1839-1923), a Chambersburg native, and William Hushire Mong (1834-1876), who hailed from Mansfield, Ohio. William had two older siblings, brother Charles William (1866-1868) and sister Lula May (1868-1880), who died in childhood. His two other brothers, Harry Warren Mong (1872-1949), a printer, and George Barnitz Mong (1878-1943), a baker, spent virtually their entire lives in Chambersburg. William's father passed away when William was less than two years old. Louisa, despite the losses of her spouse and two young children, struggled to raise Harry, William and George in a house at 338 South Main Street in Chambersburg.

Young William originally aspired to be an educator and spent several years as a district schoolteacher in and around Chambersburg. While still in his twenties, Mong made the decision to abandon teaching, instead pursuing a career in the theater. Although his middle name was Clyde, William used "V" for his middle initial throughout his acting career.

His introduction to the stage was with a barnstorming troupe in Indiana, where he learned all the rudiments of the theatrical business from performing, to building sets

Portrait (c. 1904) of William V. Mong

and promoting upcoming shows. An early theatrical reference for Mong appeared in *The Billboard* (1/23/04), wherein William reported that the Van Dyke Company, of which he was then a member, had signed former outlaw Frank James to appear with them for the balance of the season at a salary of $500 per week. The troupe, playing Independence, Missouri, at that time, was to be renamed "The Cowboy's Girl Company." Venturing to the West Coast, Mong spent a few seasons in stock in Seattle and Tacoma, Washington, eventually appearing in San Francisco, California, as well. Mong traveled constantly in stock, repertory and vaudeville, performing in many states, including Ohio, Illinois and his home state of Pennsylvania. In late September 1905, for instance, Mong played four Pennsylvania (Connellsville, Charleroi, Monongahela, Greenville) and four Ohio (Mansfield, Lima, Sandusky, Bucyrus) towns in nine days (9/19-9/27/05).

In 1905, while performing in stock in Oregon, William became friendly with Janette Stevens Kelley and her

Alias Jane Jones (1916): **William V. Mong and Ray Hanford**

unbreakable china while striving to perfect new building materials, while battling adversity, including the blindness of his daughter and capitalists that fear his creativity. Theatrical impresario Daniel Frohman accused Mong of pirating *The Clay Baker* from an existing work entitled *The Middleman*, but such claims were proven to be unfounded (although both protagonists are clay bakers or potters).

In the fall of 1909, Mong toured the Midwest in *The Devil, the Servant and the Man*, playing the Devil. Mong continued to revive *The Clay Baker* and also appeared in *Light in the Window*, bringing him to the attention of "Colonel" William Selig, whose Selig Polyscope Company was located at 20 E. Randolph Street, Chicago, Illinois. Although *The Connecticut Yankee* (1910) is generally listed as Mong's first screen credit, his first fully documented lead came in Selig's film version of *The Clay Baker* (1910). He then co-starred with Tom Mix in *The Range Riders* (1910). Among his early motion picture credits are: *Busy Day at the Selig*

daughter Marie Louise Kelley (1874- ?). Janette Stevens Kelley helped William develop and write the four-act play *The Clay Baker* (1905), which premiered in Seattle and became Mong's signature piece, regardless of which company he was affiliated with over the next seven years or so. Marie Louise Kelley would become Mong's first wife (c. 1906). At this time, Marie was part of Mong's repertory company that also included C.M. DeVere, Edwin Vivien and Clara Engersoll. Mong and his company performed such works in rep as *Till Death Do Us Part*, *The Girl of the Mountains*, *An Irish Peacemaker* and *The Prodigal Son*. Showing entrepreneurial drive, William and Marie Louise Mong opened the School of Dramatic Art in Klamath Falls, Oregon, teaching drama, elocution, public reading and speaking, while continuing their careers on stage. When Marie's father, David C. Kelley, died in October 1907, the local paper noted the Mongs were with him at his bedside. Their marriage, however, broke up soon thereafter.

Mong really achieved his first theatrical notoriety in the character of Peter Denig in *The Clay Baker* at the Chicago Opera House in March 1906, but toured extensively in the play all over the country. Reviewers in various cities and towns hailed Mong's portrayal as "exceptionally clever," as well as "remarkable, artistic and astonishing." The clay baker, an old Pennsylvania Dutchman, invents

The Girl in Lower 9 (1916): **Frequent Universal co-stars Cleo Madison and William V. Mong**

A Connecticut Yankee in King Arthur's Court (1921): **William V. Mong as Merlin, with Harry C. Myers**

General Office (1911), *Buddy, the Little Guardian* (1911) and, as Tony, in *The Survival of the Fittest* (1911), all for Selig. The latter, written by Mong, involved a love triangle among three circus animal trainers. Mong also played the father of popular Selig star Kathlyn Williams in *Back to the Primitive* (1911).

While working on *Back to the Primitive*, Mong experienced a major falling out with director Otis Turner. Mong informed Selig that, due to creative and control issues, the two men could no longer work together. Selig recalled Mong to the company headquarters in Chicago and gave him an interesting assignment. Mong was to lead a Selig film crew to Escanaba, Michigan (substituting for Labrador), making two shorts that attempted to provide an accurate illustration of Eskimo life. While also portraying a trapper, Mong directed *The Way of the Eskimo* (1911), featuring Nancy Columbia, a well-known Inuit beauty. William followed this with *Lost in the Arctic* (1911), in which he played Davis, an explorer, while utilizing native Inuit as performers in both films. Mong had played Jan Kruga, again opposite Kathlyn Williams, in *Lost in the Jungle* (1911), the last film made in Jacksonville, Florida under the Selig banner. Mong's scenes in the latter were shot prior to his recall to Chicago, but *Lost in the Jungle* was not released until after the two arctic-themed Selig films.

On April 26, 1911 Mong would wed for the second time to the former Mildred Ellen Payne (1884-1968), who was originally from Iowa. William and Mildred were married at the Centenary United Methodist Church in St. Louis, Missouri. Initially the couple established residence in Chicago, but later lived for a time in Colorado Springs, Colorado, while William worked for the Pike's Peak Company. Mildred would give birth to a son, William Lewellyn Mong (sometimes referred to as William Mong, Jr.), on March 17, 1918. The couple and child would eventually reside at 1600 Golden Gate Avenue in Los Angeles, California. Mildred died on September 18, 1968, at the age of 84. William Lewellyn Mong would live to the age of 78, passing away in Corona del Mar, California, on April 5, 1996.

From time to time, Mong would request a leave from Colonel Selig in order to return to the stage, appearing in locations like Spokane, Washington and Vancouver, British Columbia, in *The House Next Door*. One Vancouver critic opined (9/23/11):

> Mr. Mong is an actor par excellence, and what is more, he is a character painter of rare attainment—an artist who possesses the skill and intellect to interpret such a delicate character as that of Sir John Cotswold without arousing the least trace of race strife or prejudice.

An actor to whom Mong frequently drew comparisons was the late Joseph Jefferson (1829-1905), famed for his portrayal of Rip Van Winkle.

Monte Cristo (1922): **Caderousse (William V. Mong) with a vengeful Monte Cristo (John Gilbert)**

All the Brothers Were Valiant **(1923): William V. Mong as the cook**

between *The Clay Baker* and *An Unexpected Fortune*, Selig Polyscope released over 400 short films.

While working for Selig, Mong allegedly was responsible for the screen's first close-up. Filling in as assistant cameraman on a short, Mong accidentally cut off the hero just below his collar, which Selig reacted to with great indignation. Mong used to tell the story (e.g., *Picture Show*, 1/3/25) that he and Selig missed their chance to be pioneers, leaving that honor to D.W. Griffith.

After leaving Selig Polyscope, William once again returned to the stage. Mong spoke to a reporter from *The Cleveland Leader* (6/24/13) about the importance of theatrical training for a screen performer:

> I deplore the partial passing of the old-time stock company, and I consider it was far and away the best school, not only for the speaking stage generally, but for the screen platform as well. It is a hard school, but it teaches young men and women how to comport themselves and how not to move their arms and legs. It gives them poise and dignity, and instead of making them unnatural, it enables them to act as though they were ordinary human beings.

Rodney Lee (*Toledo Blade*, 12/19/12) interviewed Mong when he was in Toledo, Ohio, at the Lyceum performing as Dopie Doe, a victim of the drug habit, in *The*

In the Palace of the King **(1923): Aileen Pringle with the ingratiating William V. Mong**

Back to the film business, Mong had an interesting role as chemist Harley Abel, who rebounds from disaster mixing gases to invent a powerful illuminating light in *The Girl He Left Behind* (1912). Other Selig vehicles for Mong were *All on Account of Checkers* (1912) and *The Redemption of "Greek Joe"* (1912), which William also directed. In fact, Mong either wrote the original screenplay, adapted a story for the screen, or directed numerous Selig offerings, including: *A Summer Adventure* (1911), *Two Old Pals* (1912), *When Memory Calls* (1912), *In Little Italy* (1912), *The Slip* (1912), *Sons of the North Woods* (1912), *His Chance to Make Good* (1912), *Driftwood* (1912), *The Vagabond* (1912), *A Citizen in the Making* (1912), *On the Trail of Germs* (1912) and *An Unexpected Fortune* (1912). It is difficult to determine Mong's total output as an actor, writer and director for the studio in that, in his 2½ years

Thy Name is Woman **(1924): The brutish Pedro (William V. Mong) beats his wife (Barbara LaMarr).**

Divorce Question. Sharing his impressions of the actor, Lee noted:

> In figure Mr. Mong is tall and slender, erect and virile. His face is that of the student, a high brow accentuating the deep-set brown eyes that are serious in expression, and introspective, as though trying to fathom some great mental or spiritual problem. They betoken imagination and suggest a contemplative habit of mind. His mouth is flexible and of engaging sweetness when he smiles, yet his square chin shows tremendous will power, and invincible determination and courage. In talking with him his poise and perfect self-control are in striking contrast to the vagaries, mental and physical, of the boy who has sunk to the depths—yet still retains the leaven of good birth and breeding. He is rather diffident, possessing none of the aggressive and egotistic attributes usually associated with actors. But he talks well. His wide experience with life has given

him positive ideas and he expresses them fluently, entertainingly and convincingly.

When asked by Lee how he came to play a drug addicted youth in such a realistic manner, Mong explained:

> In the first place I built the foundation of the impersonation upon the lines of the play. They give the inner vision of the poor boy. Then I spent a great deal of time in the slums, studying types, and by combining the two processes I arrived at the result you are good enough to say what is true, convincing and artistic.

Over the next two years, interspersed with his burgeoning screen career, Mong would appear in *The Divorce Question* in many vicinities, including Chicago, Cincinnati and Brooklyn, New York.

Another vehicle for Mong in vaudeville around this time was *The Dyspeptic (*1913), in which he played a crusty old man. He briefly joined Margaret Fields' Stock Company in the summer of 1914, appearing in such works as *The Awakening of Helena Ritchie.*

What Price Glory? (1926): Dolores Del Rio with her manipulative father William V. Mong

Mong began to focus more on motion pictures at this point in time. He starred as Captain Rawley in *The Yellow Traffic* (1914). Mong also made an early appearance for Carl Laemmle's Universal (for whom he would soon be a contract player) in *Tainted Money* (1915). In early 1915, Mong succeeded George Gebhart as the assistant manager of the Pike's Peak Company studio. He was placed in charge of the scenario department, initially writing two-reel Westerns. Mong's first effort for that studio's Lariat division was *The Cost* (1915), followed by *The Parasite's Double* (1915). In a foreshadowing of things to come, Mong was paired with Cleo Madison in *Alias Holland Jimmy* (1915), which he both wrote and directed. Also for Lariat, Mong wrote and starred in *Told in the Rockies* (1915), involving mountain folk encountering Native Americans, as well as *The Word* (1915), in which he played Billy Whiskers, a religious convert who disappoints the evangelist's daughter when he returns to bank robbing. In *Out of the Silence* (1915), Mong was Fred Madison, a drug addicted young man who loses his way in the Yosemite Valley while en route to a sanitarium, but he finds his cure in nature. Other shorts Mong penned for the company were: *Montana Blunt*

(1915), *The Sins That Ye Sin* (1916) and *The Awakening of Bess Morton* (1916). Otis Thayer directed most of Mong's films with Pike's Peak. Breaking away from Pike's Peak/Lariat, Mong appeared in *The Severed Hand* (1916) with future director Edward Sloman. Mong and Sloman would become lifelong friends, with the latter utilizing William in at least 11 of his films over the next 20 years.

In the spring of 1916, in the early days of Universal, Mong signed a contract with Carl Laemmle, which would provide steady work for well over a year. *Two Men of Sandy Bar* (1916) featured Mong, as Don Jose de Castro, opposite Hobart Bosworth. Directed by the noteworthy Lois Weber, *Eleanor's Catch* (1916, a film that still exists) had Mong, as "Flash" Darcy, the town loser who attempts to lure Cleo Madison into criminal ways. Mong and Madison were a successful pairing, with the two co-directing a number of films, for which William wrote many of the scenarios. As the miserly, uncaring factory owner Henry Burke in *Her Bitter Cup* (1916), Mong is eventually redeemed by Cleo Madison's sincerity and dedication. Other Madison/Mong ventures included: *Virginia* (1916), *Alias Jane Jones* (1916), *When the Wolf Howls* (1916), *The Girl in Lower 9*

***Noah's Ark* (1928): Louise Fazenda and William V. Mong**

***The House of Horror* (1929): Louise Fazenda receives an unexpected visitor, William V. Mong.**

(1916), *The Guilty One* (1916), *Along the Malibu* (1916) and *To Another Woman* (1916). *The Crimson Yoke* (1916) had Mong as the sensitive yet avenging Phillippe Caribi of mixed race who comes to the rescue of Ms. Madison. Universal also utilized Mong as Slim in *The Iron Hand* (1916), lecherous singer "Cabaret" Charlie in *Shoes* (1916) and Kansas Reeves in *The Good Woman* (1916). Among the short films Mong directed and wrote (and sometimes starred in) for Universal were: *A Son of Neptune* (1916), *Husks of Love* (1916), *The Gates of Eternity* (1916), *The Wrath of Cactus Moore* (1916), *The Son of a Rebel Chief* (1916), *His Old Plantation Home* (1916) and *Birds of a Feather* (1916). In *The Prince of Graustark* (1916), Mong was the aide to a count (Sidney Ainsworth). He was first-billed as Colonel Morgan in *Last of the Morgans* (1916), which Mong scripted and directed. Mong was a triple threat once again in *Fighting Joe* (1916), wherein he played a bad man regenerated by his friend-

ship with a young boy (Buddy Messinger). Not only did Mong write, direct and act in *The Case of Dr. Hawley* (1916), he played the dual role of father and son, both doctors who are cursed by alcoholism. The son, however, finds the strength and courage to fight his demons as he labors to combat an outburst of infantile paralysis.

An Old Soldier's Romance (1917) had Mong as Ezra, a beloved old veteran living at the Soldiers' Home, who visits an orphan asylum and secretly takes eight babies back with him. Mong directed and starred in *The Daring Chance* (1917). As the honorable Peter Barnitz, Mong appeared in a dream to his son, who as governor is faced with a dilemma over an assassin's death sentence, in *The Girl and the Crisis* (1917). Mong had the title role in *Good-for-Nothing Gallagher* (1917), which he directed. He was first-billed (while also writing and directing) in *The Grudge* (1917), *A Darling in Buckskin* (1917) and *Chubby Takes a Hand* (1917), in which William played Mark Frawley. As John Gallagher, Mong was a wealthy, retired politician with a younger, calculating wife in *Bartered Youth* (1917).

Leaving Universal, Mong took on the ambitious project *The Chosen Prince, or The Friendship of David and Jonathan* (1917), an eight-reeler filmed in Monrovia, California, for the Crest Picture Company. The company constructed a Palestine village and other sets in Clover Leaf Canyon, with filming going on for a number of months under the auspices of Mong. In addition to directing, William played the role of Samuel, the last of Israel's Judges, who actively seeks out the shepherd David (Edward Alexander) with the realization of greatness to come. Mong had some harsh

The Sign of the Cross (1932): The villainous Tigellinus (Ian Keith) with his aide Licinius (William V. Mong, in one of two roles he assayed in the film).

lessons on location, as on one day when he had to pay 300 extras despite the fact no footage could be shot due to inclement weather.

Returning to the security of a contract employee, Mong joined Triangle, directing *Wild Sumac* (1917), starring Margery Wilson. Also for Triangle, Mong played Professor Hugo Groesback, an anarchist who dies in gruesome fashion in a metal cauldron, in *Fanatics* (1917). Mong remained with Triangle for about a year, playing the title role in *The Hopper* (1918); Petain Monest, the trapper father of Margery Wilson, in *The Law of the Great Northwest* (1918); newspaper editor William Oglesby in *The Man Who Woke Up* (1918); and florist Daniel Fanjoy, opposite Alma Rubens, in *The Painted Lily* (1918).

An item in *Motion Picture World* (2/9/18) noted that Mong's wife Mildred had been discharged from a Los Angeles hospital back to their home after undergoing a serious operation. Mong reported that his wife's condition had "greatly improved." Another *Motion Picture World*

(*MPW*) piece from April 1918 claimed that Mong had acquired several rare prints of Matthew Brady photographs of Abraham Lincoln. *MPW* added, "Mong, who has long been a student of everything pertaining to Lincoln, counts them among his cherished possessions."

In June of 1918, Mong realized a long-time dream when he purchased 10 acres of land in the citrus belt of Whittier, California. He drew up the plans and built a ranch, which he named "Your Duroc Farm." Although the land already had orange trees, Mong was more interested in raising animals, including chickens, rabbits and especially pigs. One 1918 clipping quoted Mong as saying, "This pig will be a source of support to me in my old age," as he actually bottlefed a baby pig on the set of one of his Triangle pictures. The paper noted that Mong was mourning the loss of a pet goose, making him even more protective of the baby pig, "which he now guards with anxious paternal solicitude." Soon after the ranch was completed, Mong focused on raising and breeding Duroc-

The Mayor of Hell (1932): James Cagney, Dudley Digges and William V. Mong

Treasure Island (1934): The frightening Blind Pew (William V. Mong) is escorted by Jim Hawkins (Jackie Cooper).

Jersey pigs in particular. His most famous boar was "My Partner," who sired numerous offspring, many of which William sold at auction. In addition, Mong entered many of his Duroc pigs at the California State Fair and other livestock shows, winning numerous awards, mainly from 1920-1922.

The Flame of the West (1918) reunited Mong with Cleo Madison at Universal. As the kindly bookkeeper Stetson in *The Spender* (1919), Mong took Bert Lytell into his home, only to have the man fall in love with his daughter (Mary Anderson). *Put Up Your Hands!* (1919) had William as "High-ball" Hazelitt, mistaken for a bandit by Margarita Fischer. As Larry McKean in *The Delicious Little Devil* (1919), Mong was the manager of the Peach Tree Inn where Mae Murray dances. Rudolph Valentino had a featured role in this film, which has been preserved. *The Follies Girl* (1919), starring Olive Thomas, had Mong as Edward Woodruff, a dying old millionaire who is nursed back to health by a girl posing as his imagined granddaughter. A prophetic comedy about heart transplants, *After His Own Heart* (1919), included Mong as Judah P. Corpus, a rich elderly man who wishes to remain youthful by trying to pay to receive a young man's heart. Mong played Sebastian Ritter in *The Master Man* (1919), a political drama starring Frank Keenan. *The Amateur Adventuress* (1919) featured Mong as William Claxtonbury, the lecherous head of the Working Girls' Welfare Association. Another Olive Thomas film (that fortunately still exists), *Love's Prisoner* (1919), had a third-billed Mong as Jonathan Twist, an elderly jeweler and a fence for thieves. The *New York Telegraph* (5/25/19) found that Mong "does capital work" as the caring old man who looks out for Thomas and her little sisters. As Mr. Tompkins in *Fools and Their Money* (1919), Mong is pressured by his wife (Betty K. Peterson) to use their newfound wealth to move into an exclusive neighborhood and enroll their son (Jack Mulhall) at Yale, despite their meager beginnings.

Based on a Jack London novel, *Burning Daylight* (1920) had Mong as Necessity, the old friend of Mitchell Lewis in the title role. Opposite Bessie Barriscale, Mong played Leo Goldman in *The Luck of Geraldine Laird* (1920) and Charlie Mayo in *Life's Twist* (1920). Other roles at this point of Mong's career were: Mr. Rivett in *The Turning Point* (1920), Jake Trebs in *Number 99* (1920), Professor Dillinger in *The Chorus Girl's Romance* (1920), John Gallagher in *The Dwelling Place of Light* (1920), Chapman in *813* (1920) and an old miner in *The Coast of Opportunity* (1920). Mong was in fine conniving form as Solon Hammerhead, an evil, manipulative banker, in *The County Fair* (1920), another existing silent. Hammerhead threatens to foreclose Edith

Together We Live (1935): Civil war veterans William V. Mong and Hughie Mack compete at horseshoes.

Arbuckle. *The Ten Dollar Raise* (1921) offered Mong the leading role of Wilkins, the bookkeeper who has labored for 20 years for an abusive boss who never delivered on his annual promise of a pay increase. Wilkins has been unable to marry the stenographer he has loved for years and has even more problems when his employer's son pawns off some land on him that turns out to be under water. When oil is discovered on the property, Wilkins attains wealth, buys out his employer's stock and marries his long-time sweetheart. The *New York Times* (6/13/21) commented, "William V. Mong, as the worm that turns, gives an appealing performance."

Shame (1921) featured Mong as Li Chung, the faithful servant to a missionary (John Gilbert) in China. *Pilgrims of the Night* (1921), starring Lewis Stone, gave Mong the interesting role of Ambrose, a hunchbacked street musician who escapes from prison and frames Stone for robbery. *Ladies Must Live* (1921) had Mong as Max Bleeker, the father of Betty Compson. In a film reminiscent of Mong's early work for Selig, he appeared in *Arctic Adventure* (1922). A story of India under British rule adapted by Mong, *Shattered Idols* (1922), starred Marguerite De La Motte and featured William as Rama Pal, a vengeful Hindu. For Fox and director Emmett Flynn, Mong played Boggs in *A Fool There Was* (1922) and Gaspard Caderousse, the greedy, cowardly innkeeper, in *Monte Cristo* (1922). (A print of *Monte Cristo* was located in the Czech Republic many years later and eventually released on DVD with another John Gilbert feature, *Bardelys the Magnificent*,1926.) *The Woman He Loved* (1922) was the last film written by Mong and the final motion picture he made under contract with J.L. Frothingham. Directed by his friend Edward Sloman, *The Woman He Loved* had Mong first-billed as Nathan Levinsky, a Russian Jew who immigrates to America to avoid persecution, rises from a peddler to become a successful rancher, only to lose all in a fire, before being reunited with his estranged wife.

Motion Picture (3/17/22) mentioned Mong's tragic misfortune in early 1922 as a "calamity item:"

> Half a dozen highbred pigs on the ranch of the well-known character actor, William V. Mong, were drowned during the recent record-breaking rainstorms in Southern California.

Chapman's farm and wants to marry off his weakling son (Arthur Housman) to pretty Helen Jerome Eddy, going so far as to fix the climactic horse race with an illegal battery device. As Snoop Jenkins, known as "The Rat," Mong helped Noah Beery start a mutiny during a heavy storm in *The Mutiny of the Elsinore* (1920), adapted from Jack London's novel and directed by Edward Sloman.

A Connecticut Yankee in King Arthur's Court (1920), based on the novel by Mark Twain, was brought to the screen by Fox featuring a fine cast, including Harry Myers in the lead (Martin Cavendish), Pauline Starke as his love interest, Rosemary Theby as Morgan le Fay, Charles Clary as King Arthur and George Siegmann as Sir Sagramore. Mong was in his element as Merlin the Magician, who is threatened by the presence of Martin and insists he be burned at the stake. The resourceful Martin accurately predicts a solar eclipse, escaping death and further enraging Merlin. Unfortunately, only fragments of this film exist, so Mong's villainous turn is not available for closer scrutiny.

Mong portrayed a Western villain in *The Winding Trail* (1921). He was featured in two films headlined by Anita Stewart: as Watkins in *Sowing the Wind* (1921), a tale of opium and gambling, and as Conklin in *Playthings of Destiny* (1921), both for Louis B. Mayer. He played a minor part in *The Traveling Salesman* (1921), which starred Roscoe "Fatty"

Fiercely devoted to his livestock and pets, Mong suffered great emotional distress from these losses. Because he had invested such love and effort into breeding, showing and caring for his animals, Mong never fully got over this incident.

In Metro's version of Ben Ames Williams' whaling yarn, *All the Brothers Were Valiant* (1923), with Lon Chaney, Billie Dove and Malcolm McGregor in the leads, Mong (whom Chaney fondly called "Billy") played the ship's cook. *Lost and Found on a South Sea Island* (1923), directed by Raoul Walsh, had Mong as Skinner. The film was made, in part, in Tahiti, so Mong had to secure a passport (still viewable on the internet) to travel for the location shots. *Penrod and Sam* (1923) featured Mong as Deacon Bitts, whose car accidentally runs over the beloved fox terrier of Penrod (Ben Alexander). *Wandering Daughters* (1923) provided Mong with the sympathetic role of Will Bowden, the understanding father of Marguerite De La Motte, who sacrifices the family's meager savings to assure his

The Last of the Mohicans (1936): The judicious Sachem (William V. Mong) lectures Hawkeye (Randolph Scott).

daughter's happiness. *Drifting* (1923), written and directed by Tod Browning, starred Browning favorite Priscilla Dean and Wallace Beery. *Drifting* made use of Mong's versatility as Dr. Li, the father of Anna May Wong, involved in a Chinese opium ring. (The National Film Preservation Foundation has slated *Drifting* for preservation as part of a 2012 grant.) Mong had another colorful portrayal (as witnessed by extant stills) as Don Antonio Perez in Goldwyn's lavish *In the Palace of the King* (1923), with Blanche Sweet, Edmund Lowe and Pauline Starke. The cunningly evil Perez ingratiates himself to King Phillip II (Sam De Grasse), gaining the monarch's confidence even while working his treachery on others.

Although Mong had already assayed a number of villainous film roles, his portrayal of the brutal, jealous smuggler Pedro the Fox in *Thy Name is Woman* (1924) almost typecast William as a screen "heavy." Wed to the beautiful young Guerita (Barbara La Marr), the much older Pedro showers his bride with gifts gained from his illegal activity. When she shifts her attention to a young soldier (Ramon Novarro), however, the incensed Pedro beats and finally kills Guerita, before he himself succumbs to heart failure.

Other parts for Mong at this point were: Enoch Metcalf in *Flapper Wives* (1924), the sympathetic Grandpa Sutton in *Why Men Leave Home* (1924) and factory owner Henry

McLean in *What Shall I Do?* (1924). Mong had the intriguing role of hotel handyman and part-time inventor Clem Beemis, who befriends a Jewish man (Dore Davidson), victimized by prejudice in a narrow-minded New England town, in *Welcome Stranger* (1924). Beemis encourages the man to invest in an electric light plant, which brings great benefit to the town, making heroes of them both.

Barriers Burned Away (1925), set amidst the Great Chicago Fire of 1871, had Mong as Peg-leg Sullivan. He played the meek Reverend Dr. Temple in *Excuse Me* (1925), with Norma Shearer and Conrad Nagel as lovers. *Oh, Doctor* (1925), an existing silent, included Mong as Mr. McIntosh, one of three conniving loan sharks who anticipate collecting Reginald Denny's inheritance as repayment for a debt. They need Denny to first survive for three years, however, which leads to a series of dangerous but humorous situations. *Speed* (1925) featured Mong as Sam Whipple, the father of jazz-crazed children, who must contend with fast cars and crooks who kidnap his daughter (Pauline Garon). *Up the Ladder* (1925), another surviving silent, starred Virginia Valli and had Mong as Richards. In *Alias Mary Flynn* (1925), Mong played John Reagan, a former con who provides refuge to Mary (Evelyn Brent) but then gets framed for murder, because of his past. Mong played Doc Haskell in *Under the Rouge* (1925), Philip in *Fine Clothes* (1925) and Randall in *The Unwritten Law* (1925).

Off the Highway (1925) featured Mong in a dual role, wealthy Caleb Fry and his servant Tatterly (to whom he bears a remarkable resemblance). The judgmental, miserly Fry disinherits his nephew (John Bowers) over his choice of career. When Tatterly dies, Fry assumes his identity, but is tossed from the home by the worthless cousin (Charles K. Gerrard) who comes into the money of the old man, who is believed to have died. Fry is taken in by his nephew and girlfriend Marguerite De La Motte, rebuilds his fortune, ruins his cousin and endows the young couple with his wealth. The role of Caleb Fry was said to be a tour de force for Mong.

The People vs. Nancy Preston (1925) had Mong as an abusive, lecherous criminal, who is murdered, resulting in star Marguerite De La Motte being falsely accused of the deed. As shady lawyer Robert Glaxson in *The Shadow on the Wall* (1925), Mong attempted to poison wealthy Willis Marks, with designs on his family fortune. Mong played Nicker in *Steel Preferred* (1925), while also appearing in *Lights of Old Broadway* (1925).

Shadow of the Law (1926) had Mong as sympathetic gunman and thief "Twist" Egan, who exposes Stuart Holmes as a murderer in order to vindicate star Clara Bow. Mong had no moral compass, however, as wealthy, malicious stockbroker Peter Heffner in *Fifth Avenue* (1926). As Slaney, Mong was a henchman of gang leader Montagu Love posing as a butler on an estate in *Brooding Eyes* (1926). As Michael O'Day, William was second-billed to Priscilla Moran in *No Babies Wanted* (1926). He played George, the rich capitalist father of the Bride (Martha Sleeper), in the Charlie Chase short *Crazy Like a Fox* (1926). *The Old Soak* (1926), starring Jean Hersholt, gave Mong the dastardly role of sanctimonious Cousin Webster, on the surface a pillar of the church and a bank president, but actually in league with a gang of bootleggers. Mong played Kobol in *The Silent Lover* (1926), a Foreign Legion tale with Milton Sills. *The Strong Man* (1926), directed by Frank Capra and one of the best Harry Langdon features still in existence, had Mong as Parson Brown, the Cloverdale minister known to all as "Holy Joe."

One of Mong's most noteworthy silent roles still available for viewing today was that of Cognac Pete, the father of Charmaine (Dolores Del Rio), in *What Price Glory?* (1926), directed by Raoul Walsh. Amidst the setting of a small French Village during World War I, Cognac Pete is the proprietor of an inn and bar, where Quirt (Edmund Lowe) and Flagg (Victor McLaglen) literally battle over his daughter. The innkeeper advises Charmaine to "give them nothing … free." On one level a protective father, yet more of a manipulative businessman (he claims a soldier "wrecked" his daughter and insists that the man marry her—and pay Pete 500 francs), Cognac Pete allowed Mong to show various dimensions of his acting ability.

The Magic Garden (1927), adapted from Gene Stratton Porter's classic story, had Mong as John Forrester, the father of young aspiring violinist Phillippe De Lacy. *The Price of Honor* (1927) gave Mong another complex part as Daniel B. Hoyt, an innocent man paroled after 15 years in prison. Hoyt is mistaken for a burglar when he attempts to visit his niece (Dorothy Revier) and later commits suicide while attempting to frame the son of the judge who sentenced him for murder. *Too Many Crooks* (1927) included Mong as Coxey the conman, part of a gang of criminals brought to a house party by playwright Lloyd Hughes. Mong portrayed Nosey Ricketts in *Taxi! Taxi!* (1927), a comedy starring Edward Everett Horton. *The Clown* (1927) gave Mong the tragic role of Albert Wells, part owner of a circus and a performing clown, who discovers his wife in the arms of lion tamer John Miljan. As the two men struggle, the wife is accidentally killed, with Wells sentenced to life imprisonment as a result. Years later, Wells escapes prison in a clown costume, exacts revenge on the lion tamer, saves his now grown daughter from an elephant stampede, but is killed in the process. *Alias the Lone Wolf* (1927), with Bert Lytell in the title role, featured Mong as Whitaker Monk, a jewel thief posing as a customs agent. Mong's appearance in another Charlie Chase short, *The Way of All Pants* (1927), has not been confirmed.

Mong married for the third and final time to English-born Esme Isabel Haigh Warde in 1928. (It is undetermined when and how Mong's second marriage to Mildred Ellen Payne ended.) Esme shared William's great love of animals. For a time, she maintained an aviary at their ranch, housing various birds (reportedly over 200) from all over the globe. She also spent time training dogs, winning an award for exhibiting her prized pinscher, for example, at the Oakland Kennel Club in 1932. Esme Warde worked as a librarian in the Hollywood area for many years and eventually opened her own bookshop. She was quite the bibliophile and would often seek out rare books for use by the major studios. Esme had a daughter, Barbara Esme Warde, from a previous marriage. Barbara, born March 31, 1918, would be raised by William and his wife, but would never change her name to Mong. In fact, she went by her mother's name, Esme Warde, when she went to work for the MGM publicity department in 1942. The younger Esme worked with many of MGM's stable of stars, including Judy Garland, Ava Gardner, Katharine Hepburn, Spencer Tracy and Grace Kelly. Clark Gable was so impressed by her integrity that he, as a client, followed Warde when she left MGM to join the public relations firm of Cleary, Strauss and Irvin in 1958. Eventually Esme opened her own agency in 1961, representing John Cassavetes, Gena Rowlands and a young Tom Selleck. Married to Ellis Hurst Chandlee, Esme was widowed on 9/6/88. Mong's stepdaughter Esme Warde Chandlee passed away at the age of 94 on November 23, 2012, receiving warm tributes from various trade papers and individuals, having earned great respect for her accomplishments in the film industry.

Mong portrayed Santo Bendito in *The Broken Mask* (1928) and appeared in the drama *White Flame* (1928). In *The Devil's Trademark* (1928), Mong, as Fred Benson, and Belle Bennett played an old married couple of thieves who make erratic attempts to "go straight" for the sake of their children. *Telling the World* (1928) had Mong as the city newspaper editor who gives new employee William Haines the undesirable assignment of interviewing the wealthy father who has disowned him.

Ransom (1928) presented Mong with one of his most vile roles as warlord Wu Fang, the dastardly leader of the Chinese underground. Wu Fang and his henchmen try to obtain the formula for a deadly colorless, odorless gas that destroys the nervous system of its victims from chemical genius Edmund Burns. Using kidnapping and torture in a vain attempt to reach his goal, Wu Fang eventually meets a violent end through suffocation caused by carbon dioxide that had been substituted for the more potent gas.

Mong again was a heinous evildoer in *Code of the Air* (1928), playing Professor Ross, a mad genius who has perfected a weapon that emits lethal kappa rays. Trying out his death ray on an aircraft, Ross is ecstatic when the plane loses power and plunges in flames to the ground. Moving his gang near the flight path of commercial aircraft, Ross has designs on taking down planes that carry stocks, bonds and money in fireproof metal boxes, but is thwarted by Kenneth Harlan before he can wreak greater destruction.

An early partial talkie, *Should a Girl Marry?* (1928), had Mong as a wealthy banker who denounces his son's fiancée, robs from his own bank and ends up dead in a scuffle with a detective. Mong was prominently featured in the Fox short *Forget Me Not* (1928). In the massive Warner Bros.

The Dark Hour (1936): Brothers William V. Mong and Hobart Bosworth

production *Noah's Ark* (1928), Mong had a dual role, that of a guard in the biblical scenes and the innkeeper in the modern story. The innkeeper and his tavern maid (Louise Fazenda) deal with travelers, including Dolores Costello and George O'Brien, following a massive train wreck.

The Haunted House (1928) marked the first of three comedy/mystery/thrillers in which Mong would be featured for noted Danish director Benjamin Christensen. In this first offering, William was the sinister caretaker who menaces Thelma Todd amidst the creepy proceedings, which turn out to be a ruse to test the nature of prospective heirs to the fortune of millionaire Edmund Breese. *Seven Footprints to Satan* (1929), the only surviving film of Christensen's trilogy, followed. Mong was more sympathetic this time, albeit in make-up that gave him an animal-like appearance, as the Professor. One of many bizarre characters, including a dwarf (Angelo Rossitto), a witch (Nora Cecil) and an ape (Charles Gemora), the Professor actually appears to be helpful toward the bewildered Creighton Hale and Thelma Todd in a most peculiar residence with sliding panels and hidden passageways. Again, a rational explanation follows all the strange, almost supernatural events. The final Christensen opus, *The House of Horror* (1928), had Mong as "the mystery man," who once again frightens Thelma Todd in a strange house full of unusual people. Although all of the three had a non-horror denouement, it is still a shame that *The Haunted House* and *The House of Horror* are presumed lost films, denying modern viewers the chance to witness Mong (and others) in very flashy roles.

Dark Skies (1929) included Mong as Mr. Morgan, who, with his niece (Shirley Mason), rents umbrellas in a coastal southern California town before winding up involved with rum-runners and government agents. As down and out lawyer Anthony Sommers, Mong is falsely accused and convicted of the murder of a diamond thief in *Murder on the Roof* (1930). Mong portrayed family patriarch Mr. Ward, whose sudden death greatly impacts his children, including William Haines and Frank "Junior" Coghlan, in *The Girl Said No* (1930). Another MGM film, *In Gay Madrid* (1930), starring Ramon Novarro, had Mong as Rivas. For Fox, William played Caleb in *Double Cross Roads* (1930). He then played Wellmore, interacting with young John Wayne in the early trading post sequence of *The Big Trail* (1930). Mong portrayed Colonel Marshall in *The Flood* (1931), prospector "Strike" Jackson in *Gun Smoke* (1931) and Lionel in *A Dangerous Affair* (1931). In *Bad Company* (1931), an early gangster film starring Ricardo Cortez, Mong was seen as Henry.

Having appeared in a number of Westerns during his early silent film period, Mong now would become a semi-regular in the Columbia cowboy features of Tim McCoy. Mong played Uncle John Lyman in *The Fighting Fool* (1932), record-falsifying Gafford in *Fighting for Justice* (1932), duplicitous lawyer Oscar Sikes in *Silent Men* (1933) and treacherous banker Ezra Root in *Square Shooter* (1932), all with McCoy in the lead.

In a film revealed through a series of flashbacks, Mong played the overbearing Emory Wells, who is shot in the head resulting in his son (Donald Dillaway) being tried for his murder, in *Cross Examination* (1932). *Love Bound* (aka *Murder on the High Seas*, 1932) had Mong as the crooked lawyer of Natalie Moorhead. Mong appeared in *Arm of the Law* (1932), with Rex Bell and Lina Basquette, *Widow in Scarlet* (1932) and *Rule 'Em and Weep* (1932), a Masquers Club short loaded with gifted character actors like James Gleason, Luis Alberni, Russell Simpson, Maurice Black and Matthew Betz. *Dynamite Denny* (1932), a railroad drama released by Mayfair starring Jay Wilsey, gave Mong an interesting role as William B. Marston, who used to be in charge of the company but now goes undercover as itinerant fireman Little Bill, in order to grasp the labor issues of the working men.

By Whose Hand? (1932), set on a train and displaying interesting work from Ben Lyon, Barbara Weeks and Dwight Frye as a squealer, had Mong as J.W. Martin (aka Graham). The bitter Martin had a reason for seeking vengeance on murdered womanizing jeweler Kenneth Thomson, who fired him and had him sent to jail years before. As wealthy industrialist Elias Moorehouse in *Women Won't Tell* (1932), Mong refuses to acknowledge fathering a young daughter (June Bennett), resulting in her living her early years in dire poverty. In the star-studded *If I Had a Million* (1932), Mong was briefly seen as Harry, the fence for forger George Raft, one of the recipients of a wealthy man's beneficence. Mong played Longman in the Janet Gaynor-remake of *Tess of the Storm Country* (1932) and Burkehart, a member of Walter Connolly's bank board, in *No More Orchids* (1932).

In the busy year of 1932, in which Mong was on view in at least 15 films, two titles deserve particular mention. *A Strange Adventure* (1932), produced by I.E. Chadwick and released by Monogram, had Mong as wealthy Silas Wayne, who assembles his relatives in order to read his will (and insult each member as he reveals what that relative is to receive) prior to his death. Silas appears to have a heart attack during the process and is tended to by Dr. Bailey (Jason Robards, Sr.), who covertly stabs the mean old man with a knife instead. Bailey, it turns out, was the illegitimate offspring of Wayne's tryst with his housekeeper (Lucille La Verne). *A Strange Adventure* has attained a minor cult status with the presence of Dwight Frye, June Clyde, a hooded figure and other spooky old house effects. Cecil B. DeMille's epic *The Sign of the Cross* (1932) offered Mong two distinct roles (rather than a dual role). William is first observed as Licinius (with dark hair and clean-shaven), the evil calculating aide to ruthless Ian Keith, who uses murder, abduction and torture to suit his needs. Just prior to the Christians being led up the stairs to their martyrdom at the climax, Mong is recognizable behind a long white beard, as a kindly old man comforting a young girl whose mother had been killed by Keith's soldiers.

By 1933, Mong, his wife Esme and her daughter Barbara Esme were living at 2219 Proser Avenue, Santa Monica, California. It is uncertain as to what point in time Mong was compelled to give up Your Duroc Farm, the ranch in Whittier he dreamed of and deeply loved.

The Vampire Bat (1933), another independent (Majestic) production that has achieved lasting notoriety with a wonderful cast including Fay Wray, Lionel Atwill, Melvyn Douglas, Maude Eburne and Dwight Frye, featured Mong as Sauer, the most vindictive of the angry villagers in the terror-ridden town of Kleinschloss. After the mob chases Herman (Frye) to his death, it is Sauer who insists on driving a stake through the feeble-minded youth's heart in the belief he is a vampire responsible for a series of deaths.

Mong played the executor of a wealthy unmarried woman's contested estate in *The Eleventh Commandment* (1933). *The Working Man* (1933) had Mong as the auditor for the Hartland Company, the troubled business owned by the deceased competitor of George Arliss. Mong portrayed an honest druggist in *Lilly Turner* (1933), Mr. Walter (in cahoots with vile Dudley Digges) in *The Mayor of Hell* (1933), board member (of Edward G. Robinson's father's business) Bowen in *I Loved a Woman* (1933) and an auditor (again) in *Footlight Parade* (1932), all for Warner Bros./First National. *Her Forgotten Past* (1933) featured Mong as Manners, a former butler fired from the employ of Monte Blue. Unscrupulous politicians use Manners to plant damaging evidence that will discredit Blue in his re-election campaign. *The Narrow Corner* (1933) had Mong as Jack Swan, the elderly dyspeptic father of Reginald Owen, who sadistically destroys research that his son has worked on for years.

Massacre (1934), with Richard Barthelmess coming to terms with his heritage, had Mong, as Grandy, one of the corrupt officials, including Dudley Digges and Sidney Toler, who oppose Native American rights. In *Dark Hazard* (1934), with Edward G. Robinson, Mong was Plummer, the hotel owner. Again working in a Cecil B. DeMille spectacular, Mong portrayed the court physician with a particular knowledge of snake venom in *Cleopatra* (1934), starring Claudette Colbert. Set during the Spanish-American War, Mong was involved in espionage as the cobbler who locates a code hidden in the heel of a shoe unwittingly brought to him by Hugh Herbert, in the musical *Sweet Adeline* (1934), starring Irene Dunne.

One of Mong's most memorable (although brief) sound roles was that of Blind Pew in MGM's *Treasure Island* (1934). Pew pays a visit to the Admiral Benbow Inn to confront his old double-crossing shipmate Billy Bones (Lionel Barrymore). The blind man terrifies young Jim Hawkins (Jackie Cooper) before delivering the black dot to Bones, portending imminent death. "That's done. That's done," Pew mutters before departing, only to return with hench-

Stand-In (1937): **William V. Mong as Cyrus Pennypacker**

men trying to locate "Flint's Fist," a treasure map. Looking for Jim, Pew bellows, "I should've torn his arm off. I should have put his eyes out," before being abandoned by his men. Pew suffers a pitiful fate when the carriage of Dr. Livesey (Otto Kruger) strikes him down, the wheels rolling over him and crushing him to death.

Featured with Will Rogers, Mong was folksy Uncle Eck in *The County Chairman* (1935). Directed by Robert Florey, *The Florentine Dagger* (1935) had Mong as Fishback working

Painted Desert (1938): In his penultimate screen appearance, William V. Mong is adversarial toward George O'Brien and Stanley Fields.

for detective Robert Barrat. He played Blake, the owner of an antiquated railroad line, in *Whispering Smith Speaks* (1935), opposite George O'Brien. *The Hoosier Schoolmaster* (1935), set in the post-Civil War South, featured Mong as Jake Means, one of the townsfolk dealing with their resentment toward "Yankee" teacher Norman Foster. Working for the final time with director Edward Sloman, Mong appeared as the old storyteller in the prologue of *The Perfect Tribute* (1935), a short told in flashback paying homage to Lincoln's Gettysburg Address. As an old Civil War veteran, alongside Willard Mack, Claude Gillingwater and Hobart Bosworth, Mong, as Johnny, is appalled by what he views as a growing radical movement in America in *Together We Live* (1935). *Rendezvous* (1935), an MGM spy tale of World War I with a great cast, including William Powell, Rosalind Russell and Lionel Atwill, had Mong as a hotel desk clerk.

Arguably Mong's last significant role was that of Cleon in RKO's production of *The Last Days of Pompeii* (1935), produced and directed by the *King Kong* tandem of Merian

C. Cooper and Ernest Schoedsack. Cleon, the slave dealer, first interacts with Marcus (Preston Foster) as the blacksmith is asked to repair the manacles of a huge prisoner (Bruce King) bound for the arena. As the prisoner breaks free, Marcus subdues him, saving Cleon's life. "Beat him, flog him, only don't spoil him for the arena," Cleon beseeches Marcus. As Marcus later rises in the gladiator ranks, Cleon tries to ingratiate himself to the champion. "We both furnish amusement for the people," notes Cleon, while Marcus rebuffs him as a "rat." Cleon tells Marcus that the day will come when he will need him. When Murmex (Ward Bond) injures Marcus in the arena, ending his days as a gladiator, Cleon gloats, "I've looked forward to this," offering the former blacksmith a position securing slaves in Libya. Marcus is forced to accept the sniveling Cleon's offer, triggering a major personality change. As Cleon, Mong runs the gamut from being condescending to showing fear and embarrassment, to finally displaying a sense of twisted vindication. There are many interesting character performances in *The Last Days of Pompeii*, including those by Wyrley Birch, Basil Rathbone, Alan Hale and Zeffie Tilbury, but Mong's work as Cleon is among the best.

As Professor Hendricks in *Strike Me Pink* (1936), Mong interacted with Eddie Cantor in an early sequence at Millwood University. *The Dark Hour* (1936) featured Mong as Henry Carson, elderly brother of Hobart Bosworth, who figuratively suffocates his ward (Irene Ware) before being murdered (and then stabbed in the back when already dead). Mong was Tecolote, the old Indian, who is chained to a mill wheel, in *Dancing Pirate* (1936), an early Technicolor film.

Again as a Native American, Mong was the judicious old Huron Sachem in *The Last of the Mohicans* (1936). The Sachem sits at the head of the Council as Magua (Bruce Cabot) brings Heather Angel and Binnie Barnes before him, demanding the former for his wife. The Sachem states, "Manitou has given us a law. It is for the law to say" (whether Angel becomes an unwilling squaw or dies in "the fire"). When Barnes protests, the Sachem relates, "Our fathers planted corn, hunted deer in these forests many moons before the white man's war canoe crossed the great salt water," emphasizing the fairness of the law. After Henry Wilcoxon, pretending to be Hawkeye, switches identity with Randolph Scott and goes to the Huron camp, Sachem respects Wilcoxon's offer of his life as a warrior for that of Barnes. When Scott arrives, the Sachem puts Wilcoxon and Scott to the test with a long rifle, knowing it will reveal the true Hawkeye, a sworn enemy of the Huron. The Sachem releases Barnes and Wilcoxon, but tells Scott, "Hawkeye great warrior. When sunrise, my Hurons test his strength. Find out how great." Hawkeye is tied to a tree surrounded by a burning pyre before a rescue party saves the day.

The *New York Times* (10/15/36) listed Mong as one of two-dozen screen notables, headed by Lionel Barrymore and Rosalind Russell, who had been suspended from Actors Equity Association for their unwillingness to join the fledgling Screen Actors Guild (SAG). Mong would not really be impacted in that his stage career was long over and he would only make four more films prior to his death in 1940.

Stand-In (1937), a light-hearted look at the film industry, featured interesting work from stars Leslie Howard, Humphrey Bogart and Joan Blondell. As Cyrus Pennypacker, Mong was the middle of three generations (Tully Marshall played Mong's father, with J.C. Nugent as his son) that were the powers-that-be of the bank that holds the mortgage on Colossal Studios. The Pennypackers dispatch naïve auditor Howard to Hollywood with the design of ridding themselves of the money-losing film concern, with unexpected results. Mong followed this with a brief bit as the first undertaker in *Fight for Your Lady* (1937), with

Jack Oakie as a physical trainer for singer John Boles (of *Frankenstein* notoriety). Mong's last turn at screen villainy came with his portrayal of the corrupt banker Mr. Heist, who allies himself with the heavy, Fred Kohler, against hero George O'Brien in the Western, *Painted Desert* (1938).

In his final film, *Let Us Live* (1939), Mong played Joe Taylor, Sr., the owner of an electrical repair and supply shop. When Ralph Bellamy and Maureen O'Sullivan stop in, inquiring about some particular electrical wire in an attempt to vindicate wrongly convicted Henry Fonda and Alan Baxter, old Mr. Taylor unwittingly provides the name of his murderous son and his accomplices, as well as an address where they might be found. The role was little more than a cameo, but Mong infused it with his usual skill and effort.

William V. Mong died on December 10, 1940, in Studio City, California. He had been suffering from various illnesses for the previous two years, eventually rendering him unable to work any longer in the industry for which he had such passion. Mong left behind his widow Esme, his stepdaughter Barbara Esme and his son William from his second marriage. A funeral service was held for Mong in Glendale, California, on December 13, 1940.

Included in an acting career that spanned almost 40 years and more than 200 films are many memorable performances from William V. Mong. Obviously subtracting all the lost films about which one can read but never see, there is still a substantial body of work that gives testament to the ability and range of this almost forgotten actor. From his early silent work as "Flash" in *Eleanor's Catch* and Solon Hammerhead in *The County Fair*, through rich later silent portrayals as Caderousse in *Monte Cristo*, "Holy Joe" in *The Strong Man* and the Professor in *Seven Footprints to Satan*, to his well-etched early sound characterizations of Blind Pew in *Treasure Island*, Cleon in *The Last Days of Pompeii* and the Huron Sachem in *The Last of the Mohicans*, to name but a few, there is still plenty of William V. Mong to view and appreciate.

Sources

Coughlin, Jim. "Forgotten Faces of Fantastic Films: William V. Mong," in *Midnight Marquee #30* (1981), p. 28.

Katchmer, George. "Remembering the Great Silents," in *Classic Images #229*, (July 1994), pp. 40-41.

Lee, Rodney. "Has Earned Success," in the *Toledo Blade*, December 19, 1912.

Picture Show. "The Expressions of William V. Mong," (January 3, 1925), p. 9.

The Invisible Man (1933)

E E. Clive
(1872 – 1940)

Although there are genre purists who feel that humor has no place in the horror film, a well-written and acted bit of levity often lends a nice balance to the proceedings. Famed director James Whale loved to inject offbeat humor into his films by relying on veteran performers like Ernest Thesiger, Una O'Connor and E.E. Clive to bring his eccentric ideas to life. E.E. Clive was a particularly accomplished actor, in addition to being a theatrical producer and director of note, whose dour appearance and droll delivery could evoke laughter in the most serious of situations. Clive's character in films usually possessed a misguided sense of self-importance, "harrumphing" his way through social encounters. He was equally adept at playing pompous noblemen, efficient butlers and uninsightful policemen. Clive is primarily remembered in the fantasy film genre for his skillful portrayals in two James Whale classics, *The Invisible Man* and *Bride of Frankenstein*.

Erskholme Edward Clive was born in Blaenavon, Monmouthshire, Wales, on August 28, 1872 (although some sources claim 1883). In later years, Clive reversed his first and middle names to Edward Erskholme, but he became known as "E.E." Blaenavon was an iron and coal mining town. E.E.'s death certificate lists his father's surname as Griffith and his mother's maiden name as Williams, so there is some mystery as to whether Clive or Griffith was his actual last name (Ancestry.com shows no evidence of a birth in Wales from 1870-1883 of either an Erskholme Clive or Griffith). His father was a clergyman. Young Erskholme attended Caterham School in Surrey, England. While there, he developed a yearning for a life on the stage after viewing a performance of *The Liars* at the Town Hall at the age of 12. Despite this desire, Clive decided on a career in medicine, graduating from the University of Wales and then spending four years in training at St. Bartholomew's Hospital in London. Throughout his medical studies, Clive would frequent the London theaters, until he finally summoned the courage to convince the management of the Drury Lane Theatre that he was an experienced actor. Clive made his stage debut at Drury Lane at the age of 22 in a small role in *The White Heather*. In young adulthood, Clive stood five-foot-ten and weighed 145 pounds. He had blue eyes and light brown hair.

For the next eight years, Clive toured England, Wales, Scotland and Ireland in stock and repertory, appearing early on in an old English tradition called "the Penny Gaff." This was a type of portable theater wherein the company

The Invisible Man (1933): E.E. Clive and Una O'Connor

would travel around the country in flat wagons, carrying actors, scenery, props and even benches for spectators. The company would present 36 plays over a six-week period before returning to London. While on the set of *The Earl of Chicago* (1940), Clive was quoted as saying, "No Penny Gaff player ever came away from those tours lacking experience. Because of them, I can say today that I've been in a total of 1,139 plays."

Clive spent three seasons in England under the management of Charles Frohman, appearing in such works as *Are You a Mason?* (1910). As an aside, Clive became a Mason in the Euclid Lodge in Boston, Massachusetts in 1921. In April of 1911, Clive was a lodger with the Carr family in Hammersmith, London before departing for the United States that same October. Clive sailed from Southampton, England on 10/18/11 aboard the *Majestic*, which docked in New York harbor on 10/26/11.

In the U.S., Clive made early theatrical appearances in *The Sunshine Girl*, *Mind the Paint Girl* and as Marley's Ghost in *A Christmas Carol*. Under the name of Erskholme Clive, he was seen as John Shawn on Broadway at the Booth Theatre in *The Great Adventure* (10/16/13, 52 performances). Clive toured the Northeast on the Orpheum Circuit with his own vaudeville sketch, "One Good Turn Deserves Another," before establishing residency in Boston.

The Invisible Man (1933): Constable Jaffers (E.E. Clive, center) attempts to be firm with the mysterious stranger (Claude Rains), while Ted Billings (second from left) and other villagers look on.

In 1915, E.E. Clive was married to Illinois-born Eleanor Ann Ellis (1889-1982). The couple's only child, son David John Clive (1923-2001), would be born in Boston, Massachusetts, eight years later. In their early years in Boston, the Clives lived at 500 Boylston Street. By the mid-1920s, they were residing at 333 Beacon Street. The last known Boston dwelling for the Clives was at the Maryland Apartments on 512 Beacon Street, where they lived from 1928-1931.

For a period of approximately 14 years, Clive would become a major personage in the Boston theatrical community. Clive was both an actor and director with the Henry Jewett Players from 1917 through 1924. His first appearance for Jewett came in *A Night Off* (June 1917). *Clothes and the Woman* (8/28/19) afforded E.E. the opportunity to play opposite his wife Eleanor in Jewett's company. Often Clive would have the lead, such as Sir Guy De Vere

in *When Knights Were Bold* (1920) and the title character, Mr. Carraway Pim, in *Mr. Pim Passes By* (10/15/23). He would play supporting roles as well, including the tramp in *A Message From Mars* (4/14/24). Soon after the latter play closed, Jewett moved with his company to the Arlington Theater in Boston. As a result, "Clivie," as his cronies knew him, became the manager, director and actor at the Copley Theatre with his own company, the Copley Players. *Bed Rock* (Fall 1924) was the first production at the Copley under Clive's leadership.

Over the next six theatrical seasons, Clive would produce, stage and act in numerous shows at the Copley. He directed and acted in *The River* (November 1925), which featured Richard Whorf, Alan Mowbray and Elspeth Dudgeon (of *The Old Dark House* notoriety). Other Clive productions at the Copley were Jules Romain's *Dr. Knock*, Noel Coward's *Easy Virtue* and John Galsworthy's *Strife*,

Long Lost Father **(1934): E.E. Clive with John Barrymore**

which was a financial disaster. *The Ghost Train*, which ran for 23 weeks during 1926/27, was a work of which Clive was particularly proud. *The Ghost Train* helped the Copley Players recoup their losses from *Strife*, while also giving Clive, in addition to his producing and directing, a colorful role as Teddy Deakin. During his time at the Copley Theatre on Boston's Dartmouth Street, Clive helped develop many up and coming performers, such as Fay Holden, Genevieve Tobin, Margaret Sullavan and Rosalind Russell. Clive considered Russell to be his finest pupil, telling an interviewer (Martin, 1938):

> In three years she never had to be direct-
> ed in a single line. That girl knew how to
> do things right. To my mind, Ros is the
> world's greatest comedienne, yet she has
> never had a real comedy part. Comedy is
> essentially a sense of timing, and Ros has
> that sense inborn in her to her fingertips.

Clive produced and directed *Murray Hill* (8/13/27), written by and featuring rising star Leslie Howard. How-

ard then brought *Murray Hill* to the Bijou Theatre on Broadway. Theater producers often traveled to Boston for opening nights at the Copley, with the result that a number of Clive's productions, including Sidney Howard's *They Knew What They Wanted* (1924), were imported to New York, enjoying successful runs.

Venturing to Broadway, Clive directed and produced (as he had at the Copley) *The Creaking Chair* (2/22/26, 80 performances), in which he had the role of Angus Holly. Clive produced *Sport of Kings* (5/4/26, 23 performances) in New York with O.P. Heggie (the blind hermit in *Bride of Frankenstein*). On Broadway, he also produced the mystery/ comedy *The Whispering Gallery* (2/11/29, 79 performances), which had originated at the Copley. Although he and his work occasionally surfaced in New York, Clive's main theatrical efforts were in Boston at the Copley.

John H. Wilson, Clive's press representative at the Copley Theatre, commented on Clive's directing style (Walker, 1940):

> Clive's manner in directing was always
> most gentlemanly and courteous. He

Charlie Chan in London (1934): **Warner Oland, E.E. Clive, player and Ray Milland**

Bride of Frankenstein (1935): **A portrait of E.E. Clive as the Burgomaster**

believed in letting the actor use his own intelligence upon the characterization, but if a correction was to be made, it was done quietly by drawing the actor aside. Either he would convince the actor or they would make a compromise. [He was] a fine man to work for.

Clive considered his years in Boston as the happiest time of his career. He had particularly fond memories of putting on free performances for inmates at Massachusetts State Prison. Clive continued to receive appreciative letters from inmates for many years after.

When his company at the Copley folded due to financial pressures, Clive tried New York one final time, staging and producing *The Bellamy Trial* (4/22/31, 16 performances), starring Philip Tonge. Clive also portrayed Mr. Lambert in *The Bellamy Trial*, his last Broadway appearance.

E.E., Eleanor and David Clive returned to Boston once *The Bellamy Trial* closed, but ventured to California shortly thereafter. Settling in the Los Angeles area, Clive produced *As Husbands Go* in 1931. Clive was involved in the formation of the Hollywood Playhouse, modeled on the concept of the Copley players. Some of the performers he helped develop at the Hollywood Playhouse in the early stages of their careers were Robert Taylor and Charles Locher (Jon Hall).

Although he had yet to be involved in a motion picture production, Clive was already becoming known in the Hollywood community for both his acting and producing of plays. As mentioned, even in dramatic roles Clive had the knack of evoking waves of laughter with his timing, diction and nuances given to the characters he was portraying. Clive later remarked:

The first time I ever attempted the kind of comedy I have since become identified with was as a broken-down aristocrat, who was an old fossil living in an abandoned railway carriage, in a play called *What Might Happen*. My friends advised me to stick with this type, but I never took

Bride of Frankenstein (1935): **An indignant Una O'Connor responds to the pompous E.E. Clive.**

their suggestions seriously until I repeated it in the films *Poor Rich*, *Piccadilly Jim* and *Libeled Lady*. Well, I have been doing them ever since and am quite contented as long as they want me.

E.E. Clive's initial screen appearance was in the role of a steward on an ocean line in *Cheaters at Play* (1932), starring Thomas Meighan.

James Whale knew of Clive from the theater and sensed he could provide the touch the director required for the character of P.C. Jaffers in Universal's production of *The Invisible Man* (1933). Clive, as Jaffers, makes an early impact when he is called to the Lion's Head Inn where a mysterious stranger is causing a disturbance. Jaffers haughtily disregards the threats of Griffin (Claude Rains), instructing him to come along or else he will be handcuffed. Griffin responds by unraveling his bandages, prompting Jaffers to respond, "Look! 'e's all eaten away!" Running downstairs while trying to collect his wits, the policeman utters, "'e's invisible, that's what's the matter with him. If he gets the rest of them clothes off we'll never catch him in a thousand years!" Jaffers leads some men back to Griffin's room to find just a shirt moving in mid-air. They chase the invisible man around the room, with Jaffers bemoaning, "How can I handcuff a bloomin' shirt?" As Jaffers attempts to bar his exit, Griffin, initially grandiose, becomes agitated, almost strangling the poor policeman. When Jaffers calls in the incident to his superior, he is predictably accused of drinking on the job. The special effects of John P. Fulton and the acting of Claude Rains helped shape H.G. Wells' novel into a screen classic, but the deft talent of E.E. Clive clearly marks the handiwork of director James Whale. Clive would become a part of Whale's film "stock company," appearing in seven of the director's films, including *Bride of Frankenstein*, as well as *One More River*, *Remember Last Night*, *Showboat*, *The Road Back* and *The Great Garrick*.

Within a short time, E.E. Clive found there was great demand for his services as a character player in films.

On the set of *Long Lost Father* (1934), E.E. elicited the praise of star John Barrymore, whose increasing alcohol issues often led to multiple retakes, for Clive's ability to cap-

Atlantic Adventure (1935): Lloyd Nolan, E.E. Clive and Nancy Carroll

ture a scene in one attempt. Clive portrayed Spot Hawkins in this tale of a reformed crook (Barrymore) now working as a waiter.

The Poor Rich (1934) had Clive as Lord Fetherstone, who with his wife (Una O'Connor) becomes a houseguest of Edward Everett Horton and Edna May Oliver. It turns out that the once wealthy Fetherstones are now completely destitute. *Riptide* (1934), starring Norma Shearer and Robert Montgomery, included Clive as Major Mills. James Whale's *One More River* (1934), with Colin Clive and Lionel Atwill, featured E.E. as Chayne, a private detective.

Clive was seen as a London bobby in UA's *Bulldog Drummond Strikes Back* (1934) with Ronald Colman and Loretta Young. This appearance portended of things to come, as Clive would be featured in all eight "Bulldog Drummond" films for Paramount from 1937 to 1939. *Charlie Chan in London* (1934) had Clive providing some comic relief as Detective Sergeant Thacker, who refers to Charlie (Warner Oland) as "Chang." Clive was the chief customs inspector in *The Gay Divorcee* (1934), which starred Fred Astaire and Ginger Rogers. In *Father Brown, Detective* (1934), with the underrated Walter Connolly in the title role, Clive played Sergeant Dawes. *The Little Minister* (1934), with Katharine Hepburn, included an uncredited Clive as Sheriff Greer. Rounding out a busy year, Clive appeared in two shorts, *Tin Pants* (1934) and *Service* (1934).

MGM's *David Copperfield* (1935) had Clive among a strong cast as the sheriff's man. Clive was the pompous

Bulldog Drummond Escapes (1937): A portrait of E.E. Clive as the battered valet, Tenny

Lord Mayor Thomas Sapsea, who is pressured to have Douglass Montgomery arrested, in *Mystery of Edwin Drood* (1935). *Gold Diggers of 1935* (1935) had Clive as Westbrook, the chauffeur.

Clive's most significant role in the horror genre came with his portrayal of the self-important, officious burgomaster in Universal's *Bride of Frankenstein* (1935). James Whale injected more humor in *Bride of Frankenstein* than he had in *Frankenstein*, relying on his trusted performers like Clive, Una O'Connor and Ernest Thesiger to provide quirky touches to this classic film. Clive appears early on in the film, as the burgomaster views the burning windmill. In contrast to the cackling of Minnie (O'Connor), the burgomaster encourages the townspeople to return home to

***Bulldog Drummond Escapes* (1937): E.E. Clive with Ray Milland**

has transpired. As the burgomaster again tries to dispatch the villagers to their homes, the Monster breaks free and runs amok. A scene wherein the burgomaster is pulled out of his chair and through a window, then beaten by the Monster in the street, was part of a lengthy sequence eliminated from the final print of *Bride of Frankenstein*. E.E. Clive's characterization of the burgomaster was quite vivid, being both annoying and humorous, but played completely straight.

We're in the Money (1935) had Clive as Jevons, Ross Alexander's butler. *Atlantic Adventure* (1935), which included Dwight Frye as a jewel thief, featured Clive as McIntosh, the ship's officer who does not understand the American sense of humor. Clive was the monogram shirtmaker in *Page Miss Glory* (1935) with Marion Davies. In *Three Kids and a Queen* (1935), Clive was the coachman whose vehicle, transporting wealthy May Robson, overturns while trying to avoid a jalopy. He played Higgins the pub proprietor in *A Feather in Her Hat* (1935) with Pauline Lord and Basil Rathbone. James Whale's *Remember Last Night?* (1935) had Clive as the photographer for the coroner (Frank Reicher). Clive's roles were often small, but he usually made an impact regardless of his amount of screen time. He played a waiter in *The Man Who Broke the Bank at Monte Carlo* (1935), Crane in *Stars Over Broadway* (1935), the gramophone man in *Kind Lady*

their beds, assuring them that the Monster (Boris Karloff) is dead. The burgomaster harrumphs, "Monster indeed!" and adds, "You may thank your lucky stars they sent for me to safeguard life and property." Later, the villagers alert the burgomaster that the Monster is alive and on the loose, causing him to reply, "Get out the bloodhounds, raise all the men you can, lock the women indoors and wait for me." After the Monster is trapped in the forest, the burgomaster instructs the men to bind his feet and tie him to a pole, which when raised gives the Monster the appearance of being crucified. After the Monster is chained to a chair in a dungeon, the burgomaster minimizes what

(1935), a customs inspector in *Sylvia Scarlett* (1935) and the judge in the Old Bailey in *A Tale of Two Cities* (1935), starring Ronald Colman. *The Widow From Monte Carlo* (1935), with Colin Clive, had Clive as Lord Holloway, one of Dolores del Rio's aristocratic in-laws. Clive was seen as a clerk of the court in Errol Flynn's *Captain Blood* (1935).

The Dark Hour (1936) gave Clive the interesting role of Foote, the butler of murdered William V. Mong, who tries to blackmail Hobart Bosworth but gets stabbed to death instead. *Little Lord Fauntleroy* (1936) had Clive as Sir Harry Lorridaile. He played the yacht captain in *Love Before Breakfast* (1936) with Carole Lombard. Clive portrayed

Lord Hathaway, the husband of Jessie Ralph, in *The Unguarded Hour* (1936), a murder and blackmail tale with Franchot Tone and Loretta Young.

Back at Universal, Clive played Sergeant Wilkes in the moody *Dracula's Daughter* (1936). By the time Wilkes arrives to take custody of Count Dracula's corpse from policemen Halliwell Hobbes and Billy Bevan, the body has mysteriously disappeared. Clive was a tutor in Josef von Sternberg's *The King Steps Out* (1936) with Grace Moore. James Whale managed to find a spot for Clive as the London producer in his version of *Show Boat* (1935). *Palm Springs* (1936) gave Clive a colorful part as Bruce Morgan, former explorer and British Consul in Vancouver. Other roles for Clive at this time were Walker in *The Golden Arrow* (1936), King in *Trouble for Two* (1936), Barkins in *Ticket to Paradise* (1936), surgeon Dr. Smith in *The White Angel* (1936) and Charles Fendwick in *Cain and Mabel* (1936), with Clark Gabel and Marion Davies. Clive was Bill Mechan, the annoying London gossip editor, in *Piccadilly Jim* (1936), starring Robert Montgomery. *Libeled Lady* (1936) had Clive as Evans, who tries to teach the nuances of fly casting and fishing to novice William Powell. Off screen, Clive was an avid fisherman in real life, as well as a competitive golfer. *Isle of Fury* (1936) gave Clive a more substantial role than usual as droll Dr. Hardy, a preacher who relates the story of David and Bathsheba to companion Humphrey Bogart on a small island in the Pacific.

The comedy *All American Chump* (1936), with Stuart Erwin, included Clive as British bridge champion J. Montgomery Brantley. Again opposite Errol Flynn, Clive was Sir Humphrey Harcourt, who angers Surat Khan (C. Henry Gordon) with the news that financial aid to Suristan from the British government has been discontinued, in *The Charge of the Light Brigade* (1936). *Tarzan Escapes* (1936), the third entry in the Johnny Weissmuller series for MGM, had Clive as Masters, an Englishman sympathetic to Tarzan and Jane (Maureen O'Sullivan). Clive played a magistrate in *Lloyd's of London* (1936), which seemed to feature half the British actors in Hollywood, and Saint Gaudens in *Camille* (1936), which starred Greta Garbo.

Bulldog Drummond Escapes (1937) marked the first of eight appearances for Clive in the role of Tenny, the indispensable valet to Drummond. Although Ray Milland played Drummond in this film, John Howard would assay the role in the next seven entries in this series for Paramount. In the "Bulldog Drummond" books, the character is named James Denny, but because actor Reginald Denny was a regular in these films seen as Drummond's cohort Algy, the valet was renamed "Tenny."

Maid of Salem **(1937): E.E. Clive as the village inebriate, Bilge**

Clive was Benz the cabby in the Dick Powell musical comedy *On the Avenue* (1937). As Stiles, the butler for Henry Kolker and Betty Furness, Clive chased suitor Gordon Jones around the house in *They Wanted to Marry* (1937). He played Thomas Ezekiel Bilge, amidst the witchcraft hysteria, in *Maid of Salem* (1937). *Ready, Willing and Able* (1937), a musical comedy with Ruby Keeler, had Clive as Sir Samuel Bloomington (although listed as Buffington in the credits). As Cosgrove Dabney, the owner of a woman's underwear business that goes bankrupt, Clive was Robert Taylor's father in *Personal Property* (1937). *Night Must Fall* (1937), based on the play by Emlyn Williams and starring Robert Montgomery as the murderous Danny, included Clive as the insensitive tour guide who leads visitors around the murder site. James Whale again found a role for Clive, this time as a general in *The Road Back* (1937), Universal's ill-fated sequel to *All Quiet on the Western Front*. *The Emperor's Candlesticks* (1937), with William Powell and Luise Rainer trying to outbid one another for the titled objects, had Clive as

Bulldog Drummond Comes Back (1937): E.E. Clive with John Howard (as Drummond)

the auctioneer. Set during the Spanish Civil War, *Love Under Fire* (1937) included Clive as Captain Bowden.

In *Bulldog Drummond Strikes Back* (1937), now with John Howard in the title role, Clive, as Tenny Tennison, helps Drummond avoid a bomb explosion, but he loses his boss' marriage license to the wind. *Danger: Love at Work* (1937), an early directorial effort by Otto Preminger, featured Clive as Wilbur. He played the first butler in *It's Love I'm After* (1937), with Bette Davis and Leslie Howard. *The Great Garrick* (1937), with Brian Aherne, was Clive's final appearance in a James Whale film. He was seen as the vendor selling pictures. Again with Robert Montgomery in *Live, Love and Learn* (1937), Clive played Mr. Palmiston, a wealthy horse owner who commissions a painting of himself that he ends up getting pushed through because of his arrogance. *Beg, Borrow or Steal* (1937) had Clive as Lord Nigel Braemer, who returns home from bird hunting in Scotland to find con man Frank Morgan living in his chateau.

As Tenny, Clive was taken hostage by evil Frank Puglia in *Bulldog Drummond's Revenge* (1937). In *Bulldog Drummond's Peril* (1938), Clive, as Tenny, engineers his own kidnapping in order to help rescue John Howard and Halliwell Hobbes. *Arsene Lupin Returns* (1938) had Clive as Alf Hammond, a former accomplice and friend of Lupin (Melvyn Douglas). Clive portrayed Chester Blascomb in *The First Hundred Years* (1938). He was briefly seen in *Kidnapped* (1938) as Minister MacDougall. *Gateway* (1938), with Don Ameche, had Clive as a room steward on an ocean liner bound for New York. Clive had a small bit in John Ford's *Submarine Patrol* (1938) and played Major Barclay in *The Last Warning* (1938), with Preston Foster.

On May 3, 1938, Clive was a special guest on the Al Jolson Show on WABC Radio. This is Clive's only known radio credit.

Clive returned as Tenny in *Bulldog Drummond in Africa* (1938), helping John Howard free H.B. Warner from the clutches of J. Carrol Naish. Tenny (Clive), posing as a tourist, ran afoul of an even more sinister villain, George Zucco, in *Arrest Bulldog Drummond* (1939). Staying in the mystery/detective genre, Clive was the Post Commandant General in *Mr. Moto's Last Warning* (1939), starring Peter Lorre. As Mr. Barrows, Clive wrongly informs the head mistress (Mary Nash) that Shirley Temple's father (Ian Hunter) has been killed in battle, in *The Little Princess* (1939). *I'm From Missouri* (1939) gave Clive the chance to play broad comedy as Mr. Arthur, Duke of Cricklewood, whose plane is forced down in a Missouri field and pulled from the mud by a mule.

Clive would figure prominently in both of UA's *Sherlock Holmes* films starring the newly paired duo of Basil Rathbone as Holmes and Nigel Bruce as Dr. Watson. In *The Hound of the Baskervilles* (1939), Clive was the driver of the hansom cab observed by Holmes to be following Sir Henry (Richard Greene) and Dr. Mortimer (Lionel Atwill). As a gun emerges from the cab, Holmes thwarts the potential murderer. When interviewed the next day, the cabby (Clive) reveals that his fare had claimed to be Sherlock Holmes, which amuses the actual detective. *The Adventures of Sherlock Holmes* (1939) had Clive as the rather stubborn Scotland Yard Inspector Bristol. Holmes finds the Inspector interrogating Jerrold Hunter (Alan Marshall) by the body of Lloyd Brandon (Peter Willes). Bristol states that Brandon was clubbed to death by a pistol. To Bristol's dismay, Holmes disputes his theories, positing that Lloyd was strangled, with the other blows administered after he

Arrest Bulldog Drummond **(1939): George Zucco, Sam Savitsky, player, George Regas, E.E. Clive and Reginald Denny**

Hitchcock's *Foreign Correspondent* (1940), with Joel McCrea, had an uncredited Clive as Mr. Naismith. Coincidentally, Mr. Naismith was also Clive's character name in his final film, *Flowing Gold* (1940), with John Garfield and Frances Farmer.

On June 6, 1940, Edward E. Clive suffered a heart attack at his home at 4606 Radford Avenue, North Hollywood, California. He died holding a cup of tea in his hand before wife Eleanor could take it from him. Clive had been suffering from influenza prior to his death. He was 67 years old. Clive was waked at Edwards Brothers' Colonial Mortuary, 1000 Venice Boulevard, Los Angeles, California. He was cremated and his ashes were scattered by his family. His wife Eleanor and son David John survived him.

was already dead. Nonetheless, Bristol welcomes Holmes' assistance, imploring in low tones, "You'll work on the case … in the usual way?"

Clive would assay the role of Tenny Tennison, the "gentleman's gentleman," two more times, in *Bulldog Drummond's Secret Police* (1939) and *Bulldog Drummond's Bride* (1939). He drove the barouche, a horse drawn carriage, in *Rose of Washington Square* (1939), with Alice Faye and Tyrone Power. As the Major, Clive was featured in the somber World War I saga *We Are Not Alone* (1939), starring Paul Muni. In *Man About Town* (1939), starring Jack Benny, Clive was Hotchkiss, Edward Arnold's butler. The butler roles continued for Clive in *Bachelor Mother* (1939), with Ginger Rogers and David Niven, and *Raffles* (1939), wherein he was Niven's manservant Barraclough. *The Honeymoon's Over* (1939), with Stuart Erwin and Patric Knowles, had Clive humorously on hand as Colonel Shelby, an alcoholic freeloader.

Clive portrayed Mr. Redwood in *The Earl of Chicago* (1940) with Robert Montgomery and Edward Arnold. He was sixth-billed as Horace Snell in *Congo Maisie* (1940), starring Ann Sothern. *Adventure in Diamonds* (1940), with George Brent, had Clive as Mr. MacPherson. *Pride and Prejudice* (1940), MGM's adaptation of Jane Austen's novel, included Clive as Sir William Lucas, the wealthy and self-important neighbor of the Bennett family. Alfred

When discussing horror films, the name "Clive" usually evokes "Colin." The less flamboyant, unrelated Clive who went by the initials "E.E." made his own mark in the genre in classic chillers like *The Invisible Man*, *Bride of Frankenstein* and *Dracula's Daughter*, with colorful, well-etched supporting characterizations. There may have been a number of pompous, skeptical figures in horror films over the years, but few could convey as much through subtle expression and dry delivery as E.E. Clive. "Monster indeed!"

Sources

Caftan Woman. "Clivey Rules," in http://caftanwoman.blogspot.com/2012/03/clivey-rules.html.

Chastain, George. "E.E. Clive," in *Classic Horror Players Directory* (http://myweb.wvnet.edu/-u0e53/eeclive.html)

Coughlin, Jim. "Forgotten Faces of Fantastic Films: E.E. Clive, Arthur Edmund Carewe," in *Midnight Marquee #35* (Fall 1986), pp. 32-33.

Martin, Mildred. "Stars Owe Stage Start to Guidance of E.E. Clive," in the *Philadelphia Inquirer*, 5/3/38, p. 11.

Walker, Lydia L. *E.E. Clive: The Late Actor-Producer's Record—Some Memories of his Boston Career*, uncited Boston clipping, 1940.

William Harrigan
(1886 – 1966)

Many of the roles associated with horror films have become hackneyed and clichéd over the years due to numerous repetitions and lack of novel characterizations. A film like *Young Frankenstein* (1981) lends its success to some degree by both lampooning and paying homage to such characters as the hunchbacked assistant, one-armed police inspector, eccentric servant and more. It is interesting to trace the origins of such roles within the horror genre to see how the characters were intended before they became standard plot devices and virtual parodies of themselves. *The Invisible Man* (1933) introduces the weak-willed former associate of the monster-to-be, who becomes an unwilling accomplice in the fiend's grandiose plans to wreak havoc. The character in this instance was Dr. Kemp, as craftily enacted by William Harrigan.

William Harrigan came from sturdy theatrical stock, being one of the 10 children of the legendary Edward "Ned" Harrigan (1844-1911), of "Harrigan and Hart" fame, and Annie Theresa Braham Harrigan (1860-1918), actress and daughter of composer David Braham. He was born William David Harrigan on March 27, 1886, in New York City. Reportedly, William first appeared on stage as a young child with his father's company in *Dan's Tribulations*. In 1891, at the age of five, young Billy, as he was known at the time, was seen with long golden curls in Ned Harrigan's popular *Reilly and the 400*.

By the time he was 10, William Harrigan had toured the country in a number of his father's old stage vehicles. When it came to theater, the elder Harrigan was a stern taskmaster. Ned once had young William study every move and gesture of a mediocre actor. Before William could regale his father with the techniques he had learned, Ned instructed him to "remember all those things and never do any of them!" Ned also had his son once play an entire performance without moving his arms from his sides in order to emphasize the value of face and voice in acting.

In the 1905/06 theatrical season, William played Dick in *Old Lavender* (5/21/06), another of his father's noted works. The Harrigan company toured in *Old Lavender* dur-

ing 1906/07, with William understudying his father and occasionally playing the title role when Ned was too ill to go on. While continuing to act, William Harrigan had attended New York Military Academy with aspirations of going on to West Point.

Broadway producer Charles Dillingham took note of the younger Harrigan's talent, engaging William to play the role of Jimmy Larkin in *Artie* (10/28/07). Harrigan played Michael in a revival of Yeats' *Kathleen Ni Houlihan* (early 1908), with Margaret Wycherly, and Dempsey in *The Regeneration* (9/1/08), with Arnold Daly.

Again acting with his father, William was seen as Bryan Desmond, the ambitious young Irishman, in *His Wife's Family* (10/6/08). The reviewer in *Theatre* (February 1909, p. 169) commented on William's performance, noting,

The Melody of Youth (1916 Broadway stage): **William Harrigan, William J. Kelly, Lily Cahill and Brandon Tynan**

"The boy has a youthful preponderance of animal spirits. His smile is unctuous. He sees comedy points and develops them." Ned Harrigan had taught his son well.

Opposite star Maxine Elliott, William portrayed Ed Miller in *The Chaperon* (12/30/08). Harrigan was Skinner, the cook, in the farce *Going Some* (4/12/09). With Mabel Taliaferro's company, Harrigan played the mischievous Crawley in *Springtime* (10/19/09), while also being seen as Lykon in a special matinee performance of *Ingomar* (late 1909). Johnson Briscoe (*The Green Book Magazine*, March 1910, p. 631) critiqued William's early stage efforts:

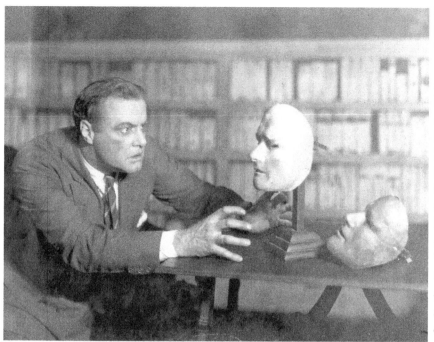

The Great God Brown **(1926 Broadway stage): William Harrigan as William A. Brown in Eugene O' Neill's potent drama**

There is a delightful sense of frank, wholesome ingenuousness about Mr. Harrigan's acting that would seem to foreshadow the development of an excellent light comedian. He is thoroughly easy and at home when in the glance of the footlights, with a preponderance of youthful spirits and a smile that bespeaks a rare sense of humor, so there is little doubt that he is destined to make a name in the field of comedy.

Again with Mabel Taliaferro, William was featured in *The Voice of the Cricket* (4/19/10). When Taliaferro took *Springtime* on tour in mid-1910, Harrigan assayed the male lead of Gilbert Steele rather than the juvenile part he played on Broadway. He remained with Taliaferro's company for two years.

After playing Mark in *The Woman* (1912) at the Republic, William succeeded Frank Craven as James Gilley in the long-running (431 performances) *Bought and Paid For* (Summer 1912). Harrigan made his silent screen debut as Phillip Warwick in *An Affair of Three Nations* (1915), which starred Arnold Daly. William then went on tour in Australia with Charles Millward's theatrical troupe, appearing in plays like *The Argyle Case* and *Ready Money.*

Back in the United States, William Harrigan was wed to Dorothy Langdon (1896- ?) on October 12, 1915. Unfortunately, not only did this marriage not work out, but Dorothy would prove to be a constant nuisance and sometime threat to Harrigan over the ensuing two decades. Harrigan appeared in *The Melody of Youth* (2/15/16), but

his stage career was about to be interrupted by the entrance of the United States into World War I.

William Harrigan enlisted in the U.S. Army in 1917. With his military school background and leadership qualities, Harrigan swiftly rose to the rank of Captain. He was attached to "A" Company of the 307th Infantry (3rd Battalion, 77th Division). Harrigan helped lead a relief column during the Meuse-Argonne Offensive to aid the so-called "Lost Battalion," who were cut off from the Allied forces for five days. Page one of the *New York Times* (8/24/18) read, "Captain Harrigan Leads Raid … Party Under Late Actor's Son Takes 14 Prisoners." The article further described William as "the hero of this effort," but he also received a number of serious wounds during the engagement resulting in a four-month stay in French hospitals. Harrigan was sent stateside for additional convalescence.

While sailing one afternoon on Long Island Sound, William docked near the residence of George M. Cohan in Great Neck, New York. Cohan supposedly remarked, "You look pretty fit, Bill. Pretty near ready to work again?"

Cohan assisted in Harrigan's return to the stage, providing William with the role of Joe Conway in *The Acquit-*

Cabaret **(1929): Tom Moore shows the evidence to William Harrigan.**

On the Level (1930): Iron-working friends William Harrigan and Victor McLaglen

tal (1/5/20). Harrigan then went on to repeat the part of James Gilley in a revival of *Bought and Paid For* (12/7/21).

Soon after his return from Europe, Harrigan secured a divorce from Dorothy on November 9, 1919. In lieu of alimony, William made an oral agreement to pay Dorothy 25% of his theatrical earnings until such time as she remarried. This was later changed to a written arrangement wherein Harrigan would pay Dorothy $50 per week when he was employed and $20 a week when he was not working. Harrigan then proceeded to marry Louise Groody (1897-1961), a showgirl who would later sing "Tea for Two" in *No, No, Nanette* (1925), on April 8, 1920. This marriage was not a success either, with William and Louise parting ways early in 1922.

As Bob Cooley, Harrigan co-starred on Broadway with Genevieve Tobin in the Guy Bolton hit (184 performances) *Polly Preferred* (1/11/23), the cast of which also included Edward Van Sloan. During the run of *Polly Preferred*, William's ex-wife Dorothy began coming to the Little Theatre, demanding her weekly pay, going so far as to attempt to

undermine his performance on one occasion. Harrigan was compelled to arrange for a third party to henceforth deliver her money to Dorothy's residence each Saturday to avoid potentially disastrous situations. Dorothy's behavior would not desist, however, as she eventually brought William to court in New York City, demanding past shortages in payments and other damages.

Harrigan continued to be active on Broadway throughout the "Roaring Twenties." William played James Darlington in *Schemers* (9/15/24) at the Bayes Theatre. David Belasco engaged Harrigan to portray Johnny Powell in *The Dove* (2/11/25) at the Empire Theatre. In the cast of *The Dove* playing Maybelle was a young actress named Grace Culbert. In May 1925, William Harrigan and Grace Culbert were married in Greenwich, Connecticut. Unlike Harrigan's previous two attempts at matrimony, the bond with Grace would be enduring, with the couple remaining happily together until William's death.

Harrigan made a significant impact in his next theatrical venture, achieving critical acclaim as the lead, Wil-

The Moon in Yellow River (1932 Broadway stage): **As Claude Rains appears dejected, William Harrigan, gun in hand, stands over the body of Henry Hull, with Egon Brecher kneeling by him.**

liam A. Brown, in Eugene O'Neill's poignant *The Great God Brown* (1/23/26). He was less successful, however, as Eddie Carpenter in the short-lived (39 performances) *Sandalwood* (9/22/26). In July 1927 William headlined the vaudeville bill (and "scored with a zoop" according to *Variety*) at the Palace Theatre, performing many of his father Ned's numbers in a sketch entitled "Memories of Harrigan and Hart." Harrigan next was seen as Robert Buchanan, newspaper editor and colleague of cub reporter Dwight Frye, in the ill-fated (15 performances) *Ink* (11/1/27).

The Cabaret (1927) presented William with his first significant film role as Jack Costigan, who runs the nightclub where singer/dancer Gilda Gray performs. After playing Joe Sanford in George M. Cohan's *Whispering Friends* (2/20/28), Harrigan ventured to Hollywood to try his luck in talking pictures. William first signed a short-term deal with Fox, appearing in four features for that studio. Harrigan played Johnny Brown, one of a pair of acrobat friends who both fall in love with Mae Clarke, in *Nix on Dames* (1929). *Born Reckless* (1930), directed by John Ford,

had William as Good News Brophy. In *On the Level* (1930), Harrigan was Danny Madden, best friend of ironworker Victor McLaglen. *Men on Call* (1930) featured Harrigan as Cap, the kindly Coast Guard officer who befriends down-and-out Edmund Lowe, before once again falling for Mae Clarke.

Returning to the stage, Harrigan played Jim Grove in *Washington Heights* (9/29/31) at the Maxine Elliott Theatre. He then toured in *Strictly Dishonorable* in late 1931. *The Moon in the Yellow River* (2/29/32) featured William as the Irish Commandant. In April 1932, Harrigan replaced William Gargan as Richard Regan during the run of *The Animal Kingdom* (1/12/32), which starred Leslie Howard. Another critical success for William came with his portrayal of Chief Inspector Detective Tanner opposite Emlyn Williams in the suspenseful *Criminal at Large* (10/10/32), written by Edgar Wallace.

Back in Hollywood, Harrigan made three consecutive appearances in Paramount productions. He played the villainous Jim Richards, gangster husband of Sylvia Sidney,

Pick-up (1933): Sylvia Sidney with murderous husband William Harrigan

who kills a guard and breaks out of jail in *Pick-up* (1933). As Peter Lawton, William was an unscrupulous mobster who has himself admitted to the hospital in order to silence Gloria Stuart in *The Girl in 419* (1933). In *Disgraced* (1933), Harrigan portrayed Police Captain Holloway, whose daughter (Helen Twelvetrees) tries to protect him after he slays her rotten fiancé (Bruce Cabot).

James Whale was busy preparing H.G. Wells' *The Invisible Man* for the screen, when Universal contract player Chester Morris, slated to play Dr. Arthur Kemp, balked at sharing top-billing with Claude Rains and left the picture. William Harrigan was called in to replace Morris and production on *The Invisible Man* (1933) ensued.

Early on in *The Invisible Man*, Harrigan as Kemp is seen consoling Flora (Gloria Stuart), the sweetheart of the erratic Jack Griffin (Claude Rains), who has mysteriously disappeared. Kemp claims, "He mettled in things man should leave alone," further noting Griffin's penchant for working behind barred doors and drawn blinds. Dr. Cranley (Henry Travers), the mentor of both Griffin and Kemp, learns that Griffin had been experimenting with "monocaine," a drug

that draws color from whatever it touches, but also made a dog insane during one experiment. Cranley swears Kemp to secrecy as they search Griffin's lab for clues.

That night, Griffin sneaks into Kemp's quarters, threatening to kill him if he tries anything. Kemp is instructed to gather surgical bandages, gown, glasses, etc. and draw the blinds. Once attired, Griffin reveals the nature of his experiments, adding, "I must have a partner … We'll begin with a reign of terror." Although horrified, Kemp drives Griffin back to the village to fetch a notebook he left behind at the inn. After securing the book and killing an inspector, Griffin orders Kemp to drive home. Waiting until Griffin falls asleep, Kemp phones Cranley and then contacts the police. After Cranley and Flora arrive, followed by the police, Griffin is forced to exit, vowing to kill Kemp for his betrayal.

Kemp tells the police of the death threat ("10 p.m., tomorrow night."), while also revealing that Griffin is "the invisible man." The next night, Kemp is escorted from his home, disguised as a policeman and brought to the police station. Kemp is then removed from the station and placed in a vehicle, only to discover Griffin has been in the car waiting for him. As Kemp pleads for his life, Griffin ties him up, describing to his former colleague how he will meet his death. Griffin stops the car, gets out and releases the brake. The vehicle plummets over a cliff bursting into flames, with Kemp trapped inside.

Keeper of the Keys (1933 Broadway stage): Dwight Frye, William Harrigan (as Charlie Chan) and Ruth Easton

***The Invisible Man* (1933): Kemp (William Harrigan) is instructed by Griffin (Claude Rains).**

Harrigan turned in an adequate performance as Kemp in *The Invisible Man*. Kemp is really a thankless, unsympathetic role. Harrigan managed to hold his own, contending with the fine special effects of John P. Fulton and the bravura acting of Rains. The character of the unwilling accomplice-turned traitor, as embodied by Kemp, later became fairly common in subsequent horror films.

Although Harrigan's next trip back to Broadway could perhaps be viewed as significant to horror film fans, critics did not herald it at the time. William was seen as Inspector Charlie Chan, playing opposite Dwight Frye, in his penultimate Broadway role of Ah Sing, in *Keeper of the Keys* (10/18/33). After a series of successful Chan films produced by Fox, *Keeper of the Keys* was the first attempt to bring Earl Derr Biggers' detective to the stage. Chan is called in to solve the murder of a prima donna at a Nevada hunting lodge. The *New York Daily News* (10/19/33) noted, "Harrigan's study of Chan is very good, particularly in the consistency of his speech and accent. Dwight Frye, elaborately made over as an ancient Chinese, is effectively

weird. Neither of the boys could conceivably get by the gatekeeper of a Tong headquarters, but they do nicely as Occidental imitations."

Also on Broadway, Harrigan was Ben Weston in *The Dark Tower* (11/25/33). William made his first appearance on the London stage at the Adelphi as Augustus McNeal in *She Loves Me Not* (4/14/34). Returning to the States, Harrigan was seen in *For Love or Money* (Summer 1934) at the Westport Country Playhouse. In New York, William played Phillip Frampton in *All Rights Reserved* (11/6/34), Jerry Morse in *Portrait of Gilbert* (12/28/34) and Didier in the powerful *Paths of Glory* (9/26/35).

During the mid-to-late 1930s, Harrigan was at the peak of his film career. William had the sympathetic role of "Mac" McKay, the racketeer who helped put "Brick" Davis (James Cagney) through law school, in *G-Men* (1935). McKay respects Davis' decision to become a federal agent and not become part of the underworld. Now retired from the rackets, McKay is forced to play reluctant host to his former cronies who hide out at his Wisconsin lodge. The

His Family Tree (1936): **William Harrigan and James Barton**

thugs, led by Collins (Broderick Crawford), tie Mac to a chair, where he is accidentally shot and killed by Davis when government agents raid the lodge.

After a small role as a henchman in *The People's Enemy* (1935), Harrigan portrayed Updyke in *Stranded* (1935). *Silk Hat Kid* (1935) had William as Brother Joe Campbell, who runs a settlement house for wayward youths and is instrumental in repairing the relationship between Paul Kelly and Lew Ayres. In *His Family Tree* (1935), Harrigan changed his name from Murphy to Murfree in an attempt to hide his Irish background and win a mayoralty race. His pub owner father (James Barton) arrives from Ireland, making Murfree's lineage public knowledge, but the Irish vote comes through (and father and son are reconciled). William played Captain Jonesy in *The Melody Lingers On* (1935), with Josephine Hutchinson. He was "Doc" Evans, the jewel-thieving partner of Robert Gleckler, in *Whipsaw* (1935), starring Spencer Tracy.

Frankie and Johnny (1936), based on the popular song and starring Helen Morgan and Chester Morris, had Harrigan as Curley. Although his love is unrequited by Frankie (Morgan), Curley remains fiercely devoted and helps her start anew after Johnny's death. *Over the Goal* (1937) included William as football coach Jim Shelly. *Federal Bullets* (1937), with *Werewolf of London* biddy Zeffie Tilbury as a supposed humanitarian who is actually a criminal master-

Back Door to Heaven (1939): **William Harrigan as the abusive, alcoholic, one-armed Mr. Rogers**

mind, had Harrigan as the Federal Agency Chief Inspector. *Exiled to Shanghai* (1937), about newsreel photographers, featured William as Grant Powell, the owner of Supreme Television, who turns out to be a swindler. As the drunken, abusive, one-armed Mr. Rogers, who beats and mistreats son Jimmy Lydon in the early going of *Back Door to Heaven* (1939), Harrigan displayed his dramatic range as a despicable character. William played the Union Army commanding officer, combating lawlessness in the territory, in *Arizona* (1940), with Jean Arthur and William Holden.

In Time to Come (1941 Broadway stage): Nedda Harrigan (William's sister) and William Harrigan

Flying Leathernecks (1951): William Harrigan as Lt. Cdr. Joe Curran

Throughout the late thirties, Harrigan still managed to find time to return to his main love, the stage. Harrigan portrayed Arthur Curtis at the Longacre in the comedy *Among Those Sailing* (2/11/36). William was seen as Andrew Rodman in *Days to Come* ((12/15/36) and Stuff Nelson in *Roosty* (2/14/38). At the Rockridge Theatre in Carmel, New York, Harrigan starred in *Away From It All* (June 1938). He played Wilmington, Delaware in *Once Upon a Night* (September 1938).

On the radio, Harrigan was heard on *The Royal Gelatin Hour* (3/24/38), performing a scene from the play *Roosty* with Jimmy McCallion. For *The Campbell Playhouse* (CBS), Harrigan was featured with Orson Welles (who also wrote the piece) in "The Things We Have" (5/26/39). William would later appear on *Arthur Hopkins Presents* (NBC) in "Yellow Jack" (8/9/44).

The Happiest Days (4/11/39), at the Vanderbilt Theatre, featured Harrigan as Alfred Chapin. He then played Mr. Slaughter, the Scottish mate, in *A Passenger to Bali* (5/14/40). Harrigan portrayed Quigley in *Snooky* (6/3/41).

Time to Come (12/28/41), directed by Otto Preminger, gave Harrigan, as Tumulty, the chance to play opposite his talented sister, Nedda Harrigan. William then spent the better part of 1942 and 1943 touring in *Death Takes a Holiday* and *Mary of Scotland*, in which he played Bothwell. A critic wrote of William's performance in the latter, "He cannot make the slightest movement on stage without creating an effect of significance and emotional power." Back on Broadway, Harrigan took to the bench as Judge Bentley in *Pick-up Girl* (5/3/44) and then replaced Howard Smith as Judge Harvey Wilkins in *Dear Ruth* (which had opened on 12/13/44 and eventually ran for 680 performances). William then went on tour with *Dear Ruth*, playing Chicago and elsewhere, in 1945/46.

Harrigan's film work began tailing off in the 1940s, with only one screen appearance between 1940 and 1947,

Francis Covers the Big Town (1953): Donald O'Connor, Yvette Duguay and William Harrigan

Broadway (4/6/48), the first television series broadcast on CBS, Harrigan, Logan and others involved in *Mister Roberts* appeared to discuss the production and enact key scenes.

For ABC Television, Harrigan was seen on *Pulitzer Prize Playhouse* in "Detour" (6/1/51, season 1, episode 35). William then returned to the big screen for two important portrayals. As Lt. Commander Joe Curran, Harrigan was the unit physician who advises John Wayne and has concerns about Robert Ryan's stability in *Flying Leathernecks* (1951). In *Steel Town* (1952), William portrayed John "Mac" McNamara, the father of Ann Sheridan. Mac, a hard-working steel company supervisor, has a heart attack on the job necessitating a dramatic rescue by John Lund.

Harrigan began to establish himself during the early days of live dramatic television. He played Captain Vansky in "You Be the Bad Guy" (8/18/52, season 2, episode 52) for *Lux Video Theatre* (CBS). For *Kraft Theatre* (NBC), William starred in "Green Cars Go East" (4/16/52, season 5, episode 32). Harrigan was seen with Una O'Connor in "The

and that one was for Poverty Row studio PRC. In *Follies Girl* (1943), William played Jimmy Dobson, the manager of Bijou Burlesque, whom Wendy Barrie aides in upgrading the quality of his entertainment. *The Farmer's Daughter* (1947), starring Loretta Young, featured Harrigan as Ward C. Hughes. *Citizen Saint* (1947), a religious production about Mother Cabrini (Carla Dare), included William as Father Vail. Harrigan was Judge Berle Lindquist in *Desert Fury* (1947), a Western crime drama that provided an early screen appearance for Burt Lancaster.

Harrigan's career received a much-needed boost when he won the role of the Captain in *Mister Roberts* (2/18/48), directed and co-written by William's brother-in-law Joshua Logan (husband of Nedda Harrigan). Although many would associate the part of the eccentric captain with a penchant for potted palm trees with James Cagney (marvelous in the 1955 screen version), Harrigan made the role his own on stage, playing Captain Morton for three years and 1158 performances. William considered the Captain a "serio-comic" character, comparing the portrayal to the "art of walking a tightrope." He felt the actor had to maintain an emotional balance and be ready at any time to shift "from instilling dread to evoking laughter" (*Mister Roberts* souvenir program notes). On the opening season's initial episode of *Tonight On*

Roogie's Bump (1954): Roogie (Robert Marriott) with the ghost of Red O'Malley (William Harrigan)

Street of Sinners (1957): **George Montgomery is cautioned by his veteran partner William Harrigan not to go strictly by the book.**

Anchorage" (2/24/53, season 3, episode 19) on *Armstrong Circle Theatre* (NBC).

William Harrigan's next two films each had a fantasy angle to them. *Francis Covers the Big Town* (1953) featured William as Deputy Chief Inspector Hansen, who confronts newspaper managing editor Gene Lockhart that his recent news articles indicate a leak in the police department. Hansen later has aspiring reporter Donald O'Connor arrested on suspicion of murder. Francis the talking mule is responsible for the hot news tips, O'Connor's troubles and, finally, his vindication. *Roogie's Bump* (1954) was an interesting effort from Republic that attempted to capitalize on the popularity of the Brooklyn Dodgers, while utilizing actual players like Roy Campanella and Carl Erskine in the cast. Harrigan portrayed Red O'Malley, the ghost of a former baseball great, who appears to young Roogie Rigsby (Robert Marriot) and attempts to help the youngster gain acceptance from his peers by accelerating his baseball

skills. Roogie progresses to the point that he reaches the major leagues with the Dodgers, but with unforeseen consequences. Red later acknowledges overstepping his ghostly powers in that a boy shouldn't be doing a man's job.

William made his first appearance (of four) on *The United States Steel Hour* (ABC) as the father in "Two" (8/31/54, season 1, episode 23), with Jack Klugman. On Broadway, Harrigan was seen as His Lordship, the Bishop of Oriel, in *The Wayward Saint* (2/17/55). William continued his television work, playing Mr. Bemis in "Happy Birthday" (6/25/56, season 2, episode 11) on *Producers Showcase* (NBC) and Emil Drucker in "The Big Vote" (8/19/56, season 1, episode 23) for *The Alcoa Hour* (NBC). He then recreated his role of the Captain for a revival of *Mister Roberts* at the New York City Center (December 1956).

Harrigan's final film role was that of Gus, the veteran cop who advises his rookie partner (George Montgomery) not to go strictly "by the book," in *Street of Sinners* (1957).

A portrait (c. 1960) of William Harrigan during his final decade

As Gus, he cautions Montgomery that gangster Nehemiah Persoff has connections in city government, while trying to impede his partner's investigation. The older officer redeems himself, however, jeopardizing his own life to save Montgomery, killing Persoff in the process.

A Shadow of My Enemy (12/11/57) represented William's last appearance on Broadway. He portrayed the First Interrogator and a Member of Congress in this show, which closed after only five performances.

Harrigan still made sporadic appearances on television before completely retiring from acting. For *The United*

States Steel Hour (which had moved to CBS), William played Father Magner in "This Day in Fear" (11/19/58, season 6, episode 6) and Ralph Henry in both "The Women of Hadley" (2/24/60, season 7, episode 13) and "Revolt in Hadley" (3/9/60, season 7, episode 14). Harrigan appeared on television one last time on the series *Brenner* (CBS), which starred Edward Binns and James Broderick, playing Arnie Carter in "Unwritten Law" (7/5/64, season 2, episode 8).

Harrigan spent most of his later years reading and pursuing other interests. In July 1962, four years prior to his death, William taped his recollections on his life and career. He also recorded his renderings of the songs of his father Ned and grandfather David Braham, such as "The Mulligan Guard."

William Harrigan died at the age of 79 on February 1, 1966, at St. Luke's Hospital, Manhattan, New York, following surgery. On February 2, members of the 307th Infantry Post of the American Legion held a memorial service for Harrigan at the University Funeral Chapel at Lexington Avenue and 52nd Street. William's solemn funeral mass was celebrated at 10:00 a.m. on February 3 at Our Lady of Peace Roman Catholic Church at 237 East 67 Street. The following day (2/4/66), Harrigan was buried with full military honors at Arlington National Cemetery, Arlington, Virginia.

Harrigan's wife Grace (1904-1968), sister Nedda Harrigan Logan (1899-1989) and brothers Philip (1892-1972) and Nolan (1894-1966) Harrigan survived him. Nedda, a fine actress in her own right, appeared in many Broadway productions and films like *Charlie Chan at the Opera* (1936) and *Thank You, Mr. Moto* (1937).

Despite being a member of a prestigious theatrical family, having a career on Broadway spanning more than 60 years and appearing in many important films, William Harrigan has been largely neglected by modern reference books. William's portrayal of Dr. Kemp in James Whale's classic adaptation of H.G. Wells' *The Invisible Man*, alongside lesser fantasy genre roles in *Francis Covers the Big Town* and *Roogie's Bump*, merit his inclusion in a work such as this. It is Harrigan's other screen efforts in films like *G-Men*, *Silk Hat Kid*, *Back Door to Heaven*, *Flying Leathernecks* and *Steel Town* that really provide evidence of this fine actor's range and versatility. It is the hope that there will be wider recognition yet to come for the career of William Harrigan.

Sources

Briscoe, Johnson. "The Younger Generation," in *The Green Book Magazine*, Vol. 3 (March 1910), p. 631.

Coughlin, Jim. "Forgotten Faces of Fantastic Films: William Harrigan," in *Midnight Marquee #38* (Spring 1989), pp. 35-37.

Forrester Harvey
(1884 – 1945)

In that the British Isles often served as the setting for many classic horror films, it is no wonder that casts of many genre offerings are laden with British, Scottish and Irish character players. Familiar Anglo/Irish faces, such as Halliwell Hobbes, Mary Gordon, Doris Lloyd, Leonard Mudie, Lumsden Hare, etc. seem to appear over and over in such films. As comic relief was frequently an ingredient for many horror pictures, directors would often call upon Una O'Connor, E.E. Clive, Billy Bevan or Forrester Harvey to provide the humor. Forrester Harvey was an accomplished comedic character player, first on stage and eventually on the screen. His ability to provide laughs amid the screams was evident in numerous fantasy/horror motion pictures including *Tarzan, the Ape Man*, *The Invisible Man*, *The Mystery of Edwin Drood*, *The Invisible Man Returns*, *The Wolf Man*, *Dr. Jekyll and Mr. Hyde* ('41 version) and *The Man in Half-Moon Street*.

Forrester Marcus Whymple Harvey was born on June 27, 1884, in Cork City, County Cork, Ireland. Whymple

***A Tailor Made Man* (1931): Forrester Harvey with William Haines**

was his mother's maiden name. Although little is known of Forrester's early years, he embarked on a career in the theater while still a young man, touring various cities and towns in the British Isles. By 1908, Harvey was regularly appearing in plays in London, in addition to playing the provinces (as touring was known at the time). Outside of acting, Forrester was a yachting enthusiast, as well as an accomplished cook.

Harvey was seen in London's Queens Theatre as Doc Gunther in *Get-Rich-Quick Wallingford* (1/14/13), which ran for 158 performances. He then appeared at Drury Lane as Edward Hay in *Sealed Orders* (9/11/13), which also enjoyed a healthy run (115 performances). Also at the Theatre Royal, Drury Lane, Harvey portrayed Duke Nemo in the pantomime *The Sleeping Beauty Beautified* (12/26/14), which starred Lupino Lane and Ferne Rogers.

By the conclusion of WWI, Harvey was a well-established comedian on stage in London's West End. He began to find demand for his talent in Britain's growing film industry, as the post-war populace began demanding more comedies to help ease their wounds and sorrows. Forrester was seen in *The Glad Eye* (1920) about the travails of a spiritualist's son. Harvey followed this with another comedy, *London Pride* (1920). *The Lilac Sunbonnet* (1922) had Forrester third-billed as Jock Gordon. Harvey starred in the comic short, *The Man Who Liked Lemons* (1923), as a burglar whose liking for that particular fruit leads to his capture. In between films, Forrester remained active on stage in produc-

A 1928 portrait of Forrester Harvey

The Man in Possession (1931): Forrester Harvey, Robert Montgomery and Irene Purcell

tions like *Other People's Worries* (April 1922) at the Comedy Theatre, Haymarket, London.

Harvey was again featured at London's Haymarket as Biddie in *Havoc* (1/16/24). This four-act play would lead to Harvey's first appearance in the United States, as the "Havoc" company crossed the Atlantic aboard the Orca, arriving in New York Harbor on August 25, 1924. Reprising his role as Biddie, Harvey opened at Maxine Elliott's Theatre on Broadway in *Havoc* (9/1/24), which ran for 48 performances. Among those in the cast who would later join Harvey in Hollywood were Leo G. Carroll, Ethel Griffies, Ralph Forbes and Claud Allister. After *Havoc* closed in New York, it was back to the English stage and screen for Harvey.

British silent film roles for Harvey included Oliver Jordan in *Somebody's Darling* (1925), Amos in *If Youth But Knew* (1926), Mr. Nippit in the short *Cash on Delivery* (1926), Dusty Miller in *The Flag Lieutenant* (1926) and Charles Hart in *Nell Gwynn* (1926), starring Dorothy Gish. Forrester appeared in two early Alfred Hitchcock-directed films, *The Ring* (1927) and *The Farmer's Wife* (1928). In *The Ring*, a boxing tale with a love triangle, Harvey had the substantial part of James Ware, the promoter for fighter Bob Corby (Ian Hunter). Forrester played Bob Ford in *That Brute Simmons* (1928), Pat in *King's Mate* (1928), Simmonds in *Glorious Youth* (1928), a tourist in *Moulin Rouge* (1928) and Watts in *Toni* (1928). As Watty the clown, Harvey was second-billed in *Spangles* (1928), starring Fern Andra. Rounding out Harvey's British screen credits are *Eileen of the Trees* (1929) and *Ringing the Changes* (1929), in which he portrayed Steve Blower.

Whether he knew it at the time or not, when Harvey returned to the United States in 1930, all of his subsequent professional work would be done in America. He first appeared unbilled as a taxi driver in *The Devil to Pay!* (1930) with Ronald Colman and Loretta Young. Harvey then played Pomeroy opposite William Haines in *A Tailor Made Man* (1931) for MGM, the major studio that would employ Forrester numerous times during the thirties.

Harvey was a jewelry store robber in *Everything's Rosie* (1931) with Robert Woolsey (of Wheeler and Woolsey fame). In *The Man in Possession* (1931), Forrester was the bailiff who takes on Robert Montgomery to assist him in collecting unpaid debts. Forrester played Joe the news vendor in *Chances* (1931), with Douglas Fairbanks, Jr. Back at MGM opposite Lionel Barrymore and Kay Francis, Harvey was Spencer Wilson in *Guilty Hands* (1931). He had a minor role as the gas inspector in *Devotion* (1931), with Leslie Howard.

Again with Robert Montgomery at MGM, Forrester played a fisherman in *Lovers Courageous* (1932). He was seen with Bette Davis and H.B. Warner in *The Menace* (1932). *Shanghai Express* (1932), starring Marlene Dietrich, offered a brief glimpse of Harvey as the Peiping ticket agent. As an innkeeper (which would become a fairly common role for Forrester), Harvey appeared with Spencer Tracy in *Sky Devils* (1932). *The Wet Parade* (1932), a Prohibition tale stressing the adverse effects of alcohol with Lewis Stone and Robert Young, had Harvey as Mr. Fortesque.

Forrester Harvey's first excursion into the realm of fantasy came with his portrayal of Beamish, the cockney

Blind Adventure (1933): The coffee wagon proprietor (Forrester Harvey) deals with the elusive burglar Holmes (Roland Young).

The Invisble Man (1933): **Jack Griffin (Claude Rains) seeks lodging from Herbert (Forrester Harvey) and Jenny Hall (Una O'Connor).**

storekeeper at the jungle post, in *Tarzan, the Ape Man* (1932), starring Johnny Weissmuller. Shortly after the film's beginning, when the British party arrives in the jungle, Beamish remarks, "Knock me for a row of ninepins if it isn't little Miss Jane (Maureen O'Sullivan)," having not seen her since she was a young girl. Harvey would later reprise the role of Beamish in the first of numerous "Tarzan" sequels, *Tarzan and His Mate* (1934), this time telling Henry Holt (Neil Hamilton), "I wouldn't trust meself in that jungle if it was me, sir!"

-But the Flesh is Weak (1932) starred Robert Montgomery and had Harvey as Gooch. *Mystery Ranch* (1932) offered a different type of role for Forrester as Artie Brower, a retired English jockey working at the Steele ranch. He had been dedicated to the father of Cecelia Parker, but when he tries to save her from the perfidy of Charles Middleton, Brower ends up strapped to a runaway horse by henchman Noble Johnson. After George O'Brien frees Brower, the Englishman is killed while warding off an Apache attack.

Mack Sennett paired Harvey, as Hawkins, with Matt McHugh as bumbling detectives in the short *Hawkins and Watkins, Inc.* (1932). To add to the absurdity, Charles Gemora appears as an ape riding a motorcycle. *Those We Love* (1932), directed by Robert Florey, had Forrester as Jake. *Young Onions* (1932), another comedy short, included Harvey as Alfred, a disinterested husband whose wife (Dorothy Granger) leaves him to seek romance. Alfred himself ends up chasing girls at the beach at Malibu. The tender *Smilin' Through* (1932), with Fredric March and Norma Shearer in the leads, afforded Forrester the part of an orderly.

Kongo (1932), a decadent remake of Lon Chaney's *West of Zanzibar* (1928) with Walter Huston impressive as the vengeful "Dead Legs" Flint, featured Harvey as Cookie Harris, one of his henchmen. Cookie displays his humanity when he helps lead Ann (Virginia Bruce) and Kingsland (Conrad Nagel) to safety through an underground tunnel when Flint is revealed to be mortal to the rampaging natives at the climax. In another film set in the jungle, *Red*

The Mystery of Mr. X (1934): Jewel thief Robert Montgomery with accomplice Forrester Harvey

Dust (1932) with Clark Gable, Jean Harlow and Mary Astor, Harvey played Limey, the English riverboat pilot.

Harvey portrayed Ring, the cook, in *Destination Unknown* (1933), set on board a ship taken over by bootleggers after the captain is killed during a hurricane. *The Eagle and the Hawk* (1933), about World War I fliers, gave Harvey the sympathetic part of Hogan, an enlisted man who is entrusted with gathering the personal effects of slain airmen for safekeeping. Harvey's roles were sometimes quite small, however, often utilizing him for a single scene in a film. Forrester was briefly seen as a barfly in *Cocktail Hour* (1933), Thomas Roberts in *Midnight Club* (1933), the coffee wagon proprietor in *Blind Adventure* (1933) and Oscar, the hotel employee with the letter, in *Lady for a Day* (1934).

Harvey was in rare form in his significant genre role as Herbert Hall, the proprietor of The Lion's Head Inn, in *The Invisible Man* (1933). After Jack Griffin (Claude Rains) enters the inn approaching Hall for a room with a fire, the innkeeper sends his wife Jenny (Una O'Connor) to take care of the accommodations for the mysterious stranger. Hall then heeds the advice of a patron and locks up his

money. After Jenny whines that Griffin must go, Herbert is dispatched both to collect the bill and rid them of the stranger. As Griffin pleads to stay, Hall accuses him of driving away customers and being bad for business. When Hall begins to pack up Griffin's chemicals and belongings, the stranger becomes enraged, hitting the innkeeper and throwing him down the stairs. One of Harvey's best comedic takes is when he is lying in O'Connor's arms in obvious pain, only to have her shrieks enhance his agony. The eccentric touch of James Whale is obvious in this particular scene.

Man of Two Worlds (1934), with Francis Lederer as an Eskimo whom British adventurers attempt to "civilize," had Harvey as Tim. Forrester played a tramp in the park in *You Can't Have Everything* (1934), with May Robson. *The Mystery of Mr. X* (1934) provided Harvey with a larger role than usual as London cabby Joseph Horatio Palmer. As Palmer, Forrester, along with Ivan Simpson, serves as a confederate to jewel thief Robert Montgomery, hiding a valuable diamond for him while displaying his clever wit. The *Cortland* (NY) *Standard* (4/13/34), reviewing *The Mys-*

Great Expectations (1934): Rafaela Otiano and Forrester Harvey

The Mystery of Edwin Drood (1935): Durdles (Forrester Harvey) leads Jasper (Claude Rains) through the cemetery.

tery of Mr. X, wrote, "Forrester Harvey is still the best cockney comedian on the screen."

Harvey again enjoyed an important role as Uncle Pumblechook in Universal's adaptation of Dickens' *Great Expectations* (1934). *The Evening Leader* (Corning, NY, 2/9/35) expounded, "The character 'Pumblechook,' enacted by Forrester Harvey, is actually better, more droll and truer to imagination on the screen than in the book." Pumblechook is partly responsible for young Pip (George P. Breakston) becoming a companion for the mysterious Miss Havisham (Florence Reed).

Menace (1934) had Harvey as Wilcox, the driver for Colonel Crecy (Paul Cavanaugh). As the genial Commissioner Waddington in *The Painted Veil* (1934), with Greta Garbo, Forrester displayed a certain fondness for alcohol. Frank Capra directed *Broadway Bill* (1934) and included Harvey as Bradshaw, the horse trainer. He played McDonald in *Limehouse Blues* (1934), with George Raft and Anna May Wong. Harvey's scenes were deleted from the final print of *Forsaking All Others* (1934).

Around this time, an unusual item appeared in various newspapers regarding Forrester. The *Troy* (NY) *Times* (1/17/34), for one, wrote, "The problem of what to have for breakfast never bothers Forrester Harvey." The piece went on to claim that Harvey had a trained hen living in a box in his kitchen that would regularly lay at least one egg every morning. Whether this was a product of studio publicists indulging in hyperbole, or if there was some substance to the story is not known.

The Best Man Wins (1935), with Bela Lugosi heading a smuggling operation, had Forrester as Harry. Harvey played Hugo, the innkeeper, in *The Gilded Lily* (1935), with Claudette Colbert and Fred MacMurray. He was unbilled as an English bobby in *The Right to Live* (1935) and as a sailor in *Captain Hurricane* (1935).

A particularly colorful role for Harvey was that of Durdles, the cemetery caretaker, in another Universal Dickens adaptation, *The Mystery of Edwin Drood* (1935). Durdles is bribed by Mr. Jasper (Claude Rains) to take him on a tour of the cemetery and crypts "by moonlight." "You bring the spirits and Durdles will show you around," the caretaker responds. When they come to a pit of quick lime essential to the plot, Durdles comments that it is "quick enough to eat your bones!" Durdles is eventually summoned to help establish that Jasper murdered young Drood (David Manners).

The Woman in Red (1935), starring Barbara Stanwyck and directed by Robert Florey, had Forrester as Mooney. Harvey played Corky Nye in *Vagabond Lady* (1935). *Jalna* (1935), based on the play *Whiteoaks* and featuring Nigel Bruce and David Manners, included Harvey as Rags, the

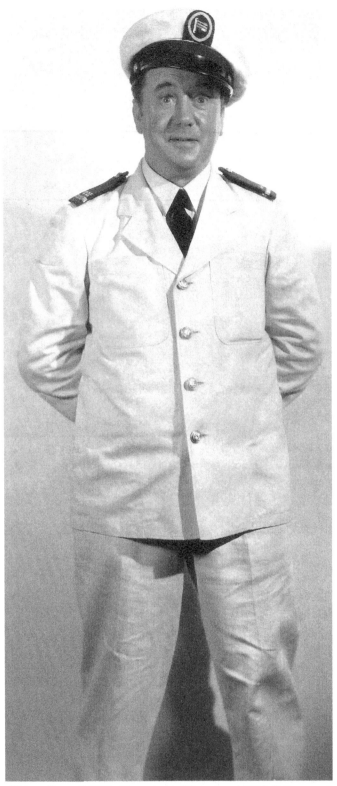

China Seas (1935): Forrester Harvey as Chief Steward Ted Gary

Captain Blood (1935): Forrester Harvey as the loyal but lazy Honesty Nuttall

family butler and chauffeur. *China Seas* (1935), with a bevy of MGM stars including Jean Harlow, Clark Gable and Wallace Beery, featured Forrester as Chief Steward Ted Gary. Harvey played the police surgeon in *Without Regret* (1935) and Wally Baxton in *The Perfect Gentleman* (1935).

Revisiting Charles Dickens, Harvey was Joe, the coach guard, in *A Tale of Two Cities* (1935).

Captain Blood (1935), which established Errol Flynn as the new screen swashbuckler, included some fine work by Harvey as Honesty Nuttall. While Peter Blood (Flynn) is treating the gout of the governor (George Hassell) of Jamaica, Honesty is brought in on the charge of vagrancy. When asked to state his occupation, Nuttall grimaces, "I'm a ship's carpenter—when the painful necessity arises." Despite his propensity for sloth and drink, Nuttall helps Blood plot his escape and becomes a valued member of his pirate crew.

Three Live Ghosts (1936), concerning a trio of British soldiers in World War I who escape from the Germans just prior to the Armistice (and have to prove they are alive to secure their back pay), had Harvey as the difficult paymaster. *Love Before Breakfast* (1936), starring Carole Lombard, featured Forrester as the chief steward. He again was on

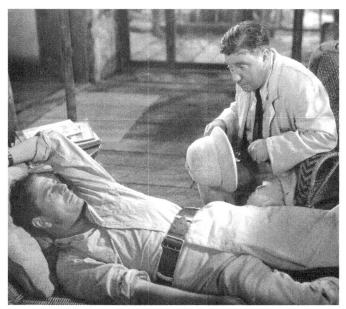

White Hunter (1936): Warner Baxter and Forrester Harvey

board, this time as the deck steward, in *The Return of Sophie Lang* (1936). *Petticoat Fever* (1936), yet another Robert Montgomery MGM feature, included Harvey as Scotty. Forrester had a minor role as a counter man in *Suzy* (1936), with Jean Harlow. Harvey portrayed Pembrooke in *White Hunter* (1936), Percival Potts in *Lloyd's of London* (1936), the "meaty man" in *The Prince and the Pauper* (1937) and the pub proprietor in *Souls at Sea* (1937).

Personal Property (1937) was, in essence, a remake of *The Man in Possession* (1931), with Harvey reprising his bailiff role. As Herbert Jenkins, Forrester represents the creditors of Crystal Wetherby (Jean Harlow) but faces a dilemma as his wife is about to give birth to their baby. Therefore, Herbert appoints Ferguson (Robert Taylor) as a deputy to live on Crystal's estate until the debts can be paid. While on the set of *Personal Property*, Forrester had a reunion of sorts with fellow cast mates E.E. Clive and Barnett Parker, as the three reminisced about touring the British provinces together 30 years earlier in *Are You a Mason?*

As Jocko Jenkins, the valet to Lawrence Fontaine (Lewis Stone) in *The Man Who Cried Wolf* (1937), Harvey hides a gun to protect his employer. He is later killed in an automobile accident before he can fully vindicate Fontaine.

Harvey was featured in a number of entries in Paramount's *Bulldog Drummond* film series, although not in a recurring role. John Howard portrayed Drummond in all four of Harvey's efforts in the series. Forrester

was the barman and innkeeper in *Bulldog Drummond Comes Back* (1937). In *Bulldog Drummond in Africa* (1938), he played Constable Jenkins. *Arrest Bulldog Drummond* (1939) included Harvey as Constable Severn at Gannett House. Harvey's best developed "Drummond" role was that of the addle-brained Professor Downie in *Bulldog Drummond's Secret Police* (1939). Downie informs Drummond that there is substantial treasure, dating back to the reign of King Charles I, buried in a cavern on the Rockingham estate, where the detective is planning to be married. Believing to have determined the location of the fortune by researching old manuscripts and clues, Downie is set to lead Drummond and his entourage to the treasure, but he is murdered before doing so.

Fight for Your Lady (1937), with John Boles and Jack Oakie, had Harvey as a wrestling referee. He was Wilkins, the horse trainer for C. Aubrey Smith's stable, in *Thoroughbreds Don't Cry* (1937), one of a number of MGM films pairing Judy Garland and Mickey Rooney. Forrester played the eager to please Scottish innkeeper in *Kidnapped* (1938). In *The Mysterious Mr. Moto* (1938), Harvey portrayed the enthusiastic George Higgins, who, with gangster partner Harold Huber, tries to ally himself with diabolical Leon Ames.

A Christmas Carol (1938), with Reginald Owen as Scrooge, had Harvey as Old Fezziwig, to whom young Ebenezer had once apprenticed. Scrooge and the Spirit of Christmas Past (Ann Rutherford) visit Fezziwig's shop, where Ebenezer realizes that business had been conducted in a moral and ethical manner.

The Man Who Cried Wolf (1937): Lewis Stone and Forrester Harvey**

The Invisble Man Returns (1940): Forrester Harvey as Ben Jenkins

A Chump at Oxford (1940): Stan Laurel with Forrester Harvey as Meredith

Harvey was the tailor's assistant in the Nelson Eddy-Jeanette MacDonald musical *Sweethearts* (1938). He played the customs inspector in the comedy *I'm From Missouri* (1939). *Let Us Live* (1939), with Henry Fonda rendering a poignant performance in the lead, had Forrester as the death row inmate requesting his music. Other roles at this time for Harvey included Nonny Watkins in *The Lady's From Kentucky* (1939), the cricket umpire in *Raffles* (1939) and a bit in *The Private Lives of Elizabeth and Essex* (1939), the latter with Bette Davis and Errol Flynn. *The Witness Vanishes* (1939) gave Forrester an important part as Alistair McNab, the reporter who forces Edmund Lowe to reveal himself as the murderer.

Harvey was one of only two performers (Harry Stubbs being the other) to appear in both *The Invisible Man* (1933) and *The Invisible Man Returns* (1940). Forrester's character in *The Invisible Man Returns*, Ben Jenkins, is clearly distinct from that of Herbert Hall in *The Invisible Man*. Jenkins, a reclusive small-scale farmer, has a long relationship with the Griffin family, including Frank Griffin (John Sutton), who is trying to develop the antidote (that eluded brother Jack) for the psychological side effects from the drug that causes invisibility. Recently escaped prisoner Geoffrey Radcliffe (Vincent Price), who has used the drug to break out of jail and evade his captors, finds safe haven for the time being at Ben Jenkins' farm.

A Chump at Oxford (1940) gave Harvey the chance to display his comic skills alongside those of Stan Laurel and Oliver Hardy. When Meredith (Harvey), the valet, spots Laurel, he declares, "Your Lordship, don't you remember me, sir?" Meredith claims Laurel is Lord Paddington, Oxford scholar and athlete par excellence, who was hit by a falling window in the midst of a victory celebration, lost his memory and soon after disappeared. As students gather to seek vengeance on the "dirty snitchers" (Laurel and Hardy), Stan is hit on the head by the same window and transforms into Lord Paddington, to Meredith's delight. Perhaps Harvey's strongest scene occurs as he marvelously extols Laurel's virtues at the same time as Hardy attempts to denigrate them.

The Mysterious Doctor **(1940): John Loder and Forrester Harvey, with villagers**

As Chalcroft, the proprietor, Harvey was once again directed by Alfred Hitchcock in *Rebecca* (1940), highlighted by the stellar performances of Joan Fontaine and Laurence Olivier. In *On Their Own* (1940), one of the Jones Family film series, Forrester played Mr. Pim. *Tom Brown's School Days* (1940) had Harvey as Sam the coachman. *Earl of Puddlestone* (1940) provided another complex comic role for Forrester as Tittington, the conman. Tittington helps perpetrate a hoax centering on James Gleason, whose family hopes to boost their social standing, being the American heir to a deceased British earl. When the conman does not get his payments as promised, he threatens to expose the charade. Instead, Tittington is kidnapped, believes he will be murdered, but eventually escapes to reveal the truth. Harvey really shone in the part.

Little Nellie Kelly (1940), with Judy Garland, had Harvey as Moriarty. He played Briggs, the landlord, in *Free and Easy* (1941). Forrester had a minor bit as a bum in Frank Capra's *Meet John Doe* (1941), starring Gary Cooper. Harvey then assayed the part of an air raid warden in *Scotland Yard* (1941).

In Paramount's remake of *Dr. Jekyll and Mr. Hyde* (1941), Harvey portrayed Old Prouty, the proprietor of the Palace of Frivolities, where Ivy (Ingrid Bergman) works as a barmaid. When Hyde (Spencer Tracy) demands that Ivy serve

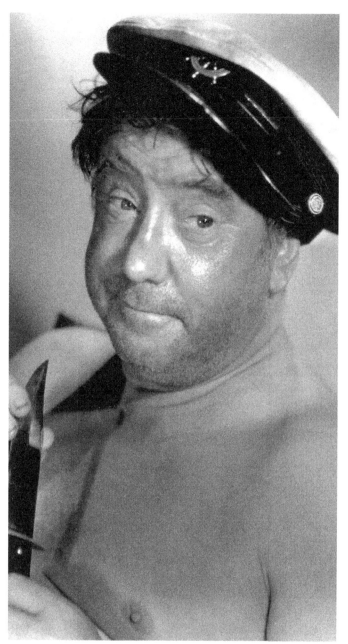

Mercy Island **(1941): Forrester Harvey as Captain Lowe**

him at his table, Prouty insists that the waiter (Alec Craig) fetch her to bring him champagne. After Hyde initiates a fight in the music hall, Prouty, who has been poked in the head by the fiend's cane, is coerced (by money) to fire the barmaid. Prouty gives in to Hyde, stating, "A troublemaker, that's what she is. Out she goes, sir." Prouty is basically a spineless character with no loyalty, but Harvey imbued him with more depth than the role required.

Mercy Island (1941) gave Harvey another important part as Captain Lowe who takes a party deep-sea fishing in the Florida Keys, only to be shipwrecked along with a complex group of characters. The Captain must contend with psychotic and murderous Ray Middleton, while helping the others survive thanks to his skills as a fisherman.

Scotland Yard Investigator (**1945**): **Injured Forrester Harvey with wife Doris Lloyd**

The Wolf Man (1941) utilized Harvey as a bit of comic relief in the character of Victor Twiddle. Twiddle is instructed by Police Captain Montford (Ralph Bellamy) to transcribe the details of the death of Jenny Williams (Fay Helm), who has been mauled by "some wild animal." Twiddle, wearing a bowler hat, shudders, grimaces and wipes his brow, offering, "I'm a little squeamish, sir." When the body of Bela the Gypsy (Bela Lugosi) is next located, Twiddle notes, in a fine cockney accent, that he was killed with "a stick with a 'orse's 'ead 'andle."

Harvey also found his way into major mainstream movies, as his roles as the proprietor in *This Above All* (1941), Mr. Huggins in the Academy Award-winning *Mrs. Miniver* (1942) and the cabby in *Random Harvest* (1942) can attest.

The Mysterious Doctor (1943), a wartime mystery with a borderline horror angle, prominently featured Harvey as ingratiating drunk Hugh Penhryn. A tavern regular, Penhryn regales Dr. Holmes (Lester Mathews), a stranger, with the legend behind the curse of Preston's Head, a tin mining town. When a man is killed and decapitated at the town mine, the victim is believed to be Holmes. It turns out that Nazis, involved in espionage, have manipulated the suspicious villagers to believe that Preston's curse has been revisited on them. Harvey helps promote the horror atmosphere in *The Mysterious Doctor*, while also injecting some humor into the plot.

The Lodger (1944), with Laird Cregar superb in the title role, had Forrester on hand as a cobbler. Harvey portrayed Alfred Morgan, a clerk, in *Secrets of Scotland Yard* (1944), with Lionel Atwill and Edgar Barrier prominent in the cast. *None But the Lonely Heart* (1944), with Cary Grant, had Forrester as the proprietor of a shooting gallery. *The Man in Half-Moon Street* (1945), with Nils Asther as a 120-year-old scientist who maintains his youth by unnatural methods, included Harvey as Harris, a cabby.

Scotland Yard Investigator (1945) gave Harvey his last substantial role on the screen as Sam Todworthy. An unscrupulous art dealer, Todworthy provides a hiding place when Miran (Georges Renavent) brings the stolen Mona Lisa to him. When Miran attempts to retrieve the painting, Todworthy shoots him. Later, Todworthy tries to extort money from Carl Hoffmeyer (Erich von Stroheim), but ends up getting murdered himself.

Set during the Spanish Civil War, *Confidential Agent* (1945) featured Forrester as Bates. Harvey played Peter Dickie in *The Green Years* (1946), which had a compelling performance by Charles Coburn. *Devotion* (1946), about the literary Brontë family, had Forrester as Hoggs. The latter two films were both released after Harvey's death. *Riding High* (1950), directed by Frank Capra, is technically another posthumous credit for Forrester (in that it utilized footage of him as a horse trainer that originally appeared in *Broadway Bill*, 1934).

On December 14, 1945 Forrester Harvey suffered a stroke and died in Laguna Beach, California. His French-born wife Helene survived him. Very little is known of Forrester and Helene Harvey's marriage or private life.

Forrester Harvey brought color and dimension to his various film roles, regardless of the size of his part. His characters were usually fraught with human frailties, easy to laugh at, identify with or just enjoy for the extra life they brought to so many films. At times, Forrester was limited to providing comic relief, but when given the opportunity he could display a much greater range and depth of emotion. Harvey's work in the fantasy genre as Herbert Hall in *The Invisible Man*, Durdles in *The Mystery of Edwin Drood*, Twiddle in *The Wolf Man*, Old Prouty in *Dr. Jekyll and Mr. Hyde* and Ben Jenkins in *The Invisible Man Returns*, among other portrayals, indicates that the actor made a significant but neglected contribution to the classic age of cinema horror.

Sources

Coughlin, Jim. "Forgotten Faces of Fantastic Films: Forrester Harvey," in *Midnight Marquee #40* (Summer 1990), pp. 35-36.

The Moonstone
(1934)

Charles Irwin
(1887 - 1969)

One of the most talented but overlooked character actors from the Golden Age of movies was Charles Irwin. He appeared in all genres of film: comedies, musicals, mysteries, dramas, sea sagas, war pictures, and horror films. Irwin worked opposite virtually every major star in Hollywood in more than 30 years on the screen. He played important roles in Oscar-winning films like *Mutiny on the Bounty* and *Mrs. Miniver*, as well as other significant motion pictures like *The Letter, The Light That Failed, Yankee Doodle Dandy* and *The King and I*. Irwin was equally adept at portraying police constables, soldiers, bartenders, drunks, emcees, announcers, reporters and even polo players, often with an Irish brogue, Scottish burr, Cockney accent or whatever the part demanded. Whether a brief, unbilled bit or a fairly lengthy featured role, Charles Irwin utilized his sense of humor

and unforced delivery to make his presence felt. A long-time nightclub comedian, Irwin predated many of today's stand-up comics who have ventured into films. It is a wonder that most film reference books have chosen to ignore Irwin and his extensive body of screen work.

Charles Wesley Irwin was in Belfast, U.K. (now Northern Ireland) on January 31, 1887 (although some sources list the Curragh region of County Kildare, Ireland as his birthplace.) He was one of 10 children born to William Henry Irwin (1861- ?) and the former Annie Elizabeth Mathers (1861- ?). The 1901 Census of Ireland lists the Irwin family as living in a house at 17 Upper Frank Street, Ormeau, County Down. At that point living in the home, in addition to 14-year-old Charles and his parents, were Charles' older brother Robert Gordon and younger siblings Florence Nightingale, Mabel, William Duncan, John Stanley, Caroline and Arthur. Youngest brother Norman Irwin would be born in 1905. Another child died in infancy. As an adult, Charles stood five-foot-10 and weighed 170 pounds, with blue eyes and brown hair. Irwin attended Queens University in Belfast. He made his theatrical debut in Great Britain in 1906 in Sir Frank Benson's production

Divorced Sweethearts (1930): Cyril Chadwick, Marjorie Beebe, Ann Christy, Charles Irwin, Tom Dempsey and Harry Dunkinson (judge, in back)

Blind Adventure (1933): John Miljan holds a gun on Roland Young, who is held by Charles Irwin.

after leaving Burnham. Hamilton, in the *N.Y. Clipper* (7/27/21), found Irwin's "dissection" and parody of the famed song "Annie Laurie" to be "very funny." Irwin then joined the noted revue *Artists and Models* (1924), playing Washington, DC; the Winter Garden on Broadway and elsewhere. *Artists and Models* showed a hint of Irwin's versatility, featuring him in numerous roles, including successful artist Charlie Famous. *Find Daddy* (3/8/26), which lasted only 16 performances at the Ritz, had Irwin as Russell Morgan. *A la Carte* (8/17/27), another musical revue, had a slightly longer run (45 performances) with Charles in the cast.

Charles made his first film appearance (as himself) in the short *The Debonair Humorist* (1928). *Ned Wayburn's Gambols* (1/15/29), another review, this time at the Knickerbocker, included Charles as "the Author" (in the Introduction), "the Host" (in "Night Life") and Jack (in "The Last Straw"). Irwin's first feature film was the early Technicolor musical *The King of Jazz* (1930), in which he appeared as himself, the announcer. Capitalizing on his reputation as a nightclub emcee and humorist, Irwin intro-

of Shakespeare's *The Merchant of Venice*. Irwin later played for a season with the illustrious Sarah Bernhardt and her company. Before venturing to the United States, Irwin was part of a theatrical troupe touring Egypt, India and northern China.

Irwin was briefly wed to Lillian M. Dyer on January 7, 1914, with the marriage ending in divorce soon after. Charles then married Kathryn Florence Henry Jolly (1895-1971) in Perth, Ontario, Canada on September 28, 1915, with that union lasting until his death in 1969. Irwin formed an act with his wife, a dancer, which was interrupted by her illness ("Chas. Irwin Playing it Alone" read a headline in the July 9, 1916 *New York Telegraph*). Irwin began to rely on his skill as a monologist, in addition to doing songs and dialects, while perfecting his solo act in clubs and vaudeville. Reviewers of the time referred to Charles as "Harry Lauter's only rival," which was high praise.

With the advent of World War I, Irwin enlisted in the Royal Inniskilling Fusiliers, saw action in the Near and Far East, including Gallipoli, and was wounded in battle. While in the service, Irwin gave a command performance of songs and comedy in Malta before the Duke and Duchess of Connaught. Charles was honorably discharged, receiving the Distinguished Service Medal. After leaving military service in Tientsin (now Tianjin, China), Irwin traveled to San Francisco, securing theatrical work with Eunice Burnham's company. Charles toured on both the Keith and Orpheum vaudeville circuits as a solo comedian for a few years

The Moonstone: Charles Irwin, John Davidson and David Manners

Mutiny on the Bounty (1935): Mutineers Charles Irwin and Pat Flaherty confront midshipmen Franchot Tone and Douglas Walton.

duced numbers by Paul Whiteman's orchestra and others. *The King of Jazz*, with its star-studded cast, was projected to be a big success for Universal. Junior Laemmle's hopes of joining the upper echelon of Hollywood producers were dampened when public and critical acclaim did not meet these expectations. Perhaps if they had, Irwin's star would have risen as well.

Charles also was seen in two shorts for Mack Sennett, as Bill Burton in *Racket Cheers* (1930) and as the wealthy Charles Renssalaer Van Buren in *Divorced Sweethearts* (1930). His prominence in the early thirties was noted in a *Los Angeles Times* (19/20/32) news item: "Charles Irwin, humorist, entertainer and MC will headline the vaudeville bill which opens today at Warner Bros. Downtown Theater in conjunction with the screening of *A Successful Calamity*." By the following year, 1933, Irwin had become a regular film performer, breaking out of the solo comedian mold, keeping active on screen for the next quarter-century.

In the dark drama *Kongo* (1932), Irwin had a small role as Carl. *Blind Adventure* (1933) had Irwin as Bill, a henchman of John Miljan, whose gang torments Robert

Armstrong and Helen Mack. Irwin was seen as the bucktoothed sergeant in *Hell Below* (1933), a steward in *The Solitaire Man* (1933), an ammunition officer in *Ace of Aces* (1933), a bridge player in *If I Were Free* (1933), a drunken passenger in *Luxury Liner* (1933) and Mr. Burton, a clerk, in *Looking Forward* (1933). He also appeared as Nikki the Prime Minister in *Kickin' the Crown Around* (1933), a Masquers short. As Willis, Charles served as the aide to the inspector (Lewis Stone) in *The Mystery of Mr. X* (1934), a clever mystery with Robert Montgomery.

Monogram assembled a fine cast, including David Manners and Herbert Bunston of *Dracula* fame, for their adaptation of Wilkie Collins' *The Moonstone* (1934). Viewing the film over 80 years later, Irwin's acting appears to hold up as well as that of anyone in the film. As Inspector Cuff, friend of Franklin Blake (Manners), Irwin is brought to the Verinder mansion from Scotland Yard to help unravel the disappearance of the "moonstone," a beautiful, precious gem. Charles brightens up the proceedings with his witty questioning of suspects like Jameson Thomas and John Davidson. *Variety* (9/18/34) noted, "David Manners

Candid photo (c. 1935): Helen Hayes and Charles Irwin at a party for Joseph Cawthorne

Mutiny on the Bounty (1935), MGM's epic adaptation of Nordhoff and Hall's classic novel, featured an all-star cast, not only of leading players, but also some of the best character actors of the time (Donald Crisp, Henry Stephenson, Herbert Mundin, Stanley Fields, Dudley Digges, Ian Wolfe and Ivan Simpson, to name but a few). Irwin portrayed Matthew Thompson, able seaman, who early on experiences the injustice of Captain Bligh (Charles Laughton) and later becomes one of the most prominent mutineers. This was a straight dramatic adventure role for Irwin, different than most of his earlier parts, but he was able to convey just what director Frank Lloyd and the story itself required.

And So They Were Married (1935) provided Irwin a comic bit as Tom Phillips, a drunk in the jail. Charles portrayed Carlton the polo player in *Spendthrift* (1936), a sympathetic soldier waiting to say goodbye in *The White Angel* (1936) and the mounted policeman who tickets Jean Arthur in *More Than a Secretary* (1936). Irwin's scenes as Larry King in *Whipsaw* (1936) were deleted from the final print. Some of Irwin's other roles at the time could almost be missed if one happened to blink: the subpoena server in *The Unguarded Hour* (1936), John, the head waiter, in *Small Town Girl* (1936), the steward in *Libeled Lady* (1936), the information clerk in *Wife vs. Secretary* (1936), the master of ceremonies in *Go West, Young Man* (1936) and the movie cameraman in *Love on the Run* (1936).

The League of Frightened Men (1937), with Walter Connelly as Nero Wolfe, included Irwin as Augustus Farrell, one of 10 former Harvard students being systematically murdered years later, supposedly for their roles in the crip-

and Phyllis Barry head the cast, but it all goes to the detective, with Charles Irwin getting more out of the role than was put into it."

In *The Little Minister* (1934), Irwin, as Jon Mac-Laren, tells the parishioners of the disappearance of the title character (John Beal). Irwin played a cockney drunk on the street in *Bulldog Drummond Strikes Back* (1934), the master of ceremonies in *The Key* (1934), Mr. Chisholm in *Long Lost Father* (1934), a customer in *College Rhythm* (1934) and the St. Louis emcee in *Belle of the Nineties* (1933). As Abraham Gray, the ship's carpenter in *Treasure Island* (1934), Irwin sided with the loyalists against the pirates led by Long John Silver (Wallace Beery). *China Seas* (1935), starring Clark Gable, Jean Harlow and Wallace Beery, featured Irwin as Bertie, the ship's purser. Irwin was Oscar the orchestra leader in *The Gilded Lily* (1935), a staff announcer in *Page Miss Glory* (1935), an officer in *Clive of India* (1935) and the purser in *I Found Stella Parish* (1935). In his first of many appearances with Errol Flynn, Irwin was unbilled as a seaman in *Captain Blood* (1935).

Let's Get Married **(1937): Sympathetic bartender Charles Irwin commiserates with Ralph Bellamy.**

Lord Jeff (1938): Dialogue coach Charles Irwin (seated) gives tips to young actors Peter Lawford, Walter Tetley, Terry Kilburn and Mickey Rooney.

The Light That Failed (1939): Soldier model Charles Irwin, artist Ronald Colman and Walter Huston

pling of another student during a hazing incident. Irwin displayed his aptitude for playing drunks in both *Double or Nothing* (1937) and *Wings Over Honolulu* (1937). Charles was the replacement steward in *Think Fast, Mr. Moto* (1937) and a fire drill steward in *Shall We Dance* (1937).

For MGM, Irwin played a court usher in *Parnell* (1937), the emcee at the ship's party in *Mama Steps Out* (1937) and a magazine salesman in *Live, Love and Learn* (1937). Charles was seen as Kelly in *Another Dawn* (1937), Editor Black in *The Devil is Driving* (1937), the ringside radio announcer in *Fight for Your Lady* (1937) and Mike, the compassionate bartender who listens to Ralph Bellamy, in *Let's Get Married* (1937). Irwin was on hand as Sergeant Ellis, who accompanies vile tax collector Leonard Mudie, in *Kidnapped* (1938), First Mate Palmer in the short *Captain Kidd's Treasure* (1938), one of King Richard's returning crusaders in *Adventures of Robin Hood* (1938), a highlander in DeMille's *The Buccaneer* (1938) and Mr. Burke in *Lord Jeff* (1938). In addition to acting in the film, Charles worked with Freddie Bartholomew, Mickey Rooney and other young performers from *Lord Jeff*, instructing them on their accents and dialogue.

The year 1939 was a noteworthy one in cinema history and a busy one for Irwin, who had at least 15 screen credits. Irwin was the sergeant of marines in *The Adventures of Sherlock Holmes* (1939). Charles played opposite Shirley Temple in both *The Little Princess* (1939), as a wounded soldier outside the hospital, and *Susannah of the Mounties* (1939), as Sgt. MacGregor, who discovers Temple as the only survivor of an Indian massacre. Irwin again was a drunk in *Charlie McCarthy, Detective* (1939) and then a hangover victim in *I'm From Missouri* (1939). Other Irwin roles included: the theater manager in *I Stole a Million* (1939), the mounted police sergeant in *Wolf Call* (1939), an announcer in both *Little Accident* (1939) and *Sweepstakes Winner* (1939), a working man in an apron in *We Are Not Alone* (1939), Detective Phillips in *Raffles* (1939), a staff person at the Ireland airport in *The Flying Irishman* (1939) and the hotel desk clerk in *Man About Town* (1939). As the soldier model in *The Light That Failed* (1939), Irwin objected to artist Ronald Colman's sanitized depiction of him for commercial purposes. Irwin is not often credited, however, with his appearance in one of the most famous and popular fantasy films of all time, *The Wizard of Oz* (1939). With Gerald Oliver Smith, Irwin is one of the metal polishers (he sings, "Rub, rub there.") who work on the Tin Man (Jack Haley) at the "Wash & Brush Up Co." upon the arrival of Dorothy and her friends at the Emerald City.

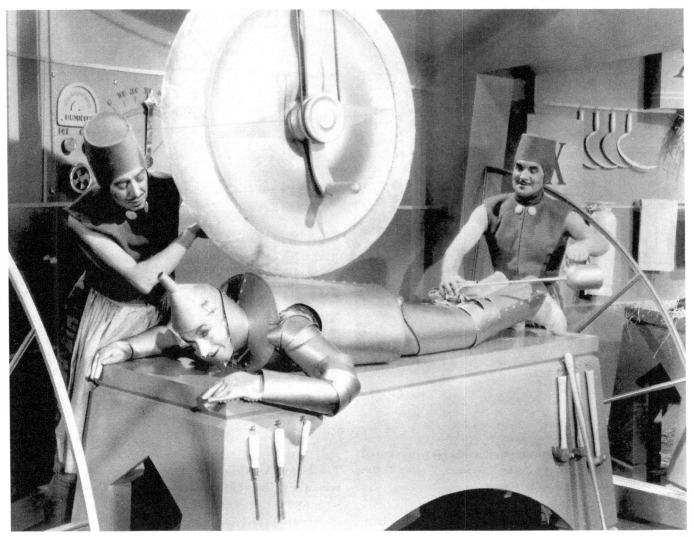

***The Wizard of Oz* (1939): The Tin Man (Jack Haley, center) is polished by Ozmites Gerald Oliver Smith and Charles Irwin.**

Irwin continued to show up in major films, such as *The Letter* (1940), in which he played a friend of Herbert Marshall, *The Great Dictator* (1940), as a banquet waiter and the remake of *Waterloo Bridge* (1940), as the announcer at the Candlelight Club. Charles was a telegraph operator in *A Dispatch from Reuters* (1940), a drunk in *Kitty Foyle* (1940), Constable Gervin in *South of Suez* (1940), Nelson, in *Adventure in Diamonds* (1940), a townsperson in *Rangers of Fortune* (1940) and had an unaccredited bit in *The Man I Married* (1940). In the Robert Benchley short *That Inferior Feeling* (1940), Irwin had a humorous turn as a tailor. Irwin worked in another Errol Flynn swashbuckler, *The Sea Hawk* (1940), wherein Charles played loyal crew member Arnold Cross.

Shadows on the Stairs (1941), an atmospheric murder mystery with horror genre familiars like Turhan Bey, Frieda Inescourt, Heather Angel, Miles Mander and Lumsden Hare, had Irwin as the police constable. Irwin played the sergeant at the base in *They Met in Bombay* (1941), Eddie the reporter in *Singapore Woman* (1941), the casino manager in *The Blonde from Singapore* (1941), the apartment manager in *Married Bachelor* (1941), the first man sitting with Kay in *Blues in the Night* (1941), the Chemin de Fer Croupier in *Free and Easy* (1941) and the concert announcer in *Dr. Kildare's Wedding Day* (1941). Charles was the second detective in *The Devil and Miss Jones* (1941), a uniformed man in *A Yank in the R.A.F.* (1941), the dance hall emcee in *A Girl, a Guy and a Gob* (1941), Biddle in *International Squadron* (1941) and the radio announcer in *San Antonio Rose* (1941).

Irwin played a number of officers around this time, such as the captain in *Son of Fury* (1942), a sea captain in *The Black Swan* (1942), the regimental commander in *This Above All* (1942) and Captain Coswick in *Desperate Journey* (1942), another Errol Flynn starrer. The Academy Award-winning *Mrs. Miniver* (1942) offered Irwin the colorful role of Mac, who, although inebriated and attired in evening clothes, joins Walter Pidgeon and other civilians in small sea crafts aiding in the relief of Dunkirk. Charles was the carnival batting game operator in *Pride of the Yankees* (1942), Fairoaks in *Journey for Margaret* (1942), Sir Benjamin Trask

The Devil and Miss Jones (1941): Detective Charles Irwin (right) handcuffs Robert Cummings.

Son of Lassie (1945): Donald Crisp reviews documents with Charles Irwin.

in *Eagle Squadron* (1942), Gelson the horse groom in *A Yank at Eton* (1942), Yardly in the remake of *The Great Impersonation* (1942), a reporter in *To Be or Not to Be* (1942) and the chief ground instructor in *Captains of the Clouds* (1942). *The Man Who Wouldn't Die* (1942), with Lloyd Nolan as Michael Shayne, featured Charles as Gus, aka the Great Merlini, a magician. He played the old Irishman in *This Gun for Hire* (1942) and Mr. Whittaker in *On the Sunny Side* (1942). An astute film observer can pick out an unbilled Irwin from the play-within-a-film portion of *Yankee Doodle Dandy* (1942) as the track announcer who calls the horse race in the *Little Johnny Jones* sequence.

The Gorilla Man (1943), which involved Nazi spies masquerading as doctors, had Irwin as Inspector Cady. Irwin was a pub patron in the Errol Flynn number of *Thank Your Lucky Stars* (1943). He played the second cop who questions James Cagney in *Johnny Come Lately* (1943), and again assayed a drunk in *Wintertime* (1943). Irwin portrayed English traveler Hotchkins in *Background to Danger* (1943), a commando lieutenant in *Assignment in Brittany* (1943), orchestra leader Ray Irwin in *Thumbs Up* (1943), a noncommissioned officer in *The Immortal Sergeant* (1943), the spieler in

The Crystal Ball (1943), O'Conner in *No Time for Love* (1943), Tom in *Lassie Come Home* (1943) and the groom in *The Constant Nymph* (1943). As Captain Lungden in *First Comes Courage* (1943), Charles led troops to destroy Nazi supplies and armaments, while rescuing Brian Aherne. Irwin showed a comedic touch as waiter Patrick Aloysius O'Conner in *No Time for Love* (1943). Other roles included an English bobby in *Sweet Rosie O'Grady* (1943), the ring announcer in *The Man From Down Under* (1943), Corporal Charlie in *Forever and a Day* (1943), a creditor in Moscow in *They Got Me Covered* (1943) and a bit in *The London Blackout Murders* (1943). *Jane Eyre* (1943), with Orson Welles and Joan Fontaine, included Irwin as an auctioneer.

Frankenstein Meets the Wolf Man (1943) provided Irwin with his only appearance in a Universal horror film. After the opening sequence with grave robbers in the Talbot family crypt, Irwin is viewed as a Cardiff police constable who spots a man lying on the ground. "Here now, come off it!," he chides Lawrence Talbot (Lon Chaney, Jr.). "Come on, laddy. Wake up and get along with ya. You've got a home, haven't you? Or do you want me to take you to the station?" The constable then turns the body over, sees the wound on Talbot's head, utters, "Good heavens!" and blows his whistle for assistance.

Irwin was able to bring some warmth and humor to the role of the jailer, Zachariah Smith, whose wife is expecting their 13th child, in *Frenchman's Creek* (1944). Charles was fifth-billed and in comedic form as a wacky psychologist, Professor Jasper Cartwright, in *Sing, Neighbor, Sing* (1944).

The Foxes of Harrow **(1947): Portrait of Charles Irwin as Sean Fox**

Bomba, the Jungle Boy **(1949): Peggy Ann Garner, Charles Irwin and Onslow Stevens**

Other mid-1940s parts for Irwin were: Patterson in *Practically Yours* (1944), the starter in *National Velvet* (1944), Farmer Kenney in *The White Cliffs of Dover* (1944), the policeman at the crash site in *None But the Lonely Heart* (1944), Carl in *Nothing But Trouble* (1944) and a British reporter in *Adventures of Mark Twain* (1944). Charles also played the marshall of the hunt in *The Canterville Ghost* (1944), a reporter in *Passport to Destiny* (1944), Harry Gage in *My Best Gal* (1944), a doctor in *Marine Raiders* (1944), McGregor in *An American Romance* (1944) and an Aussie sergeant in *Abroad With Two Yanks* (1944). In the Laurel and Hardy film *Nothing But Trouble* (1944), Irwin appeared as Karel.

Hangover Square (1945), featuring an intriguing performance by Laird Cregar as George Harvey Bone, had Irwin as the manager of the King's Head Arms. As singer

Netta Longdon (Linda Darnell) completes her rendition of "Have You Seen Joe?," the manager cajoles her with, "They want another song!" When Netta declines, stating she doesn't have one prepared, the manager insists, "Well, sing anything!" After she raises the issue of money, the manager begrudgingly pays Netta, who exits without acceding to his wishes for another song. Charles played a drunk at the bar in *Wonder Man* (1945), army officer Captain Grey in *Son of Lassie* (1945) and Barrows in *Kitty* (1946).

After a long absence from the Broadway stage, Irwin signed to appear in *Up in Central Park* (1/27/45), a Mike Todd-produced musical, which enjoyed a lengthy run (504 performances) at the Century Theatre. Irwin played Timothy Moore, a minor Tammany Hall official and the father of Rosie (Maureen Cannon).

Returning to the screen, Irwin secured some fairly substantial roles at 20th Century Fox: Sean Fox, the adoptive father of the baby who grows up to be Rex Harrison, in *The Foxes of Harrow* (1947), Long Kirby in *Thunder in the Valley* [aka *Bob, Son of Battle*] (1947) and Cornelius, the tavern owner, in *The Luck of the Irish* (1948). In the biopic of tenor Chauncey Olcott (played by Dennis Morgan), *My Wild Irish Rose* (1947), Irwin played Foote, the actor-manager of Haverly's Minstrels. Irwin appeared opposite Johnny Sheffield in the first two of 12 films in the "Bomba" series, *Bomba, the Jungle Boy* (1949) and *Bomba on Panther Island* (1949). Irwin's part of the benevolent Andy Barnes was

Captain Pirate (1951): **Louis Hayward shares a drink with his crew, Charles Irwin and Sven Hugo Borg.**

(Deborah Kerr) and her son Louis (Rex Thompson) to Siam. Captain Orton conveys concern and compassion for the widow and her child, while also providing some cultural and historical information to help set the scene for the ensuing story.

After appearing as Captain Pat O'Shea in *Beau James* (1957) with Bob Hope, Irwin essentially retired from films, remaining active, however, as a nightclub emcee and comedian. Charles was seen on a number of television programs around this time, including *The Gale Storm Show* (4/20/57, as Barker in "Singapore Fling" and 3/1/58, in "Bye Bye Banshee"), *The Adventures of Rin Tin Tin* (4/4/58, as Terence X. McClanahan in "Wind-Wagon McClanahan"), *Broken Arrow* (5/27/58 as Quincannon in "Backlash"), *The Restless Gun* (1/19/59, as Lem in "The Lady and the Gun"), *Rescue 8* (3/3/60, as Cappy in "Lifeline") and *The Real McCoys* (12/3/62, as Dr. Johnston in "The Girl Veterinarian"). Irwin had a moving role as O'Toole in "Elephant Sitters" (5/20/62), an episode of *Lassie*.

taken over by horror genre familiar Leonard Mudie in the later "Bomba" entries.

Challenge to Lassie (1949) had Irwin as the Sergeant Major. Charles' portrayal of the sheepherder McKenzie in *Montana* (1950) marked his final appearance alongside Errol Flynn. Irwin returned to the high seas as Smitty in *Fortunes of Captain Blood* (1950) and Angus McVickers (for which Charles received fourth billing) in *Captain Pirate* (1952), both of which starred Louis Hayward. *Charge of the Lancers* (1953), set during the Crimean War, had Irwin as Tim Daugherty, who disguises himself as a Gypsy to spy on the Russians. Irwin was the golf starter in the Dean Martin-Jerry Lewis comedy *The Caddy* (1953). Charles played Mountie Sergeant Saxon in *Fort Vengeance* (1953), James O'Toole in *The Iron Glove* (1954) and was seen in *Son of the Renegade* (1953).

[The Charles Irwin who appeared in the British films *Mystery Junction* (1951) and *A Tale of Five Women* (1951) was actually a different actor with the same name, as was the case with the performer who played Luke in *The Sheriff of Fractured Jaw* (1958).]

Two of Irwin's latter screen appearances bear witness to his accomplished acting skills. In the Danny Kaye comedy *The Court Jester* (1956), Irwin was the knight who spies for Sir Griswold (Robert Middleton). It is Irwin's character who overhears the hilarious exchange between sorceress Mildred Natwick and Kaye regarding the "pellet of poison" in "the vessel with the pestle" (and Charles has to report this tongue-twister back to his leader). *The King and I* (1956) had Irwin in the film's opening as Captain George Orton, whose ship has transported Anna Leonowens

The Iron Glove (1954): **Robert Stack, Charles Irwin and Richard Wyler**

Fever in the Blood (1961): **The doctor (Nelson Leigh) provides news of the condition of Don Ameche to Charles Irwin, Efrem Zimbalist, Jr., Angie Dickinson and players.**

Irwin returned to the screen with a small role as Angus in *Walk Like a Dragon* (1960). He then had a more substantial part of Itchy Forst, loyal aide to a senator (Don Ameche), in Warner Bros.' *A Fever in the Blood* (1961), starring Efrem Zimbalist, Jr. and Angie Dickinson. While in "retirement," Irwin wrote the story and adapted the screenplay (with Robert Creighton Williams) for the Western *He Rides Tall* (1964), which featured Tony Young and Dan Duryea. In *He Rides Tall*, Irwin was also seen onscreen for the last time, unbilled as a townsman.

For many years, Irwin resided in Palm Springs, Riverside, California. During the late 1960s, Charles became progressively ill due to cancer. He eventually entered the Motion Picture Country Home in Woodland Hills, California, where he remained and was cared for until his death at the age of 81 on January 12, 1969. *Variety* (1/15/69) reported that his widow Kathryn, two brothers and two sisters survived him.

Perhaps unrecognized by many modern film buffs, Charles Irwin was clearly liked and respected by his peers, some of whom would make special requests for his presence in the cast of their films. For example, by no coincidence, Irwin was seen in seven films with Errol Flynn, while making multiple appearances each with Clark Gable, James Cagney, Tyrone Power, Danny Kaye and others.

Charles Irwin is long overdue for some recognition of his lengthy screen legacy. Although his contributions to the horror genre in particular might not be that noteworthy, Charles still was seen in important fantasy-related motion pictures like *The Wizard of Oz*, *Frankenstein Meets the Wolf Man*, *The Canterville Ghost* and *Hangover Square*. When one of Irwin's films surface on television, the viewer has the opportunity to rediscover this entertaining character player. It might be his nightclub emcee persona, displayed in *The King of Jazz*, or a colorful portrayal in a costume drama, like *Mutiny on the Bounty*, *Treasure Island*, *The Sea Hawk* and *Kidnapped*. He manages to stand out in minor roles in major productions like *Yankee Doodle Dandy* and *Mrs. Miniver*. Note Charles' comic touches in *The Court Jester*, or his warmth and sincerity in *The King and I*. Irwin's distinct voice and engaging Irish countenance, with the proverbial twinkle in his eye, are likely to make the screening of an old film just that much more enjoyable.

Bride of Frankenstein (1935)

Ernest Thesiger
(1879 – 1961)

Arguably the most memorable performance turned in by a supporting player in the horror film genre was that of Ernest Thesiger as Dr. Pretorius in *Bride of Frankenstein*. The vision of Thesiger offering a cigar to Boris Karloff as the Monster in the crypt without allowing the scene to degenerate into the ridiculous is a thing of beauty. There was a particular appeal to Thesiger's characterization, despite his haughty tones, sardonic nature and evil, chiseled features. Director James Whale was able to put Thesiger's eccentric traits to effective use in two classic offerings, *The Old Dark House* and *Bride of Frankenstein*. Thesiger, a very complex, talented individual, would also make fantasy genre appearances in *The Ghoul*, *The Man Who Could Work Miracles*, *The Ghosts of Berkeley Square*, *The Man in the White Suit*, *A Christmas Carol* (1951) and *Meet Mr. Lucifer*.

In all actuality, Thesiger does not qualify as a "forgotten face" in that his whole manner and appearance were so unique and memorable. Anthony Slide (1998, p. 146) summed him up thusly:

> With his distinctive beaklike nose, waspish and aristocratic demeanor, and tall, slim body, Ernest Thesiger was an impressive, if slightly repellent, figure.

Ernest Frederic Graham Thesiger was born in London, England on January 15, 1879, the son of Sir Edward Pierson Thesiger, K.C.B., and the former Georgina Mary Stopford. Among his illustrious ancestors were his grandfather, the First Baron Chelmsford, and uncle, Sir Frederic Augustus Thesiger, who figured prominently in the Zulu War of 1879, including the tragic battle of Isandlwana. He was also the cousin of explorer Wilfred Patrick Thesiger, who traveled and wrote extensively about the Near East.

Young Ernest received a public school education at Marlborough College, before studying at the Slade School of Arts at University College, London. Thesiger aspired to be a painter, initially specializing in watercolors. While at Slade, Ernest became proficient at and passionate about needlepoint, eventually becoming a leading authority on embroidery. Thesiger spoke of his training in a 1934 interview (uncited clipping):

> My entire education was designed to point me toward a career as a painter. It was my only ambition. At college I

Ernest Thesiger: a signed and inscribed portrait from 1920

> played in amateur theatricals, but only as a diversion. And then, my education completed, I started to paint. Each work left me more discouraged. I felt I wasn't good enough—that there was no future for me unless I had greatness.

A family member who had seen him in college plays encouraged Ernest to try the stage as a career. Theater (and, to a lesser degree, film) became Ernest's primary focus for over 50 years, although Thesiger never gave up his involvement with painting and embroidery, both of which

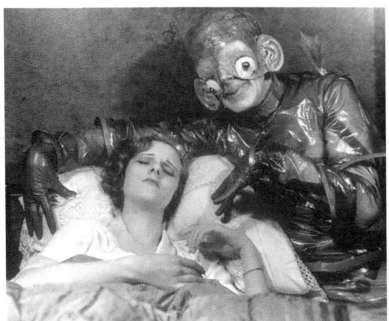

Too Good to Be True (1932): George Bernard Shaw's play, with Ernest Thesiger as the Microbe and Leonora Corbett as the Patient

he practiced until his death. In later years, for example, Thesiger enjoyed a successful showing of his creative efforts at a 1933 Bond Street art gallery exhibition, at which he sold a number of his paintings.

Thesiger was 30 years old when he made his professional stage debut at the St. James Theatre in London on April 23, 1909, as James Raleigh in *Colonel Smith.* At Wyndham's Theatre, Thesiger was seen as Franz Pepo in the musical *The Little Damozel* (October 1909). Ernest's first real theatrical success came with his portrayal of Dumby in Oscar Wilde's *Lady Windermere's Fan* (1911). Other prewar British stage appearances for Thesiger came in *Othello, Inconstant George, Very Much Married* and *The Seven Sisters.*

Thesiger's career was put on hold with England's entrance into World War I. Ernest was a rifleman in D Company of the 9th County of London Territorials. Ernest was injured at the front in combat in the summer of 1915, leading him to fall back on his avocation of needlepoint as part of his rehabilitation while in the hospital. He shared his passion for embroidery with other wounded soldiers, aiding many of them in their recovery as well. After the war, Thesiger helped establish the "Disabled Soldiers Embroidery Industry," while also becoming involved with the "Church Army League of Friends of the Poor." For all his perceived lofty ways, Thesiger was acutely aware of the suffering of others and desired to give back where he could. Queen Mary, the consort of King George V, took notice of Thesiger's work with disabled soldiers in particular. She frequently requested his presence at Buckingham Palace, where they would do needlepoint and crochet together.

Ernest opted to return to the stage, in part to keep his mind off his slowly healing wounds. A role with which Thesiger became firmly associated was that of Bertram Tully in *A Little Bit of Fluff* (October 1915). Although he supposedly told a friend that he did not expect the show to last a week, Thesiger went on to appear as Tully in over 1200 performances.

While he studying at the Slade School, Thesiger became enamored with a fellow student, Scottish born William Bruce Ellis Ranken (1881-1941), who would achieve fame of his own as a painter. Ranken actually painted a portrait of Thesiger in 1918. The two would become life-long friends and lovers, interrupted for a time by a significant life event for Ernest. As was a fairly common practice of the day for homosexuals, gays would often arrange a marriage of convenience to mask their actual lifestyle and avoid public scorn. Thesiger chose to marry William's sister, Janette Mary Fernie Ranken (1878-1970). The wedding, which took place on May 29, 1917, so enraged William that he shaved his head and lived as a recluse for a time. Janette reportedly (Hadleigh, 1998, p. 41) was also gay, associating with Margaret Jourdain and Ivy Compton-Burnett. Regardless of their respective sexual orientations, the marriage of Ernest Thesiger and Janette Ranken lasted for 44 years, ending only with Ernest's passing.

The Old Dark House (1932): Ernest Thesiger, as Horace Femm, insists that Raymond Massey be quiet.

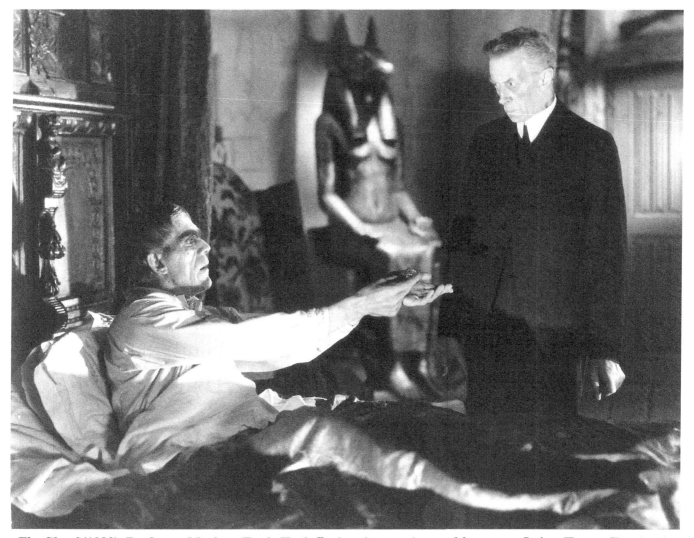

The Ghoul **(1933): Professor Morlant (Boris Karloff) gives instructions to his servant Laing (Ernest Thesiger).**

The Real Thing at Last (1916), a comedy short about a play within a film, had Thesiger, in his screen debut, in drag as a Witch in "Macbeth." *Nelson* (1918), with Donald Calthrop as Horatio, featured Thesiger as William Pitt. Ernest played Joseph Chamberlain in *The Life Story of David Lloyd George* (1918), before repeating his stage success as Bertram Tully in the film version of *A Little Bit of Fluff* (1919). Additional early silent film roles for Thesiger were Israfel Mondego in *The Bachelor's Club* (1921), Mr. Jingle in *The Adventures of Mr. Pickwick* and Mr. Peabody in *Number 13* (1922), the latter the first film ever directed by Alfred Hitchcock (and reportedly never completed).

Thesiger was appearing in a Christmas production of Shakespeare's *The Merry Wives of Windsor* (December 1919) in Manchester, England, where he became acquainted with James Whale. This association would prove to have a significant impact on the fantasy film genre some years later.

By the early 1920s, Ernest Thesiger was an established figure on the London stage. Ernest played Giannetto Malespini in *The Love Thief* (1920), a reworking of *The Jest*,

in which John Barrymore starred on Broadway. Some of Thesiger's important roles around this time were Cameron in *Mary Rose* (1920), Arnold Campion-Cheney, M.P., the husband in Maugham's *The Circle* (March 1921), Captain Hook in Barrie's *Peter Pan* (December 1921), Mr. Bly in Galsworthy's *Windows* (April 1922), Sir George Orreyd in *The Second Mrs. Tanqueray* (1922) and Piers Gaveston in *Edward II* (1924). Thesiger's portrayal of the Dauphin, opposite Sybil Thorndike, in George Bernard Shaw's *Saint Joan* (March 1924) was particularly noteworthy.

In an article in the *London Times* (11/17/58) entitled "The Inimitable Mr. Thesiger Remembers," Ernest stated:

> The Dauphin in *Saint Joan* was offered to me as a small part he (Shaw) wants you to play. The salary was insufficient but I bluffed him into increasing it by saying, "You don't want actors in your plays. You only want loud-voiced gramophones." After the first reading Shaw said, "There's something I want you to do for me. I want

A Sleeping Clergyman (1933 England stage): A 1938 Ogden's cigarette card of Ernest Thesiger, depicting him in (as Dr. Marshall) and out (inset) of character.

you to go home and stay in bed till the first night. You know all there is about the part already."

Critical response to Thesiger as the Dauphin was laudatory. James Agate (Slide, p. 149) remarked that the Dauphin was "beautifully played by Mr. Thesiger, who showed beneath his astonishing grotesquerie the pity and pathos of all weakness." The *Stage* wrote, "His height, his slender silhouette and his wailing voice helped to make this interpretation unique in theatrical history." After enacting the diabolical role of Mephistopheles in *Dr. Faustus* (October

1925), Thesiger received a postcard from G.B. Shaw with but one word—"Magnificent!"

Thesiger appeared at the London Pavilion in drag, along with British female impersonator Douglas Byng, in the C.B. Cochran review *On With the Dance* (1925) by Noel Coward. One scene concerned two elderly women (Thesiger and Byng) sharing a room in a boarding house, trying to maintain their modesty as they prepare for bed. Thesiger was not shy about making his own fashion statements, even in public, being a founding member of "The Men's Dress Reform Society."

Other mid-to-late twenties' theater roles for Thesiger were Lord Foppington in *A Trip to Scarborough*, Hans Christian Andersen in *The Emperor of Make Believe*, Henry Higgins in *Pygmalion*, Malvolio in *Twelfth Night*, Finch McComas in *You Can Never Tell*, Mr. Vanhattan in *The Apple Cart* and the chief statistician in *Under the Sycamore Tree.*

In 1927, Thesiger penned his autobiography entitled *Practically True*, published by William Heinemann. Reviewers made note of Thesiger's highbrow wit and colorful story telling ability. The title itself hints that Ernest may have indulged in some hyperbole along the way.

In the London West End, Thesiger was an effective Henry Spofford in *Gentlemen Prefer Blondes* (1928). Although Thesiger focused most of his energy on the stage at this point, he occasionally did some film work in England. Ernest played Lidoff in *The Vagabond Queen* (1929), Bertram in *Week-End Wives* (1929) and the announcer in the short *Ashes* (1930).

Journeying to the United States in late 1931, Thesiger made his first Broadway appearance at the Selwyn Theatre as Cosmo Penny, an unsuccessful novelist, in the comedy *The Devil Passes* (1/4/32, 96 performances), which also featured Basil Rathbone and Diana Wynyard. During the run of *The Devil Passes*, James Whale contacted Thesiger, who was bringing J. B. Priestley's *Benighted* to the screen, stating he had a role in mind for Ernest in his new production, *The Old Dark House*.

Whale's *The Old Dark House* (1932) concerns a group of travelers (including Charles Laughton, Melvyn Douglas, Raymond Massey, and Gloria Stuart) who are forced to seek shelter at the decaying Femm residence due to a terrible storm. Thesiger was truly marvelous as Horace Femm, the head of the household, who presents himself with an air of breeding, while looking upon the uninvited guests with contempt. "My sister was on the point of arranging these flowers," Horace smiles to the visitors, before hurling the bouquet into the fire. When the lights go dim, Horace apologizes to Margaret (Stuart), claiming, "We make our own electricity, but we're not very good at it." When there is an interruption during dinner, Horace coldly gazes at Sir William (Laughton), adding, "Have a potato." As if giving a preview of Dr. Pretorius in *Bride of*

Frankenstein, Femm queries, "Do you like gin? It's my only weakness!" Noted film historian William K. Everson, in his *Classics of the Horror Film* (1974, p. 83), opined that Horace Femm was Thesiger's finest screen characterization, even surpassing his Dr. Pretorius. Horace Femm nicely blends Whale's offbeat humor with Thesiger's own peculiar style. The camerawork, using close-ups in various angles, seemed to enhance Thesiger's skeletal appearance in the role. Even when grouped with many fine performers, including Boris Karloff as the demented butler, Thesiger managed to steal the acting honors of *The Old Dark House*.

Back in England at the Festival Theatre of Malvern, Worcester, Thesiger appeared in the unusual and neglected G.B. Shaw comedy *Too True to Be Good* (1932). Wearing a monstrous costume, Thesiger played the Microbe who threatens the patient (played by Leonora Corbett).

Thesiger rejoined Karloff in Gaumont's production of *The Ghoul* (1933). As Laing, Thesiger was the servant to the elderly Professor Morlant (Karloff), a lifelong scholar of Egyptology. Morlant, knowing the end of his life is near, hopes for immortality through "The Eternal Light," a precious jewel stolen from an Egyptian tomb. Laing is directed to bury the jewel with Morlant, who cautions the servant not to remove the jewel or disobey his instructions. The club-footed Laing, however, has plans of his own and pilfers the jewel before the tomb is sealed. In a well-constructed death scene (for Laing), Morlant returns to life and strangles the disobedient servant. Perhaps due to the script or the direction, Thesiger did not appear as comfortable with his role in *The Ghoul* as he did with his more flamboyant portrayals.

The Only Girl (1934), with Lilian Harvey and Charles Boyer, featured Thesiger as the Chamberlain. *My Heart is Calling* (1935), the English language version of *Mon couer l'appelle* (1934), included Ernest as Fevrier. Jan Kiepura and Martha Eggerth played the leads in both versions.

Ernest Thesiger originated the role of Dr. William Marshall in *A Sleeping Clergyman* (7/29/33) at the Festival Theatre of Malverne. He would regularly be seen at Malvern, usually under the direction of Sir Barry Jackson, for many years, frequently in plays by G.B. Shaw. Over the next year, Thesiger toured in *A Sleeping Clergyman*, only interrupted by intermittent film work. When the Theatre Guild brought *A Sleeping Clergyman* (10/8/34, 39 performances) to the United States (at the Guild Theatre on Broadway), Thesiger again took on the part of Dr. William Marshall. *A Sleeping Clergyman*

***A Sleeping Cleryman* (1934 Broadway stage): Ruth Gordon and Ernest Thesiger**

dealt with the theory of inherited evil and its relationship to genius. Ruth Gordon headlined the Broadway cast of *A Sleeping Clergyman*, which included Helen Westley and Glenn Anders.

As James Whale was in preparation for *Bride of Frankenstein* (1935), Universal's sequel to *Frankenstein* (1931),

Bride of Frankenstein (1935): Minnie (Una O'Connor) is unnerved by Dr. Pretorius (Ernest Thesiger).

there was controversy as to who would play the pivotal role of Dr. Septimus Pretorius. The studio was said to have wanted Claude Rains for the part. Whale, despite having directed Rains in *The Invisible Man* (19330, felt that Thesiger, his former associate from the London stage, would provide just the touches he was looking for in that cunning, malicious character.

Early on in *Bride of Frankenstein*, the mysterious Dr. Pretorius (Thesiger) pays a call on the recuperating Henry Frankenstein (Colin Clive), but he first must contend with the shrill servant Minnie (Una O'Connor). Pretorius, a former professor of Henry's at Goldstadt University, tells Frankenstein of how he was "booted out" of the school for his theories and an autopsy on a woman who turned out to still be alive. Accompanying Pretorius to his residence, Henry views his former teacher's experiments with creation. Pretorius removes seven glass bottles from a coffin, each containing a tiny creature: a queen, king, archbishop, baby, ballerina, mermaid and devil (to whom Pretorius notes a personal resemblance, "or do I flatter myself"). Offering Henry a glass of gin (naturally, his "only weakness"),

Pretorius toasts, "a new world of gods and monsters!" The former mentor suggests that the two collaborate to create a woman ("That should really be interesting!").

Later viewed with two grave robbing associates (Dwight Frye and Neil Fitzgerald), Pretorius examines the remains of a young woman in a crypt. Left alone by the ghoulish pair to dine amidst the dead, Pretorius encounters the Monster (Boris Karloff), who has learned to speak. When the Monster exclaims "love dead ... hate living," Pretorius retorts, "You're wise in your generation!" Pretorius offers the creature a cigar (again, his "only weakness'), realizing he has secured a valuable ally. When Henry later balks at fulfilling his part of their bargain, Pretorius produces his trump card, the Monster, who subsequently kidnaps Henry's fiancée Elizabeth (Valerie Hobson).

Under duress, Frankenstein returns to work on their project and soon exhibits his usual fervor. Karl (Frye) is dispatched to secure a heart for the new creation (originally planned to be that of Elizabeth), which he fulfills by murdering a young woman of the street. The two scientists complete their experiment, with lightning flashing and

Bride of Frankenstein (1935): **Dr. Pretorius (Ernest Thesiger) with his lackey Karl (Dwight Frye)**

machinery (designed by Kenneth Strickfadden) crackling. As their creation is unraveled to the sound of wedding bells, Pretorius exclaims, "The Bride of Frankenstein!" The "Bride" (Elsa Lanchester) and the Monster, however, quickly prove to be incompatible. Gazing at Pretorius, the Monster states, "We belong dead!" The forlorn Monster then pulls the switch, destroying the laboratory and its occupants (although Henry and Elizabeth were permitted to survive in the altered finale).

Thesiger's performance as Pretorius has stood the test of time as one of the highlights of all the classic Universal horror films. He is sardonic, condescending and grandiose, taking delight in his defiance of convention and God Himself. Thesiger's appearance was further accentuated by the creative camera angles utilized by John Mescall, who filmed Ernest in ways that managed to have him appear even more skeletal and evil. In *Universal Horrors* (p. 121), Tom Weaver and the Brunas brothers wrote: "Thesiger delivers the goods in a rich, fruity performance that is at once pompous and slightly perverse; one wonders to what degree Pretorius' character is modeled on the actor himself."

Thesiger was somewhat of an enigma, with his on-screen persona at times matching aspects of his own personality. Acquaintances varied in their response to his quirkiness. Elsa Lanchester, in an interview with Greg Mank (*It's Alive!*, p. 59), noted: "Ernest Thesiger was a delightful laugh for anyone who saw him or talked to him—a weird, strange character. Very acid-tongued—not a nasty person at all, just acid!" On the other hand, Whale's longtime companion David Lewis remarked to author James Curtis (1982, p. 125), "I thought he (Thesiger) was the most loathsome man I ever knew. He was very nasty to me. He treated me like some kind of servant in my own home. He was a terrible snob, but he was related to the aristocracy and that's what Jimmy (Whale) liked about him."

Back in England, Thesiger appeared as Chiddiatt in *The Murder Party* (1935), directed by Michael Powell and starring Leslie Banks. Ernest had been cast to play the sculptor Theotocopolous in the screen adaptation of H.G. Wells' *Things to Come* (1936), directed by William Cameron Menzies. However, Cedric Hardwicke replaced him in the role. It remains uncertain if it was Wells' opposition to Thesiger playing the part, or other factors that resulted in

The Murder Party (1935): Ernest Thesiger as Chiddiatt

tion as Walter Hoover, a former schoolmaster and student of psychology. He keeps a scrapbook related to horrid murders, purporting to be an amateur criminologist as well. Appearing benign, serving milk to kittens, Hoover is revealed to be the "silk-stocking murderer," who has been committing the heinous slayings in serial-like fashion. Thesiger rendered a clever portrayal of the effete yet psychopathic Hoover.

Ernest was back in the U.S., appearing at the Broadhurst Theatre on Broadway as Lheureux in *Madame Bovary* (11/16/37, 39 performances). *Madame Bovary* featured Constance Cummings and Eric Portman.

Thesiger returned to England, where he continued to work both on the London stage and the U.K. film industry. He appeared as Carter in *The Ware Case* (1938), with Clive Brook. *Lightning Conductor* (1938), directed by Maurice Elvey, had Ernest as the professor. The British television presentation of George Bernard Shaw's *Geneva* (4/23/39) featured Thesiger as Sir Orpheus Midlander.

In 1941, Thesiger saw his *Adventures in Embroidery* published by The Studio. Edited by C.G. Holme, *Adventures in Embroidery* contained many illustrations of Ernest's artistry and passion. Thesiger, a talented writer, had penned the introduction to T.W. Bamford's *Practical Make-Up for the Stage* (1940) a year earlier.

Although WWII seriously impacted the British film industry, Thesiger was involved in a few films during the war years. Ernest played Ferris in the Will Hay comedy *My Learned Friend* (1943). Again directed by Maurice Elvey, Thesiger was the chairman in *The Lamp Still Burns* (1943) with Stewart Granger. *Don't Take It to Heart* (1944), a comedy involving a castle ghost, included Thesiger as the justices' clerk. Laurence Olivier's ambitious *Henry V* (aka *The Chronicle History of King Henry the Fifth with His Battell Fought at Agincourt in France*, 1944), with a strong cast including Leslie Banks, Robert Newton, Felix Aylmer and Niall MacGinnis, had Thesiger as the Duke of Berri, the ambassador from France.

Directed by Bernard Knowles, the atmospheric *A Place of One's Own* (1945) starred James Mason and Barbara Mullen as a couple who purchase an old haunted mansion. They hire a young woman (Margaret Lockwood) to join them, but she gradually becomes possessed by the spirit of an invalid girl who had died there years before. Dr. Marsham (Thesiger), the old physician who had treated the dead girl 40 years earlier, returns to help the Lockwood character regain her sanity and release the spirit possessing her. It is revealed back then that Dr. Marsham spurned the poor girl's love, and his departure led to her death. Strangely, Thesiger was filmed almost exclusively from behind, thus not making use of his remarkable features.

Shaw's *Caesar and Cleopatra* (1945), with Claude Rains and Vivien Leigh, had Thesiger as Theodotus. He played

this change. In any case, Thesiger was then signed to appear in another H.G. Wells tale, *The Man Who Could Work Miracles*.

Starring Roland Young as George McWhirter Fotheringay, a meek clerk who has been granted extraordinary powers, *The Man Who Could Work Miracles* (1936) featured Thesiger as the Reverend Silas Maydig, a Baptist minister. Maydig, a philosophical preacher, realizes the potential for good in Fotheringay's powers. He envisions the eradication of disease and poverty, preaching "peace and prosperity for all." Unfortunately, other forces have opposite viewpoints, leading to cataclysm before Fotheringay relinquishes his powers, returning to his previous mundane existence.

They Drive By Night (1936), starring Emlyn Williams, provided Thesiger with another intriguing characteriza-

The Robe **(1951): Jean Simmons, Richard Burton, Ernest Thesiger (far right) and players**

the Baron Emil de Kekesfalva, the father of crippled Lilli Palmer, in *Beware of Pity* (1946). The British TV movie *Androcles and the Lion* (9/3/46), with Andrew Leigh and Torin Thatcher, featured Ernest as Caesar. Thesiger played Farne in Graham Greene's *The Smugglers* (1947), with Michael Redgrave and Richard Attenborough. He was Sir Edward Follesmark in *Jassy* (1947), featuring Margaret Lockwood and Dennis Price.

The Ghosts of Berkeley Square (1947) concerned two British officers (Robert Morley and Felix Aylmer) who, as a result of their accidental suicides, have received a heavenly sentence to haunt a house until it is visited by royalty. Thesiger had the role of Dr. Cruickshank, an investigator from the Psychical Research Society, who is among those exploring the phenomenon of the haunting.

Based on the play by Terence Rattigan and directed by Anthony Asquith, *The Winslow Boy* (1948) showcased a powerful performance by Robert Donat, with Thesiger in support as Mr. Ridgeley Pierce. In the fourth segment ("The Colonel's Lady") of Somerset Maugham's *Quartet* (1948), with Cecil Parker, Thesiger played powerful literary critic Henry Dashwood. Ernest was Ryder-Harris in *Brass Monkey* (1948), the final film of Carole Landis prior

to her tragic suicide. Thesiger's footage as Bloomfield in *Lost Daughter* (1948), directed by Terence Fisher, was regrettably deleted. Ernest again played one of Shakespeare's three witches, this time in the U.K. television presentation of *Macbeth* (2/20/49).

At Broadway's Cort Theatre, Thesiger was part of the Theatre Guild's production of Shakespeare's *As You Like It* (1/26/50, 145 performances), featuring Katharine Hepburn, Robert Quarry, William Prince and a young Cloris Leachman. Thesiger, with his name listed under the play's title as "Also starring," portrayed Jacques.

The Bad Lord Byron (1950), with Dennis Price in the title role, featured Thesiger as Count Guiccioli. *The Last Holiday* (1950), based on a story by J.P. Priestley, had George Bird (Alec Guinness) allegedly suffering from the fatal Lampington's Disease, until he meets Sir Trevor Lampington (Thesiger), for whom the disease was named. Sir Trevor then convinces Bird that he has been misdiagnosed. *Laughter in Paradise* (1951), with Alistair Sim and George Cole, had Thesiger as Endicott, the executor of a prankster's estate.

Thesiger had an important fantasy-related role as Sir John Kierlaw, the ruthless capitalist and powerful elder

The Man in the White Suit (1951): Ernest Thesiger as Sir John Kierlaw

statesman of the cotton industry, in *The Man in the White Suit* (1951). In this Ealing black comedy, Alec Guinness portrayed Sidney Stratton, a textile chemist who invents a synthetic fabric that never wears out nor requires cleaning. Stratton's invention results in great turmoil and resistance from both management and labor, whose businesses and jobs are threatened. The greedy, controlling Sir John, with the mill owners behind him, attempts to suppress the invention and manipulate Stratton, to no avail. His efforts prove wasted, however, as the prototype suit disintegrates.

A Christmas Carol (1951), with Alistair Sim marvelous as Scrooge, had Thesiger as an undertaker grabbing at the late Ebenezer's property in the "Christmas yet to come" segment. Thesiger was seen as an Earl in *The Magic Box* (1951) with Robert Donat and Laurence Olivier. He played the judge in *The Woman's Angle* (1952). In "Thought to Kill" (3/4/53), a TV episode of Rheingold Theatre hosted by Douglas Fairbanks, Jr., Thesiger was seen as Burdon Sr., the father of John Vere.

The Robe (1953), with Richard Burton, Jean Simmons and Victor Mature involved in the aftermath of Christ's Crucifixion, featured Thesiger as the Emperor Tiberius. In a poignant scene, Tiberius questions the visibly shaken Marcellus (Burton), the Roman tribune who came into possession of Jesus' garment and remains tormented by His death. Thesiger played Montané in "The Public Pros-

ecutor" (10/4/53), an episode of *BBC Sunday-Night Theatre*. *Meet Mr. Lucifer* (1953), another Ealing comedy with Stanley Holloway, included Thesiger as Mr. Macdonald. *Man With a Million* (1954), starring Gregory Peck, had Ernest as Mr. Garrett, the bank director. As the Vicomte de Verdigris, Thesiger was a somewhat senile elderly librarian in *The Detective* (1954), with Alec Guinness. Thesiger played Lord Dewsbury in *Value for Money* (1955), with Diana Dors helping rugby fan John Gregson spend his large inheritance.

As the Scottish Lord Crawford, Thesiger played the elderly, now impoverished uncle of the title character (Robert Taylor) in *Quentin Durward* (1955). Lord Crawford dispatches Quentin as an emissary to French Countess Isabella (Kay Kendall), with the hope of a future profitable alliance. The musical comedy *An Alligator Named Daisy* (1955), with Diana Dors and Donald Sinden, had Thesiger as Notcher.

In late 1955, Thesiger had the opportunity to journey to the Soviet Union to appear as Polonius (his favorite role) in Peter Brooks' production of *Hamlet*. Thesiger also assayed the part of Polonius in an *ITV Play of the Week* presentation of "Hamlet" (2/27/56), with Paul Scofield as 'the melancholy Dane." Thesiger played Sir Walter in *Who Done It?* (1956), a comedy featuring Benny Hill as a private eye. *Three Men in a Boat* (1956), with Laurence Harvey, had Ernest as one of three old gentlemen (A.E. Matthews and Miles Malleson being the other two). He also played opposite Laurence Harvey as the judge in *The Truth About Women* (1957). Thesiger was the first examiner in *Doctor at Large* (1957), starring Dirk Bogarde. Ernest was seen in the first episode of the British TV drama *Joyous Errand* as the title character in "Mr. Skaife" (4/6/57). After James Whale died on May 29, 1957, Thesiger contributed to the director's obituary in the *London Times* (5/30/57).

Thesiger's last New York stage appearance came with his portrayal of Sir Jasper Fidget, in a revival of *The Country Wife* (11/27/57), at Henry Miller's Theatre. This production of *The Country Wife* starred Julie Harris and Laurence Harvey.

At this time, Thesiger was acting more on British television than on stage or screen. For *ITV Television Playhouse*, Thesiger was seen in at least five episodes. He was Phipps in Robert E. Sherwood's "The Queen's Husband" (4/18/57), in which Dwight Frye was featured on Broadway in early 1928. Ernest also appeared in "Do as I Do" (3/14/58, as Colonel Gyll), "The Touch of Fear" (6/6/58), "The White Sheep of the Family" (7/3/59) and "Night Run to the West" (6/30/60, as Calvin Broderick). For the U.K. series *Armchair Theatre*, Thesiger played the reclusive oil millionaire in "Invitation to Murder" (8/30/59), Professor Galton in "Suspicious Mind" (11/22/59) and the Dean in "Lord Arthur Saville's Crime" (1/3/60).

***The Horse's Mouth* (1958): Kay Walsh, Alec Guinness and Ernest Thesiger**

Chaucer's England (1958), a short, had Thesiger in the role of Death. Thesiger then had the prominent part of Hickson in the Alec Guinness comedy *The Horse's Mouth* (1958). Eccentric artist Gulley Jimson (Guinness), recently released from jail, continually harasses Hickson, his former patron, to return his 18 canvasses. The paintings had been given to Hickson by Jimson's ex-wife Sara (Renee Houston) to settle Gulley's debts. Soon after Jimson is thwarted trying to steal back his paintings, word comes that Hickson has died, leaving the artwork to the people of England. Although Guinness and Thesiger had drastically different acting styles, they played off one another extremely well in a number of films together.

Thesiger still cherished appearing before live audiences. He was seen as Shrewsbury in the Old Vic production of *Mary Stuart* (November 1958). Interviewed in this latter stage of his career, Thesiger waxed philosophically about the relation between acting and emotion (the *Times*, 11/17/58):

> Acting is the reproduction of an emotion once felt, but it is not the emotion itself.

You've got to be under control, and if you are carried away by emotion that cannot be so. At rehearsal you can work yourself up to a tremendous pitch of emotion. In performance you must remember what it felt like and be able to cold-bloodedly reproduce it.

The Battle of the Sexes (1959) featured Ernest as Old MacPherson, the patriarch of a long-standing manufacturing concern of Scottish tweeds. The old man dies, leaving the business in the hands of son Robert Morley, who is woefully unprepared for the responsibility. *Sons and Lovers* (1960), with Oscar-nominated Trevor Howard, Wendy Hiller and Dean Stockwell, had Thesiger as art collector Mr. Hadlock. Thesiger's final film appearance came in *The Roman Spring of Mrs. Stone* (1961), which was based on a novella by Tennessee Williams. Vivien Leigh and Warren Beatty starred in *The Roman Spring of Mrs. Stone*, while Thesiger portrayed Stefano.

Thesiger continued to act, nearly to the end. He appeared as the sinister confidante in *The Joke* with John

Ernest Thesiger contended that his background in painting gave him a pronounced advantage as an actor in that his acquired knowledge of anatomy enabled him to make effective use of make-up, postures and expressions. Without a doubt, Thesiger used his acting skills to paint lasting impressions in the fantasy genre with his portrayals of Horace Femm, Dr. Septimus Pretorius, Laing the Scottish servant and Sir John Kierlaw, among others. Thesiger's collaboration with James Whale in *The Old Dark House* and *Bride of Frankenstein* in particular resulted in characterizations so distinctive, eccentric and flamboyant that they may never be duplicated on film again.

Sons and Lovers **(1960): Dean Stockwell, Wendy Hiller and Ernest Thesiger**

Gielgud and Ralph Richardson at the Phoenix Theatre in London just a few weeks prior to his death. On January 14, 1961, on the eve of what would have been his 82nd birthday, Ernest Thesiger passed away in his sleep due to natural causes. His widow Janette Rankin, who in later years had become a chronic invalid, survived him. Janette followed Ernest in death on May 21, 1970. Ernest Thesiger was buried in Brompton Cemetery in West London, in a plot with his parents and sister.

In 1960, a year prior to his death, Ernest Thesiger had been granted the Order of Commander of the British Empire (C.B.E.), based on his more than 50 years in the theater and general contributions to the arts. In addition to all his surviving films, Thesiger also left a legacy of needlework and paintings. His "Ruins of Old Chelsea Church" is still on display at the Victoria and Albert Museum in London. Thesiger also donated an extensive collection of his letters, papers, photographs and memorabilia, as well as an unfinished manuscript for a second autobiography, to the University of Bristol Theatre Collection, where it is housed to this day

Gods and Monsters (1998), Bill Condon's fictionalized account of the last days of director James Whale (as played by Ian McKellen), featured a flashback sequence on the set of *Bride of Frankenstein*. Arthur Dignan, portraying Ernest, failed to capture the multifaceted flamboyance of Thesiger in the scene, however. Nonetheless, the film in part served as a tribute to those who contributed to Universal's "golden age" of horror.

Sources

Brown, Barry, & Coughlin, Jim. *Unsung Heroes of the Horrors*, Unpublished manuscript, 1978.

Chastain, George. "Ernest Thesiger," in *Classic Horror Players Directory* (http://myweb.wvnet.edu/-u0e53/ernest thesiger.html)

Coughlin, Jim. "Forgotten Faces of Fantastic Films: Ernest Thesiger (18979-1961)," in *Midnight Marquee #38* (Fall 1988), pp. 179-181.

Curtis, James. *James Whale*, Metuchen, NJ: The Scarecrow Press, 1982.

Everson, William K. *Classics of the Horror Film*, Secaucus, NJ: Citadel Press, 1974.

Fischer, Dennis. "The Fantastic Films of Ernest Thesiger," in *Wet Paint #24* (Winter 1998), pp. 6-10.

Hadleigh, Boze. "The Importance of Being Ernest Thesiger," in *Scarlet Street #30*, 1998, pp. 40-45.

The Importance of Being Ernest ... www.classichorror.free-online.couk/ernest20%thesiger.htm.

"The Inimitable Mr. Thesiger Remembers," in the *Times*, 11/17/58.

"A Painter Comes Here to Act and An Actor Arrives to Paint," uncited clipping, 1934.

Slide, Anthony. *Eccentrics of Comedy*, Metuchen, NJ: The Scarecrow Press, 1998

Neil Fitzgerald
(1892 - 1982)

Although a busy actor in the theater, film, radio and television for approximately 50 years, Neil Fitzgerald never had the one role on film that established his name and face for posterity in the memory of movie buffs. Fitzgerald did make significant appearances in classic motion pictures, however, such as *Bride of Frankenstein* and *The Informer*. The fact that he departed Hollywood in 1940 to focus on stage and radio (and later, television) limited the scope of Fitzgerald's body of screen work. In watching a Neil Fitzgerald performance in films like *The Plough and the Stars* and *Parnell*, one cannot miss the expertise and nuance he brought to every role.

He was born Cornelius James (Neil) Fitzgerald in County Tipperary, Ireland (some sources report near Emly on the County Limerick-Tipperary border) on January 15, 1892. Ireland at the time was still under British rule. Cornelius was one of nine children born to James Joseph Fitzgerald and his wife Ellen. Four of the nine died in either infancy or early childhood. In the 1901 Census of Ireland, the Fitzgerald family was living in a home at 5 William O'Brien Street in Tipperary West Urban. In the house at that time were Neil, his parents, sister Kathleen and older brothers John and Gerald. Young Neil spent his early years in Tipperary, Dublin and a seaside resort on the west coast of Ireland. Fitzgerald's father James, a member of Parliament, wanted his son to pursue a career as a doctor. Neil graduated from Trinity College in Dublin with a degree in pharmacy. He had long been enamored of the stage, however, having traveled whenever possible to Dublin, London and Paris to view theatrical productions. Fitzgerald was convinced by no less a luminary than George Bernard Shaw that his future was in acting rather than medicine. Shaw reportedly told Fitzgerald, "You will do better with greasepaint than with blood." Whether this story is apocryphal or not, Neil eventually gave up other pursuits to focus on learning the craft of the theater. Neil's father had opposed his son's choice of an acting career, while helping him get established in business. When the elder Fitzgerald died, Neil abandoned pharmacy and formed a theatrical troupe in Ireland.

By the late 1920s, Fitzgerald was an established figure, as both an actor and director on the London and Dublin stage. Part of Neil's early training had been at Dublin's famed Abbey Theatre. He ventured to America in 1929, landing in Boston, where he found work at a pioneer television station. Supposedly, Neil, along with the Abbey Theatre's Denis O'Dea, was handpicked by John Ford to come to Hollywood and be among the native Irishmen featured in *The Informer*. Fitzgerald's first film, however, was the Helen Hayes vehicle *What Every Woman Knows* (1934), which

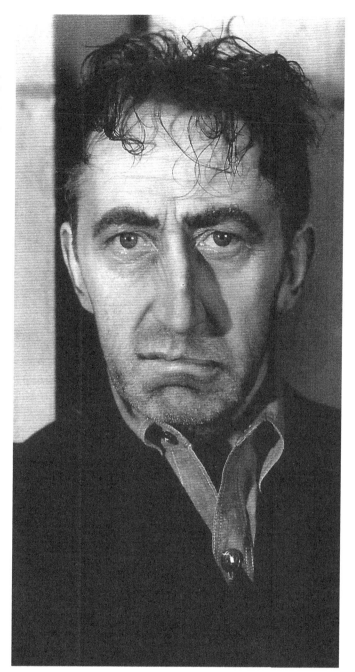

***Bride of Frankenstein* (1935): Neil Fitzgerald as Rudy**

offered him the minor role of a friend of Shand (Brian Aherne). Also for MGM, Fitzgerald played an Army doctor in *Vanessa: Her Love Story* (1935). He was an English waiter in *The Gilded Lily* (1935).

Fitzgerald's character in *Bride of Frankenstein* (1935) is referred to as the "second ghoul" in the script and Rudy in the cast listing. Hiding in a crypt from irate villagers, the Monster (Boris Karloff), unseen, views the activities of three interlopers. Led by the prissy Dr. Pretorius (Ernest Thesiger), Karl (Dwight Frye) and Rudy (Fitzgerald) comment on their macabre surroundings. As Karl notes he "can smell the ghosts already," Rudy adds, "I never could stand graves." Pretorius chides them to get about their

A September 1929 photo taken at a costume ball aboard the ocean liner *Republic*, with Neil Fitzgerald near the center in drag with long black pigtails.

work, threatening them with the gallows. Rudy claims such a fate "could be no worse than this." They pry the lid off the coffin of a young woman to reveal the skeleton that will provide the internal structure for the "Bride." Their work completed, the two grave robbers depart, bantering with the doctor and themselves. Outside the crypt, Karl recommends that if there is more call for work of this nature that they turn themselves in and "let them hang us." Rudy assents, "That goes for me, too!" Many fans and even film researchers have lumped the characters of Rudy and Ludwig (Ted Billings, seen only in the *Bride* creation sequences) together, wrongly crediting Billings with Fitzgerald's efforts on the film.

The Informer (1935), based on the Liam O'Flaherty novel, was a very personal undertaking by director John Ford, who made salary concessions in order to maintain a high degree of creative control. This included the casting of the stars, like Victor McLaglen and Preston Foster, to his Irish imports, to Ford's usual stock players. Fitzgerald played the steady Tommy Connor, reliable lieutenant to IRA Captain Dan Gallagher (Foster). Along with the more aggressive Mulholland (Joe Sawyer), Connor monitors every move made by Gypo Nolan (McLaglen) during his partying spree, which follows the betrayal and death of their comrade Frankie McPhillip (Wallace Ford). Connor observes and notes every coin Gypo spends and with whom he interacts, before the brutish yet sympathetic Nolan is held accountable for his actions. Fitzgerald's interpretation

of Tommy Connor matched Ford's patriotic view of the IRA.

Fitzgerald freelanced mostly with major studios like MGM, Paramount and Fox, often securing small roles with minimal dialogue. Neil was a warehouse workman in *Ten Dollar Raise* (1935), the hotel waiter in *The Perfect Gentleman* (1935) and a soundman in *Anything Goes* (1936). As Dakin in *Charlie Chan in Shanghai* (1935), he was a police official following the directives of the Commissioner of Police (Halliwell Hobbes) in Shanghai. *The Unguarded Hour* (1936), with Henry Daniell as a detestable blackmailer, had Fitzgerald as Larkin, the chauffeur to Lady Helen (Loretta Young). He played a captain in *The King Steps Out* (1936), directed by Josef von Sternberg. In *The White Angel* (1936), with Kay Francis as Florence Nightingale, Fitzgerald was seen as an officer in the barracks. *Charlie Chan at the Racetrack* (1936) is a credit often listed for Fitzgerald, but his presence in the finished film is not confirmed.

John Ford called upon Fitzgerald to appear in his next two features. Neil was billed last (42nd!) as a nobleman in *Mary of Scotland* (1936). Fitzgerald's character arrives with soldiers at the cottage of fisherfolk Lionel Belmore and Doris Lloyd, who have been harboring Queen Mary (Katharine Hepburn). He genuflects and kisses Mary's ring, assuring her, "I've come to conduct you to a place of security." Fitzgerald, however, is part of a trap and turns Mary in to the custody of Robert Warwick, who imprisons her. In *The Plough and the Stars* (1936), based on Sean O'Casey's play and set amidst the Easter Rebellion of 1916 in Ireland, Fitzgerald played Lieutenant Jim Langon. With the occupied Post Office heavily under siege and communications severed, the Irish commander (Moroni Olsen) asks for three officers to volunteer to contact the other rebel positions. Langon, along with Clitheroe (Preston Foster) and Brennan (F.J. McCormick), bravely agrees, but the lieutenant is wounded by machine gun fire soon after hitting the streets of Dublin. For *The Lux Radio Theatre* on CBS, Fitzgerald appeared in "The Brat" (7/13/36) with Joel McCrea and "Beloved Enemy," (12/23/37) starring Brian Aherne.

Another film set in Ireland offered Fitzgerald one (actually two) of his most substantial screen characterizations. *Parnell* (1937), with Clark Gable in the title role as the Irish statesman and patriot, was neither a critical nor a financial success. The film is loaded with noteworthy character players, however, like Donald Crisp, Edna May Oliver, Montagu Love, Berton Churchill, Murray Kinnell and many more. Interestingly, Fitzgerald played two distinct roles, although he is only billed for one. When Parnell speaks before Parliament, Fitzgerald, as an Irish Party member (with a short reddish beard) seated to his left, blurts out, "Ireland for the Irish!" Later, Neil deftly portrays Richard Pigott, a rogue journalist and calligrapher. Pigott is the key

Bride of Frankenstein (1935): Dr. Pretorius (Ernest Thesiger) observes as Rudy (Neil Fitzgerald) and Karl (Dwight Frye) open a young woman's coffin.

witness against Parnell, who has been accused of sedition and complicity in an assassination. Now wearing a long white beard and a monocle in his right eye, Fitzgerald finds defense attorney George Zucco grilling him. The self-described "scribe" is accused of writing to Parnell in order to obtain a handwriting sample from which to forge the seditious document. Pigott is adamant that he is not a forger, but Zucco has him spell "hesitancy," which he misspells ("hesitency") as he did in the forged letter. Pigott's monocle falls from his eye as he complains that he "is not feeling very well," asking the court to briefly be excused. As soon as he exits the courtroom, Pigott shoots himself. Near the film's conclusion, Fitzgerald returns as his original character, who actually is a doctor attending to the dying Parnell.

Fitzgerald played the constable who prevents the departure of the mysterious professor (Lal Chand Mehra) in the remake of *The Thirteenth Chair* (1937). *London by Night* (1937), with Leo G. Carroll in perhaps his most villainous role, had Neil as Inspector Sleet, who assists George Zucco

in his investigation. Fitzgerald was a radio operator in the chaotic early airport sequence in *Lost Horizon* (1937). The small roles continued: an orderly in *Lancer Spy* (1937), a British clerk in *International Settlement* (1938) and an English officer in *Kidnapped* (1938). At least *Holiday* (1938), directed by George Cukor and starring Katharine Hepburn and Cary Grant, gave Fitzgerald a larger, more dimensional part as Edgar, the butler at the party. Neil also had an interesting bit as a forensic assistant in the MGM "Crime Does Not Pay" short, *They're Always Caught* (1938).

Fitzgerald had the distinction of appearing in four offerings, in four distinct roles, in Paramount's *Bulldog Drummond* series in 1938 and 1939. John Howard starred as Drummond in all four features. In *Bulldog Drummond in Africa* (1938), with J. Carrol Naish supplying the perfidy, Neil played McTurk. Entering the British Consulate in Arbi, Morocco, disguised as an Arab, McTurk informs Major Gray (Matthew Boulton) that he has discovered where the fiendish Lane (Naish) is harboring kidnapped Colonel

***Bride of Frankenstein* (1935): "This is no life for murderers!"—Neil Fitzgerald and Dwight Frye**

Nielson (H.B. Warner) of Scotland Yard. The duplicitous Anthony Quinn pulls a gun on both men, capturing them before they can initiate the raid to free Nielson. Drummond and Algy (Reginald Denny) later discover Gray and McTurk in "pretty bad shape." Fitzgerald was Sir Malcolm McLeonard, the Scotland Yard medical examiner who determines Leonard Mudie was killed by the venom of a "giant sting ray," inside a British flat, in *Arrest Bulldog Drummond* (1938). He played the Rockingham stationmaster who deals with the confused queries of absent-minded professor Forrester Harvey in *Bulldog Drummond's Secret Police* (1939). Fitzgerald was Evan Barrows, the manager who shows Heather Angel her new flat, in *Bulldog Drummond's Bride* (1939). Barrows comes upon thief Eduardo Ciannelli, disguised as a demented painter, determines him to be "mad as a hatter" and sends for an ambulance. Later, Barrows, armed with a pistol, confronts Ciannelli, who has returned for the hidden money. Barrows attempts to negotiate a financial split, but he is shot to death with his own gun.

Mostly minor roles continued to come Fitzgerald's way. He was seen as the first councilor in MGM's lavish *Marie Antoinette* (1938). Fitzgerald was an English Sergeant in *Mr. Moto's Last Warning* (1939). As Casey, Neil was the police dispatcher who communicates via radio with Wallace Beery near the climax of *Sergeant Madden* (1939). *The Adventures of Sherlock Holmes* (1939) included Fitzgerald as the clerk of the court. Fitzgerald next portrayed Dr. Taylor on the steamship in *Rulers of the Sea* (1939).

Fitzgerald opted to leave Hollywood and return to his first love, the theater. He established residence in Manhattan prior to securing the Broadway role of Martin Reardon in *Leave Her to Heaven* (2/27/40). *The Wookey* (9/10/41), starring Edmund Gwenn, won critical acclaim and included Fitzgerald as Walt Gibbs. Other wartime theater efforts for Fitzgerald came as Brigadier Husted in *Plan M* (2/20/42), Novakovich in *The Merry Widow* (7/15/42) and Robert Emmett Riordan in *Without Love* (11/10/42).

Agatha Christie's *Ten Little Indians* (6/27/44) featured a fine cast including Estelle Winwood, Halliwell Hobbes,

The Informer (1935): Joe Sawyer, Leo McCabe, Gaylord Pendleton and Neil Fitzgerald determine who will execute Victor McLaglen.

Harry Worth and Fitzgerald (as Rogers). The clever mystery enjoyed a lengthy run (426 performances). While appearing in *Ten Little Indians*, Neil staged an exhibit of his watercolors at the Blue Bowl on 48th Street in Manhattan, in November 1944. On display were Fitzgerald's portraits of Wendell Wilkie, Katharine Hepburn and Estelle Winwood, among his other works of art.

Fitzgerald was also featured on Broadway as Reverend Guilford Melton, along with Montgomery Clift, in *You Touched Me!* (9/25/45). He later played Alcott in *The Survivors* (6/19/48). In the fall of 1948, Neil replaced Francis Compton in the role of the footman Johann Dwornitschek in a revival of Molnar's *The Play's the Thing* (4/28/48), starring Louis Calhern.

Residing in New York City, Fitzgerald busied himself with radio work. One of his earliest roles was that of Timothy J. Brandon, a former Abbey Player (art imitating life), in *Beyond These Valleys* (CBS, 1940). Fitzgerald was heard on the Blue Network in a radio segment of *Renfrew of the Mounted* (5/25/40).

Neil also was a semi-regular on *Arthur Hopkins Presents* for NBC Radio. Fitzgerald was featured on the following broadcasts:

"The Last of Mrs. Cheyney" starring Mary Phillips and Roland Young (episode 12, 7/12/44)

"The Lady With a Lamp" with Helen Hayes (episode 13, 7/26/44)

"Justice," featuring Estelle Winwood (episode 18, 8/30/44)

"Escape," starring Dennis King (episode 24, 10/11/44)

"Berkeley Square," with Neil playing Mayor Clinton opposite Dennis King (episode 30, 11/22/44)

On *The Cavalcade of America*, Fitzgerald appeared in "Conquest of Quinine" (7/31/44) and "Remember Anna Zenger" (10/18/49), with Rosalind Russell. For WMCA, he was on *The Eternal Light* ("The Microscope and the Prayer Shawl," 2/4/45) and *New World A' Coming* ("The People Next Door," 3/12/46, and "Trouble in the Galley," 4/9/46). Fitzgerald was heard on *The Ford Theatre* productions of "A Connecticut Yankee in King Arthur's Court" (10/5/47) and "Of Human Bondage" (10/29/48), starring Ray Milland. On *Grand Central Station* (CBS), Fitzgerald was in "A Sprig of Mignonette" (3/13/48). Along with Una O'Connor, Neil was one of the original film cast members who performed in *The Ford Theatre* (NBC) presentation of "The Informer" (3/28/48). For CBS Radio, Fitzgerald was featured on at least two serial dramas: *Aunt Jenny* and *Our Gal Sunday*.

Fitzgerald often indulged his creative muse, painting, writing articles for magazines and newspapers and writing songs. One of Neil's songs, *Two Little Pigs*, was heard on a broadcast of *Beyond These Valleys*. Fitzgerald's other interests were said to be gardening, swimming, horseback riding, tennis and badminton. Neil even provided acting lessons for aspiring performers, such as Jane Withers and Laraine Day.

In addition to radio and theater, Fitzgerald was beginning to find a niche in the relatively new medium of television. For *NBC Presents*, Fitzgerald was featured in "Alison's Lad" (3/14/49). He also was seen on *The Philco Television Playhouse* (NBC) in "The Pupil" (12/24/50), starring John Newland, later to be the host of *One Step Beyond*. Fitzgerald was seen in "Victoria Regina" (1/15/51), starring Helen Hayes, for *Robert Montgomery Presents* (NBC) and "The Stolen City" (5/25/51) for *Pulitzer Prize Playhouse* (ABC). On *The Lux Video Theatre*, he was featured in "Ferry Crisis at Friday Point" (5/19/52), starring Fredric March, and as the bartender in "The Man Who Struck it Rich" (11/17/52), with Barry Fitzgerald and Una O'Connor. For the Melvyn Douglas series *Steve Randall*, Fitzgerald played Bender in the episode "The Trial" (9/11/52). Neil made appearances for all the networks, mostly in dramas, such as *Studio One*.

On stage, Fitzgerald played Henry Maye in *Design for a Stained Glass Window* (1/23/50), Melling in *The High Ground*

The Plough and the Stars (1936): **F.J. McCormick, Neil Fitzgerald and Preston Foster receive their orders from Arthur Shields and Moroni Olsen.**

even made an appearance in the noteworthy early television comedy *The Goldbergs*, starring Gertrude Berg. Neil was also seen on *The Jackie Gleason Show* as a bartender in the "Curse of the Kramdens" (3/2/57) episode.

Most of Fitzgerald's acting efforts in the 1950s and 1960s were on the stage. He was seen as Holiday in the revival of *Abie's Irish Rose* (11/18/54). Neil took over as Carter during the run of *Witness for the Prosecution* (1955). Fitzgerald, as the venerable judge, played opposite the Gish sisters, Lillian and Dorothy, in *The Chalk Garden* in the summer stock season of 1956. Of his role as the Priest in *The Tinker's Wedding* (3/6/57), Brooks Atkinson wrote in the *New York Times*, "Since Neil Fitzgerald has the most experience, it is not surprising that he gives the finest performance." In *Oscar Wilde* (4/19/57), Neil was the Solicitor General. Robert Coleman in the *New York Mirror* commented on his portrayal of Gouttez in *Monique* (10/22/57), stating, "Neil Fitzgerald has a few effective moments as a garrulous carpenter." With Irish theater making a comeback in New York, Fitzgerald found work in *On Baile's Strand* and *The Death of Cuchulain* (both 4/12/59). As Father Curran, Fitzgerald acted with Julie Harris and a young Robert Redford in *Little Moon of Alban* (12/1/60).

On television, Neil related the ghost story in "Lost Hearts" (6/27/59), concerned with an old English manor house, as part of the CBS anthology *Camera Three*. For *The Play of the Week*, Fitzgerald portrayed Fintry in "The White Steed" (11/23/59), set in Ireland and starring Tim

(2/20/51), a variety of roles in *To Dorothy, a Son* (11/19/51) and Mr. Wardle in *Mr. Pickwick* (9/17/52). On tour, Neil was featured in *Two Blind Mice* (1950), starring Melvyn Douglas.

After a 14-year hiatus from films, Fitzgerald had a memorable scene in the early moments of *Niagara* (1953), which starred Marilyn Monroe. As the Canadian Customs Officer, Neil questions Ray (Max Showalter) and Polly Cutler (Jean Peters) about their backgrounds and visit to the Canadian side of Niagara Falls. After learning that they are "honeymooners," the customs man inquires, "That isn't liquor you have in that case under your coat, is it?" After Ray assures him that he is carrying books to catch up on his reading, Fitzgerald's character does a marvelous take, as he incredulously adds, "Reading?"

As part of an essentially Irish ensemble, Fitzgerald was seen on TV's *Hallmark Hall of Fame* in "The Harp of Erin" (3/15/53), about the life of poet Thomas Moore. He acted with Dane Clark and Werner Klemperer in "The Hangman in the Fog" (1/10/54) on *The Philco Television Playhouse* (NBC). "Second Dawn" (2/4/54), an installment of *Four Star Playhouse* (CBS) starring Charles Boyer, had Fitzgerald as Hodgins. As Mr. Classens in "Moving Day" (9/22/55), Fitzgerald

Lancer Spy (1937): **Lionel Atwill addresses Virginia Field as Neil Fitzgerald stands by.**

The Play's the Thing (1940 Broadway stage): Louis Calhern and Neil Fitzgerald

O'Connor. In a 40-minute film produced by the Colonial Williamsburg Foundation, Fitzgerald was Miller in *Music of Williamsburg* (1960). He portrayed the Doctor in "I Heard You Calling Me" (5/5/61), with Constance Ford, on television's gripping anthology *Way Out*.

Fitzgerald still did radio drama, such as "Turnabout" (1/24/60) and "Weekend at the Gleebes" (7/29/62), both for *Suspense* and "The Doniger Doniger Matter" (9/2/62) for *Yours Truly, Johnny Dollar*, on CBS. On 9/30/62, Fitzgerald had the distinction of being heard on the final broadcast of the long-running radio anthology *Suspense* (which had aired 945 episodes over 20 years). This last episode, entitled "Devilstone," had Fitzgerald as the butler to star Christopher Carey, who is investigating a haunted house with unexpected results.

A news item in the *Long Island Star-Journal* (2/21/62) announced that Neil Fitzgerald would be appearing at the Bryant Center in Astoria, Queens on Friday, February 23, 1962. He was to provide a lecture, entitled "All About Picturesque Ireland," while regaling the audience with stories about the theater, Irish writers and music, as well as "a bit of the old blarney."

Other Fitzgerald stage performances came in *A Portrait of the Artist as a Young Man* (5/28/62), *The Barroom Monks* (5/28/62) and *Roar Like a Dove* (5/21/64). During the summer of 1963, he toured Connecticut and Rhode Island in a road company of *Kiss Me Kate*. Fitzgerald was seen with Carroll Baker at the Tappan Zee Playhouse, Nyack, New York in a production of *Anna Christie* (6/23/66). As part of *Three Hand Reel*, Neil played Sean O'Donoghue in *The Bridal Night* and the man in *The Eternal Triangle* (both 11/7/66). Fitzgerald was in the Irish review *Carricknabauna* (March 1967) and played both Mr. Casey and the Confessor in *Stephen D* (9/24/67).

Fitzgerald appeared in two episodes of television's *East Side/West Side* (CBS) starring George C. Scott: "Not Bad for Openers" (11/18/63) and "The Name of the Game" (3/23/64). E.G. Marshall's fine TV drama *The Defenders* (CBS) featured Fitzgerald as Stacey, along with Bramwell Fletcher, in a program entitled "Claire Chevel Died in Boston" (1/4/64).

Fitzgerald secured another interesting role in his intermittent film career in *Mirage* (1965), starring Gregory Peck. Shot on location in New York City and cleverly directed by Edward Dmytryk, *Mirage* was a suspenseful thriller from

***Niagara* (1953): Neil Fitzgerald, as the border customs official, questions Jean Peters and Max Showalter.**

A Portrait of the Artist as a Young Man (1962 Off-Broadway stage): **Michael Kane, Sarah Cunningham, Margaret DePriest, Robert Brown and Neil Fitzgerald**

its confusing beginning to the exciting climax. Fitzgerald played Joe Turtle, the night elevator operator at the Unidyne Corporation skyscraper, which figures prominently in the plot. After Walter Abel falls from the skyscraper to his death, an amnesiac Peck, who turns out to be a physiochemist who has discovered the secret of neutralizing radioactivity, struggles to regain his memories and avoid hit men, as vying factions attempt to steal his formula.

Back on television, Fitzgerald reprised his earlier role on *The Jackie Gleason Show* (10/29/66) as Terrance the bartender in "The Honeymooners: The Curse of the Kramdens" segment. *The Thanksgiving Visitor* (1968), a poignant tale written and narrated by Truman Capote, starred Geraldine Page in an Emmy-winning performance and included Fitzgerald as Uncle B. Fitzgerald also was seen on daytime television in *Search For Tomorrow.*

Hadrian VII (1/8/69) was Fitzgerald's last long-running (359 performances) Broadway show. In this play that made a star of Alec McCowen, Neil was effective as the Rector of St. Andrew's College. In the short-lived (10 performances) *The Mundy Scheme* (12/11/69) by Brian Friel, Fitzgerald played Charles Hogan, opposite Jack Cassidy.

The late film historian Richard Bojarski vividly recalled an appearance by Fitzgerald in the 1960s on the Joe Franklin television show, seen on WOR (Channel 9) in the New York City area. Fitzgerald was about to recount an anecdote regarding the filming of *Bride of Frankenstein*, when Franklin, in his inimitable manner, cut him off and went to a commercial. "After the commercial was completed," Bojarski wrote, "Joe didn't get back to Fitzgerald, but to another guest." Fitzgerald never got to relate his story and sat silently for the remainder of the show. This constituted a lost opportunity to hear a first-hand account of a classic film!

Nearing the age of 80, Fitzgerald continued to work his craft in television, theater and film. In 1970/71, Fitzgerald had a recurring role as Clifford, the Whitney chauffeur, on the daytime TV soap opera *The Edge of Night* (CBS). On stage, Fitzgerald was nominated for a Drama Critics Circle Award for his performance as the doctor in Edward Albee's *All Over* (3/27/71). He played Viscount Tomworth in *Murderous Angels* (12/20/71), with Louis Gossett, Jr. In David Storey's award-winning play *The Contractor* (10/17/73), Fitzgerald was seen for the final time on Broadway as Old Mr. Ewbank.

For his last film appearance, Fitzgerald found himself in the unusual, to put it mildly, *Savages* (1972), directed by James Ivory, produced by Ismail Merchant and co-written

The Barroom Monks (1962 Off-Broadway stage): Sarah Cunningham goes after Neil Fitzgerald in the bar.

by Michael O'Donoghue (of *Saturday Night Live* notoriety). This allegorical tale concerns the primitive Mud People, who follow the path of a bounding croquet ball to come upon a lavish, deserted mansion. While there, they take on the clothing, dialogue and habits of upper crust society, only to deteriorate to their tribal beginnings, all in the space of 24 hours. Fitzgerald is first seen as the tribal elder, who, soon after the encounter with the spherical object, assumes the persona of Sir Harry. The nouveau aristocrat makes droll comments with a deadpan delivery, amidst an unlikely cast, including a young Susan Blakely, Sam Waterston, Lewis J. Stadlen, and even Ultra Violet. *Savages* represents a rather strange cap to the atypical acting career of Neil Fitzgerald.

Retiring from acting in 1973 at the age of 81, Fitzgerald maintained his residence in Manhattan until about a year before his death. He moved to the Ten Acre Nursing Home in Princeton, New Jersey, at that time. Neil Fitzgerald, now at the age of 90, passed away at that facility on June 15, 1982.

Although never a major performer and unbilled in many of his films, Neil Fitzgerald had the good fortune to

Mirage (1965): Neil Fitzgerald as Joe Turtle

work well into his 80s, achieving some degree of success in four different media: film, theater, radio and television. A bright, witty Irishman, Fitzgerald made career choices that limited his cinematic career. Fortunately, Neil's entertaining performances in *Bride of Frankenstein*, *The Informer*, *Parnell*, *Mirage* and *Savages*, among others, provide a minor legacy for this neglected actor.

Sources

Coughlin, Jim. "Forgotten Faces: Neil Fitzgerald," in *Mad About Movies #6* (2007), pp. 47-54.

Mark of the Vampire (1935)

Ivan F. Simpson
(1875-1951)

A true Renaissance man, Ivan Simpson was once labeled by George Arliss "as one of the ablest actors on the stage or screen" (*Film Weekly*, 6/23/33, p. 12). Not only was Simpson a skilled character player, he was also a sculptor, writer and teacher. A modest man with strong ideals and values, Simpson was well respected by his peers for his integrity. He was one of the founding members of the Screen Actors Guild and helped serve as a moral

Disraeli (1929): Ivan Simpson greets George Arliss.

conscience for the union during its early development. Simpson's performances enhanced many major motion pictures, including *Mutiny on the Bounty* and *The Man Who Played God*, and helped salvage some minor films, like *The Phantom of Crestwood* and *The Past of Mary Holmes*. He had noteworthy roles in several horror/fantasy genre movies, including *Mark of the Vampire*, *The Monkey's Paw*, *The Invisible Man Returns*, *The Body Disappears* and *The Uninvited*. Simpson's sincerity, passion and warmth always brought a note of truth to whatever character he was enacting.

Ivan Freebody Simpson was born in Thanet Isle, Kent, England (although many sources note Glasgow, Scotland as his birthplace) on February 4, 1875. Freebody was the maiden name of Ivan's maternal grandmother, Elizabeth. Ivan was the fourth of five children born to Robert Simpson (1834-1883) and Jane Freebody Rowe (1841-1930). The others were sister Eliza Jane (1868-1960) and brothers Malcolm MacLean (1868-1945), Allan Charles (1874-1918) and John T. Simpson (1877-?).

Ivan Simpson was educated in London. An avid sportsman in school, being particularly proficient at cricket, Simpson initially embarked on a career as a newspaperman. He was working as a reporter for the London society newspaper *The Herald* when it went out of business. A school friend, who knew Ivan had experience in amateur theatricals, suggested Simpson try working in the theater until another newspaper position came along. Simpson learned the rudiments of the theater from the bottom up,

The Green Goddess (1921 Broadway stage): Ivan Simpson as Watkins

Forgotten Faces

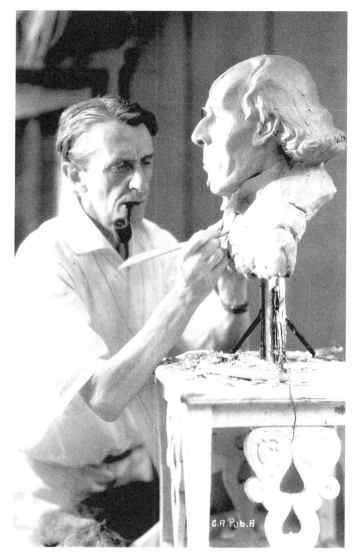

Candid photo (1929) of Ivan Simpson sculpting a bust of George Arliss as Disraeli.

Old English (1930): Ivan Simpson as Joe Pillin

beginning as what he called a "humble *super*, with no influence at all." Within a few years, Simpson was appearing in major productions both in London and in regional theaters in Great Britain. He toured the provinces, performing comedies, melodramas and Shakespearean works, with Sir Henry Irving's company. Ivan was married at St. George's Anglican Church, Hanover Square, London, England circa 1904, but no known references list the name of his wife nor the date of their divorce.

Simpson first came to the United States in 1905 while on tour with E.S. Willard's theatrical company. Willard's troupe disembarked from the Arabic in New York on 1/21/05 and opened at the Knickerbocker Theatre the following evening in *Lucky Durham* (1/22/05). Simpson was also seen with the Willard Company in *The Brighter Side* (2/6/05). Returning to England for the birth of his daughter Pamela Joy Simpson (1905-2002) in Headington, Oxfordshire on July 22, 1905, Simpson was soon to rejoin Willard in *The Man Who Was*, which opened at the New

Amsterdam in New York on 12/5/05. Ivan appeared in the tragicomedy *The Evangelist* (9/30/07, 19 performances) at the Knickerbocker. Much of Simpson's early stage work came under the management of Charles Frohman, including the long-running *Arsene Lupin* (8/26/09, 144 performances), Arthur Conan Doyle's *The Speckled Band* (11/21/10, 32 performances) and the comedy *A Single Man* (9/4/11, 104 performances), starring John Drew and featuring Ivan as Henry Worthington. Simpson was seen in the farcical romance *Love Among the Lions* (8/8/10, 48 performances), with A.E. Matthews. Opposite Mrs. Fiske and Henry E. Dixey, Simpson was featured in the revival of *Becky Sharp* (3/20/11, 16 performances).

Simpson joined the famed theatrical club, the Players, in 1910 and would remain a member for 40 years. Very

The Sea God (1930): **The cast takes a break on the golf course: Richard Arlen, Eugene Pallette and Ivan Simpson.**

the stage. He portrayed an English derelict in *Inside the Lines* (2/9/15, 103 performances), written by Earl Derr Biggers, the creator of Charlie Chan. Simpson also was part of an impressive company, including Margaret Anglin and Holbrook Blinn, in the revival of Oscar Wilde's *A Woman of No Importance* (4/24/16, 56 performances).

Although 41 years old, Simpson enlisted in the Canadian Army upon the outbreak of World War I. He was assigned to the Sixteenth Battery of the Canadian Field Artillery and served almost four years in France and Belgium. Wounded at the Battle of Vimy Ridge in April 1917, Simpson later returned to the front and eventually was given a commission as an officer.

After being mustered out of the Canadian Army, Simpson journeyed to New York and found theatrical work as the English consul in *Her Blue Devil* (1920). He also cowrote (with Oliver Herford) a farce entitled *What's the Matter With Father*, which Simpson had copyrighted on 1/29/20. Simpson had an important role as David MacKenzie, the Scotsman, in *The Charm School* (8/2/20, 88 performances), with Sam Hardy and James Gleason. His portrayal of Hewston, the harried but efficient butler of Roland Young, in *Rollo's Wild Oat* (11/23/20, 228 performances) brought Simpson both critical acclaim and popular recognition.

Simpson built on this success by forging an alliance with actor George Arliss that would span many years, significant plays and 10 films. Arliss and Simpson first appeared together in William Archer's *The Green Goddess*, which opened in Philadelphia on 12/27/20 before moving to Broadway on 1/18/21, where it ran for 175 performances. Simpson portrayed Watkins, the English-born

much concerned with the rights of performers, Simpson became part of Actors Equity in 1913 (he later would play a significant role in the founding of the Screen Actors Guild). In addition, Simpson belonged to the Lambs, the Episcopal Actors Guild, the New York Athletic Club and the Hollywood Athletic Club.

Hawthorne of the USA (11/4/12, 72 performances), produced by Cohan and Harris, included Simpson in a cast with Douglas Fairbanks (soon to achieve fame in films). Simpson was seen in three New York productions with brief runs: *Nan* (1/13/13, 1 performance), *Shadowed* (9/24/13, 6 performances) and *Miss Phoenix* (11/3/13, 8 performances). Like many Broadway performers of the time, Simpson ventured into silent films, portraying a character named Simpson in *The Dictator* (1915), starring John Barrymore. As Martin, Simpson played opposite Marguerite Clark in the society film drama *Out of the Drifts* (1916). Simpson was not sold on the cinematic medium, however, continuing to concentrate his efforts on

The Man Who Played God (1932): **George Arliss and Ivan Simpson**

The Monkey's Paw (1933): C. Aubrey Smith, Ivan Simpson, Bramwell Fletcher and Louise Carter gaze at the title object.

The Past of Mary Holmes (1933): Ivan Simpson with Eric Linden

valet to the Rajah of Rukh (Arliss), in a tale of colonialism and conflicted loyalties. The demure and correct Watkins is enticed by captive Britishers to transmit a message via Morse code to aide in their rescue. Unknown to them, however, is that Watkins spent time in an English reformatory, left the country under questionable circumstances and would rather deceive his countrymen than betray the

Rajah. As a result, the valet is bound by the Englishmen and thrown to his death. In a January 1936 article for *The Screen Guild's Magazine*, Simpson reminisced, "I shall go to my grave grateful to the late William Archer for writing and giving me the part of Watkins in *The Green Goddess*."

While playing in *The Green Goddess* on Broadway, Arliss was presented by the company with a bronze bust of himself that had been sculpted by Simpson. The following year, when the show was touring in Chicago, *The Green Goddess* company repeated the ritual, apparently for publicity, again giving Arliss the bust. The gesture caused playwright Archer to quip, "There have been, however, no accounts of the intervening festivities in the course of which Mr. Arliss seems to have given the bust back to the company." Some years later, Simpson would sculpt a bust of Boris Karloff. A photograph of Simpson modeling the bust while Karloff poses remains in existence. The bust itself, according to the Karloff family, has long been lost.

"Ivan Simpson, as an old servant, is particularly pleasing," wrote the *New York Times* (10/2/22) of his portrayal of Carter, appearing with Arliss on screen for the first time, in *The Man Who Played God* (1922). For Goldwyn, he recreated his role of Watkins in the first film adaptation of *The Green Goddess* (1923), again starring George Arliss. The *New York Times* (8/14/23) noted Simpson's "splendid screenacting" as Watkins. Also with Arliss, Simpson played James Pettison in *$20 a Week* (1924). Arliss (1940, pp. 141-142) described his fondness for working with familiar players:

> I like acting with the people I know and who have worked with me before. I suppose if I had no one to control me, I should have almost the same cast in every picture I make. As it is, the casting director always says, "I suppose you want Simmy" (that is Ivan Simpson). Of course I want Simmy. I know that he will give a fine performance; and the better the actor I work with, the better I shall appear to be.

Simpson played Mr. Willis, the father of Dorothy Mackaill, in *Twenty One* (1923), with Richard Barthelmess. Back to the stage, Simpson initiated what would be a long-time association with actress/producer Katharine Cornell, being featured as Bennett Lomax opposite her in the dra-

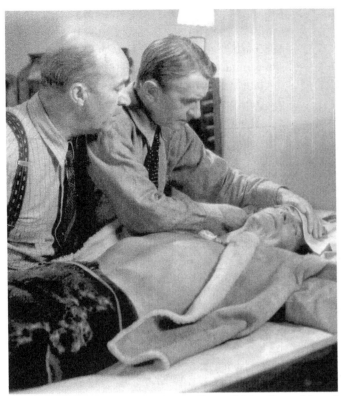

A Man of Two Worlds (1934): J. Farrell MacDonald and Ivan Simpson examine Francis Lederer.

ma *The Way Things Happen* (1/28/24, 24 performances). John Galsworthy's *Old English* (12/23/24, 183 performances) again paired Simpson, as shipping magnate Joe Pillin, with George Arliss.

As Bounds in *Miss Bluebeard* (1925), starring Bebe Daniels, the *New York Times* (1/28/25) exclaimed, "Ivan Simpson is splendid in the role of a butler." Simpson also appeared with Ms. Daniels in *Wild, Wild Susan* (1925), as Malcolm and *Lovers in Quarantine* (1925), as "the silent passenger." In *A Kiss for Cinderella* (1925), with Betty Bronson, Simpson played Mr. Cutaway. He then took on another butler role in *Womanhandled* (1925).

Simpson remained prominent on Broadway in the late 1920s. The Players Club did a brief revival (8 performances) of *Julius Caesar* (6/6/27), with a solid cast, including Basil Rathbone, Harry Davenport and Pedro de Cordoba. Simpson was the Soothsayer who told Caesar to beware "the Ides of March." He played Uncle Herbert in *The Garden of Eden* (9/27/27, 23 performances), starring Miriam Hopkins. *The Command Performance* (10/3/28, 29 performances), with Ian Keith, featured Simpson as Paul Masoch. Simpson portrayed Edward Laverick in the successful drama *The Perfect Alibi* (11/27/28, 255 performances).

Back on screen, Simpson played Sir Hugh Meyers, the international Jewish lawyer who helps

finance the efforts of Benjamin Disraeli (George Arliss) in *Disraeli* (1929). Sir Hugh, however, goes bankrupt, forcing Disraeli to bluff regarding his finances. *Evidence* (1929), starring Pauline Frederick, included Simpson as Peabody.

During the early days of the transition from silent to talking pictures, Simpson found work as a coach at Warner Bros.' dramatic school. Warner Bros. and First National expanded the concept to that of a training school, with Simpson as one of the directors where aspiring young performers would learn all aspects of the film acting craft. According to the *New York Times* (5/10/31), "The course laid out by Mr. Simpson for his young hopefuls embraces a very thorough coaching in the various phases of dramatic art—diction, bearing, pantomimic expressions and gestures, the details of make-up and so on." Warner Bros. intended the school to be a permanent institution, with a maximum of 25 students on the roster at any one time.

In 1930, Warner Bros. remade *The Green Goddess*, with Arliss and Simpson recreating their roles of the Rajah of Rukh and Watkins respectively. *Isle of Escape* (1930), with Myrna Loy and Monte Blue, included Simpson as the judge. Ivan had a small bit in *The Golden Dawn* (1930). The World War I spy tale *Inside the Lines* (1930), starring Betty Compson, had Simpson as Capper. He played Morson, opposite Claudette Colbert and Fredric March, in *Manslaughter* (1930). As Joe Pillin, the father of Reginald Sheffield in *Old English* (1930), Simpson was induced to sell ships to cunning George Arliss and turn over a percentage of his profits to Arliss' grandchildren. Arliss noted in his second autobiography, *My Ten Years in the Studios* (p. 87), "I was fortunate in having Ivan Simpson once more in the part that he had so successfully played in the theater."

The Mystery of Mr. X (1934): Partners-in-crime Ivan Simpson, Robert Montgomery and Forrester Harvey

Among the Missing (1934): **Arthur Hohl with a skeptical Ivan Simpson**

Simpson portrayed Higgins in *The Way of All Men* (1930), with Douglas Fairbanks, Jr.

The Sea God (1930), with Fay Wray and Richard Arlen, offered Simpson the colorful role of Pearly Nick. While Arlen is engaged in a seagoing race with villain Robert Gleckler, he begrudgingly comes about to rescue the nearly dead, parchment-skinned Pearly Nick, who was flying a white flag on his small vessel. The grateful Nick tries to convince Arlen of the existence of a rich pearl bed that will more than compensate the skipper for the loss of his ship in the race. Later that year, Simpson staged the dialogue for the Ronald Colman film *The Devil to Pay* (1930). Back on stage, Simpson had a comedic role as Arthur Dupin in A.A. Milne's *A Kiss of Importance* (12/1/30, 255 performances), in a cast that included Montagu Love, Frederick Kerr (the Baron in *Frankenstein*) and Basil Rathbone.

As Davis the butler in *The Millionaire* (1931), Simpson was found by the *New York Times* (4/9/31) to be "up to his usual standard of excellence." In the cast of *The Millionaire* was a young James Cagney, who listed Simp-

son first among his favorite screen performers in an article in the *New York Times* (6/28/31). Again as a butler (this time villainous, however) in *The Lady Who Dared* (1931), Simpson takes photos of Betty Compson in a compromising position with Conway Tearle for the purpose of blackmail. Simpson provided some comedy relief as Stevens, Conrad Nagel's butler, in *The Reckless Hour* (1931) and again was seen as a butler in *I Like Your Nerve* (1931), with Loretta Young. As Crunch in *Safe in Hell* (1930), Simpson played one of the seedy denizens of a Caribbean island who cannot be extradited despite their criminal histories. Speaking with a pronounced Cockney accent, Crunch chews on nuts and spits out the worms while describing how he killed a robbery victim by walloping him "over the nebber."

Simpson was Battle (named Carter in the silent version), the compassionate butler who helps avert the suicide of his employer, George Arliss, in *The Man Who Played God* (1932) [aka *The Silent Voice*]. Battle pleads with his master, then gives the man binoculars. Arliss' character uses them to read the lips of strangers from his window, thus realizing there are others with far more difficult problems and situations than his own. Simpson played Simms in *A Passport to Hell* (1932) and was Hodge, Ruth Chatterton's butler, in *The Crash* (1932). As Mr. Vayne, the alias of character Henry T. Herrick in *The Phantom of Crestwood* (1932), Simpson sends a death mask of his late son to Karen Morley. He had hoped to terrify the woman in retaliation for spurning his son, who subsequently committed suicide. Vayne/Herrick dies from a heart attack, however, before enacting further vengeance. Simpson was seen as Mr. Faulkner, the banker whose daughter is abducted by Professor Moriar-

Shadow of a Doubt (1935): **Constance Collier plays cards with her butler, Ivan Simpson.**

Mutiny on the Bounty **(1935): Franchot Tone, Clark Gable, Dudley Digges and Ivan Simpson**

ty (Ernest Torrence), in *Sherlock Holmes* (1932), with Clive Brook in the title role.

Perhaps Simpson's most significant fantasy film part came in *The Monkey's Paw* (1933), of which no complete version is believed to exist. Simpson portrayed Mr. John White, a timid old clerk who yearns for the best for his family. He steals the title object from an old military friend (C. Aubrey Smith), hoping to utilize the alleged three wishes from the paw to provide some money for his daughter's wedding and other family needs. When White uses the first wish to ask for money, however, the calamities begin. The money comes from the insurance from the death of his son (Bramwell Fletcher), who is mangled in a work accident. White then wishes his son to be alive again. The clerk, now tormented by what he has unleashed, realizes that his son would be coming back in a butchered, traumatized state. As the young man, in a presumed horrid condition, arrives at the door, White must spend the final wish to return his son to the grave. It is unfortunate that this version of *The Monkey's Paw*, with its fine cast and an elaborate prologue,

has not survived. For Ivan Simpson, a large and important fantasy role is not available for contemporary viewing and evaluation.

C. Aubrey Smith, a former England Cricket International member, founded the Hollywood Cricket Club in 1932. There were numerous British expatriates in the film colony who were cricket enthusiasts. *The Monkey's Paw* cast members Simpson and Fletcher were prominent members, as were Boris Karloff, Nigel Bruce, Clive Brook and Murray Kinnell, among others. Out of the ranks of the Hollywood Cricket Club would emerge many of the founders and earliest members of the Screen Actors Guild (SAG).

Shortly after the release of *The Monkey's Paw*, Simpson would appear as the subject in a feature article by John K. Newnham in the British periodical *Film Weekly* (6/23/33). The piece, entitled "Hollywood's Least-Known Celebrity," lauded Simpson's acting skills and personality. Newnham wrote, "It doesn't matter how big or how small his part is, he is always distinctive … His acting ability has carried him a long way without the assistance of high-powered public-

Maid of Salem (1937): Ivan Simpson as Reverend Parris

The Earl of Chicago (1940): Robert Montgomery and Ivan Simpson

ity boys, without any undue effort on his part to attract attention." Newnham characterized Simpson as "quiet, gentle, artistic," adding Ivan could have "gone much further in the acting world if he cared to push himself forward more." Simpson, however, impressed as content "to rise on one's own merits." Newnham claimed that even though "everyone in Hollywood knows him and admires him," outside the film community, "few people know anything about him."

The Past of Mary Holmes (1933) had Simpson as Jacob Riggs, the theater doorman who shoots and kills employer Clay Clement after witnessing him mistreat young women. In *The Secret of Madame Blanche* (1933), Simpson played Lionel Atwill's lawyer. The two men travel together to Paris to take away Irene Dunne's son and have her declared an unfit mother. *Lost in Limehouse (1933)*, a Masquers Club short, included Ivan as the Duke of Dunkwell. Simpson played Johnson, the secretary to silk importer Neil Ham-

ilton, in *The Silk Express* (1933). *Midnight Mary* (1933) featured Simpson as Tindle, the head clerk who is caught by Franchot Tone accosting Loretta Young at her job. Reunited with George Arliss, Simpson portrayed Lelain, the old merchant in the play within the film, in *Voltaire* (1933). Simpson played Lathrop in *Her Secret* (1933) and a butler in *Blind Adventure* (1933). *Charlie Chan's Greatest Case* (1933) provided Simpson with the pivotal role of T.M. Brade, who arrives in Hawaii attempting to reclaim jewels stolen from his father 35 years prior and intending to exact revenge on Robert Warwick.

In the early 1930s, the Hollywood studio system was at its strongest. The major studio moguls, like MGM's Louis B. Mayer and the Warner brothers, were not above exploiting actors, exacting long hours while abusing contracts. On 7/12/33, a group of performers met at the home of Kenneth Thomson to discuss the formation of a new actors' union that would offer greater protection, unity and industry leverage than did Actors Equity. Out of this meeting would arise the Screen Actors Guild. Among the initial members were James and Lucile Gleason, Ralph Morgan and Arthur Vinton. The Hollywood Cricket Club supplied a significant contingent of SAG founding members: Boris Karloff, Alan Mowbray, Noel Madison, Claude King and Ivan Simpson among them, soon to be followed by C. Aubrey Smith, Murray Kinnell and more.

The Invisible Man Returns (1940): Cobb's staff experiences the presence of invisibility: player, Boyd Irwin and Ivan Simpson.

Ivan Simpson wrote the first SAG dues check in July 1933. He designed the original SAG logo, considered the union's coat of arms, featuring a torch (symbolizing liberty, knowledge and the light of truth) with two halves of a laurel wreath (symbolizing victory) and the SAG initials. Simpson also developed the motto of SAG: "He best serves himself who serves others." Simpson reportedly was very passionate at the early SAG meetings, speaking out on behalf of the minor, often neglected, performers.

Man of Two Worlds (1934), an interesting tale of the attempt to "civilize" a Greenland Eskimo (Francis Lederer), had Simpson providing able support as Dr. Lott. *Variety* (2/27/34) referred to Simpson as "a highly expert character player" in his role of "Hutch" Hutchinson, a grouchy insurance agent and colleague of jewel thief Robert Montgomery and cabbie Forrester Harvey, in *The Mystery of Mr. X* (1934). "Ivan Simpson does creditably as Amschel Rothschild," reviewed the *New York Times* (3/15/34) of his portrayal of one of the banking brothers of Nathan (George Arliss) in *The House of Rothschild* (1934). Other roles for Simpson at this time were: Smeed in *Among the Missing* (1934), the first doctor in *Murder in Trinidad* (1934), Clumber in *The World Moves On* (1934), "Poohbah" Evans in *British Agent* (1934), Sanders Webster in *The Little Min-*

ister (1934) and a bit as a bearded man in *Stingaree* (1934).

MGM's elaborate production of *David Copperfield* (1935) included Simpson as Littimer. He played Morse, Constance Collier's butler and cribbage partner, in *Shadow of Doubt* (1935). As Mr. Grantham, the father of Maureen O'Hara in *The Bishop Misbehaves* (1935), Simpson is the victim of Reginald Owen who cheats him out of a valuable patent for his invention. *Variety* (11/27/33) stated, "Ivan Simpson is a standout as the butler," Fletcher, in *Splendor* (1935). Simpson was Moss in *The Perfect Gentleman* (1935), a resident in *East of Java* (1935) and the prosecutor who tries Errol Flynn for aiding the rebellion against King James II, in *Captain Blood* (1935).

Working with director Frank Lloyd on one of their six films together, Simpson was the sympathetic botanist Morgan, whose mission it is to secure breadfruit plants for British colonies in the West Indies, in *Mutiny on the Bounty* (1935). After the death of the Bounty's surgeon (Dudley Digges), Morgan helps ease the grief of Christian (Clark Gable) and Byam (Franchot Tone) with an impromptu eulogy:

A drunkard, yes—but everybody loved him. The welfare of men on shipboard depends on things that seem small: a joke at the right moment, a glass of grog, a kind word would do more with seamen than the cat-o-nine tails. This ship will be worse, if possible, for his death.

Following the mutiny, Morgan begs the men to care for his plants, prior to his being put into a longboat with Captain Bligh (Charles Laughton) and the loyalists by the mutineers. During the courageous open boat voyage to Timor, a very weak Morgan refuses his meager ration of food, telling Bligh to "Give it to the youngsters. They need it more." Simpson provided a splendid characterization of Morgan amidst a cast of stalwart character players in *Mutiny on the Bounty*.

Universal's atmospheric *The Great Impersonation* (1935) had Simpson as the kindly Dr. Harrison, who is lawn bowling when spotted by Lord Dominey (Edmund Lowe). Harrison, who has been treating the mentally unbalanced Lady Dominey (Valerie Hobson) since her husband's departure five years earlier, advises Dominey to take a cautious and gentle approach in re-establishing a relationship with his wife. When Dominey is about to burn the "black bog," Harrison must attend to the distraught Mrs. Unthank (Esther Dale), whose "dead" son Roger (Dwight Frye) allegedly haunts the grounds. After Roger is really killed, Harrison, assisting Dominey with his unconscious wife, wonders if the shock of the incident will actually cure her hysteria or drive Lady Dominey further into madness.

Simpson had an important role as Jan the butler in *Mark of the Vampire* (1935), MGM and Tod Browning's remake of *London After Midnight* (1927). Jan is first seen being questioned by inspector Lionel Atwill about the mysterious death of Sir Karell Borotyn. With Leila Bennett, he later provides some modulated comic relief, reacting to the eerie visages of the "vampires." Jan also plays a role in helping recreate the night of Sir Karell's death in a plot designed to expose Jean Hersholt as the murderer.

Simpson served in many positions with SAG, including being one of the first trio (with C. Henry Gordon and Murray Kinnell) comprising Actors' Magazine Advisory Committee. He regularly contributed thoughtful articles to *The Screen Guild's Magazine*, including a piece entitled "For the Good of Your Soul" (September 1935). In it, Simpson endorsed the concept of actors regularly returning to the stage to further hone their craft. Simpson stressed:

> There is something fine about taking the written words of the author and turning them into a living character, the careful, even meticulous care with which a character is developed during rehearsals in the theater is a healthful contrast to the haphazard methods of the screen where a complete characterization may be changed a few minutes before shooting or even during the shooting itself. Then, too, when a full day is devoted to one scene, and the chronological order of events is sacrificed for the mechanical technique of the screen, the player loses perspective of the character. Particularly for young people, the learning to sustain a part through an entire evening is excellent training. It helps to give them poise and weight. This does not mean stodginess, but grip, command and repose. And the same is good for the older player who may have become stale.

The Male Animal (1942): Ivan Simpson as Dean Frederick Damon

In the January 1936 issue of the SAG magazine, Simpson submitted "An Actor Looks at Screen Writers." With part tongue in cheek, Simpson wrote:

> All intelligent actors know (and when I say intelligent actors, I naturally refer to those who think as I do. The others, of course, are morons) that however good the actors, directors, supervisors, producers, cutters and script girls (bless their hearts) may be—the big mogul or chief cheese

Jane Eyre (1943): Orson Welles, Joan Fontaine, Erskine Sanford and Ivan Simpson

is the writer. Given a good story, we are all happy and our road is comparatively easy. With a bad story, everybody has a bad case of jaundice. Casting a bad play or picture is a heart-breaking job. With a good property, you can almost shut your eyes and pluck the cast out of the air.

Another significant article by Simpson entitled "An Old Actor's Home in the West" graced the pages of the May 1936 *The Screen Guild's Magazine*. Simpson built a strong case for the movie industry taking care of its own in their retirement and infirmity. The efforts of SAG and the Motion Picture Relief Fund led to the building of the Motion Picture Country Home and Hospital in Woodland Hills, California.

A man of strong moral principles, Simpson submitted his resignation from the Actors Committee of the Guild Magazine due to SAG's proposal to publish a letter from the Drivers Union advocating use of forceful means to bring non-member performers, such as Ronald Colman,

into the still fledgling Guild. Simpson wrote (1/16/36) to the Secretary of SAG, Kenneth Thomson:

I dislike coercion and abominate tyranny and I find no difference between the tyranny of capital and that of labor. The publication of the letter and the threat of the streetcar conductors I consider ill advised—more than that, grotesque. Colman is no friend of mine—(though of course I know him). In my opinion he is a very fortunate young man, with very little acting ability but endowed with a certain charm of personality that appeals to women. He has been extraordinarily lucky and being destitute of a sense of humor, takes himself over seriously. Just the same, if we cannot bring him into the fold with moral persuasion—we should not descend to mean tricks such as coercion. You will probably ask why I didn't say all this last night. The answer may be that there is some foundation for the belief that Britishers think slowly. Anyway I required more time to deliberate the matter.

Thomson and SAG refused to accept Simpson's resignation and, more importantly, unanimously voted not to publish the letter recommending the coercive measures.

Simpson portrayed Reverend Mordaunt in *Little Lord Fauntleroy* (1936), with Freddie Bartholomew. He was the Hyde butler in *Small Town Girl* (1936) and an irate old man in *Lloyd's of London* (1936). In *Mary of Scotland* (1936), starring Katharine Hepburn, Simpson was one of many judges that appeared to be borrowed from the casts of '30s horror films (Lawrence Grant, Nigel de Brulier, Murray Kinnell and Barlowe Borland being among the others). As Collins, Simpson yielded an "effective performance ... as the hotel menial who artfully steers the prince into one of the nihilists' traps" (*Variety*, 6/3/36) in *Trouble for Two* (1936). Collins, a waiter, solicits the help of Robert Montgomery, tearfully telling the prince that his dog is to be put to sleep for killing a bird. This ruse leads to Montgomery having to contend with the ranks of "The Suicide Club."

Maid of Salem (1937) had Simpson in fine form as the Reverend Parris, who speaks out in church about parishioners being overly concerned with appearances, including "fancy bonnets." This event is prior to the witch hysteria that soon engulfs the community. Simpson played Clemens in *The Prince and the Pauper* (1937), Sproot in *Night of Mystery* (1937), Burroughs in *London by Night* (1937) and Chamberlain in *45 Fathers* (1937).

The Baroness and the Butler (1938), starring William Powell, featured Simpson as Count Darno. *Invisible Enemy* (1938) had Simpson as Michael, a henchman of unscrupulous C. Henry Gordon. At one point, Michael knocks out star Alan Marshal when he tries to learn of Gordon's activities. In *Booloo* (1938), Simpson played the first Governor. He had small roles in three major films, as well: the proprietor of the Kent Road Tavern in *The Adventures of Robin Hood* (1938), an old man in *Kidnapped* (1938) and Sauce in *Marie Antoinette* (1938).

The Lux Radio Theatre (CBS) provided Simpson with another venue to act with his esteemed colleague George Arliss. Ivan was heard on three installments of this noted radio series, all recreating Arliss films, plays or both: "Disraeli" (1/17/38), "The Man Who Played God" (3/21/38) and "Cardinal Richelieu" (1/23/39).

On October 4, 1938 Ivan Simpson was discovered in his automobile suffering from carbon monoxide poisoning in a garage at the Riviera Country Club in Pacific Palisades, California, in the Santa Monica Valley. An inhalator squad worked on an unconscious Simpson for more than an hour, before transporting him by ambulance to Santa Monica Hospital. The cause was revealed to be a failed suicide attempt. The *New York Times* (10/5/38) reported that Simpson's friends had noted that he "had been bitter because he thought he had not gained the screen recognition he deserved." Simpson's psychological condition was likely far more complex than that. Fortunately, he quickly recovered and threw himself back into his craft.

Simpson was Simon, the brother of Judge Doolittle (Charles Coburn), in *Made for Each Other* (1939). He appeared in the two Fox Sherlock Holmes films, as a shepherd in *The Hound of the Baskervilles* (1939) and Gates in *The Adventures of Sherlock Holmes* (1938). Simpson played Kretsky in *Never Say Die* (1939), with Bob Hope; a doctor in *The Sun Never Sets* (1939) and the second secretary in *Rulers of the Sea* (1939). As the retainer, Simpson was the protector of Anne (Rose Hobart) in *Tower of London* (1939).

Although Simpson had remained active in the theater in California, he returned to Broadway for the first time in 10 years with his portrayal of Dean Frederick Damon in Elliot Nugent and James Thurber's comedy *The Male Animal* (1/9/40, 243 performances). Brooks Atkinson in the *New York Times* (1/10/40) wrote, "Ivan Simpson is amusing as an ancient professor who deplores trouble but lives in it." Writing to Kenneth Thomson of SAG on 1/21/40, Simpson requested:

> As I have to pay dues to Equity, I'm writing to ask if I can have an excuse card from the Guild. It looks as if the play might run for a year—it's too bad they felt it necessary to mutilate my part. It was so successful in the Coast version.

Thompson gladly granted Simpson an honorable withdrawal, noting on 2/14/40:

> I am delighted that the play is a hit. I tried to get to see it during my recent trip to New York but found it impossible. Elliot (Nugent) promised me his house seats but on the only night I could go you were all sold out for a benefit. I went to the Players' Pipe Night and was sorry not to have seen you there. Best to both you and Pamela (Ivan's daughter).

He would reprise the role of Damon when the play was brought to the screen in 1942.

The Earl of Chicago (1940) had Simpson on hand as Hargraves, while *New Moon* (1940) featured him as Guizot. Simpson also was cast in two films dealing with the theme of invisibility. He was Cotton, the butler, in *The Invisible Man Returns* (1940), featuring an early horror genre ap-

My Girl Tisa (1948): Ivan Simpson plays the concertina, as Lilli Palmer gazes soulfully in his direction.

pearance by Vincent Price. Simpson then played Dean Caxton in *The Body Disappears* (1941), with Edward Everett Horton dabbling in experiments with invisibility.

Simpson portrayed Professor Jim Sterling, friend of bookstore owner Conrad Veidt, in *Nazi Agent* (1942). In the screen adaptation of *The Male Animal* (1942), Simpson again was Dr. Frederick Damon of Midwestern University, who comes to defend Henry Fonda's freedom of speech despite holding disparate views. He was Dr. Cassell, who provides a sedative for Joan Crawford, in *They All Kissed the Bride* (1942). *Eagle Squadron* (1942), with Robert Stack, had Simpson as Simms. Simpson played Arnold, a moneychanger, in *Nightmare* (1942) and the Vicar in *Random Harvest* (1942), starring Ronald Colman.

As Dean Andrew Wharton of Cotchatootamee College, Simpson reinstates professor John Hubbard and permits a musical show to proceed in *Youth on Parade* (1943). Amid a huge cast in RKO Radio's *Forever and a Day* (1943), Simpson was Dexter, an elderly bachelor. He played the eccentric Professor Albert Frisby, who offers Abner Pea-

body $10,000 to travel in a rocket ship to Mars, in the Lum and Abner comedy *Two Weeks to Live* (1943). *This Land is Mine* (1943) included Simpson as the judge in the courtroom where Charles Laughton gives an impassioned speech. *Variety* (3/17/43) noted, "Ivan Simpson registers in a character bit." Simpson was a porter in Oxford in *Above Suspicion* (1943), Professor Harlow in *My Kingdom for a Cook* (1943) and Judge Leonard in *Government Girl* (1943).

In the 20th Century Fox remake of *Jane Eyre* (1944), with Joan Fontaine and Orson Welles, Simpson lent support as the minister, Mr. Woods. He was the magistrate in *The Hour Before the Dawn* (1944), featuring Franchot Tone and Veronica Lake. Simpson's last appearance in a fantasy film came with his role of the tobacconist, Will Hardy, in *The Uninvited* (1944), with Ray Milland.

Simpson again went back to the Broadway stage, playing Dr. Sewell in *Bright Boy* (3/2/44, 16 performances). *Sleep, My Pretty One* (11/2/44, 12 performances), starring Pauline Lord, had Simpson as Dr. Ogden Pomfret. As Doctor Ford-Waterlow, Simpson rejoined old friend Katharine Cornell in her revival of *The Barretts of Wimpole Street* (3/26/45, 88 performances).

On 9/9/45, Simpson was seen in the very first televised episode of *The Theater Guild on the Air* for ABC's *United States Steel Hour*. He appeared with Burgess Meredith in "Wings Over Europe."

Now in his early seventies, Simpson seemed to be focusing his efforts on his first love, the theater. Ivan had written some years earlier (*The Screen Guild's Magazine*, September 1935), "The rising of the curtain on the first night is a thrill never to be forgotten, be it your first or your fiftieth *first night*; while going before the camera can become a nerve-racking ordeal at each instance if one is sensitive, sincere and earnest."

Simpson had a challenging role as Dr. Jackson, who tries to a cure a woman traumatized by her stay in Dachau during World War II, in *The Secret Room* (11/7/45, 21 performances). He played Titogh in the drama *Swan Song* (5/15/46, 22 performances). In *The Haven* (11/13/46, 5 performances), a play written by and starring actor Dennis Hoey (Inspector Lestrade from Universal's "Sherlock Holmes" series), Simpson enacted the role of the coroner.

Old colleague Katharine Cornell summoned Simpson to appear in her elaborate revival of Shakespeare's *Antony and Cleopatra* (11/26/47, 126 performances). Simpson portrayed Lepidus, first on tour and then on Broadway. Ivan's daughter Pamela played Octavia in this production.

Simpson returned to the screen for the first time in four years in the minor role of the old man with the concertina in *My Girl Tisa* (1948), a turn-of-the-century immigrant tale with Lilli Palmer. This turned out to be his final film appearance, although Simpson continued to perform in both the theater and television.

In *Make Way for Lucia* (12/22/48, 29 performances), a comedy by John van Druten, Simpson portrayed Mr. Wyse. The revival of George Bernard Shaw's *Caesar and Cleopatra* (12/21/49, 151 performances) at the National Theatre won raves for Sir Cedric Hardwicke as Caesar and provided Simpson with his final stage role as Theodotus.

While working on *Caesar and Cleopatra*, Simpson made some contacts that resulted in appearances in television dramas. He was featured on the *Philco-Goodyear Television Playhouse* (NBC) in "The Last Tycoon" (10/16/49) and "Bethel Merriday" (1/8/50), the latter starring Grace Kelly. For *Kraft Television Theatre* (NBC), Simpson was seen with George Reeves in "Storm in a Teacup" (episode 158, 5/17/50). Simpson made two significant appearances on *Robert Montgomery Presents* (NBC) as Frith in "Rebecca" (5/22/50) and in "Victoria Regina" ((1/15/51), starring Helen Hayes. As part of a fine cast including Anna Lee and Margaret O'Brien, Simpson played Professor Adams in "To the Lovely Margaret" (episode 21, 2/19/51) for *Lux Video Theatre* (CBS). "The Professor's Punch" (3/15/51),

with John Beal, had Ivan on hand for the final episode of *Nash Airflyte Theatre* (CBS). Simpson was featured in "The Open Heart" (episode 49, 5/8/51) for *Armstrong Circle Theatre* (NBC). As the Duke of Towers, he was part of *The Ford Theatre Hour* (CBS) presentation of *Peter Ibbetson* (season 3, episode 26, 5/18/51), with Richard Greene. Simpson's final acting credit came with his role in "The Adventures of Hiram Holliday" (6/3/51), a production of *NBC Philco Television Playhouse* that starred E.G. Marshall.

In the late summer of 1951, Simpson became progressively ill, eventually necessitating his being hospitalized in New York City. On Friday evening, October 12, 1951 Ivan Simpson passed away at the age of 76 at Lenox Hill Hospital in Manhattan. His daughter, actress Pamela Simpson, who was touring with Olivia de Havilland in *Candida* at the time of her father's death, survived him. Pamela was in a number of theatrical productions in the late 1940s and 1950s, as well as some early television dramas. Pamela Simpson retired from acting in the mid-1960s, returning to England where she died in Buckinghamshire on April 15, 2002, at the age of 96.

Although Ivan Simpson might not have received the proper recognition for his body of acting work during his lifetime, he did not suffer the ignominy of many of his colleagues who were reduced to walk-on bits or drifted into obscurity. Simpson remained a busy actor for more than 50 years, from his early 20s on stage until months before his death, when he was appearing in live television dramas. "Simmy," as his cronies knew him, made his mark in the film industry in particular by more than just his roles on screen. Simpson played an important part in the development and philosophical shaping of SAG. His self-effacing humor, intelligence, artistic ability, integrity and loyalty to friends and co-workers indicate that Ivan Simpson was a special individual whose place in Hollywood history should not be forgotten.

(Special thanks to Ms. Valerie Yaros, an archivist from the Communications Department of SAG, who provided copies of Simpson's correspondence with the Guild, as well as articles he wrote for *The Screen Guild's Magazine*.)

Sources

Arliss, George. *My Ten Years in the Studios*, New York: Little, Brown and Company, 1940.

Coughlin, Jim. "Forgotten Faces: Ivan Simpson," in *Mad About Movies #5* (2006), pp. 39-48.

Newnham, John K. "Hollywood's Least-Known Celebrity," in *Film Weekly* (6/23/33), p. 12.

The Last Days of Pompeii (1935)

Wyrley Birch
(1883 – 1959)

As a child, one of this writer's favorite films was *The Last Days of Pompeii*. The character Leaster, who embodies the voice of moral reasoning in the film, made a lasting impression on me. It was some years later that I made the connection between that character and the man who played him, Wyrley Birch, spurring me to learn more about this sensitive performer. Although Leaster probably represents the cinematic highpoint for Wyrley Birch, the actor had a varied and interesting career in stock, Broadway, film and television that merits some overdue recognition.

He was born Ernest Home Wyrley Birch, the son of Richard Jacob Wyrley Birch (1838-1901) and the former Catherine Leonora Margaret Vass (1843-1931), on May 7, 1883, in Montreal, Quebec, Canada. Richard was originally from Roxholme, Lincolnshire, England, while Catherine was a native of Montreal. Ernest was baptized shortly thereafter at the Anglican Christ Church Cathedral. Young Ernest had four siblings, sister Emily Frances (1868- ?) and brothers George (1871- 1955), Anthony (1876- ?) and Richard Fielding Home Wyrley Birch (1873-1873), who died in infancy.

Wyrley, as he later chose to be called, became enamored of the theater at an early age and, while in his teens, made his stage debut in Montreal with Thomas Shea in *Richelieu*. He then became a member of the Minnelli Brothers Troupe that toured the Ohio Circuit, playing cities like Fostoria, Tiffin, Medina, and Wapakoneta. The leading lady was Mina Minnelli, the mother of film director Vincente Minnelli. Not only was Birch the company juvenile, but he served as a scene painter, stagehand and general handyman, learning his theatrical rudiments the hard way. Wyrley loved to reminisce about his early acting days, telling Lucius Beebe of the *New York Herald Tribune* (1941):

> I remember splitting my breaches in some improbable one-night town just as I dashed onto the on-stage deck to save the heroine in *Little Nugget*, and having to save the situation and my modesty by doing a record-breaking high dive off the pier and out of sight.

On May 24, 1905 Wyrley was wed to Grace Bullock (1870-c. 1956), 13 years his senior, in Newton, Massachusetts.

A 1913 newspaper clipping of Wyrley Birch

Birch eventually made his New York City debut on January 1, 1906 as Eddie Hudson in *Julie Bonbon*, written by and starring Clara Lipman. Wyrley played the passionate son and then toured in Charles Frohman's production of *The Thief*. He continued to hone his craft in stock, joining Lindsay Mortson's Company, which toured New England in 1908. During his time with Mortson's troupe, Wyrley's wife Grace gave birth to their only child, Richard Wyrley Birch (1911-1988), in Massachusetts. Wyrley remained with Mortson for four years, often receiving superior notices to the company stars. Of his role of Judge Prentice in *The Witching Hour* (5/6/12), the *Boston Transcript* noted, "… he gives it a sympathy and at the same time a distinction that is rare in stock companies." In the fall and winter of 1912/13, Birch successfully managed the Anna Cleveland Stock Company in New Britain, Connecticut, presenting standard plays like *A Woman's Way* and *Merely Mary Ann*. Wyrley was noted for his sound business judgment, making the season an artistic and financial success. He would later manage and direct stock companies in Baltimore, MD

Another Language (1934 Broadway stage): The Hallams play cards: Margaret Wycherly, Wyrley Birch, Herbert Duffy and Glenn Anders.

flected that the South Africa experience was "fraught with more dangers than the Brewster household" (of his current play). Soon after his return from South Africa, Birch joined the New York cast of *Fair and Warmer* (1917). Wyrley also served for a time (c. 1918) as the special New York representative of the International Variety and Theatrical Agency, Ltd., with which he had become involved during his time in South Africa.

Re-establishing himself with the theatrical profession in New York, Birch was elected to the Actors' Equity Association on January 15, 1918, in a ceremony held at the Longacre Building in Manhattan. At the Empire Theatre in Syracuse, New York Birch directed and played the Church elder in *The Puritan* (June 1919), which starred Minna Gombell.

Although not in the original Broadway casts, Birch was seen in New York (where his troupe included Roland Young, Tallulah Bankhead, Chester Morris and Wallis Clark), Syracuse, NY and Dayton, Ohio. Hired to manage the Eleanor Gordon Players at Boston's famed Plymouth Theatre in 1913, Birch directed and acted in such works as *Divorcons, The Second Mrs. Tanqueray, Her Husband's Wife* and *Sham*. Commenting on Wyrley's work as the irritable, selfish English baronet in *The House Next Door*, a Boston critic wrote (6/24/13), "If Mr. Birch never makes another special characterization, he will be remembered by the art which made his Sir John a real human being."

Wyrley resided in a theatrical rooming house in Manhattan in 1914, appearing in plays like *Twin Beds*, later remembering that he resisted the opportunity to move from the stage to the fledgling motion picture industry:

> Vitagraph was offering actors the unheard-of salary of $90 a week. Most of us at the time turned up our noses at such sideshow and carnival claptrap. "No 10-cent entertainment for us," we said. "It would ruin us professionally to be connected with anything like that."

Birch spent the better part of 1915-1916 touring South Africa. He made his unofficial screen debut while in South Africa, billed as E. Wyrley Birch as the Reverend Francis Owen in *De Voortrekkers* (1916), a silent film directed by Harold M. Shaw. While on Broadway with Boris Karloff in *Arsenic and Old Lace* (in the early 1940s), Wyrley re-

A 1935 character portrait of Wyrley Birch

Air Hawks (1935): **Aviator Ralph Bellamy makes a strong point to Wyrley Birch.**

miles. The company rotated at least seven plays during their tour of Australia (with Birch's role in parenthesis): *New Brooms* (as Thomas Bates, successful, but harassed father), *The Family Upstairs* (as Joe Heller, the irascible head of the family), *Six Cylinder Love* (as Richard Burton, kind and dignified man who can't handle the financial burden of his new car), *White Collars* (as Mr. Thayer, family patriarch), *Saturday's Children* and two plays by George M. Cohan, *Whispering Friends* (as Joe Sanford, insurance salesman) and *The Baby Cyclone* (as Robert Webster). In fact, the Adelaide press (*The Advertiser*, 11/16/29) referred to Birch as "a second George Cohan." While in Perth, Birch was interviewed about his thoughts on the new fad, talking pictures (*The Daily News*, 10/7/29):

> I do not think any shadow shape will ever do that (kill the stage) but the talkies will always be interesting as a means of conveying the voice and appearances of famous men to all parts of the world.

When it came time to leave Australia for New Zealand, the next stop on the tour, the ship on which the company was sailing, the *Manuka*, encountered dense fog, was damaged and ended up sinking on December 17, 1929. All 118 passengers aboard were saved, but not before spending over five hours in open boats. Birch not only lost most of his

in *Shavings* (1920) and *The Bat* (1920), in which he played Richard Fleming, the spendthrift nephew who is murdered. Birch later reprised the role of Fleming in *The Bat* (11/23/22) at the Parsons Theatre in Hartford, Connecticut. He succeeded Robert McWade as Cousin Webster Parsons, the village banker, in *The Old Soak* (1923). As Mike Connell, the rheumatic and imbibing Irishman, Wyrley opened in the successful (390 performances) *Laff That Off* on 11/2/25. Birch played Michi in *Menace* (3/14/27), the Rev. Ezra Hale in *Jacob Slovak* (10/5/27) and Jacob Harrington in *The Silent House* (2/7/28). Throughout most of the 1920s, Birch and his family lived in New Rochelle, New York. Wife Grace, an accomplished cellist, played with various ensembles over the years in the Westchester County, New York area, including the Grosskopf Trio and the Huguenot String Trio.

In June of 1928, Birch traveled by sea to Australia as part of The American Comedy Company. Birch served as producer and lead actor for the troupe that included Leona Hogarth, Leonard Doyle and Mary Curtain. Landing in Sydney, Australia on June 23, 1928, Birch and his colleagues toured the continent for the ensuing 18 months, playing Melbourne, Canberra, Sydney, Brisbane, Perth and Adelaide in succession, reportedly covering 3600

The Last Days of Pompeii (1935): **Soothsayer Zeffie Tilbury predicts important events concerning Preston Foster and son David Holt, while Wyrley Birch listens attentively in the background.**

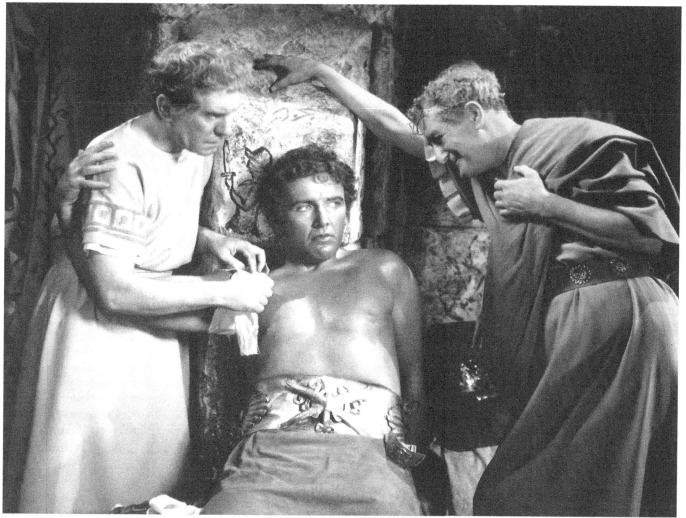

The Last Days of Pompeii (1935): **Wyrley Birch tends to the wounds of Preston Foster, while William V. Mong makes a business proposition.**

worldly belongings, but also all the props and items of his theatrical company. Relying on borrowed scenery and costumes, Birch and the American Comedy Company opened in Dunedin, New Zealand, just seven days after the shipwreck. The theatergoers treated them to a thunderous ovation, and Birch himself received a gift he treasured thereafter: a cane fashioned from a salvaged door of the sunken Manuka.

Wyrley returned to the United States, arriving by ship in San Francisco, California, from Wellington, New Zealand, on March 14, 1930. Birch was back on Broadway as the stage manager in *In Times Square* (11/23/31). In the long-running (348 performances) *Another Language* (4/25/32), Wyrley excelled as the patriarch of the ornery Hallam family. Birch was seen to advantage as Don Sebastian de la Fresneda in *Spring in Autumn* (10/24/33), cheerful town physician Dr. Stirling in *Wednesday's Child* (1/16/34), honest managing editor Joe McGuire in *Kill That Story* (8/29/34) and theater doorman Mac Mason in *Small Miracle* (9/26/34). Wyrley also appeared with Dwight Frye in

The Pursuit of Happiness (6/4/34) at the Boulevard Theatre in Jackson Heights, Queens.

Despite his earlier reluctance to make films, Birch had a successful screen test for Columbia Pictures on February 15, 1935. He signed a contract right after and departed from New Rochelle to Hollywood on February 20, 1935. Wyrley's first film was *The Awakening of Jim Burke* (1935), starring Jack Holt. Birch played general store proprietor Lem Hardie, the father of Florence Rice. *Air Hawks* (1935), which included Edward Van Sloan as the evil inventor of a destructive ray gun, had Wyrley as Holden. Birch was the auctioneer at Grace Moore's family's estate at the beginning of *Love Me Forever* (1935). He played the understanding prison warden who makes George Murphy a trustee, enabling the convict's escape, in *After the Dance* (1935).

Guard That Girl (1935) proved that Birch was capable of portraying villainy and duplicity on screen. As Joshua Scranton, the lawyer to heiress Florence Rice, he hires detectives to protect her, as well as a woman to act as her double. Scranton, however, later turns out to be an embezzler,

The Last Days of Pompeii (1935): Servant and master now aged: Wyrley Birch and Preston Foster

guages and knows "thousands" of stories, as a tutor for his adopted son Flavius (David Holt), refuting Leaster's earlier claim that "Money doesn't matter." Leaster becomes friend and confidant to Marcus, helping him prepare for his gladiator battles and nursing his injured shoulder when he is defeated in the arena by Murmex (Ward Bond). His fighting days over, Marcus, to the horror of Leaster, now aims to be the head of the arena. "You would be responsible for the slaughter of helpless slaves," Leaster cautions. In Judea, where Marcus runs a clandestine mission for Pontius Pilate (Basil Rathbone), Leaster breaks the news that Flavius is injured and near death. Leaster knows transporting Flavius to a doctor would kill the boy, so he implores Marcus to take his son to the "healer" (Christ). The unseen Lord cures Flavius.

Years pass and Leaster is the steward of the wealthy household of Marcus, the most powerful man in Pompeii. The now grown Flavius (John Wood) despises Marcus' lifestyle and confides in Leaster his plan to rescue Christians and slaves, taking them to a "free" island of which his Greek tutor had told him. Leaster then must inform Marcus that Flavius has been captured with the slaves intended for the arena, meaning the "death penalty" for the young man. As Vesuvius erupts and Pompeii is destroyed, allowing Marcus a final chance for redemption, Leaster is slain as he struggles to release the female slaves from their cell. Wyrley Birch captured Leaster perfectly, displaying his wisdom, loyalty and, even in the face of materialism and corruption, a clear sense of moral values, which inevitably impact both Marcus and Flavius.

Following his work on *The Last Days of Pompeii*, a reporter from Adelaide interviewed Australia-born John Wood, who played Flavius as a young man, regarding the actor's experience with the American Comedy Company back in 1928. Wood remembered, "My first grown-up roles were with a touring company under the management of Wyrley Birch and, in my very first Hollywood film, Mr. Birch played the part of my tutor" (*The Advertiser*, 3/7/36).

Despite his well-etched characterization of Leaster while on loan to RKO, Columbia was providing Birch with smaller and smaller roles. Wyrley was uncredited as a committee man in *Too Tough to Kill* (1935), which starred Victor Jory amid tunnel construction and sabotage. Again

seeking the fortune for himself, and also a murderer, killing an undercover policeman. In *Grand Exit* (1935), starring Edmund Lowe, Wyrley again played a warden. Birch was seen as Dr. Schaeffer in *She Couldn't Take It* (1935), with George Raft and Joan Bennett.

Birch was loaned out to RKO to appear in Merian C. Cooper's production of *The Last Days of Pompeii* (1935), developed by the creative team responsible for *King Kong* (director Ernest B. Schoedsack and effects wizard Willis O'Brien).

As the Greek slave Leaster, Birch represented the conscience of the protagonist Marcus (Preston Foster), who constantly struggles between his innate goodness and need for worldly goods. When first introduced to Foster's character at the arena, Leaster observes, "So even the great Marcus cannot yet kill with a light heart." Marcus later purchases the gentle, scholarly Greek, who speaks four lan-

After the Dance (1935): Wyrley Birch as the warden, with Jack Daley, George Murphy and Nancy Carroll

unbilled, Birch appeared as the manager of the art office in *One Way Ticket* (1935) with Lloyd Nolan. Wyrley played a minister in *If You Could Only Cook* (1935). Rounding out a busy year as a Columbia contract player, Birch was Mr. Cole in *The Lone Wolf Returns* (1935), with Melvyn Douglas starring as the clever jewel thief.

The Music Goes 'Round (1936), a musical with Harry Richman and Rochelle Hudson, had Wyrley as Josh, part of a showboat acting troupe. *Panic on the Air* (1936), with sports reporter Lew Ayres getting mixed up with gangsters and secret codes, included Birch as Major Bliss.

Wyrley had a significant, albeit unbilled, role as a psychiatrist in Frank Capra's clever social comedy/drama *Mr. Deeds Goes to Town* (1936). Birch's character sits on the board of the sanity hearing of Longfellow Deeds (Gary Cooper), presided over by Judge May (H. B. Warner). When the two spinster sisters from Deeds' hometown testify that Longfellow is "pixilated," Birch turns to Judge May and offers:

> Perhaps I can explain, your Honor. The word "pixilated" is an early American expression, derived from the word "pixies," meaning elves. They would say the pixies had got him, as we nowadays say a man is "barmy."

The psychiatrist, who shares the Judge's concern about Deeds' condition, catches himself tapping his fingers as Longfellow attempts to show "everybody does silly things to help them think."

The Devil's Squadron (1936), a tale of courage and redemption among pilots, starring Richard Dix, gave Birch the minor part of a farmer. Wyrley then played Turner in *Trapped by Television* (1936), with Lyle Talbot as a TV inventor. *Blackmailer* (1936) offered Birch the meaty role of Nelson, the butler to wealthy H.B. Warner. Nelson is discovered to be the killer of contemptuous extortionist Jack Donovan (Alexander Cross) and another man. Donovan had been responsible for corrupting and causing the death of Nelson's daughter, motivating the butler's vengeful reprisal. *Shakedown* (1936), starring Lew Ayres, had Wyrley on hand as Mr. Morrison.

Birch returned to his main passion, the stage, in the Theatre Guild's production of Maxwell Anderson's *The Masque of Kings* (2/8/36). In a star-laden cast including Henry Hull, Dudley Digges and Pauline Frederick, Wyrley portrayed Sceps.

Birch completed his Columbia contract with his appearance in another major Frank Capra film. In the early scenes of *Lost Horizon* (1937), Wyrley, as a missionary, is

The Music Goes Round (1936): Harry Richman is shown an acting job opening by Wyrley Birch.

Panic on the Air (1936): Wyrley Birch is approached by Florence Rice and Lew Ayres.

Mr. Deeds Goes to Town (1936): Two members of the Board at Gary Cooper's sanity hearing: Wyrley Birch and H.B. Warner

viewed with the panic-stricken Westerners clamoring to be airlifted out of revolution-torn China to Shanghai.

Although Wyrley would not make another feature length film until 1947, he did appear in two Vitaphone shorts for Warner Bros. that were filmed at the Kaufman Astoria Studios in Queens, New York. *Your True Adventures: Dear Old Dad* (1938), part of a series of shorts presented by renowned reporter Floyd Gibbons, had Birch as an elderly father who has been a missing person for over a year. In flashback, it is revealed that "Dad" was hit by a car, suffered memory loss and wandered aimlessly looking for work, until he ended up in a convalescent home. The doctors and nurses at the facility assist in his recovery, but it is not until his picture runs in the newspaper that "Dad" is reunited with his searching daughter and family (whereupon his memory is restored). Birch also appeared in *Broadway Brevity No. 10: Little Me* (1938), with star Wini Shaw realizing through a dream that her childhood ambition to be a great singer has gone unfulfilled.

Back on Broadway, Wyrley was featured as Uncle Ernest in *Whiteoaks* (3/23/38), with star Ethel Barrymore yielding a powerful performance. Birch then went on tour with Barrymore in both *Whiteoaks* and *The School for Scandal*. *Whiteoaks* had its final performance at the Ridgeway Theater in White Plains, New York on August 12, 1939. Afterwards, the cast threw a 60th birthday party (three days early) for Ethel Barrymore. During a brief hiatus from the

Barrymore tour, Wyrley was seen as Josh in *The Old Homestead* (8/1/38) at the Rockridge Theatre in Carmel, New York. At the Berkshire Playhouse in Stockbridge, Massachusetts Birch portrayed Carter Hibbard in *First Lady* (8/21/39), starring Violet Heming.

Wyrley always felt fortunate to have been in the original cast, along with Boris Karloff, of Joseph Kesselring's enormously successful *Arsenic and Old Lace* (1/10/41). In the first act, Birch, as the Reverend Dr. Harper, sat in the seemingly serene Brooklyn home of the Brewster family, chatting and sipping tea with Josephine Hull and John Alexander. His character's function was to help establish a mood of peace and quiet, despite a body being hidden in the window seat behind him, prior to the hilarious mayhem that would soon follow. When Edgar Stehli, who played Karloff's sidekick Dr. Einstein, missed a number of performances due to illness, Wyrley switched gears and assumed the role of the erratic plastic surgeon.

Even with the stability of a hit show, Birch still missed the lure of the road, as he told reporter Lucius Beebe (1941):

> There was a charm and excitement about being with a touring company, which has never existed in a long Broadway run with a single success. Heaven forfend that I should

Blackmailer (1936): **William Gargan and Florence Rice struggle to restrain prone Wyrley Birch.**

ing parishioners and then pausing by a lamppost to light his pipe. A gun is put to the back of his head and the priest is shot dead, setting in motion a drama of not only murder, but political intrigue, ambition, family strife and moral principle. Dana Andrews, Lee J. Cobb, and wrongly accused Arthur Kennedy headed the cast of this complex mystery.

Having already appeared in one of the longest running plays of the 1940's, *Arsenic and Old Lace* (1,444 performances), Birch concluded the decade in another: Mary Chase's whimsical Pulitzer Prize winning *Harvey* (1,775 performances). When Birch joined *Harvey* on 9/6/48, Joe E. Brown was starring as tippling Elwood P. Dowd (the role originated by Frank Fay), whose best friend is an invisible six-and-a-half-foot rabbit. Wyrley delighted in playing Judge Omar Gaffney opposite Brown, and toured with him when *Harvey* went on the road.

Wyrley and his wife Grace moved from their 30 Westminster Court, New Rochelle, New York residence to Katonah, New York, in early 1950. Now approaching 70 years of age, Birch resided in a Victorian boarding house in Katonah, within walking distance of the train station. He would usually travel by train to Manhattan to

cry down a New York hit or the good luck to be in one, since from the economic point of view it is an actor's dream, and there were inconveniences on the road that I daresay I forget with the passage of time, but I can tell you I'd like to tour Australia again, or sit down to a table at some of the boarding houses I knew in Philadelphia, Omaha or Salt Lake.

After departing *Arsenic and Old Lace*, Wyrley went on to play Mr. Daniel Drum, the banker, in *All for All* (9/29/43). He was Reverend Wilson in another successful play (319 performances), *Chicken Every Sunday* (4/5/44). In the fantasy *How I Wonder* (9/30/47), with Raymond Massey as an astronomy professor searching for ways to prevent the earth from being destroyed by atomic war, Birch portrayed Henry Harkside.

Wyrley Birch made his first and only return to the big screen after the 1930's to appear in *Boomerang* (1947). Filmed by Elia Kazan in Stamford, CT and White Plains, NY, *Boomerang* was based on the brutal unsolved murder of a priest that shocked Bridgeport, CT in 1924. In the film's opening sequence, much-loved, civic-minded Father George M. Lambert (Birch) goes for his nightly stroll, greet-

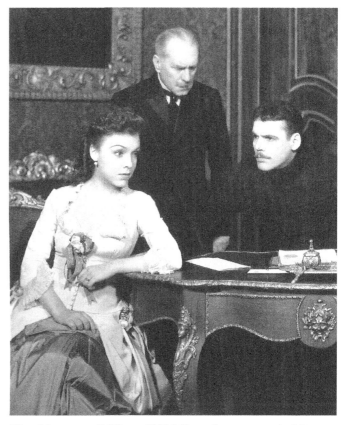

The Masque of Kings **(1936 Broadway stage): Margo, Wyrley Birch and Henry Hull**

Arsenic and Old Lace (1941 Broadway stage): At the Brewster household, with John Alexander, Josephine Hull and Wyrley Birch (as the Rev. Dr. Harper)

appear in plays, spend time at the Lambs Club (of which he was a long-time member) or perform in the relatively new medium of television. Sadly, Wyrley's wife Grace passed away c. 1956.

Working in New York City, Birch performed on the radio in the late 1940s and early 1950s. For WNBT Radio, Wyrley was heard on an episode of *The Clock* entitled "William and Mary" (2/8/50), featuring Helen Kingstead and Byron Russell.

Birch returned to the Berkshire Playhouse in Stockbridge, playing Wingblatt, an "unreconstructed" Southern congressman, in Maxwell Anderson's *Both Your Houses* (7/24/50).

An early television role for Birch came in "The Great Merlini" (5/23/50, season 1, episode 2) on *Cameo Theatre* (NBC). For *The Philco-Goodyear Television Playhouse* (NBC), Birch was seen in "Semmelweis" (4/28/50, season 2, episode 39). In the initial offering of NBC's *Musical Comedy Time*, Wyrley supported Martha Raye in "Anything Goes" (10/2/50, season 1, episode 1). He also was featured in an

eerie episode of *Lights Out* (NBC) entitled "Benuili Chant," starring Ed Begley and involving a magical parchment that enables the possessor to read the minds of others. Birch had a part in "Mountain Song" (7/31/51, season 2, episode 50), a segment of *The Armstrong Circle Theatre* (NBC).

Birch made three appearances on *Hallmark Hall of Fame*, the famed dramatic staple of the early days of television (and which still exists to this day). In the noted show's first season, Wyrley was seen in "The Last Command" (8/10/52, episode 33). Birch was featured with Cliff Robertson and Peggy McKay in "The Bride's Teapot" (9/21/52, season 2, episode 5). "The World on a Wire" (4/19/53, season 2, episode 34) had Russell Hardie as inventor Samuel Morse and included Wyrley in its cast.

"Medal of Honor" (1/11/53, season 1, episode 21), a segment of *The Doctor* (NBC) directed by Robert Aldrich, involved Birch in a small Maine town where the police constable is fired because there has not been a crime in over 10 years. Also for NBC, Wyrley was seen on *Goodyear Television Playhouse* in the episode "Printer's Measure"

All for All (1943 Broadway stage): Wyrley Birch and Jack Pearl

ance" came as the voice of Grandfather Holly in *Sixth Finger on a Five Finger Glove* (10/8/56), which closed after only two performances.

One of Birch's latter dramatic parts was that of Reverend James Hardin, the father of Old West gunfighter John Wesley Hardin (Richard Boone), in "Dead of Noon" (1/28/57, season 9, episode 16) for *Studio One in Hollywood* (CBS). Always proud of his comedic training in stock, it is fitting that two of Wyrley's last television efforts were on *The Phil Silvers Show* (CBS). He was seen in "Bilko on Wall Street" (5/15/56, season 1, episode 34). Birch's penultimate television role was that of Uncle Jasper in "Bilko's Double Life" (10/22/57, season 3, episode 76). When Bilko, on furlough in Manhattan, takes advantage of his uncanny resemblance to multi-millionaire Herbert Penfield (also Phil Silvers), the rich double has to contend with Bilko's annoying relatives, including Uncle Jasper, back in Kansas. Birch's last known television appearance came with his portrayal of Burr in "And a Merry Christmas to the Force on Patrol" (12/23/58, season 1, episode 13) on *Naked City* (ABC). The episode aired just weeks before Wyrley's death.

Wyrley Birch passed away at the age of 75 on February 7, 1959, at Northern Westchester Hospital in Mount Kisco, New York. Birch was interred at Ivandell Cemetery in Somers, New York.

His son Richard and his brother, Anthony Home Wyrley Birch, survived him. Son Richard had an interesting

(4/26/53, season 2, episode 15) written by Paddy Chayefsky. Birch portrayed a judge in "Force of Circumstance" (7/2/53, season 3, episode 44), starring Robert Alda, for *Lux Video Theatre* (CBS). Written by Rod Serling, "Nightmare at Ground Zero" (8/18/53, season 5, episode 43) was part of the excellent *Suspense* series. Set at the Nevada Proving Grounds, "Nightmare at Ground Zero" starred O.Z. Whitehead, who adds his nagging wife to the mannequins in a house to be destroyed by a nuclear bomb test. Birch played a painter, preparing the home to look proper prior to its destruction.

In the late summer of 1953, Wyrley was engaged to appear in *The Trip to Bountiful* (9/7/53) at the Westport Country Playhouse in Westport, Connecticut. Based on the story by Horton Foote, the production of *The Trip to Bountiful* starred Lillian Gish and featured a strong cast including Eva Marie Saint, John Beal, Jo Van Fleet, Jean Stapleton and Birch. After additional out of town tryouts, *The Trip to Bountiful* opened on Broadway on November 3, 1953. Unfortunately Wyrley was not retained for the Broadway cast. Birch was back on Broadway, however, portraying Mr. Patterson in *The Desperate Hours* (2/10/55, 212 performances) amidst a cast featuring a young Paul Newman and Karl Malden. Wyrley's final Broadway "appear-

Boomerang (1947): Wyrley Birch, as Father George Lambert, faces imminent death.

The Desperate Hours (1955 Broadway stage): Escaped convict George Grizzard holds a gun on Nancy Coleman, while Wyrley Birch (as Mr. Patterson, the garbage collector) awaits his payment.

her life, although somewhat distant. He would visit her family at their home in Carmel, New York almost every Sunday in the 1950s, but was "not the down-on-the-floor-to-play kind of grandfather as grandfathers are more likely to be today." She still has fond recollections of their time together, stating:

> I do remember long walks and conversations, especially about acting, which was something I thought for a while I wanted to do. He advised me strongly not to choose it as a career, but he also taught me theatrical diction! I wish now that I had talked to him more about his life and especially his travels, which were extensive. I certainly inherited my love of travel and adventure from someone and it was probably him. He was a good man, warm and loving.

Certainly not a prolific screen actor, Wyrley Birch was a very talented performer who made his presence felt in almost any size role. Much of his avoidance of film work in deference to the stage was of Wyrley's own choice. It is a shame, though, that more directors didn't follow the lead of Elia Kazan, who brought Birch back to the screen in 1947 in *Boomerang*. Wyrley Birch's varied, clever portrayals as Leaster in *The Last Days of Pompeii*, Scranton in *Guard That Girl*, Nelson in *Blackmailer* and the board psychiatrist in *Mr. Deeds Goes to Town* provide evidence that the screen efforts of this underutilized talent should not be forgotten. What is more apparent, however, is that Wyrley Birch had an extensive, diverse body of work in many areas of the performing arts. He acted, directed and produced on stage, performed on both television and radio, in addition to his film credits. It is the whole of Wyrley Birch's career that is worthy of recognition, as is the case for so many neglected performers.

life as well. While in his twenties, he worked as a photographer, doing both studio and magazine work. It was in New Rochelle that Richard met Norman Rockwell, the famed artist. For six years, Richard took reference photographs for Rockwell's paintings. He also held a patent on the Dubl-Chek camera. Richard, who had studied at the University of Melbourne in Australia, later became a mechanical engineer, working for companies in Pleasantville and Thornwood, New York, and Danbury and Cornwall Bridge, Connecticut. Richard Wyrley Birch passed away in Kent, Connecticut on February 25, 1988. Richard's wife, Alison Wyrley Birch (1922-2002), achieved her own fame as a poet and author, with *Poetry for Peace of Mind* (1978) being her most recognized work. Richard and Alison Wyrley Birch had two daughters, Wendy and Laurie, Wyrley's only grandchildren.

In correspondence with the author, Laurie Birch Kendall noted that her grandfather Wyrley was a presence in

Sources

"An Australian in Hollywood," in *The Advertiser*, Adelaide, 3/7/36, p. 24.

Beebe, Lucius. "The Good Old Days, According to a Man Who Lived Them," in "Stage Asides," *New York Herald Tribune,* January ?, 1941.

Coughlin, Jim. "Forgotten Faces: Wyrley Birch," in *Mad About Movies #2* (2001), pp. 36-39.

"Stage Adventurer Settles Down to Peace and Quiet—in 'Arsenic'," clipping source unknown.

Murray Kinnell
(1889 - 1954)

As is the case with many of the performers dealt with in this volume, Murray Kinnell has been all but ignored by film historians and reference works. Even his important role as the carnival barker in *Freaks* is not credited to him in most of the movie books that provide a cast listing for that Tod Browning cult film. Kinnell had a relatively brief (1930-1937) film career, but was a significant presence in noteworthy motion pictures, including *The Public Enemy*, *Grand Hotel* and *Lloyds of London*. His main contribution to the horror genre was his work in MGM's *Freaks* and *Mad Love*, but Kinnell was also prominent in four of the first seven Warner Oland *Charlie Chan* films, as well as the first entry in the Peter Lorre *Mr. Moto* series. Kinnell made his mark in a number of borderline-horror/mystery offerings such as *The Great Impersonation*, *Secrets of the French Police* and *The Avenger*. Murray Kinnell, who stood five-foot-10-inches and weighed 145 pounds, had brown-gray hair and gray eyes, but, above all, a very distinctive speaking voice that always lent authority to his roles (including his unusual didactic appearance in the semi-exploitation work, *Damaged Lives*).

Murray Kinnell was born in Sydenham, Lewisham, London, England on July 24, 1889, one of eight children of John Kinnell (1862-1913) and the former Rose Taylor (1860-1946). Murray had an older brother Donald (1888-1950), as well as younger siblings John Lindsay (1891-1957), Alan (1892-1948), Gilbert (1894-1961), Eileen Mary (1897-1897), Brian (1899-1960) and Charles Ellis Kinnell (1901-1950). He was educated at Mill Hill School in Hertfordshire, England, as well as Seaford College. Kinnell made his stage debut at the age of 18 in 1907, performing in Shakespearean repertory with the Florence Glossop Harris Company. He spent three years honing his acting craft with Sir Frank Benson's company, in essence a touring dramatic academy that served as a training ground for numerous British performers (including Ronald Colman, Basil Rathbone and Robert Morley, to name a few). In 1912, Kinnell journeyed across the Atlantic to appear in New York in the play *Pomander Walk*, which had opened on Broadway in December 1910. Returning to England after a few months, Kinnell joined Annie Russell's troupe, then known as the Old English Comedy Company. Back on Broadway, Kinnell was featured in *The Garden of Paradise* (11/28/14), based on Hans Christian Andersen's *The Little Mermaid*.

Kinnell was married to Henrietta Goodwin (1890-1978), formerly of Tacoma, Washington, in Philadelphia, Pennsylvania on April 14, 1914. Henrietta gave birth to their only child, Peter Kinnell (1916-1963), in Woking, Surrey, on June 5, 1916. Both mother and son would later

Portrait of Murray Kinnell in the British Army (c. 1918)

have a minor connection to the entertainment industry. Henrietta would serve as the dialogue director on the film *Moss Rose* (1947). Peter, who attended UCLA and played cricket there under the tutelage of coaches C. Aubrey Smith and Boris Karloff in 1934, eventually appeared on Broadway in *Escape This Night* (4/22/38), with Hume Cronyn.

On October 14, 1916, in the midst of World War I, Kinnell enlisted in the London Regiment of the British Army, serving with the 14th Battalion of the London Scottish. Although wounded twice in combat, Kinnell remained on active duty throughout the war, until his discharge in 1918. Murray Kinnell was awarded the British War Medal and the Victory Medal in recognition of his service. After the war, Kinnell eagerly reinvolved himself in the theater in plays like Doris Keane's production of *Romeo and Juliet*, gradually becoming a well-known face on the London stage.

The Secret Six (1931): **Murray Kinnell is questioned by D.A. Theodore von Eltz.**

Kinnell's return engagement in the United States came in 1923 with the prominent theatrical company of E.H. Sothern and Julia Marlowe, who brought a number of classic works to the Broadway stage and on the road. Kinnell had the following roles during the Sothern/Marlowe tour: the raucous Guiderius in *Cymbeline* (10/2/23), Tranio in *The Taming of the Shrew* (10/15/23), Sebastian in *Twelfth Night* (10/22/23), Lorenzo in *The Merchant of Venice* (11/5/23), Benvolio in *Romeo and Juliet* (11/12/23) and the First Player in *Hamlet*.

Kinnell decided to stay on in America after the Sothern/Marlowe Company departed. On Broadway, Murray was seen as Ishak the Poet in *Hassan* (9/22/24) and Falnall in *The Way of the World* (11/17/24). In 1925, Kinnell succeeded Stafford Dickens in the role of Charles Ventnor, the unpleasant, troublesome lawyer, in *Old English* (12/23/24 original opening) starring George Arliss. Kinnell's interpretation of the villainous Ventnor so impressed the venerable Arliss that the two became good friends. Kinnell would become part of Arliss' theater company and would later be featured in six of the actor's films as well. When Arliss brought his production of *The Merchant of Venice* (1/25/28) to Broadway, he utilized Murray as the tragic Bassanio, Antonio's friend and Portia's suitor.

Murray Kinnell became a naturalized United States citizen on October 24, 1928.

Other 1920s theatrical work for Kinnell included parts in *Simon Called Peter*, *Young Love* and *The Constant Wife*, which

starred Ethel Barrymore. Kinnell secured positive reviews as Sutton in *Sign of the Leopard* (12/11/28). Murray's final Broadway appearance came as Robert Cecil (Lord Burleigh), in *The Royal Virgin* (3/17/30). From 1925-1933, Kinnell belonged to the prestigious theatrical club, the Players, in Manhattan. After 1930, however, his career took him to Hollywood, where he would remain, for the most part, until his death in 1954.

Recreating his stage role of the villain Charles Ventnor, Kinnell ventured into motion pictures with *Old English* (1930), when Warner Bros. brought the George Arliss vehicle to the screen. Murray then assayed the part of Worthing in *The Princess and the Plumber* (1930), starring Maureen O'Sullivan and Charles Farrell.

The Public Enemy (1931), which helped catapult James Cagney to stardom, provided Kinnell with the important, meaty role as Putty Nose. A Fagin-like character, Putty Nose runs a pool hall, while inducing young boys from the street into a life of crime. He fences the stolen goods that the youths have been encouraged to pilfer. Providing two of his protégés, Tom Powers (Cagney) and Matt Doyle (Edward Woods) with guns, Putty Nose helps plan the robbery of a fur warehouse. When

The Public Enemy (1931): **Murray Kinnell (center, as Putty Nose) begs for his life with Edward Woods and James Cagney.**

the robbery goes awry and a policeman is killed during Powers' and Doyle's escape, the young men find mentor Putty Nose has deserted them and left town. Years later, Powers, vowing vengeance, locates Putty Nose, who tries to placate him, playing on the piano and singing *Hesitation Blues* as he had done for the boys in the past. The attempt fails, so Putty Nose resorts to begging, also to no avail, before being executed by Powers for his perceived betrayal. *The Public Enemy* gave evidence that Kinnell was capable of playing seedy and despicable, yet believable, villain roles.

As Dummy Metz (aka Fink), Kinnell was a hitman for gang lord Wallace Beery in another crime opus, *The Secret Six* (1931), featuring Jean Harlow and Clark Gable. Murray played Captain Elek in *Honor of the Family* (1931), set in Budapest. Kinnell was seen as Alf in *Reckless Living* (1931). As Jerry Baxter, Kinnell was a henchman and advisor to crime boss Leo Carrillo in *The Guilty Generation* (1931). Baxter, displaying some semblance of morality, defies his boss' orders to eliminate the son (Robert Young) of a rival gang leader (Boris Karloff). Kinnell portrayed Breckinridge in *The Deceiver* (1931) and was Peterson the butler in *Under 18* (1931), starring Marian Marsh.

The Black Camel (1931), the second of Fox's *Charlie Chan* series starring Warner Oland, had a strong cast, including Bela Lugosi, Dwight Frye and C. Henry Gordon. Kinnell portrayed an artist-turned beachcomber whose name "might be Smith" ("Might also be Jones," counters Chan). Resting on a pavilion outside a window, Archie Smith overhears a conversation between Fyfe (Victor Varconi) and the soon-to-be-murdered Shelah Fane (Dorothy Revier), which he later attempts to use for his own benefit. Smith tries to get Fyfe to purchase one of his paintings, claiming, "I assure you it isn't blackmail. It's merely that I thought you might welcome the opportunity of becoming a patron of the arts." Eventually, the devious Smith gets shot in the back for his efforts. The role of Smith represented a nice piece of character work by Kinnell.

Murray Kinnell would become somewhat of an Oland *Chan* series regular, resurfacing (as different characters) in the fifth, sixth and seventh Fox entries. As Martin Thorne in *Charlie Chan's Courage* (1934), Kinnell claimed to be the secretary of wealthy businessman Paul Harvey. Thorne unwittingly aids the detective by hiring Chan, believing Charlie to be an out-of-work cook. *Charlie Chan's Courage* is believed to be a lost film. In *Charlie Chan in London* (1934), Kinnell purports to be Phillips the butler, but is actually

The Black Camel (1931): **Murray Kinnell, Victor Varconi and Warner Oland (as Charlie Chan)**

Captain Seton, a military intelligence officer who has been planted in the home of Alan Mowbray. As the fussy and meticulous bank teller Henri La Touche, Murray was involved in bond forgery and murder in *Charlie Chan in Paris* (1935).

While playing Carr in *The Menace* (1932), directed by Roy William Neill of horror and *Sherlock Holmes* notoriety, Kinnell became impressed with the talent of young Bette Davis. He recommended Davis to his friend George Arliss, arranging for the two to meet. Arliss recalled in his second autobiography (1940, pp. 178-179):

> We were having difficulty in finding a girl with some ability, who looked a little different from the average ingénue. It was Murray Kinnell who suggested Bette Davis; that same Murray Kinnell who had done such valuable work in *Old English* both on the stage and screen. He had played with Bette Davis in a picture called *The Menace*; he thought she had possibilities and urged me to let her rehearse … I think that only two or three times in my experience have I ever got from an actor at rehearsal something beyond what I realized was in the part. Bette Davis proved to be one of these exceptions.

Davis was cast in the major role of Grace Blair in *The Man Who Played God* (1932), while Murray was seen as the aide

Grand Hotel **(1932): Tully Marshall looks over the "stenographer" (Joan Crawford), while Murray Kinnell (center) gives a knowing smirk.**

Finally, the hideously disfigured Cleopatra (Olga Baclanova) is revealed. Kinnell's unbilled character, in essence, provides *Freaks* with a prologue and an epilogue (although some versions have a happy ending scene tagged on after the revelation).

After appearing in a film that MGM virtually disowned, the studio still included Kinnell as Schweimann in its all-star gala, *Grand Hotel* (1932). Also for MGM, Kinnell was Carson in *Are You Listening* (1932), starring William Haines in one of his last films. Kinnell played Smitty, the fence, in *The Expert* (1932), with Chic Sale. Murray was Thompson, Warren William's butler, in *The Mouthpiece* (1932). He had a minor role as an escaping prisoner in *While Paris Sleeps* (1932). Returning to evil-doing as Spike Forgan, Kinnell assisted David Landau in burning the wheat crop of Barbara Stanwyck and George Brent in *The Purchase Price* (1932). Kinnell was Collins in *The Painted Woman* (1932), an early Spencer Tracy film. Rejoining George Arliss, Murray portrayed broker Alfred Curtis in the stock market tale, *A Successful Calamity* (1932). Kinnell, as Professor Kropotkin, was on

to a visiting king (Andre Luquet). After playing the judge in *The Beast of the City* (1932), Kinnell would appear in a controversial film that has achieved cult status over the years.

As stated in the introduction to this chapter, Murray Kinnell rarely receives credit for his fine work in MGM's *Freaks* (1932), directed by Tod Browning. The film opens with the sideshow barker (Kinnell) stating:

> We didn't lie to you, folks. We told you we had living, breathing monstrosities. You laughed at them, shuddered at them and yet, but for the accident of birth, you might be even as they are.

Providing a clue of things to come, the barker adds, "Their code is a law unto themselves. Offend one and you offend them all." He then leads the carnival patrons to the pit containing "the most astounding living monstrosity of all time." Before the film audience can view what the sideshow gawkers have witnessed, the focus shifts as the story begins to unfold. Much later, after the horrific, climatic storm chase sequence, the scene returns to the barker, who now states:

> How she got that way will never be known. Some say it was a jealous lover. Others, it was the code of the freaks. Others, the storm. Believe it or not, there she is.

Voltaire **(1933): George Arliss, Theodore Newton and Murray Kinnell**

The House of Rothschild (1934): **Murray Kinnell as James Rothschild**

played from 1932-1938. Founded by former cricket great and marvelous character actor C. Aubrey Smith, the HCC featured many noted actors in its early years, including David Niven, Errol Flynn, Claude King, Ivan Simpson and Boris Karloff. Kinnell, as both a batsman and bowler, played in a series of matches against a touring Australian team in August 1932. He remained an active part of the HCC squad when it toured Canada in July 1938. The Hollywood Cricket Club would be instrumental in the formation of the Screen Actors Guild in 1933.

Today We Live (1933), with Joan Crawford and Gary Cooper, had Kinnell as the Padre. He was Gabrosh in *Zoo in Budapest* (1933), directed by Rowland V. Lee. *Voltaire* (1933), again with George Arliss, included Murray as Emile, the servant to the noted philosopher.

Directed by Edgar G. Ulmer, *Damaged Lives* (1933) focused on the risk and dangers of venereal disease, with Kinnell as Dr. Vincent Leonard, an infectious disease specialist. Dr. Leonard confirms the feared diagnosis of VD for the lead characters, before providing a presentation of which *Variety* (6/16/37) commented (note the film was released in some areas four years after being made):

The House of Rothschild (1934): **Murray Kinnell assists his mother, Helen Westley.**

hand in another major MGM work, *Rasputin and the Empress* (1932), featuring, among others, all three Barrymore siblings (John, Lionel and Ethel). *The Match King* (1932), starring Warren William, had Kinnell as Nyberg, a banker.

Secrets of the French Police (1932), with Gregory Ratoff as an evil hypnotist who dabbles in espionage and making statues out of his victims, offered Murray a borderline horror genre role. As Bertillon, the French chief of detectives of the "Surete Nationale," Kinnell supervised Ralph Morgan in solving a series of grisly murders.

An avid cricketer, Kinnell was one of the early members of the Hollywood Cricket Club (HCC), for whom he

Affairs of a Gentleman (1934): Murray Kinnell with his employer, Paul Lukas

hours and unreasonable conditions. As stated, the Hollywood Cricket Club supplied many of the driving forces of SAG, including Boris Karloff, Ivan Simpson, C. Aubrey Smith, and Claude King. Kinnell was one of the pioneering members, as well, being awarded SAG card #37. [Boris Karloff had SAG card #9, while Bela Lugosi was #28.]

George Arliss utilized virtually his entire screen "stock company" in the historical drama, *The House of Rothschild* (1934). Kinnell played James Rothschild, one of the prestigious banking brothers. *The House of Rothschild* had Boris Karloff in a colorful non-horror role as the family's adversary. Murray would later make his sixth and final film with George Arliss, *Cardinal Richelieu* (1935). Kinnell portrayed the Duke of Lorraine opposite Arliss' powerful, manipulative title character.

Affairs of a Gentleman (1934) gave Kinnell the interesting role of Fletcher, Paul Lukas' valet, who opportunely murders his employer after the man's suicide attempt fails. Kinnell

The 29-minute lecture, delivered by Murray Kinnell, specialist of the story, is forceful, dignified and informative. His spiel is crammed with facts, plus frequent use of diagrams and illustrations.

The straight lecture portion of *Damaged Lives* was likely an attempt by Ulmer to have it regarded more as public information vehicle than exploitation film.

The Avenger (1933), a Monogram "update" of *The Count of Monte Cristo*, featured Kinnell as Cormack, henchman to the vile Arthur Vinton. *The Solitaire Man* (1933), a lighthearted crime tale starring Herbert Marshall, had an unbilled Kinnell as Inspector Harris. Murray played Davenport in *I Loved a Woman* (1933), with Edward G. Robinson. *Ann Vickers* (1933), headlining Irene Dunne in a courageous role, had Kinnell as Dr. Slenk, the warden of Copper Gap women's prison. Murray had relatively minor parts as Horton in *From Headquarters* (1933), Dr. Clairbourne in *If I Were Free* (1933) and the first trial defendant in *The Women in His Life* (1933). Somewhat more substantial was his role of Luigi Malatini in the musical *I Am Suzanne* (1933), an unusual tale involving puppeteers with Leslie Banks as the villain.

A series of meetings in early 1933 led to the formation of the Screen Actors Guild (SAG) in direct response to exploitation of performers with excessive

Charlie Chan in Paris (1935): Murray Kinnell points to a document held by Warner Oland.

Mad Love (1935): **Sara Haden, Frances Drake and Murray Kinnell examine the gifts delivered to the theater dressing room.**

portrayed Major Bruce Cassell in *Murder in Trinidad* (1934), Jan Paris in *Such Women are Dangerous* (1934) and the judge in *Hat, Coat and Glove* (1934). Showing a sadistic side, Murray was the abusive schoolteacher Mr. Phillips in *Anne of Green Gables* (1934) with Anne Shirley. *The Silver Streak* (1934), a railroad drama involving a super train and a medical emergency, had Kinnell as Dr. Flynn.

Mad Love (1935), an MGM horror film starring Colin Clive as Stephen Orlac, included Kinnell as Charles, the theater manager of Les Theatre des Horreurs. It is Charles who alerts Yvonne Orlac (Frances Drake) for her final scene of the last performance of their production. Charles then comes to Yvonne's dressing room to escort her to the closing night party, only to find her with Dr. Gogol (Peter Lorre), who has sat transfixed in the same box every night during the show's run. Charles invites Gogol to the party as well. He later unknowingly feeds the doctor's obsession

with the actress, stating, "Doctor, no champagne, no cake and no kiss. Yvonne, don't forget the public." Although Charles is not a major horror role, it still afforded Kinnell the chance to show his skills in an interesting, atmospheric production.

The Three Musketeers (1935) had Kinnell as the lustful landlord Bernajou, who first is manipulated by Heather Angel and later by the Musketeers as well as they cite an imaginary law in order to secure free lodging for D'Artagnan (Walter Abel). *Rendezvous* (1935), a tale of espionage during World War I with Lionel Atwill on the side of good, had Kinnell as de Segroff. Murray played Dean James Churchill in *Fighting Youth* (1935), a football yarn concerning radical subversion in U.S. colleges. *Kind Lady* (1935) had Kinnell posing as a smooth talking doctor, but actually he is part of a gang of thieves headed by Basil Rathbone. Kinnell's "doctor" is not above murder,

Cardinal Richelieu **(1935): A portrait of Murray Kinnell as the Duke of Lorraine**

and his own safety over his debt to the Master and possible intervention on Jesus' behalf. Kinnell did a fine job portraying Simon's mounting despair and anger as Marcus flees the scene.

The Great Impersonation (1935), one of a number of versions of E. Phillips Oppenheim's novel, featured Edmund Lowe in the dual role of ne'er-do-well Lord Dominey and the evil Baron Leopold von Ragastein. The film is essentially an espionage tale, with a taste of horror, aided by having gaunt genre veterans like Brandon Hurst and Leonard Mudie on board, along with Dwight Frye playing Roger Unthank, the "creature" of the Black Bog (whose nocturnal screams have embellished the local legends). Kinnell played Seaman, an operative of unscrupulous munitions baron Sir Ivan Brunn (Charles Waldron). Erroneously believing Dominey to be von Ragastein, Seaman brings Princess Stephanie (Wera Engels) in on their diabolical plans. Seaman then compiles a list of all Sir Ivan's spies and saboteurs. He prepares to transmit the orders for all the operatives to fulfill their nefarious roles via radio, but is thwarted by Dominey, who redeems himself in the process.

In an article for SAG's in-house periodical, *The Screen Guild's Magazine* (October 1935), Kinnell penned a piece entitled "Let's Adopt the Orphan," in which he explained the negative impact that the film industry had on the theatrical experience on the West Coast:

> There is no really first-class theatrical organization in Los Angeles. There is a wish among back-stage folk to see such a theater established, and an audience for the front of the house if only it could be rounded up. There is one great obstacle, the fact that moving pictures claim the entire time and attention of all actors, writers and directors of real prominence.

as he slays the maid (Nola Luxford) when she attempts to contact the police. Kinnell had the minor part of the clerk in Governor Steed's court in *Captain Blood* (1935), starring Errol Flynn.

The Last Days of Pompeii (1935), which featured many well-crafted supporting bits including those of Edward Van Sloan and Ward Bond, had Kinnell as Simon, an old Judean peasant. In the Holy Land on mercenary business, Marcus (Preston Foster), carrying his seriously ill son (David Holt) in his arms, has the smiling Simon direct him to "the Master." When Marcus attempts to pay Jesus for curing his boy, Simon stops him, stating, "The Master won't take money." Simon refutes the material appearance of poverty, adding, "He's the richest man in the world." Later, as Jesus is being led for crucifixion, Simon spots Marcus in the crowd and pleads for his help. This is a dramatic moment in the film, as Marcus chooses his need for wealth

Kinnell believed the Screen Guilds (not just SAG) should play a major role in establishing "a permanent commercial establishment of the highest class," while providing all professionals the time and opportunity to explore and develop their creative skills in a theatrical setting.

Kinnell played Conrick, the defense attorney who defends Walter Abel in a murder case, in *The Witness Chair* (1936). Murray's roles, however, seemed to be diminishing in size and importance. He portrayed the theater manager in *One Rainy Afternoon* (1936), a judge at the trial of Katharine Hepburn in *Mary of Scotland* (1936), the Dean in *The Big Game* (1936), Dr. Barnes in *Make Way for a Lady* (1936) and Professor Dean Liggett in *Winterset* (1936). *Fifteen Maiden Lane* (1936), a mystery tale involving jewel thieves, gave Murray the part of Fingers Garson, kind of an homage to some of his earlier 1930s screen work in films like *The Public Enemy* and *Kind Lady*. Kinnell gave a fine interpretation of the stern Reverend Nelson, the father of young Horatio (Douglas Scott), in *Lloyds of London* (1936). *Four Day Wonder* (1936), based on a story by A.A. Milne, had Murray on hand as Morris.

Outcast (1937), a tale of vengeance directed by Robert Florey, featured Kinnell as crippled Anthony "Tony" Stevens. His appearance in *The Soldier and the Lady* (1937) remains unconfirmed. As Hugo, Murray appeared once again opposite Errol Flynn in Warner Bros.' *The Prince and the Pauper* (1937). Kinnell was seen near the conclusion of *Captains Courageous* (1937), as the minister at the seaside tribute. Amid a stellar supporting cast (Donald Crisp, Montagu Love, Edna May Oliver, George Zucco, Billie Burke, Donald Meek, et al.) of a mediocre film, Kinnell was the accusatory prosecutor Sir Richard Webster in *Parnell* (1937), with Clark Gable in the title role.

Kinnell's final film was the first entry in the Peter Lorre *Mr. Moto* series. In *Think Fast Mr. Moto* (1937), Murray played Mr. Joseph Wilkie, the Shanghai branch manager of a major ocean cruise line. Near the climax, Wilkie bumps into Moto, causing the detective to accidentally shoot himself in the stomach. Wilkie also kills the other antagonist, Sig Ruman, appearing to be helpful while actually protecting his own true identity. Moto eventually unmasks Wilkie as the mastermind of a gang of international smugglers (gems and drugs). It seems rather fitting that Kinnell would conclude his movie career in such a villainous role, while also ushering in a new Oriental detective series, having previously appeared in four *Charlie Chan* films.

In 1937, Kinnell became the assistant treasurer of the Screen Actors Guild (SAG). Giving up his career as an actor, Murray concentrated much of his time and energy into the union's negotiations with the major studios, which resulted in a new SAG contract in November 1938. Kinnell continued to gain greater prominence in the hierarchy of SAG, eventually becoming the administrator of SAG's agency division. Murray retired from that position in 1952.

In more recent times, Murray Kinnell's name has emerged as possibly being linked to young Norma Jean Baker (who would become Marilyn Monroe). Some of

***The Great Impersonation* (1935): Murray Kinnell as Seaman**

Monroe's biographers list a man named "Mr. Kimmell" as among those suspected of sexually abusing young Norma when she was about eight years old. Lois Banner in *The Passion and the Paradox* refutes the contention of other authors that Murray roomed in the Baker household in January of 1935. Banner confirms that Kinnell and his wife Henrietta lived on 1264 Beverly Glen Boulevard in Westwood in 1933 and at 279 Glenroy Avenue in Westwood from 1934-1936—not as alleged boarders at the 6812 Arbol Drive home of Gladys Baker during that time frame. [I have copies of personal correspondence between Kinnell and SAG from 1933-1936, all of which confirm the two Westwood addresses for the Kinnells]. Other writers (e.g., Keith

Kind Lady (1935): **Murray Kinnell, Basil Rathbone and Dudley Digges contemplate their next move.**

Badman, p. 7) go so far as to contend that Murray Kinnell definitely molested young Norma, despite Monroe's later description of the attacker not matching that of the actor in either age or appearance. Monroe stated "Kimmell" was an elderly man, while Murray was then in his mid-forties and quite athletic. In fact, Monroe's account fits more with George Atkinson, the stand-in for George Arliss, who did reside for a time with the Baker family. Both Kinnell and Atkinson were connected with Arliss, with all three working together on *Cardinal Richelieu* (1935), which fits the time period in question. Sarah Churchwell, in *The Many Lives of Marilyn Monroe* (pp. 161-163), challenges others, including Donald H. Wolfe in *The Last Days of Marilyn Monroe*, who made the judgment call that Kinnell had any connection to Monroe as a child. Monroe's biographies are numerous and the subject matter is likely fascinating for many. But for writers to smear the character and person of Murray Kinnell with such vicious accusations based on supposition and interpretation is truly detestable. It is sad indeed that

Kinnell should be remembered for something in which he likely had no involvement, rather than the fine body of work of which he has provided lasting evidence on film.

On Wednesday, August 11, 1954 Murray Kinnell passed away at his home in Santa Barbara, California. He was 65 years old. His widow Henrietta and his son, Peter Kinnell, survived him. Funeral services were held on Saturday, August 14, 1954 at the Santa Barbara Cemetery Chapel. He was interred there, in the Vista Del Mar Section.

Murray Kinnell has unfortunately and regrettably drifted into film obscurity. Some recognition for his career is long overdue, as Kinnell was a colorful, talented actor, who held his own with major players of his time, earning the esteem of George Arliss and others. Kinnell enacted some excellent villainous parts, like Putty Nose in *The Public Enemy*, Dummy Metz in *The Secret Six* and Spike Forgan in *The Purchase Price*. While appearing quite comfortable as a despicable character like Putty Nose, Kinnell was equally

Outcast (1937): Tony Stevens (**Murray Kinnell**) with his daughter (**Karen Morley**)

adept as the sympathetic Simon, the Judean peasant, in *The Last Days of Pompeii.* Horror and fantasy genre fans can

Lloyd's of London (1936): Douglas Scott, Murray Kinnell and Lumsden Hare

still appreciate how his efforts enhanced *Freaks, Mad Love* and *The Great Impersonation.* It is the hope that reexamination of Murray Kinnell's career can help rectify some of the neglect.

Sources

Arliss, George. *My Ten Years in the Studios*, New York: Little, Brown and Company, 1940.

Badman, Keith. *Marilyn Monroe: The Final Years*, New York: St. Martin's Griffin, 2013.

Banner, Lois. *The Passion and the Paradox*, New York: Bloomsbury, 2013.

Churchwell, Sarah. *The Many Lives of Marilyn Monroe*, New York: Picador, 2005

Coughlin, Jim. "Forgotten Faces of Fantastic Films: Murray Kinnell," in *Midnight Marquee #45* (Summer 1993), pp. 79-82.

Kinnell, Murray. *Wikipedia.com*

Wolfe, Donald H. *The Last Days of Marilyn Monroe*, New York: William Morrow, 2012.

Snow White and the Seven Dwarfs (1937)

Lucille La Verne
(1869 – 1945)

One of the more frightening images from my childhood memories was that of the Wicked Witch in the animated classic *Snow White and the Seven Dwarfs*, which I first viewed when Disney re-released the 1937 feature in 1958. Albeit a cartoon character, the Evil Queen/Wicked Witch (with voice provided by Lucille La Verne), with her narcissistic, envious need to be "the fairest in the land," is as chillingly depicted as any Disney villain, devoid of any positive attributes or comic relief. The impact of La Verne's cackling tones as the Witch provided many restless nights and bad dreams for a seven year old.

Lucille La Verne's ability to play grotesque, menacing hags in films like *Orphans of the Storm* and *A Tale of Two Cities* makes one wonder why she was never utilized as an antagonist in the horror genre. There were virtually no significant villainous roles for women in the suspense and fantasy films of the early sound era. Those that do come to mind (Gloria Holden in *Dracula's Daughter*, Myrna Loy in *Thirteen Women*, Gale Sondergaard as the Spider Woman, etc.) all seem to be younger, dark-haired, lean women. When it came time to cast the Wicked Witch of the West for *The Wizard of Oz* (1939), MGM, after passing on Sondergaard, chose thin, bony-faced Margaret Hamilton (who was wonderful in the role). Perhaps even then, Hollywood was prejudiced against heavier, older women. Whatever the reasoning, it was a loss for the moviegoers of the time that Lucille La Verne never had the opportunity to be a prominent villain, as she could convey evil and menace with the best. Lucille would have been a sensational mad scientist, twisted murderess or other monstrous personage, had only studios taken a risk considering females in roles of these natures. It is a shame that La Verne's best chance to display her malevolent side came in an animated film, although certainly an historic one.

She was born Lucille La Verne Mitchum on November 7, 1869 (or 1872), near Memphis, Tennessee (although some references claim Nashville as her birthplace). She was the daughter of William Erwin Mitchum (1811-1880) and Jenny MacDowell (1838-?). Young Lucille had auburn hair and brown eyes. Having made her first stage appearance as a young child (in a play called *Centennial* in honor of the 100th birthday of the U.S.A. in 1876), La Verne had played both Juliet and Lady Macbeth by the age of 14. La Verne apprenticed with the Fanny Ellsner Company

ENGRAVED BY A. GLASGO

Yours always,
Lucille La Verne.

An early cabinet photo (c. 1890) of Lucille La Verne

beginning with the 1887/88 theatrical season. Lucille first appeared on stage in New York City in *La Tosca* (1888), but spent most of her early performing days on the road. La Verne, years later, reflected:

> I used to think when I was slaving along in unknown stock companies that the world was made up of blizzards, thermometers that registered a hundred in the shade, icy cold dressing rooms, bumpy iron bedsteads, fried steaks, one-night stands and salary ghosts that never walked.

After receiving strong notices as Corin, the old shepherd, in an all-woman production of Shakespeare's *As You Like It* (1894), Lucille ventured to Broadway. With Frank Mayo's company, La Verne scored an even greater success as Patsy in *Puddin' Head Wilson* (1895). She had major roles in touring productions of *Notre Dame* (1895) and *Uncle Tom's Cabin* (1897). Lucille gained acclaim as the title character

A portrait (c. 1910) of Lucille La Verne

in *Lady Windermere's Fan* (1897) and played Betsy in *Way Down East* (1897). In San Francisco in the late 1890s, La Verne was seen at the leading theaters, like the Grand and Columbia, in plays like *The Dancing Girl*, *The Two Orphans*, *Camille* and *Frou Frou*. When she took on the title role in *Carmen*, one critic raved:

> I have seen Carmens great and Carmens small, from the average stock actress to Olga Nethersole, but Lucille La Verne is second to none. She is under the skin of Merimee's Gypsy—the child, the co-quette, the witch, the woman, the tiger, the devil, all in one.

Aphrodite **(1919 stage): Lucille La Verne as Chimeris, the Oracle**

For many years a leading player in stock companies in both major cities and small towns, Lucille also spent a number of seasons managing her own company at the La Verne Theatre in Richmond, Virginia. This commenced in 1898 when La Verne was named director of the recently constructed Empire Theater in Richmond. There, Lucille

Orphans of the Storm **(1921): Lucille La Verne exploits blind Dorothy Gish.**

a perfect thing! She was unimpeachable and irresistible. Her audience loved her, laughed and cried with her.

A revival of *Uncle Tom's Cabin* (5/20/07) represented La Verne's next Broadway appearance. She once made the claim that she was the first woman to ever take on the role of Uncle Tom (years earlier with a touring company). Lucille was prominently featured in New York in both *The Easterner* (3/2/08) and *The Blue Mouse* (11/20/08), the latter as a replacement in the role of Mrs. Lewellyn. She was seen as Selina in the farce *Seven Days* (11/10/09). La Verne authored and starred, as Jane Hemmingway, in the original play *Ann Boyd* (3/31/13), which closed after only seven performances. Also in the mid-teens, Lucille appeared on Broadway as Mrs. Owen Denbigh in *The House of Bondage*

would play leading roles in *Hedda Gabler* and *Antigone*. In Richmond, La Verne again portrayed the wretched, abusive La Frochard in *The Two Orphans*. La Verne would dabble in playwriting from time to time, as when she adapted Charles Dickens' *A Christmas Carol* for the stage in 1900. So prominent was La Verne on the Richmond stage and community that she was named "Woman of the Year" by the Virginia Women's Society in 1901.

La Verne was renowned for her portrayals of black characters (with whites playing in blackface, a common practice at the time), including Clancy, "the Old Negress," in *Clarice* (1905), which represented her London, England debut. Lucille also appeared in New York in *Clarice* (10/16/06), about which critic Roland Burke Hennessy wrote, "She made blasé Broadway sit up and take notice." Chicago critics were equally favorable when *Clarice* toured the Midwest in early 1907. James O'Donnell Bennett stated:

> Miss La Verne's Clancy was a masterpiece of Negro characterization. It was

Sun-Up **(1923 Broadway stage): Lucille La Verne as the Widow Cagle**

Sun-Up (1923): As George K. Arthur looks with apprehension, Lucille La Verne encourages son Conrad Nagel to shoot the stranger.

(1/19/14) and in *The Cinderella Man* (1/17/16). In regional theater, La Verne played Aunt Mary Watkins in *The Rejuvenation of Aunt Mary* and Ayah in *East of Suez*.

La Verne reportedly made her film debut as the Mammy, billed as "Laura La Varnie," in the Biograph short *Butterflies and Orange Blossoms* (1914). She next had an undetermined role for William Brady and his World Pictures in *Over Night* (1915). Perhaps because of her prominence on the stage, Lucille was hesitant to use her actual name on screen. La Verne was billed as "Lucille La Varney" in her next two film roles, playing Lady Maria in *Sweet Kitty Bellairs* (1916) and Mme. Batavia in *The Thousand Dollar Husband* (1916), with Blanche Sweet. The first time "Lucille La Verne" was actually listed in the screen credits was when she portrayed Mandy in *Polly of the Circus* (1917), starring Mae Marsh. As she often had enacted on stage, La Verne was the "Old Mammy" in the Olga Petrova film, *Tempered Steel* (1918). As Sarah Harden in *The Life Mask* (1918), Lucille was the nurse who murders the husband of Anita

Courtland (again, Olga Petrova) to free her from a bad marriage. *The Praise Agent* (1919) had La Verne as Mrs. Eubanks, a Suffragette leader.

The stage remained Lucille's passion, as witnessed by some of her work on Broadway in the early 1920s. In the comedy *Come Seven* (7/19/20), La Verne portrayed, again in blackface, Elzevir Nesbit. She had a longer run (79 performances) as Lottie in Fanny Hurst's drama *Back Pay* (8/20/21). *The Goldfish* (4/17/22) featured La Verne as Magnolia. It was her next vehicle, *Sun-Up*, however, that would establish La Verne in the upper echelon of American stage actresses.

Sun-Up, which opened at the Provincetown Playhouse on 5/25/23, provided La Verne her most famous characterization, Widow Cagle, the Spartan matriarch of a clan of southern mountain folk. With an occasional hiatus for a film role, Lucille appeared in *Sun-Up* almost continuously over the next four years in New York, Chicago, London, Paris and elsewhere in Europe, playing before many heads

An American Tragedy (1931): Convicted Phillips Holmes is given comfort by his mother, Lucille La Verne.

D.W. Griffith's *Orphans of the Storm* (1921) stands up well to this day. Wild haired, sporting a moustache and missing teeth, the beggar woman Frochard abuses and uses the blind sister Louise (Dorothy Gish) to suit her purposes. Frochard not only lies to Louise, stating her beloved sister Henrietta (Lillian Gish) has died, the old woman locks the blind girl in a cellar full of rats. Louise is coerced by Frochard to sing and beg in the streets of Paris. At one poignant moment, Frochard, eager to obtain more money, snatches the shawl from Louise's shoulder in the midst of snow and freezing weather, with the title card claiming, "You'll shiver better without that shawl." The evil Frochard, who finally gets her comeuppance, remains one of the most memorable villains of the silent screen. Griffith was so impressed with Lucille's efforts that he would also use her as the compassionate "Auntie" Easter in *The White Rose* (1923), the dramatic refugee mother in *America* (1924) and, later, as the midwife to the president-to-be's mother, Nancy Hanks Lincoln (Helen Freeman), in the opening sequence of *Abraham Lincoln* (1930).

La Verne was the rollicking drunken Aunt Rosa in *Zaza* (1923), starring Gloria Swanson and directed by Alan Dwan. In a film started by D.W. Griffith (but finished by John W. Noble), Lucille played Aunt Lucy, better known as "Darktown's Cleopatra," in *His Darker Self* (1924).

Sun-Up (1925) gave La Verne the opportunity to recreate her great stage success as the Widow Cagle, a homesteader in the hills of North Carolina. The embittered widow blames the U.S. government for her husband's death and wrongly believes her son Rufe (Conrad Nagel) has now been killed in action in the War. As her anger and resentment mount, Widow Cagle plans to enact her vengeance on the government representative en route to their backwoods dwelling at "sun-up." Perhaps the silent screen did not capture her tour de force as the Widow Cagle as much as the live stage, but *Sun-Up* still gave La Verne the vehicle to display her great dramatic presence. Following *Sun-Up*, La Verne would revert to the stage, making only one other film in the ensuing five years: *The Last Moment* (1928), in which she played the innkeeper. In the fall of 1927, La Verne purchased the proprietary rights to *You Can't Win* by Jack Black and Bessie Beatty, a portion of which was adapted for the stage under the title

of state, including Edward VII of England, Leopold of Belgium and Kaiser Wilhelm of Germany. Queen Marie of Romania called La Verne "the greatest artiste I have ever seen." Lucille would portray Widow Cagle over 3000 times (this may be hyperbole—other sources claim 500 performances) in her career. Thoroughly familiar with the plight of the underprivileged, often illiterate Appalachian mountain people, La Verne, during the run of *Sun-Up*, helped raise more than a million dollars to establish schools in Southern mountain regions. As a result of her success in *Sun Up*, New York's Princess Theatre was renamed (for a time) the Lucille La Verne Theatre.

La Verne's performance as Mother Frochard (which she had previously done on stage in *The Two Orphans*) in

Forgotten Faces

24 Hours (1931): Regis Toomey and Lucille La Verne

During the run of *Sun-Up*, Lucille adopted an Appalachian mountain girl named Grace. She took Grace with her to England and later decided to educate her adopted daughter there. La Verne had much earlier given birth to two sons while she was married to a Mr. Wald, but unfortunately both boys died during infancy.

Lucille soon after ventured to Hollywood to try her hand in the medium of talking pictures. La Verne's return to the screen came as Ma Delano, the owner of the Coney Island boardwalk penny arcade, who tries to protect her three children (including James Cagney in his film debut) in *Sinners Holiday* (1930). Ma bemoans the illegal booze trade that allegedly killed her husband, as she rules her family in a tough, opinionated, almost tyrannical manner. She even attempts to pin the murder by her son (Cagney) of a hoodlum (Warren Hymer) on her own daughter's boyfriend (Grant Withers) in order to preserve what she has left of a family. Although Ma Delano's values are twisted, La Verne was certainly convincing in the part.

Following two minor roles in *Du Barry, Woman of Passion* (1930) and *The Comeback* (1930), a "Leather Pushers" short, La Verne would make her mark in a memorable early talkie. In another "old hag" portrayal, La Verne was the unscrupulous Ma Magdalena who shields and later cheats Rico (Edward G. Robinson)

Salt Chunk Mary. Black's story was semi-autobiographical, dealing with a powerful, charismatic, criminal woman who had influenced his life. Black did not get along with La Verne during the play's development, finding her bossy and belligerent. *Salt Chunk Mary* opened at the Egan Theatre in Los Angeles in late 1927 to a poor critical response. Jack Black later filed a complaint against La Verne and her production, bringing the case to arbitration and voiding her rights to his story.

On 10/22/28, La Verne, again portraying the Widow Cagle, opened at the Lucille La Verne Theatre in a revival of *Sun-Up*, which ran for 101 performances. Lucille then produced, directed and starred (as "Duckie" aka Jessica Dale) in *Hot Water* (1/21/29), which ran for 32 performances, also at the house bearing her name. With the theater losing money, La Verne was released as manager, with the site reverting to its earlier name as the Princess Theatre (as it was called when it opened in 1913). Discouraged, La Verne received a boost when she was invited to play Shylock in *The Merchant of Venice* (1929) in London, a real chance to exhibit her versatility.

The Last Trail (1933): Claire Trevor, Lucille La Verne and George O'Brien

Kentucky Kernels (1934): The feud between Noah Beery, Sr. and Lucille La Verne turns to romance.

in *Little Caesar* (1931). Lucille was Elvira Jarvis, a pioneer woman and mother of Johnny Mack Brown, in *The Great Meadow* (1931). Her death at the hands of Indians sparks the conflict for the new settlers. La Verne played Mrs. Dacklehorse in *24 Hours* (1931) and was Lucie Villars, the owner of the Palais Royale, in *The Unholy Garden* (1931), starring Ronald Colman.

Based on the novel by Theodore Dreiser, *An American Tragedy* (1931) afforded Lucille the complex role of Mrs. Ada Griffiths. The zealous Mrs. Griffiths runs a mission, obsessed with the saving of souls, yet neglects the development of her own son, Clyde. That son (Phillips Holmes) grows up to be a scheming psychopath and eventual murderer, causing his mother great torment as she blames herself for his nefarious deeds. Mordaunt Hall in the *New York Times* (8/6/31) opined, "Lucille La Verne does quite well with the part of Clyde's mother."

La Verne had a cameo appearance as the lady with the pipe at the bustling metropolitan railroad station in *Union Depot* (1932). Her scenes were deleted from the final print of *She Wanted a Millionaire* (1932). Lucille's ability to portray mothers involved in moral dilemmas was again put to the test in *Alias the Doctor* (1932). As Frau Martha Brenner, she allows foster son Karl (Richard Barthelmess)

to take responsibility for a medical mishap caused by her biological son Stephan (Norman Foster), resulting in Karl doing prison time and foregoing a promising medical career. When Stephan dies, Karl performs life-saving surgery on a child. Martha encourages Karl to assume his dead brother's identity, leading to many issues, including his love for Stephan's sister (Marian Marsh). In the midst of Karl's crises, Martha has a stroke. Karl begs for the opportunity to operate and save his foster mother, before giving up the medical profession altogether. Mordaunt Hall found La Verne "effective" in a "chameleon-like" role (the *New York Times*, 3/6/32).

Early 1930s roles for La Verne included: Mme. Golden Bonnet in *While Paris Sleeps* (1932), Mrs. Sneider in *Hearts of Humanity* (1932) and Mrs. Flynn in *Breach of Promise* (1932). In *Wild Horse Mesa* (1932), Lucille was Ma Melberne, better known as "the General." *A Strange Adventure* (1932), featuring Dwight Frye, included La Verne as Mrs. Shean, the housekeeper to murdered millionaire William V. Mong. It is eventually revealed that the doctor (Jason Robards, Sr.) tending to Mong is actually the illegitimate son of Shean and her employer—and is later disclosed as the murderer! A formulaic old dark house film, *A Strange Adventure* is also known as *The Wayne Murder Case*.

On occasion, La Verne would return to the stage in California. She starred as Aunt Mallie, a mammy in black-

The Mighty Barnum (1934): Janet Beecher and Wallace Beery (as Barnum) gaze upon Lucille La Verne, as the purportedly 161-year-old "mammy" of George Washington.

A Tale of Two Cities (1935): **Fritz Leiber, Barlowe Borland, Blanche Yurka, Lucille La Verne, Mitchell Lewis and player plot their revenge.**

face, in *Shining Blackness* (2/13/32), at the Mason in Los Angeles. Lula Vollmer, the playwright of *Sun-Up* scripted the play. Of note was that Dwight Frye, appearing shortly after the release of *Frankenstein*, played the murderer. Lucille also played the comic lead in *Love's Passport* (February 1933) at the Los Angeles Theatre Guild.

In 1932, Lucille was involved in a serious car accident while driving in Los Angeles. While attempting to avoid another vehicle, La Verne hit a telephone pole, resulting in her dislocating five vertebrae. The following year brought more health concerns, when Lucille was first diagnosed with cancer, leading to two surgeries.

John Ford's *Pilgrimage* (1933) featured La Verne as Mrs. Hatfield, the mountaineer mother of a slain WWI soldier. Hatfield, one of the "Gold Star" mothers visiting their sons' graves, befriends anguished Henrietta Crosman, while also causing a stir by smoking her corncob pipe. As Mrs. Wilson, La Verne was the wife of a judge (Edward Le Saint) in *The Last Trail* (1933), starring George O'Brien

and Claire Trevor. The musical *Beloved* (1934), with John Boles and Gloria Stuart, had Lucille as Mrs. Briggs. It was back to screen perfidy for La Verne, however, with her portrayal of Miss Keeble in *School for Girls* (1934). Keeble, the sadistic head matron of a girls' reformatory, mistreats her residents and deceptively funnels money from their agricultural work to herself, before being killed during an escape by girls from her facility. *Kentucky Kernels* (1934), a Wheeler and Woolsey comedy, had La Verne as dowager Hannah Milford, the head of the clan feuding with the Wakefields, led by Noah Beery, Sr. As Joice Heth in *The Mighty Barnum* (1934), Lucille was purported by the famous showman (Wallace Beery) to be the 160 year-old former nurse to George Washington, but is exposed as a fake.

La Verne's last significant in-person onscreen role was that of the colorful "La Vengeance" in the Ronald Colman version of *A Tale of Two Cities* (1935). Lucille's flamboyant old crone cackles with delight as the guillotine descends on the heads of the French aristocrats. La Vengeance later

A Tale of Two Cities (1935): **Lucille La Verne, Fritz Leiber and Blanche Yurka out of character at a party during the production of the movie**

expresses dismay that her friend Mme. De Farge (Blanche Yurka) might actually miss an execution for the first time and would never fail to attend that of the perceived nephew of the hated Marquis St. Evremonde (Basil Rathbone). La Verne's performance not only echoed her work as Mother Frochard on stage in *The Two Orphans* and film in *Orphans of the Storm*, but also foreshadowed her animated effort still to come in *Snow White and the Seven Dwarfs.*

Lucille had a small part in the U.K. film *Hearts of Humanity* (1936), which featured Wilfred Walter ("Jake" in *The Human Monster*). Her next two roles involved only voice work (as would her final film). La Verne's threatening tones were very much on display as she voiced "the Bomber" in *The Blow Out* (1936), a Porky Pig cartoon. Well-meaning Porky picks up items that people drop and hands them back, which causes unforeseen problems for the mad bomber. In the film *Ellis Island* (1936), Lucille's handiwork is clearly detectable as the voice on the radio.

Returning to Broadway one final time, La Verne played the heinous Dr. Emma Koloich in *Black Widow* (2/12/36). The "good" doctor murders pregnant young women who seek her help, disposes of their bodies in either the incinerator or an acid bath, stabs her chemist-partner (who helped her kill her husband) and, when found out, leaps to her death in her own vat. Unfortunately, the play only lasted seven performances, but it gave audiences the chance to witness La Verne in a role worthy of Lionel Atwill or George Zucco. It is too bad La Verne never had the chance to play the horrible Dr. Koloich on the screen.

It is fitting, in a way, that Walt Disney chose Lucille La Verne to provide the voice for the Evil Queen, who is consumed with jealousy toward her stepdaughter, in the animated classic *Snow White and the Seven Dwarfs* (1937). Reportedly when her intonation as the old hag was not as distinct from her well-delivered diction as the Queen, Lucille left the recording session to shortly return with a raspier, older voice, surprising the animators. La Verne informed them the trick was removing her false teeth to obtain the effect. What the Disney technicians captured was truly one of the great early voice-over performances for an animated film.

In the early stages of *Snow White and the Seven Dwarfs*, the Evil Queen keeps Snow White dressed in rags, working as a scullery maid. Frustrated by her dialogues regard-

hag goes after the dwarfs ("I'll crush your bones," La Verne intones), but is destroyed when lightning strikes the cliff on which she is lurking.

Although an animated character, La Verne's expressive voice work in *Snow White and the Seven Dwarfs* resulted in the Queen/Witch being ranked #10 by the American Film Institute (AFI) in the villains' list of 100 years of "The Greatest Heroes and Villains." That level of respect and recognition only makes one yearn for how much more Lucille could have done in the horror genre, in particular, if given the opportunity.

Snow White and the Seven Dwarfs proved to be La Verne's farewell performance. In 1937, Lucille received the terrible news that her cancer had recurred, requiring further surgery. She retired from acting, but still kept active as the co-owner of a nightclub. On 12/31/44, La Verne broke her hip and was admitted to Culver City Hospital in California. While hospitalized in January 1945, she learned that she was again afflicted with cancer. Complications ensued and her condition worsened. Lucille La Verne died on March 4, 1945 at the age of 75. She was interred at Inglewood Park Cemetery in Los Angeles County. Although married three times, all of La Verne's husbands had predeceased her and she left no survivors. What became of her adopted daughter is not known.

Generally regarded as one of the finest stage actresses of the early 20th century (she has been nominated multiple times, although not elected, to the Theater Hall of Fame), Lucille La Verne sadly left behind only a limited legacy on film. Her frightening efforts as Mother Frochard in *Orphans of the Storm*, La Vengeance in *A Tale of Two Cities* and the detestable Miss Keeble in *School for Girls* bear witness to her talent for malevolence. It is her nightmare-inducing voice work in *Snow White and the Seven Dwarfs* that has provided the greatest evidence of what a wonderful evildoer this actress could enact, only making movie buffs pine for what might have been—perhaps one of the most fearsome villainesses of them all!

Snow White and the Seven Dwarfs **(1937): The animated and real-life Lucille La Verne meet (Lucille modeled for the Evil Queen)**

ing comparative beauty with the Magic Mirror, the Queen dispatches a huntsman to kill the girl and bring back her heart as proof. La Verne, however, is at her best when the Queen, after earlier methods have failed, takes a potion and is transformed into a hideous old peddler, referred to by many as a wicked witch. She raves, "When she (Snow White) breaks the tender peel to taste the apple in my hand, her breath will still, her blood congeal. Then I'll be fairest in the land!" With Snow White in the "sleeping death," the

Sources

Coughlin, Jim. "Forgotten Faces of Fantastic Films: Lucille La Verne," in *Midnight Marquee #58* (Fall/Winter 1998), pp. 26-28.

La Verne, Lucille. *Wikipedia.com*

Walter, Brett. "Lucille La Verne." IMDb mini biography.

References and On-Line Sources

References

American Film Institute of Feature Films, 1921-1930. Edited by Kenneth Munden, New York: R.R. Bowker Co., 1971.

American Film Institute of Feature Films, 1931-1940. Edited by Patricia King Hansen, Berkeley & Los Angeles, CA: University of California Press, 1993.

Best Plays and Year Book of the Drama in America: 1909-1919; Edited by Burns Mantle and Garrison P. Sherwood; 1919-1920 to 1943-44, New York: Dodd, Mead and Co., various.

The Biographical Encyclopedia and Who's Who of the American Theatre. Edited by Walter Rigden, New York: James H. Heineman, Inc., 1965.

Bordman, Gerald. *The Oxford Companion to the American Theatre,* New York: Oxford University Press, 1984.

Brunas, Michael; Brunas, John; and Weaver, Tom. *Universal Horrors: The Studio's Classic Films, 1931-1946,* Jefferson, NC: McFarland & Co., Inc., 1990.

Everson, William K. *The Detective in Film,* Secaucus, NJ: The Citadel Press, 1972.

Everson, William K. *Classics of the Horror Film,* Secaucus, NJ: The Citadel Press, 1974.

Everson, William K. *More Classics of the Horror Film,* Secaucus, NJ: The Citadel Press, 1986.

Hanke, Ken. *Charlie Chan at the Movies: History, Filmography and Criticism,* Jefferson, NC: McFarland & Co., Inc., 1989.

Hoey, Michael A. *Sherlock Holmes & the Fabulous Faces: The Universal Pictures Repertory Company,* Albany, Georgia: BearManor Media, 2011.

Mank, Gregory William. *It's Alive! The Classic Cinema Saga of Frankenstein,* New York: A.S. Barnes & Co., Inc., 1981.

Mank, Gregory William. *Karloff and Lugosi: The Story of a Haunting Collaboration,* Metuchen, NJ: The Scarecrow Press, Inc., 1989.

Mank, Gregory William. *Women in Horror Films, 1930s,* Jefferson, NC: McFarland & Co., Inc., 2005.

Mank, Gregory William. *Women in Horror Films, 1940s,* Jefferson, NC: McFarland & Co., Inc., 2005

Skal, David J. *The Monster Show: A Cultural History of Horror,* New York: W. W. Norton and Co., 1993.

Weaver, Tom. *Poverty Row Horrors! Monogram, PRC and Republic Horror Films of the Forties,* Jefferson, NC: McFarland & Co., Inc., 1993.

Weaver, Tom. *Attack of the Monster Movie Makers,* Jefferson, N.C.: McFarland and Company, Inc., 1994.

On-Line Sources

Ancestry.com
Findagrave.com
Fultonhistory.com
IBDB.com (Internet Broadway Database)
IMDb.com (Internet Movie Database)
Radiogoldindex.org (J. David Goldin)
Wikipedia.com

Note: The above-cited references are in addition to the sources listed after each chapter, which are actor or actress specific.

Acknowledgments

I would like to express my sincere appreciation to Gary J. and Susan Svehla, without whose encouragement, support, creativity and guidance this book would not have been possible. Not only did they provide the impetus for *Forgotten Faces of Fantastic Films*, but they nurtured my writing in general over these many years.

My gratitude goes out to the following, all of whom had a role in bringing this book to fruition: Dr. Dave Baldwin, James Brown, George Chastain, Dr. Ron Delehanty, Jayne Dwyer, Mike Dwyer, Catherine Hagele Elmore, Bob Esposito, Emily Feldman, Harry Groener, Laurie Birch Kendall, Leonard Maltin, Richard Maturi, Donald Maurer, Dr. Russell A. Potter, Rick Pruitt, John P. Quinn, Dennis Van Sloun, Tom Weaver, Scott Wilson and Valerie Yaros (Screen Actors Guild historian).

Thanks to these individuals who unfortunately are no longer with us: Robert Bloch, Richard Bojarski, Barry Brown, Frank Coghlan, Jr., Randye Cohen, Dwight David Frye, Richard Gordon, James Hagele, Doug McClelland and Linda Miller.

My appreciation goes out to the various shops, individuals, and businesses (many of which are no longer in existence) who have assisted me in amassing the stills to help illustrate the lives and careers of these actors and actresses: Ronald V. Borst, Cinemabilia (Ernest Burns), Film Favorites, Jay Parrino's the Mint, Jerry Ohlinger's Movie Material Store, Larry Edmunds Bookshop (Mike Hawks), Ron Harvey, Kenneth G. Lawrence, the Memory Shop (Marc Ricci), Movie Star News (Ira Kramer, the late Paula Klaw and Jack Kramer), Stephen Sally, Bob Scherl, Kay Shackelton, Richard Stoddard and the University of Washington (J. Willis Sayre Collection).

To my two main research centers in the pre-internet days: The Billy Rose Theatre Collection, Library of the Performing Arts, New York Public Library (especially the late Donald Madison) and SUNY College at Purchase Library (Robert Evans).

To six primary Internet databases: Ancestry.com, Findagrave.com, IBDB.com (Internet Broadway Database), IMDb.com (Internet Movie Database), Radiogold-index.org (J. David Goldin) and Wikipedia.org.

Special thanks go to my colleague, Gregory William Mank, for his support and encouragement in addition to providing the forward to this volume.

My sincere thanks go to my sister, Marianne Coughlin, her husband, Dr. Robert Davis and her daughter (my niece), Kate Coughlin Davis.

My love and eternal gratitude extend to my late parents, Jane Frances and Thomas Patrick Coughlin, who respected my interest in films while always spurring on my quest for knowledge.

My deepest appreciation and love go out to my wife, Dr. Mary E. Quinn, and children, Kerry and Brian Quinn Coughlin, for their understanding, patience, caring and kindness, putting up with my research and writing, as well as my quirks. They have been my anchors through stormy seas.

Author Biography

James Thomas Patrick (Jim) Coughlin was born in Rye, New York. He spent his childhood with his sister Marianne on the grounds of Playland Amusement Park in Westchester County, where his father Thomas served as General Superintendent. Jim's mother Jane, an expert typist and former WAC, nurtured his love of old movies and zest to learn more about the character players who inhabited these films. Initially aspiring to be an electrical engineer, Jim changed career focus and obtained his Master's and Doctorate in Clinical Psychology from Fordham University. Presently the Program Director, he has worked for more than 35 years at Lincoln Hall, a residential treatment center for disadvantaged youth.

Jim has been married for 34 years to Mary E. Quinn, a Clinical Psychologist. Jim and Mary have two children: Kerry, a graduate of Hamilton College and former Peace Corps volunteer in Moldova, who is currently working on her Master's at the University of Pennsylvania; and Brian, who received his Bachelor's and Master's from Villanova University and is presently working in analytics for Decision Resources, while also serving as the Director of Lacrosse Operations at Villanova.

For more than 40 years, Jim has contributed numerous career studies on actors and actresses to *Midnight Marquee* and *Mad About Movies*, as well as Leonard Maltin's *Film Fan Monthly* and *The Real Stars*. With the late actor Barry Brown, Jim co-authored the unpublished *Unsung Heroes of the Horrors*. Jim collaborated with noted genre writer Gregory William Mank and Dwight David Frye, the actor's son, on the biography *Dwight Frye's Last Laugh*, published by Midnight Marquee Press in 1997. In addition to his long-time fascination with film and performers, Jim is an avid sports aficionado, compulsively loyal to the Texas Rangers (baseball), St. Louis Rams (football), Toronto Maple Leafs (hockey), Detroit Pistons (basketball), Chelsea F.C. (soccer) and the New York Lizards (lacrosse), as well as Villanova lacrosse and basketball.

Author Jim Coughlin sings and plays the bodhran at an Irish music festival. Photo credit: Frank Contreras

**If you enjoyed this book,
write for a free catalog of
Midnight Marquee Press titles
or visit our website at
http://www.midmar.com**

**Midnight Marquee Press, Inc.
9721 Britinay Lane
Baltimore, MD 21234
410-665-1198
mmarquee@aol.com**